THE FRANCHISE

by Cameron Stauth:

The Sweeps
The New Approach to Cancer
The Dealmakers
The I.R.A.
Modern Folk Remedies, with Mark Bricklin
The Franchise

THE
FRANCHISE

Building a Winner
with the World Champion
Detroit Pistons,
Basketball's Bad Boys

Cameron Stauth

WILLIAM MORROW AND COMPANY, INC.
New York

Recognizing the importance of preserving what has been written, it is the policy of William Morrow and Company, Inc., and its imprints and affiliates to have the books it publishes printed on acid-free paper, and we exert our best efforts to that end.

Library of Congress Cataloging-in-Publication Data

Stauth, Cameron.
    The franchise : building a winner with the world champion Detroit Pistons, basketball's bad boys / Cameron Stauth.
        p.   cm.
    Includes bibliographical references.
    ISBN 0-688-09573-9
    1. Detroit Pistons (Basketball team)—History. I. Title.
GV885.52.D47S73   1990
796.323'64'0977434—dc20   89-78000
                                                                                         CIP
            133048

Printed in the United States of America

First Edition

1 2 3 4 5 6 7 8 9 10

BOOK DESIGN BY PAUL CHEVANNES

For my parents, Vernon and Lorraine Stauth

Acknowledgments

There are four people without whose help I could not have written this book: Dave Stauth, Jack McCloskey, Richard Pine, and Adrian Zackheim. Dave Stauth did all the groundwork for the book and turned a vague idea into a workable project. Jack McCloskey generously agreed to be the focus of the book and gave a great deal of himself during its preparation, always pleasantly, even during difficult times. Richard Pine, of Arthur Pine Associates Literary Agency, represented the project with his usual skill and enthusiasm. And Adrian Zackheim, of William Morrow and Company, turned the project into a book. I am particularly grateful for these indispensable contributions.

Also of great help in the preparation of the book were Bob Wolfe, my research assistant on this project and collaborator on others; Jeanne Withrow, who did an excellent job transcribing interviews and word processing the manuscript; and Lorraine Stauth, who helped organize the material in its early, chaotic form. Thanks, too, to transcribers Glenda Jones, Judy Close, Marilyn Huckstep, Megan Nolan, and Eileen Adams for their hard and high-quality work.

Virtually everyone in the Piston franchise was extraordinarily friendly, cooperative, and professional. I particularly enjoyed the time I spent with Tom Wilson, John Ciszewski, Ron Campbell, and Dave Auker, and also appreciated the assistance of Dan Hauser and Harry Hutt. Stan Novak and Will Robinson, two of the great scouts in NBA history, were a pleasure and an education to get to know. Nancy Maas was extremely efficient and cheerful, and made my job much easier. Matt Dobek and Debbie Mayfield of the public relations department were helpful at all times, and I also enjoyed the kindness of Eric Randolph, Pete Skorich, Sue Emerick, Andy Appleby, Lorrie Sanders, and Michelle Yaros.

Of course, the cooperation of the players and coaches was absolutely vital. My appreciation goes to Chuck Daly, Brendan Suhr, Brendan Malone, Mike Abdenour, Adrian Dantley, Fennis Dembo, Joe Dumars, James Edwards, Vinnie Johnson, Bill Laimbeer, Rick Mahorn, Dennis Rodman, John Salley, Isiah Thomas, Michael Williams, Jim Rowinski, Pace Mannion, and Dave Popson. Also players on other teams, particularly Michael Jordan, Kareem Abdul-Jabbar, Jim Paxson, Danny Ainge, Bill Cartwright, Terry Tyler, Buck Williams, Charles Barkley, Brad Daugherty, and Mark Price.

A number of writers and broadcasters went out of their way to share their expertise with me, which was invariably greater than my own. Especially helpful were Charlie Vincent, Terry Foster, Steve Addy, George Blaha, Joe Tait, Terry Pluto, Leo Martinosi, Jeff Coplon, Fred Waitzkin, Clark Attebury, Steve Kelley, and David Kahn. Also publicists John Lashway, Bob Price, Tim Hallam, and Jeff Twiss, and the NBA's Brian McIntyre.

As a group, the NBA's general managers impressed me with their intelligence and forthrightness. Special thanks to Donnie Walsh, Harry Weltman, Bucky Buckwalter, Bob Whitsitt, Jack McMahon, Jerry West, Wayne Embry, Stan Kasten, Jan Volk, Bob Ferry, Jerry Krause, Rick Sund, and Ed Gregory.

I appreciated the hospitality of Bob and Donna Gibson, proud parents of Detroit favorite Kirk Gibson and proprietors of the Beachside Motel resort.

Last but not least, thanks to my wife, Shari Levine, for her love and support throughout this project, those before it, and those to come.

Contents

Sports is like life—with the volume turned up.
—Mike Reid
professional golfer

Winners are losers who just won't quit!
—Jack McCloskey
Detroit Pistons

Prologue

IT BEGAN with a kiss. But the man with gunmetal-gray hair wasn't fooled. He knew there was no love in the kiss. At least not now. Later there would be love, but now there were just two men trying to destroy each other. They each had the same dream. Only one could achieve it.

Isiah Thomas dropped the hand of his best friend Magic Johnson and pulled his lips away from Johnson's cheek.

Four days ago, Thomas had been smashed to the floor by his best friend Buck—"Magic" was just a media name. Johnson had delivered the blow knowing that Thomas's back was injured and that further assault might cause grave damage. In the same game, Johnson had bludgeoned his forearm into Thomas's throat, again knocking his friend to the floor. At one point, Thomas had had to be restrained as he'd tried to attack Johnson. They both loved the essence of their profession—winning—more than they loved each other. But that trait was the primary reason they'd made it here. Nobody got into the NBA Finals without it.

At the moment, Isiah Thomas had a wrenched knee and an injured back. But the man with the gray hair wasn't worried about Thomas. Thomas was possessed. He was the one person in the arena who was as obsessed with winning the Championship as the man with gunmetal-gray hair. They were ahead in the series 3–2—one game from their goal.

But—two hours later: Isiah Thomas lay writhing on the floor. His teeth were clenched into a grotesque parody of his famous high-beam smile. He looked like a snarling dog. He'd just landed from a sky-leap onto the side of his ankle, and now it felt as if someone were sawing it off. He grabbed for the leg of a nearby referee, mute with pain but desperate to stop play. His mind screamed, *"Not now! Not now!"* He was in the midst of the most extraordinary performance of his life, having scored 14 points in the first seven and one-half minutes of the third quarter.

Thomas inched toward the bench like an old man. He sat there in agony and misery. Blood was dripping from a wound under his eye, one of his fingers had been dislocated, and his vision was wavy from a finger that had knifed into his eye. At his feet, a trainer mummified his ankle, which was beginning to bloat and puff with blood. As soon as the trainer had finished, Thomas said, "Tell Chuck I'm ready to go back in." Before the game, Thomas had told himself that he was going to take control. He was still determined to do it.

Thomas hobbled onto the floor and the inspiration continued. When the buzzer finally blared, he had scored 25 points in one quarter—the most in Finals history. The Detroit Pistons—who had existed without a Championship longer than any other sports franchise in America—were poised, at last, to win.

Thomas, who looked tiny and fragile next to the other players, continued to dominate the game in the last quarter. In Cleveland, Ohio, a vice president of the Cleveland Cavaliers watched with grim satisfaction. He hated the Pistons. He thought they were brutal and would do anything to win. And he thought Isiah Thomas was, at this moment, destroying them. In the first five games, Thomas's teammate Adrian Dantley had starred. The Cleveland executive had told a friend, "When Isiah can't stand Dantley being the star anymore, the Pistons will go down the toilet." Now the executive was thinking, "It's over. I don't care *how* many points Isiah scores. He just ripped the chemistry right out of this team." "Chemistry" was a concept most basketball fans paid little attention to, but the men who ran the NBA were haunted by it. In its simplest sense, it meant teamwork. But it covered every interaction among all the players—emotional as well as physical. In this game, the emotional chemistry of the Pistons was soured. There was tension between several of the Detroit stars and high-scoring Adrian Dantley. It was over money. Promo money. The Walt Disney Company was going to give the Most Valuable Player of the Finals $35,000 to say, "Now I'm going to Disneyland!" Piston center Bill Laimbeer and Isiah Thomas had said that if they won the award, they would split the money with the team. Dantley wanted to keep it. Dantley was easily the richest man on the team, earning $1,250,000 per year, plus endorsements. No matter. If he earned thirty-five thousand bucks, it was *his*. They'd finally compromised by agreeing that the winner would keep half the money and share half. But it had caused friction—mostly because it was part of a larger, ongoing argument about selfishness. Right now, friction was the last thing the Detroit Pistons needed. Basketball, more than any other sport, required an almost psychic sense of togetherness—good chemistry—and the Pistons' chemistry was slightly off. The man with gunmetal-gray hair was aware of it, and there was nothing he could do about it. For now.

But Detroit struggled on, and stayed slightly ahead of the Lakers, who had one of the finest teams ever to play. At courtside, Laker coach Pat Riley looked glassy-eyed and frantic. The Lakers were a storybook team: Kareem, Magic, Worthy, the fast break, the glamorous coach, the celebrities. But Detroit had a mysterious quality that gravitated toward victory—a mix of hunger, anger, and love of the sport. This quality was new to the franchise, though. For many years, they had been a joke and a disgrace. The Detroit front office—the men who ran the franchise and had been there longest—had become numb and defensive during the long years of humiliation. Now they almost never opened themselves to emotion. They had a saying about the team: "They'll break your heart."

But now, after so many years . . . one minute to go. Three-point lead. Tom Wilson, thirty-nine-year old chief executive officer of the Pistons, felt a painful, unusual stirring. It was optimism. "You know," he said to himself as he sat behind the bench, "we've got a *chance*. To *win*.'' It was the first time he had ever allowed himself to believe that his team could beat the Los Angeles Lakers. A few more seconds ticked by—in slow motion, for Wilson—and L.A.'s Byron Scott hit a jump shot to shrink the lead to 1 point. Detroit coach Chuck Daly jerked his eyes toward the game clock: 37 seconds. "If we get *one defensive stop*,'' thought Daly, "we're World Champions.''

The Championship Trophy was wheeled into the Detroit locker room. CBS Sports had found Piston owner Bill Davidson and had brought him to the locker room. He stood now, waiting, next to the lustrous gold trophy. Tubs of champagne and ice were being carried into the room.

On the floor, young Piston Dennis Rodman told himself, "We've *got it.''*

Bill Laimbeer swung around a pick. He had a shot but passed it up. He rifled the ball to Thomas. Thomas sprang off his crippled ankle over defensive genius Michael Cooper. He snapped off the shot. No good.

Laker James Worthy erupted off his tree-stump thighs to grab the ball.

Fourteen seconds left. One-point lead. Worthy tried to find Magic Johnson, failed, and hurled the ball to Kareem Abdul-Jabbar. Jabbar was Riley's second choice for the shot, after Johnson. Jabbar no longer had the skills for the situation, but he had the mind for it, and that was almost as important. Jabbar shot his skyhook. A whistle. Laimbeer had bumped Jabbar's left arm during the shot. Daly's body went rigid. He was horrified. It violated NBA protocol to call a soft foul in an all-important situation. Laimbeer's eyes popped and his jaw dropped.

Jabbar stepped to the line. He breathed deeply. Cleared his mind. Almost went into a trance. He made both shots.

Daly called time-out. 14 seconds left—plenty of time. Daly diagrammed a play for Isiah Thomas. Thomas felt confident.

They fired the pass inbounds. Thomas darted into his route—and ran headlong into Adrian Dantley. Guard Joe Dumars threw up an errant shot. Dantley was angry. He'd wanted to shoot.

In Cleveland, the Cavaliers' executive smiled.

Time elapsed. They wheeled the trophy and champagne out of the Detroit locker room and left the owner of the Detroit Pistons standing by himself.

Isiah Thomas labored into a meeting room at L.A.'s Airport Marriott for a press conference. It was the day before Game Seven. Thomas was on crutches, and he had a Band-Aid big as a playing card covering the gash under his eye.

About seventy-five sports reporters, almost all casually dressed in sport shirts and warm-up suits, crowded around as Thomas worked his way to a small podium. As he put his crutches aside, one of them shouted, "How bad *is* the ankle, Isiah?"

"It's pretty fucked up, I know that," said Thomas. Some of the reporters looked taken aback at the profanity—even some of the Detroit reporters. Most of the out-of-town writers weren't aware that Thomas had a tough, ghetto-hardened core beneath his thousand-dollar suits and million-dollar smile. Detroit reporters knew it, but they weren't used to seeing it surface. Two years earlier, Thomas had disastrously agreed with a teammate that Larry Bird was overrated because he was white. After that fiasco, Thomas had talked less and smiled more.

"At this point in time," said Thomas, "I doubt I'll play. Most people who have looked at the ankle don't think there's a chance."

Thomas had just come from an L.A. Raiders training facility. Raider boss Al Davis had struck up a friendship with the Pistons, calling them "the Raiders of the NBA," because they played rough. Now, on occasion, the CBS announcers were calling the Pistons the Bad Boys. Thomas had spent almost forty-eight straight hours at the Raider facility, much of it wearing "the Boot"—a hated, bootlike device filled with ice and water that acted as a cold-compression unit. While the Raiders had offered their facilities and an around-the-clock medical staff, all that the host-team Lakers had given Thomas was a bucket of ice. The Lakers' general manager, former star Jerry West, was famous for his own obsession with winning.

After the press conference, one of the reporters asked Detroit assistant coach Dick Versace if the Pistons could win without Thomas. "If there ever was a team that can win without its star," said Versace, "it's this one." The Pistons' lack of dependence upon a single player was the cornerstone of the franchise's strategy. The strategy had been devised by the man with gunmetal-gray hair.

"Strictly drama for television." The Pistons' chief financial officer, Ron Campbell, was only thirty-four but he'd had his heart broken by the team so often that now he considered the seventh game already lost: "Strictly drama for television." He sat quietly in the stands behind the bench as his prophecy came to life before his eyes. The Laker fans were screaming, Pat Riley was standing with his arms laced in a knot over his chest, Jack Nicholson was shaking his fist, and the Pistons were falling further and further behind—10 points . . . 15 points. Campbell didn't feel a thing. It wasn't that he didn't care. His entire identity was wrapped up in the Pistons. It was just: "They'll break your heart."

On the floor, Bill Laimbeer began to feel a sick flush of shame. He couldn't stand for this game to turn into a blowout. It didn't matter that Isiah was hobbled and was contributing almost nothing, or that power forward Rick Mahorn couldn't play. The Pistons didn't make excuses. The man with gunmetal-gray hair didn't accept excuses. Laimbeer, who had a tremendous ego, began to battle back. He was getting superb help from young John Salley. Salley had talked to his college coach before the game and the coach had told him that no one would ever be able to take this forty-eight minutes away from him, so he should just enjoy the game and have fun. It was the kind of advice Salley was glad to hear. Salley was friends with Eddie Murphy, Arsenio Hall, and other comedians, and he tried to keep every situation—even Championship games—as light as possible. His motto was "Don't get the blues when you lose, and keep the same grin when you win." So far, he had prospered with that approach, and now he was having the best game of his life. The lead melted away. The game clock surged forward. Pat Riley was beginning to look tortured and to move in fast-forward.

A minute and a half to go. Four-point Laker lead. Bill Laimbeer—broad-butted, sunken-chested, and white—dove gracelessly for the ball as it sailed toward the sidelines. He clutched it with his fingertips and flipped it backward over his head as he belly flopped onto the floor. Joe Dumars darted over to grab it and heaved it to Vinnie Johnson, who was playing for Isiah. Johnson, who was so strong he looked like he'd been molded out of clay and then squashed, charged for the hoop. At the last second, he snapped the ball behind him to Dumars. Dumars locked his eyes onto the hoop, ignored the huge defenders screaming toward him, jumped, and swished it. Two-point lead. 1:19 to go.

James Worthy picked up the ball. Piston CEO Tom Wilson muttered, "Holy shit, it's possible." Worthy called over Laker guard Byron Scott and passed in to him. Full-court press. The Lakers brought the ball over the halfcourt line. A whistle! The referee pointed at Dennis Rodman. Rodman, skittish and tightly wired, had bumped Magic Johnson. Rodman, gifted with enthusiasm, often made dumb mistakes—Dumb Dennis mistakes. Rodman gripped his fists together in front of his chest, radiating frustration. Coach Chuck Daly grabbed his face and turned his head away. Rodman looked at the scoreboard, took a deep breath, and pulled at his jersey. Magic Johnson looked serene—but he missed his second free throw. Three-point lead. 1:17 left.

Vinnie Johnson passed to Bill Laimbeer at the 3-point line. Laimbeer, with the best jump shot of any center in the league, launched a 3-pointer. But it had too much force behind it—an adrenaline miss. The ball ricocheted all the way to the free-throw line, where Dumars tapped it up and backward. It floated toward out-of-bounds as Laimbeer raced over and grabbed it near the Laker bench. But his foot was on the line. Pat Riley pointed at Laimbeer's foot and the referee hit his whistle and shot a finger toward the Laker end. Laker ball. Magic Johnson clapped his hands in a short, hard burst. 49 seconds. The Laker fans were standing, screaming, and the Laker bench was up.

Worthy got the ball and drove toward the hoop. Worthy was in another world, a state of concentration athletes call "the zone of altered consciousness." And he had 34 points, 16 rebounds, and 10 assists—almost every move he made was in perfect rhythm. But Vinnie Johnson jabbed his arm into the blur that was Worthy and knocked the ball away. It skittered free and Johnson pounced on it. Again, for CEO Tom Wilson, the scene began to unfold in slow motion. Vinnie Johnson dribbled over the halfcourt line. Daly thought about calling a time-out. But he felt confident; he told himself, "Vinnie's an uncomplicated player. He'll make the right pass. Save the time-out." Johnson spotted Dennis Rodman just inside the 3-point line. He whipped the ball to Rodman. Dumars jetted to the opposite corner and waved for the ball. He was open. But Rodman had a clear path to the basket. Rodman hesitated. Drive or pass? Rodman couldn't make a jump shot to save his life, but he was good on the drive. Four Laker rebounders clotted around the hoop. Then . . . Rodman *shot*. An ugly, awkward Dumb Dennis jump shot. Daly's eyes went wild. He screamed, "Shit!" The ball hit the rim. John Salley hurtled toward the basket from out of nowhere, soaring so high his feet were almost level with everyone's crotch. Salley lunged toward the ball. But it took an odd hop and dropped into the hands of Laker Byron Scott. Rodman couldn't bear to look at Daly. As soon as he'd let go of the ball he'd wanted to reach out and pull it back.

Now it was too late. It was over.

A long time later, after the noise had died away and the fans had drifted off, the members of the Detroit Pistons front office slowly climbed out of the stands. They began to collect—for no reason and with no plan—on the now-still court. The empty arena echoed with the hollow drum of paper cups being swept down stairs. Occasionally, someone would begin to utter a cliché, along the lines of "Well, we didn't quit." But no one paid attention, and the remarks got stuck in silence.

After a while, they were all there. Except one. The man with gunmetal-gray hair. Jack McCloskey, the general manager of the Detroit Pistons—the man who ran the franchise—had left quickly. He had gone to see the team, and had then hurried out of the building. He needed time to think. About next year.

THE FRANCHISE

ONE

"Showdown at Windsor" Fall Camp

"OVER HERE a second, guys!" The young men dropped their basketballs immediately. Jack McCloskey wanted them.

They gathered around him. He was dressed like them—shorts and a T-shirt. But there was something very distinctive about him. It wasn't his age. Take away the gunmetal-gray hair, a few creases in the face, and he looked a lot like them: thin, tall, hard. The special thing about him was his eyes—their intensity, their focus.

"None of you guys were with us last month when we lost to the Lakers." His voice was stern. "Except for Dennis." McCloskey looked at Rodman, the only veteran on the team who'd chosen to join the Detroit rookies and free agents at the midsummer rookie camp. "The thing is, we were a much better team than they were. *We shouldn't have lost.*" McCloskey let the thought sink in. He wasn't angry, and he wasn't cheerleading. Mostly, he sounded grim—and dead certain. "This year," he said, "we're not *going* to lose." He locked eyes with the players. "*This* year," he said, "we're going to the Finals *again*. And this year, we're going to kick their *butts.*" He sounded absolutely positive, as if he'd seen the future. The players had all heard rah-rah speeches before, but this wasn't one of those. This was more a statement of fact. It was a little chilling.

Dave Popson, one of the young men gathered around McCloskey,

23

had been around competitive people all his life. Popson had gone to the University of North Carolina, alma mater of players like Michael Jordan, Brad Daugherty, and J. R. Reid. He knew all about the special fire of men who loved to compete.

But as Dave Popson stood before Jack McCloskey, he thought, "My god! *This is the most competitive man I've ever seen.*"

Most of the players wouldn't make the team, and they knew it. But—for just a moment—they were a team. They were the team that had lost to the Lakers. And that was going to win the 1989 World Championship.

Two young men, one black and one white, both tall, shot baskets in a cold, shadowy field house in Windsor, Ontario, just across the Detroit River from downtown Detroit. They were remarkably skilled. The ball was light in their hands and they feathered it through the net so softly that it barely ripped the strings. One would stand deep in the corner sinking shots in rhythmical cadence while the other rebounded, then they would switch places. With obvious pleasure, they would drift into dancing sets of one-on-one. They seemed almost never to miss, and when they did miss they would leap after the ball and ram it through the rim with violent grace. Every so often, they would punctuate their play with a trick shot—bouncing the ball off the floor into the basket, or standing with their backs to the hoop and flipping it up backward.

At the other end of the court, an older man tossed up hook shots. He wasn't particularly good, but he seemed to be enjoying himself. Sitting near him, just off the court, a very large black man teased him, offering advice and criticism, making jokes. Sometimes the older man paid attention, and sometimes he didn't.

Then there was a stirring in the gym and the sound of deep voices and heavy footsteps. A line of men in shorts and T-shirts emerged from a runway that led to the rocker room. They were, unmistakably, professional basketball players.

On television, or even from a tenth-row seat in a stadium, professional basketball players look like other athletes—tall and muscular. But that's the view from a distance, and from the perspective of seeing them next to one another. Up close, and from one's own perspective, they are the most physically remarkable people in the world.

To a basketball fan, seven feet no longer sounds exceptionally tall. It's basically the minimum height for a center. Ralph Sampson and Mark Eaton are seven feet, four inches, and Manute Bol is seven-seven. But the eyes of a relatively tall man—someone six-one or six-two—hit a seven-footer in the middle of his chest. A six-footer must crane his neck to look at a seven-footer like a child looking at an adult. And much more than height, it is size that sets pro basketball players apart. Every part of a man who is six-eight to seven feet is of unusual proportion: hands, neck, arms, feet—even eyes and ears. Hands are like baseball gloves, eyes can be as huge and round as those of a stallion, and arms are stacked with muscle and are long as tree limbs. All this size and strength, though, is carried with the silky grace of a professional dancer. Because of this unusual combination of size, strength, and grace, pro basketball players are often called "the best athletes in the world." Their physical presence—which they have been trained to expand for intimidation—is overpowering. And in a group—even a relaxed, quiet group like the one that was loping into the gym in Windsor—the collective physical presence is unparalleled.

"Okay!" yelled the older man—Detroit Piston coach Chuck Daly— "Everybody off the floor but players! Dawkins, let's go!" The large black man who'd been teasing Daly eased out of the stands, and the two men at the other end of the court put down their ball and took a seat in the bleachers. They were high school basketball coaches who'd come to watch the big time. Skilled as these two men were, they were no better than one million other young men at the game of basketball. The men who were gathering around Daly, though, were of a wholly different category. They were among the 250 best basketball players in the world. They all moved with a sense of strength, gracefulness, confidence—and arrogance—that is present only in the movements of a few hundred men.

Even some of the players—the rookies—were in awe of their colleagues. Now that the season was approaching, only the best young prospects had been allowed to join the members of last year's team for fall camp. Most of the players from rookie camp were long gone. Only Dave Popson and six others had survived McCloskey's first cut.

Daly and McCloskey were ready to get down to serious business. But to Michael Williams, McCloskey's second pick in last summer's college draft, the situation had an odd, dreamlike quality. Just three months ago, in late June, Williams had been watching these players fight for the World Championship on television. Now they stood on either side of him, and he felt not as if his dreams had become real, but as if he'd jumped into the television, and were just watching his dream from another angle. He couldn't possibly feel like he'd achieved his dream of playing in the NBA, because he still had to survive the final roster cuts. Right now there were seventeen players gathered around Daly, and only twelve would make the team. To earn a spot, Williams would have to win the approval of McCloskey, who, as general manager, had authority over all personnel decisions. McCloskey wasn't on the floor with Daly. He was in the stands, watching quietly. Always watching. Williams's agent, Bill Blakely, had not been able to persuade McCloskey to guarantee Williams's $100,000 salary, the league minimum. That put Williams at a significant disadvantage, because McCloskey had nothing invested in him. Williams had been chosen in the second round as the forty-eighth pick, and picks that low virtually never got guaranteed salaries.

That disadvantage was a cruel twist of fate for Williams, because McCloskey had actually been more interested in Williams than he'd been in Detroit's first pick, Wyoming guard Fennis Dembo, who *had* gotten a guaranteed salary.

Williams's future had become threatened because of publicity. Dembo had made the cover of *Sports Illustrated* last year—getting the attention of everybody in the league. Williams, playing in relative obscurity at Baylor, had gained little national attention. But McCloskey had seen things in Williams that others hadn't. McCloskey had a reputation for uncovering diamonds in the rough, and he had been willing to stake that reputation on Williams. But he'd gambled. He'd wanted both Dembo and Williams, so he'd taken Dembo first, hoping that no one else valued Williams as much as he did. The gamble had paid off. Williams had still been available at the forty-eighth pick.

But once McCloskey had gotten Williams, he hadn't given him a guaranteed salary. Simple reason. He didn't have to. Williams didn't have the bargaining power to demand it.

So now Williams was having to scrap his way onto the team. He was doing a good job of it, though. He'd played well in rookie camp, and had then made the All-League Team of the NBA's Summer League, which had just concluded. At first, Williams had been shocked at the skill level in the Summer League, a preseason proving ground for rookies and free agents. Williams was only six-two and 175 pounds—slight by NBA standards—but he was bullet-fast and had blown right past everyone in college. In the Summer League, however, players six-nine and 225 were blowing past *him*. He'd seen players like that on television and had thought he was ready for them. But TV just didn't convey it: the ungodly whoosh of a huge player whistling past like a semi. You couldn't prepare for that—you just endured it.

At the moment, Williams was bringing the ball downcourt. Daly had split them into two groups for a scrimmage. There was no time to screw around with orientation and conditioning drills and pep talks—McCloskey would make his final roster cuts in a couple of weeks. It was time to try to become a millionaire—the average salary in the league was about $500,000, and in about twenty months, when the new TV contract kicked in, it was expected to rise to $1 million per year. If the rookies didn't become millionaires, they'd drop back into the real world—the world of the two high school coaches who'd been shooting baskets. The NBA was an all-or-nothing proposition, because America really had no minor leagues. There was only the Continental Basketball Association, and its players made less than high school coaches. The real minors were the colleges, and they didn't pay—at least not after four years.

Williams eyed the defense—Isiah Thomas was guarding him, and Bill Laimbeer and Rick Mahorn were under the hoop. The prudent move: pass off to Adrian Dantley. But that wasn't the way into the league. First and last, the NBA was a shooter's league. If you couldn't shoot the ball . . . Williams ducked his head and drove toward Laimbeer. He flew into the air with the ball in front of him. He had a clear shot off the glass. Then: *bash!* Laimbeer, seventy pounds heavier and nine inches taller than Williams, shifted suddenly and heaved his weight into Williams, knocking him to the floor so hard he bounced twice. Williams lay on the floor, feeling dizzy and sick as pain shuddered up and down his body. Trainer Mike Abdenour ran up and put his hand on Williams's arm to keep him from getting up. But Williams wasn't going anywhere. He was spread-eagled and choking for breath. Laimbeer turned and walked away. No apology: Welcome to the NBA. For about two minutes, Williams lay panting and twitching. Gradually, he worked his way upright, then found the free-throw line. His right hand was beginning to throb and turn purple, but he didn't favor it. He didn't want to show anyone he was hurting. He just wanted to make his free throws. He wasn't trying to impress McCloskey or Daly. It was instinct. But it was the instinct that McCloskey had drafted him for.

After the scrimmage, Isiah Thomas approached Williams. "You know," said Thomas, "if you're going in on a big guy like that, you got to know how to protect yourself. In college, you just *go.* You jump over them, and you dunk on them. But at this level, everybody's so much bigger and so much stronger and so much taller that you got to find ways to protect your *body* while you get your shot off. That's why even a guy like Michael Jordan—he can jump over a *lot* of people—but he turns his back to a guy while he's in the air, and then flips it over his shoulder. That's to protect his *body.*"

Williams was grateful, not just for the advice but for the attention. But he didn't react effusively. That wouldn't be cool. Besides, he was worried. His hand was getting fatter and more blue by the minute, and trainer Mike Abdenour had told him he'd better get it X-rayed. If it was broken, he was in trouble. They didn't save roster spots for forty-eighth picks. McCloskey would probably be sympathetic. Then he'd go out and find another body.

Darryl Dawkins was *pissed.* "Don't you *ever* turn that TV off again!" Rookie Dave Popson rubbed sleep out of his eyes and stared at Dawkins. Popson and Dawkins—competing for the same spot on the roster—were rooming together, and Dawkins, who had a $300,000 guaranteed salary, insisted on having the TV on all night, every night, as he slept. Last night, after Dawkins had fallen asleep, Popson had gotten up and turned it off. But now it was morning, and Dawkins had just realized the TV wasn't on. He glared at Popson.

"Hey, okay, no problem," said Popson. Why argue with a guy who was six-eleven and 280? Besides, Popson had sympathy for Dawkins. Dawkins's life was a mess. Last November, his wife Kelly—a beautiful twenty-eight-year-old woman—had killed herself. They had been separated, but seemed to be reconciling when she'd swallowed a bottle of Propacet, a pharmaceutical painkiller. On top of that, Dawkins was almost broke. For most of his thirteen-year career, he'd been near the ceiling of the NBA salary schedule, peaking at about the $1-million level over the past two years. But he'd been ripped off, and he'd screwed up, and he'd been too generous, and now he was just about at ground zero again. In addition, he had serious injury problems. He was recovering from back surgery, trying to rebuild the strength he'd had when he'd first entered the league, and trying to melt the roll of blubber that was roped to his waist. So now Dawkins—fighting for his career—was a born-again Christian and fitness fanatic. Every night, he said his prayers and went to sleep in front of the friendly white glow of the television.

Despite his problems, Darryl "Chocolate Thunder" Dawkins was an NBA legend. He, Moses Malone, and one other player had been the only three men ever to enter the NBA straight out of high school. He'd done it for the money. While a great many NBA players had grown up poor—particularly the black players—Dawkins had been not just poor but the only viable means of support for a large family. They'd been living in the humid, beaten-down eastern section of Orlando, Florida, and when a scout from the Philadelphia 76ers had come to their shack with an $80,000 offer, Dawkins had wanted to scrap college. The only dissenting voice was that of the Reverend W. D. Judge, pastor of the family church and a surrogate father for Dawkins, whose dad had left the family. The Reverend Mr. Judge argued that Dawkins needed the ma-

turing influence of college, and that at the very least they should enter-
tain offers from other teams. But overnight the offer had grown to
$160,000, and Dawkins had pounced. He'd bought himself a sports car
and had never looked back. He'd been on the excellent 76er team
centered around Julius Erving in the late 1970s, but he'd never lived up
to the team's monstrous expectations. He'd become famous mostly for
shattering glass backboards with his dunks, accounting almost single-
handedly for an innovation in basketball technology—the hinged rim.
He'd also achieved notoriety as one of the great flakes in professional
sports, contending, among other things, that he was not of this earth but
a refugee from the planet Lovetron. He made up poems, told jokes, and
was generally very well liked. But he never did average 15 points a
game, and Philadelphia had gotten so sick of him that they'd dumped
him for just a draft pick. He'd labored with the horribly run New Jersey
franchise—the New Jersey "Nuts"—for five years before they'd lost faith
and dealt him to Utah. By that time, he'd been tagged as "the biggest
waste of space since Greenland." But then his wife had killed herself,
and he'd lost the heart to play. Jack McCloskey had entered the scene
at that point, picking up Dawkins for two future second-round picks.
Dawkins had taken the year off to recover from surgery and stitch
together his psyche. His joyous personality had taken a hell of a beating.
The Reverend Mr. Judge had again become a central figure in his life,
serving now not only as spiritual adviser but also as agent. Judge, now
almost eighty, had traveled to Dawkins's home in New Jersey and had
put Dawkins through a spiritual boot camp, reviving Dawkins's desire to
play basketball. He'd badgered Dawkins into exercising, and worked out
a $300,000 deal with McCloskey for 1988–89.

However, despite Dawkins's guaranteed money, he didn't have any
guarantee of making the team. McCloskey was suspicious of Dawkins.
He questioned Dawkins's desire. He liked Dawkins—who didn't—and
he felt compassion for him, but McCloskey was a businessman. His
business was basketball players. He couldn't afford to be sentimental
about them any more than a steelmaker could be sentimental about
steel. When McCloskey had first entered the NBA in 1972 as head coach
of the Portland Trail Blazers, he'd had to release a skinny kid named
Charlie Davis. Davis weighed 145, and in the NBA that made him little
more than lunch meat. But Charlie Davis had been on the college team
McCloskey had coached at Wake Forest. He'd thrown his little body into
the jaws of hell for McCloskey, the team had done well, and McCloskey
had ascended to the NBA. McCloskey was closer to Davis than he'd ever
been to any other player. When he'd sat down to give Davis the news,
he'd started crying. Still, he'd shipped him out. Ended the guy's career.

McCloskey's first loyalty had been to the franchise. It was the last time he'd ever cried over releasing a player. So it wouldn't be sentiment that would save Darryl Dawkins.

As far as sentiment went, Dawkins was in direct competition with another young player McCloskey felt emotionally close to, William Bedford. Bedford was big, strong, smart, handsome, gifted—and a junkie. He'd gotten involved with drugs in college, and several professional teams had found out about it through research by private investigators. Ever since Boston Celtic draftee Len Bias had died of an overdose, general managers had become deadly serious about drug problems. Phoenix, though, apparently had not done its homework—the Suns said they were "surprised" that Bedford, the best center in the draft, had slipped down to their number six pick. They grabbed him. Bedford had continued to use drugs in the NBA, and the league had busted him. But McCloskey had given a first-round pick to Phoenix for Bedford in 1987. McCloskey was close to someone who'd developed a drug problem—with disastrous results—and he felt a great deal of compassion for addicts. But not enough compassion to screw up the franchise. If he had to, McCloskey would dump both Bedford and Dawkins and keep Dave Popson.

Popson never would have the skills of Dawkins or Bedford, but he was an intelligent, hardworking, clean-cut kid. He'd just spent a year in Monaco, playing in a French league, and McCloskey was impressed with his progress. McCloskey had chosen him two years ago, as the eighty-seventh pick in the fourth round—basically, a throwaway pick. Popson hadn't even tried to make the team that year, because the odds were so bad. But in Monaco he'd picked up 25 pounds—now he was pushing 250—and he'd learned a few offensive moves. He knew they didn't want him to be a scorer, but in the NBA—a shooter's league— everybody had to be able to put up points. He was now playing beyond McCloskey's expectations, and had been good enough to survive the first cut.

After calming Dawkins down following the TV incident—promising to leave it on all night, even though it was driving him crazy—Popson had a quick breakfast in their cafeteria at the University of Windsor. Major league food: pancakes, eggs, fruit, cereal, juice, rolls, coffee, sausage. The Pistons didn't skimp. But most of the players were eating carefully; the days of hot dogs and Coke on the way to the ballpark were long gone. Adrian Dantley seemed to be particularly picky about what he ate. Dantley was thirty-two—an old man. But he was resisting age with furious intensity, and was wearing a cutoff shirt that exposed his stomach, which was as flat as a sidewalk. The bare midriff had a purpose. It told rookies: Don't go after *my* job.

After breakfast, Popson walked over to the field house. Just outside it, he hit the herd of fans who came for autographs. Right now, they'd pinned down Dennis Rodman—he seemed to be a favorite, even more than Isiah. They didn't care that his Dumb Dennis shot in the seventh game had blown the Championship. They just loved the way he played: like a kid, fist in the air, cheerleading, leaping over bigger guys. They didn't understand that he was of little more value to the team than the unspectacular Rick Mahorn, who was the anchor of the defense. Or that Rodman was worlds away from having the value of Isiah Thomas, who was obsessed with *winning,* and not just playing. The average fan, for all his or her love of the game, saw it very differently from someone like McCloskey. The fan, for the most part, saw the team from two primary vantage points: box scores, and video cameras that were usually isolated on the ball. Those two vantage points gave the fan some drama and enough information to talk coherently about the team. *And that was enough*—that was all most fans wanted. After all, basketball was little more than a temporary diversion for practically all the people who followed it, even "big fans." The whole point of being a fan was to have something to get excited about, but forget an hour after the game.

But for Jack McCloskey and Chuck Daly, basketball was a consuming passion. It was the sole source of their income, which was considerable. Daly made $500,000 a year. McCloskey's salary, which was undisclosed, wasn't a half-million dollars, but it was substantial. Basketball was also the source of their fame. Aside from money and fame, though, basketball gave each of them an opportunity for stark, kick-ass competition. Competitiveness was at the core of their personalities. It had attracted them to sports in the first place, when money and fame had been nonexistent.

That passion gave them a very different perspective on the team from that of the average fan. McCloskey was only marginally concerned—as he sat in the Windsor field house, watching practice begin—with box scores or highlight film acrobatics. His primary concern—now and always—was mix and chemistry. You had to have talent, but all good franchises had talent. It was mix and chemistry that won Championships.

A good mix meant having enough of each necessary ingredient. A team had to have a mix of youth and age—teams with too many young players made too many mistakes and teams with too many old players were too slow and prone to injury. You also needed the right mix of skills—the proper number of shooters, rebounders, defensive stars, ball handlers, and shot blockers. A fan who saw a box score with five players at 20 points thought, Great team! McCloskey saw it and thought, Nightmare! You couldn't have five guys all trying to do the same thing. They got in each other's way. You also had to have a balance of heights and sizes, and a balance of personalities. You wanted some players who were unshakable, and others who ran on emotion. You wanted some who were were hot in the relaxed early stages of a game and others who loved the crunch time. You wanted players who were slow and deliberate and players who were fast and freewheeling. You needed some tough, kick-ass guys, and others who kept the game fun.

Those things didn't show up in the box socres or highlight film. But McCloskey was convinced they were the keys to the Championship.

The way that the various aspects of the mix fit together produced a team's chemistry. Chemistry was the most indefinable aspect of a basketball team, but, according to McCloskey, it was probably the most important. "Right now," McCloskey said, "we're trying to find the right chemistry among ten primary players, with two more who will develop as time goes by. It isn't really important that those two help the team right now. Because there are only so many people you can put in your regular rotation.

"It's hard to manufacture the right chemistry. You really can't do it. You have to allow it to develop, and then you'll know it when it happens. It'll show up in the flow of the ball. It's part of the rhythm and the communication."

Chemistry was hard to force because a lot of it depended on how the players felt about each other. They had to trust each other, respect each other, understand each other—and hopefully, like each other. You couldn't win without generosity, self-sacrifice, and excellent communication. But all of those qualities were complicated by basketball having become a business. It was a coldhearted and brutal business. Mostly because it was a very *good* business. It offered enormous financial reward; successful players were treated almost like gods. And it didn't take long for them to realize that there was only so much money and godhood to go around.

Dennis Rodman had finally broken from the fans outside and was ready to work. Part of that work was talking to reporters. The business of basketball was totally dependent upon the media. It was the media that made the league rich. The print media created a vast reach of interest and the electronic media cashed in on that interest. Recognizing that, the league now insisted that its teams' locker rooms be open to the press at all times, except for forty-five minutes before a game. Such easy access had helped to make the NBA big news. And there was no bigger story within the NBA this year than the Pistons. Jack McCloskey wasn't the only one who thought the Pistons would win the Championship. So did the editors of *The New York Times Magazine*. They'd sent a writer to do a piece on the NBA's hottest team.

The writer, a longtime fan named Fred Waitzkin, had been struck by the adulation he'd seen Rodman receiving outside the field house. So he'd asked Rodman what it was like to be a role model.

"It's weird," said Rodman. "I gotta be *careful*. You know, I feel like *I'm* just a kid." To Waitzkin, who wasn't a sports reporter, that seemed like a fairly forthright answer. He'd expected something more like the postgame interviews he read in the papers and saw on TV: "I'm just glad to be able to do something for the youth of America, because the game's been very good to me." Sports interviews always seemed to have the same elements—for one thing, they stated the obvious: "I think we won because, to be frank, we scored more points than them. That's how I see it." And they were thicker with clichés than any other form of communication: "We have a much maligned defense but we really stepped up and played our game, stayed within ourselves, keyed on their mistakes and didn't lose sight of our objectives. But you've gotta give them credit, 'cause they have a good work ethic and gave a hundred ten percent." Lastly, all sports interviews, often even those with female athletes, were almost painfully masculine: "You've gotta be willing to play hurt in this league, because everybody has a job to do at gut-check time. Sure, I'll miss the ear that got bit off, but that's part of the game." In short, all you ever seemed to hear from athletes was mantalk: obvious, trite virility. But: "I've gotta be careful; I'm just a kid"—that wasn't bad. That was pretty honest. Waitzkin, who'd been hanging around for a couple of days, was beginning to believe that the players let it hang out more at fall camp than during the regular season. But even when the players tried to open up, it seemed like most of the sportswriters preferred to lapse back into mantalk. The sports reporters needed heroes for their stories, not complex characters. Also, the beat writers didn't want to open any cans of worms. They had to work with the players year in and year out, and it wasn't too hard to antagonize a rich, moderately educated twenty-five-year-old god.

Today's scrimmage started, and it was fierce: Not enough money and godhood to go around. Big Rick Mahorn, crippled in the playoffs, was back from disk surgery and renewing his reputation as the league's most aggressive—or violent, depending on your point of view—player. Mahorn kept slapping his body against John Salley so hard it made a sick, fleshy *crack!* in the near-empty gym. Then Popson, who felt he had to show McCloskey that he'd learned to be a "banger" overseas, got in the game and went to work on Salley and Bill Laimbeer. Popson knew his only hope of making the team was to be a role player, to fit a niche that

McCloskey needed for the proper mix. For Popson, that role wouldn't be scorer or rebounder—it would be hit man, the guy who came in and sacrificed his body for a few minutes to soften up the other team, so that a more skilled player, like James Edwards or Vinnie Johnson, could come in and employ his finesse. Michael Williams wasn't playing today. His X ray had revealed no break—to his vast relief—but his hand was still fat and misshapen. That opened up a few more minutes for Williams's friend Fennis Dembo—they'd been buddies since their high school days in Texas—but Dembo was enduring a lot of wrath. Dembo had been an invincible brick of muscle in college, but six-six and 215 didn't make much of a forward in the pros, so he was having to learn to play guard. Being a "bastard size" was a common problem, one that kept many rookies out of the NBA. Now, every time Dembo made a mental error, Bill Laimbeer jumped all over him. Laimbeer had a loud, petulant voice, and it seemed to drill into Dembo. Dantley and Rodman were also battling each other savagely. Dantley had the moves—he was the eleventh highest scorer in NBA history, mostly because of a repertoire of maneuvers that opened up easy shots or drew fouls. But Rodman had ungodly spring in his phone-pole thighs, and a fervor that was almost impossible to match.

When Daly called a halt, they all walked off the court wet with sweat. Fred Waitzkin, the guy from the *Times*, approached Dantley, who was sitting quietly on a table. It was a little disconcerting. To Dantley, Fred Waitzkin was *The New York Times*. Big deal. Dantley had been dealing with major media all his adult life. To Fred Waitzkin, Adrian Dantley was not a god—not quite. But Dantley was the kind of superstar he'd idolized as a kid. So Waitzkin led off with a fairly innocuous line of questioning.

"It seems like you and Rodman are competing pretty hard out there," said Waitzkin.

The next thing Waitzkin knew, Dantley was up and in his face. Dantley looked furious—his mouth was twisted up. "Isn't it the same between Laimbeer and Edwards?" he snarled. "Isn't it the same between Isiah and Joe Dumars?" Dantley stalked off. Waitzkin was shocked, even a little disillusioned. Athletes were packaged as heroes—that was their *job*. It was easy to say, "But they're just people, like you and me." But who believed that?

The other reporters commiserated with Waitzkin. They'd all been there. Not necessarily with Dantley—Dantley was generally quite polite, though frustratingly quiet. Dantley, they explained, was scared as hell of losing his job. Not only was Rodman threatening his minutes, but Dantley was starting to just generally feel like the odd man out. Everybody on the team was trying to play it cool, but something was wrong. The feud over the Disneyland money had carried over from last season, and it symbolized the larger conflict between Dantley and some of the other players. Joe Dumars was in Dantley's corner—they were both shy and thoughtful—but many of the others were lining up against him. They thought he was selfish, and cared more about himself than the Championship. In an odd way, their grievance wasn't personal. He was a genuinely decent guy, very generous about teaching players like John Salley the finer points of the game. He'd even gotten the nickname Teacher. But guys like Isiah Thomas and Bill Laimbeer were obsessed with the Championship, and had no patience for anyone who wasn't. After they'd lost the Championship last spring, Thomas had found Laimbeer sitting on the floor of the shower, weeping. It had been totally out of character for Laimbeer, who minimized victories and rationalized defeats. At that moment, Thomas and Laimbeer had promised each other that this would be the year. Even before that, though, Thomas and Laimbeer had placed a tremendous premium upon winning. Thomas had sacrificed his chance to be one of the game's statistical leaders. He had the skills to push Chicago's Michael Jordan and Boston's Larry Bird for the scoring title, but he'd never ever tried to. In fact, every year for the past six years—of his seven years in the league—his scoring average had declined slightly. Last year, he hadn't even averaged 20 points. But every year, his team had won more games, and every year he'd been of more value, becoming increasingly well rounded. As the point guard, in charge of bringing the ball down the floor, he often decided who shot. He'd willingly pass up his own shot to win. But when Team-First Thomas saw someone who wouldn't sacrifice his own glory, it ignited his fierce, ghetto-boy anger. During the 1985 All-Star Game, some of the veteran stars had thought rookie Michael Jordan was glory hogging. So Thomas, playing the point, had frozen Jordan out. It was the last time Jordan had tried to take over an All-Star Game.

After Dantley had cooled off, Waitzkin talked to him about selfishness. "Players today, they're for themselves," Dantley said. "Coaches are that way. They're selfish. Players got to be selfish, too."

But then Waitzkin talked to Thomas, and got a different story. "You know Dantley wants the ball all the time," Thomas said. "But, damn it, I ain't going to give it to him all the time. It's not that I don't like him. It's just that sometimes I'm going to Dumars or to Salley." Thomas told Waitzkin he wasn't feuding with Dantley. It sounded untrue.

To an extent, Isiah Thomas had adopted his obsession with winning from Jack McCloskey. McCloskey was an important influence on Thomas—the only general manager Thomas had ever played for. But the searing desire to win had always been a big part of Thomas. That was why, in 1981, Jack McCloskey had tied his fate to Thomas. And that was why, in 1988, it was a mistake to get on the wrong side of Isiah Thomas. It meant that you weren't just on the wrong side of one man. You were on the wrong side of the franchise.

When Jack McCloskey became general manager of the Detroit Pistons in the spring of 1980, the team's two stars were locked in a feud. The issue was selfishness.

For ten years, Bob Lanier had been the superstar of the team. He was one of the early dominating centers of the NBA, averaging about 22 points and 10 rebounds. At six-eleven and 265, he was the "big man" around which—in theory—every team had to be built. Lanier, the first pick of the 1970 draft, was hardworking and popular, and was good friends with Piston owner Bill Davidson. By 1980, Lanier wasn't as good as he'd once been. But he still played hard. He was just starting to make big money—about $300,000 per year—as NBA salaries were beginning to soar. Lanier wanted badly to hang on for a few more years of big paydays.

But the team had just acquired another star, Bob McAdoo, who had even stronger credentials than Lanier: 26-point average, 1975 Most Valuable Player, 1973 Rookie of the Year, and NBA scoring leader for three years. Piston coach Dick Vitale had traded away two first-round draft picks, along with free agent M. L. Carr, to get McAdoo. He'd made the trade with Boston's Red Auerbach, the most adroit general manager of the era. The trade helped put Boston in the NBA Finals five times over the next nine years. One of the two picks became Kevin McHale and the other was traded for Robert Parish. But Vitale had his star big forward in McAdoo. Conventional wisdom held that after a franchise had its star center, it went after its power forward, and then everything else took care of itself. Guard positions were considered easy to fill—there were lots of little guys out there.

But the trade was a disaster for Detroit. Just 12 games into the season, Vitale was fired, with a record of 4–8. For the season, the team went 16–66. It was one of the worst seasons for any team in NBA history. Detroit looked great in the box scores—McAdoo and Lanier both put up good numbers, and so did guards John Long and Terry Tyler. And nobody had better highlight film than the Pistons. But they won *16 games*—because McAdoo and Lanier hated playing together.

Lanier, after almost a decade as top dog, couldn't stand the idea of McAdoo coming in and stealing his spotlight. Lanier launched a whispering campaign to urge the franchise to get rid of McAdoo, but it got totally out of hand and caused an ugly public rift. Lanier lunched with owner Bill Davidson and tried to politick McAdoo off the team.

McAdoo, unlike Lanier, was quiet, introspective, and moody, and was not close to Davidson. McAdoo had a working-class North Carolina background, and didn't have the tools or desire for politicking. But McAdoo was just as proud as Lanier, and just as self-centered.

McAdoo was also one of the earliest beneficiaries of the NBA's salary explosion, and that didn't make him any less selfish. From the late 1960s to the middle 1970s, basketball salaries had gone up 700 percent. That happened partly because of the bidding war between the NBA and the American Basketball Association, and partly because television had decided that basketball was a "hot" sport, more in step with the younger audience than slow-moving baseball. In 1978, CBS gave the NBA $78 million for four years, and changed pro basketball forever. TV brought more money to all players in general, but a great deal more to the stars, who were "good video." Television also brought a new kind of fan to the sport, one who was much less astute than the aficionados who packed the crumbling, smoky, inner-city arenas. The new fan didn't know much about a pick-and-roll, but he did know a flashy dunk when he saw one. So the salaries of stars rocketed from the $75,000 range to the $600,000 range over just a few years. Suddenly, stars were being paid four or five times as much as their coaches. The big money undermined the desire to win of many of the stars—all of a sudden, the primary goal of some stars, like Lanier, was avoiding injury. It was the only thing that stood between them and wealth. That wealth, in turn, further engorged their egos. Virtually every player in the NBA had, from grade school on, dominated his peers—he'd been the king of the playground.

Bob McAdoo was one of the players who was accused of going soft, of just hanging on to cash his fat checks. A piece of doggerel was written about him: "McAdoo, McAdon't—McAwill, McAwon't." At one point, he told a member of the Detroit front office—headed by coach Dick Vitale, who was the de facto GM—that he was going to remain "injured" until the Pistons traded for a better point guard. Lanier, though, was a little more of the old school. He was hanging on for money, but he still believed that basketball, first and foremost, was just a game, and should be played with maximum intensity. Even this late in his career, he busted his ass every night. So Lanier and McAdoo, both proud and enormously talented, were at each other's throats, and were struggling through a hellish 16–66 season.

In the middle of that 1980 season, Jack McCloskey became general manager of the Detroit Pistons.

Virtually no general manager had ever inherited such a mess. Not only was Detroit bad, it had *always* been bad. The franchise was founded in 1948 in Fort Wayne, Indiana, by an industrialist named Fred Zollner, who manufactured automobile pistons. At that time, most of the teams were owned by companies that used them for promotion, as companies today sponsor softball teams. The league they played in, a predecessor of the NBA, had teams in Oshkosh, Sheboygan, Chicago, Toledo, Syracuse, Rochester, and Indianapolis. It was a region with cold winters, not much night life, and thousands of indoor gyms. The region had long taken great interest in its high school and college basketball teams, and had gradually become the country's Basketball Belt. The Fort Wayne Pistons played in a high school gym that held thirty-eight hundred people, and they had some reasonably successful teams.

But when they sought a larger market, moving to Detroit in 1957 as members of the National Basketball Association, they went to hell. They played to small, poor crowds in downtown Detroit, a deteriorating area that reached its nadir in 1967, when the worst race riot of the 1960s claimed forty-two lives. From 1957 to 1971, the Pistons had losing seasons every year. From 1957 until McCloskey took over in 1980, they had only one truly successful year—1973—when they went 52–30. But that was it—one little island of success.

Jack McCloskey held a news conference soon after being named GM. Charlie Vincent, a *Detroit Free Press* sportswriter at the time, was impressed by McCloskey. "Jack McCloskey will never be the hyper type of salesman Dick Vitale was," wrote Vincent. "You'll never catch him passing out Pistons' T-shirts in a restaurant, plastering Pistons' bumper stickers on automobiles in a television station parking lot, or throwing basketballs to kids in the stands." Vincent wrote that McCloskey ended the conference "without shouting a single slogan, without any reference to 'Piston Pride,' and without promising a new era of basketball excitement." But Vincent was also skeptical. He thought McCloskey's plans sounded "vague."

But McCloskey had big plans. Too big to reveal.

The first thing McCloskey did was to make a deal with another new GM—Stan Kasten of the Atlanta Hawks—who was also trying to build a good team out of practically nothing. McCloskey picked up Ronnie Lee from Kasten. It wasn't a big trade, but it was revealing. Ron Lee was the Kamikaze Kid, noted mainly for diving after loose balls. He'd dive at *anything*—body be damned.

Then came the big move. Two months into the job, McCloskey traded Lanier. The whole town howled, because Lanier looked *so* good in the box scores and in highlight film. All McCloskey got was a decent young center, Kent Benson, and a first-round pick. The fans thought McCloskey was crazy. Lanier for *Benson?* But the trade dissolved the poisonous chemistry of the team, and the following year they won about one-third more games—21, to be exact. Toward the end of the 1981 season, McCloskey executed the second half of his plan.

McCloskey had been trying for over a year to reignite Bob McAdoo. He'd played a lot of tennis with McAdoo, and they'd had long talks. But McAdoo had kept removing himself from games, complaining of a series of minor injuries. This was at the tail end of an era in which Piston players regularly came down with mysterious injuries in the middle of winter, went off to rehabilitate—and came back with a tan. They were called "Florida injuries."

McCloskey wouldn't stand for it. After a rash of midwinter injuries, McAdoo came back in April raring to play. At season's end he'd be a free agent, ready for the highest bidder. But he needed a month of hard play to strut his stuff.

McCloskey told him to go home. Go home and recover. He was no longer a Piston. McAdoo's release shocked the team even more than Lanier's trade. A new era had begun.

Two months later, McCloskey drafted Isiah Thomas with the second pick of the 1981 draft. A more highly rated player was also available in that draft—Mark Aguirre. Dallas took Aguirre with its first pick, which was fine with McCloskey. Aguirre had a reputation for selfishness. Thomas had a reputation for being obsessed with winning. And that was exactly what had obsessed McCloskey all his life.

One of Jack McCloskey's earliest memories was of his mother wrapping his father's feet for work. McCloskey's father had been a coal miner in Jackson's Patch, Pennsylvania, a company town, or "patch," based around an Allegheny Mountain colliery—a coal mine and processing plant. The mines were cold and wet, so McCloskey's mother rubbed Vaseline on his father's feet and wrapped them in waxed paper before he put on his boots. Even with that protection, they looked like raw meat. When the local deep mine played out, Jackson's Patch was devoured by a strip mine, and the McCloskeys moved to nearby Mahanoy City. McCloskey's father took Jack down into the mines just one time. That was enough. Jack McCloskey realized he had to escape that life. His way out, he believed, was sports. Not professional sports—that was a dream for people who could afford to be unrealistic. McCloskey thought that sports could get him into college.

For as long as McCloskey could remember, he'd had a talent for sports. He was good at all of them—baseball, basketball, football. He was fairly tall—eventually he'd be six-two—and his body was strong and supple, with good reflexes and excellent coordination. Everybody around him was competitive—you couldn't survive in a mining town in the Depression without being competitive. But McCloskey was more competitive than any of the kids he grew up with. There were no deep Freudian reasons for it—his parents hadn't pushed that hard and he didn't have any siblings to compete with. It was just part of him. It felt good. And he usually won. In high school, he played three sports and was on three championship teams. Local sports helped keep Mahanoy City alive. You didn't win anything other than "bragging rights" with a win over some desperate little town like Minersville or Blue Mountain, but bragging rights were important. They meant: My town's better than your town (so I'm better than you). More important to McCloskey, though, he got a scholarship to the University of Pennsylvania.

At Penn—always a strong sports school, filled with tough mining town kids—he won All-American honorable mention on the football team, played guard on the basketball team, and pitched baseball. But sports weren't the height of manhood. World War II had begun.

McCloskey dropped out to enlist in the Navy. He'd been in officer training school at Penn, so he became a lieutenant junior grade and skipper of a landing craft. At age nineteen, he was one of the youngest skippers in the Navy, with authority over men much older. But he found he had a talent for leadership. He served in the Pacific, and was part of the invasion of Okinawa. After Okinawa was secured, he was based there with a friend from Penn, Stan Novak, who was also an excellent basketball player. Novak and McCloskey played a lot of basketball, and talked about making their living at it. From coaching. There was no such thing as professional basketball. Novak, an avid tennis player, tried to teach tennis to McCloskey, but McCloskey thought it was a "pussy sport."

After McCloskey got home and finished his degree at Penn, he shifted his emphasis to baseball. Connie Mack, the great Philadelphia Athletics manager, had scouted and signed him. For three years he was a promising fastball pitcher in the A's farm system, but it all fell apart in a game in North Carolina against the Durham Bulls. His arm had gotten tired in that game, then had ached the next morning. His team doctor had rubbed some hot liniment on it and another doctor had shot it full of Novocaine and told him to go pitch the soreness out. McCloskey took the advice and ruined his arm. He tried to throw sidearm and under-handed. He even learned to throw left-handed, but didn't have enough speed. He was through.

While that was happening, the NBA was being created. An early branch of it, which later became part of the Basketball Association of America, was the Eastern League. McCloskey and his buddy Stan Novak joined one of the teams, along with another Penn grad, Jack Ramsay, who would later coach more NBA victories than anyone but Red Auerbach. They played for the Sunbury (Pa.) Mercuries in a town just down the road from Mahanoy City.

The Eastern League was rough as hell, playing basically with no-blood, no-foul rules. McCloskey liked that style—the Coalminer Style. In place of raw talent, it emphasized aggressiveness, tough defense, and teamwork. It wasn't really that bloody—it was still more civilized than mining town football—or Okinawa. The money was paltry. They played about thirty-five games a year and in a good year made $1,500—collecting a small fee after every game. McCloskey, Novak, and Ramsay would all drive to the games together in an old car, and the drives turned into coaching clinics. They all wanted to coach, since that was the only way to make a living from basketball.

In one of their games, Ramsay hit the deck for a loose ball and banged open his head. When he finally became conscious, about an hour later, he asked, "What happened?"

"You got knocked out and the game's over," McCloskey told him.

Ramsay, still groggy, paused only briefly. "You get my money?" he asked.

While McCloskey continued to play guard in the Eastern League—where he won the MVP award twice—he began to coach. He got a job coaching basketball at the small but prestigious Germantown Academy, which had always had terrible teams. Only after he had signed on, for $3,000 a year, did he find out that they were terrible because they had no gym to practice in. He found an unheated barn with wooden floorboards and a leaky roof and forced the kids to practice there. The boys—rich kids—bitched like crazy. McCloskey's only concession was to let them wear gloves. McCloskey taught the kids Coalminer Style basketball and they started beating the teams that had gyms. After three years, though, Germantown wouldn't give him a raise, so he left. He had a wife and child now, and $3,000, even in the early 1950s, was still poverty.

He found another coaching job in Collingswood, New Jersey, just across the Delaware River from Philadelphia. Again, he took over a losing team and made it into a winner, teaching them aggressiveness, hard defense, and teamwork. Without stars, that was the only way to win. By his second year, they'd won their group's state championship.

In 1954, McCloskey went back to Penn as assistant basketball and football coach and head baseball coach. Two years later, he took over the basketball team. At first, his team was terrible—7–19. But over the next four years they went from fourth in the Ivy League to second. By 1966, they won the league championship and held the longest winning streak in major college basketball. McCloskey left the job to Dick Harter, who learned the Coalminer Style and later was the college coach of Ronnie Lee, the Kamikaze Kid. After Harter left, the job and the style were assumed by another young coach from rural Pennsylvania, Chuck Daly. Daly had started out coaching for $3,600 a year at Punxsutawney, another Allegheny Mountain town not too far from Mahanoy City. They played pretty rough at Punxsutawney, too.

McCloskey moved on to another loser—Wake Forest, by far the smallest school in the rugged Atlanta Coast Conference. After six years, Wake Forest had become an ACC title contender. They didn't have any superstars, but their leader, skinny Charlie Davis, was scrappy as hell.

By 1972, Jack McCloskey was ready for the NBA. Now firmly established, the NBA was in its first throes of struggling with big money. McCloskey became head coach of the expansion Portland Trail Blazers. McCloskey was hired because of his reputation for making winners out of losers, and because he was known as a tough disciplinarian. Portland had a bad boy: Sidney Wicks, one of the NBA's first million-dollar rookies and a notorious prima donna. McCloskey and Wicks clashed from the start. The first time McCloskey asserted himself, Wicks told him, "I've checked you out and you're nothing but a loser! You've been a loser every place you've coached, and I've been a *winner* every place I've played."

McCloskey answered, "All-Star? Sidney Wicks an All-Star? The only team you could make is the all-*dog* team."

But the NBA, by that time addicted to its television money and television exposure, had become "a players' league." Coaches could no longer lay down the law. They had to peacefully coexist with their stars. McCloskey was gone after his second year.

He went to L.A., as assistant coach to former Laker star Jerry West, another tough, small-town Allegheny Mountain product. In 1977, the Lakers won the Pacific Division title, and when West became general manager McCloskey wanted the head coaching job. He was fifty and making $28,000 a year. But new owner Jerry Buss wanted a new coaching staff. McCloskey was out of a job.

McCloskey had to take another assistant coaching job with the down-and-out Indiana Pacers. The NBA was a very difficult place to work. There were only twenty-three head coaching jobs, and every basketball coach in the world wanted one. It was easy to get pigeonholed as an assistant, or a scout, or a college coach, or a coach who was too old. It was especially hard to nail a top job once you'd reached middle age. The players were all young, and in a players' league, you had to speak their language. McCloskey loved the NBA, because it was the zenith of basketball. But time was slipping away.

In November 1980, the job of general manager of the Detroit Pistons opened up. Detroit, of course, was the ultimate loser franchise. That didn't bother McCloskey. He applied.

When he got the job, he was fifty-three and still hungry—he'd yet to taste real success in the NBA. A year and half later, he still hadn't. But he'd cleaned house, corrected the team's chemistry, and instituted a new style of play: Coalminer Style, featuring Ronnie Lee.

And he had drafted a brilliant, obsessed college sophomore named Isiah Thomas.

TWO

"Cut from the Team"
The Exhibition Season

FRED WAITZKIN, *The New York Times Magazine* writer, sat down to a fall camp lunch between Isiah Thomas and Piston center James Edwards, feeling horrible and fantastic. It was a thrill to be sitting between two NBA stars. But Waitzkin felt dismal about the job he was trying to do. He wanted to talk to some of the players about personal subjects, but it was like pulling teeth. The Piston beat writers had begun to crank out their feature stories about camp, and the players were already starting to clam up. Waitzkin had asked Dennis Rodman for an interview this morning, but Rodman had scheduled it just before practice, and then he'd steered Waitzkin over by several of this buddies, to keep things light and safe. Rodman was spooked by the press. In 1987, the media had portrayed him as the NBA's worst racist—and no one in the press had even realized what an ironic portrayal that was.

Dennis Rodman had grown up in a tough part of Dallas, raised by just his mother. He'd been too small for sports in high school, and had been dominated by his athletic older sisters. After high school, he'd cleaned cars, worked as a janitor, and hung out in the streets. He'd landed in jail for stealing some watches. An eleven-inch growth spurt had made him feel like a freak, but it had also gotten him onto the basketball team of a tiny Oklahoma university. Still, he had little focus or ambition. Then he'd met Bryne Rich. Rich, an Oklahoma farm boy, was thirteen—six years younger than Rodman—but like Rodman he also seemed lost. The year before, Rich had been hunting with his best friend, Brad Robinson, and had stopped by a tree to reload. Rich had snapped his shotgun shut, but the firing pin had stuck and the gun had gone off, shooting Robinson. Rich had held Robinson as others went for help, telling him how sorry he was and how much he loved him. Robinson had said, "I love you too"—but he died. For months, Rich was sick with depression; he couldn't even sleep in his own room. All his parents could do was tell him to pray for a brother.

At a basketball camp, though, he'd met Rodman and they'd immediately become close. Rich had taken Rodman home one evening, shocking his parents. Their farm community was overtly racist and Rich's parents were against the relationship. But that night, for the first time since the shooting, Bryne Rich had slept in his own room. The relationship blossomed, Rodman moved in with the family, and now he lived there in the off-season, doing farm labor all day long. The Rich family has not been the only white influence in Rodman's life—his longtime girlfriend, and mother of his baby daughter, is also white.

Then, in 1987, Rodman had sat amid a group of reporters after the Pistons had lost the seventh game of the Eastern Finals to Boston. He was hurt and angry. A reporter had mentioned Larry Bird and Rodman had said, "Larry Bird is overrated in a lot of areas. Why does he get so much publicity? Because he's white." There was an uproar, but Rodman had assumed it would subside as he drove from Detroit to Oklahoma, to spend the summer with the Riches. It didn't. Rodman was branded as racist. So now Dennis Rodman tried to limit most of his communication with reporters to mantalk and stats.

Most of the other players did, too. Especially when they were around their buddies. Waitzkin had been waiting to talk to Isiah Thomas—who seemed to be the resident Big Thinker on the team—about money and how it affected the game. But Thomas had insisted they talk over lunch. So Waitzkin sat there unhappily, thinking, "This is your chance. Get it over with."

Isiah, though, seemed to read Waitzkin's mind. Thomas said, "Tell you what. Why don't you eat your food then we'll go up to my room to talk." Waitzkin was impressed. Any of the other players, he believed, would have been oblivious to his mood and would have bulled through with the interview.

In the quiet of Thomas's room, Thomas opened up with Waitzkin about money, and what it had done to pro basketball. "Most of the guys in professional sports come from poor backgrounds," said Thomas. "Overnight a guy's making a million a year, and this is a guy who doesn't know how to balance a checkbook. He's probably never *had* a checkbook. Overnight, instead of being a college kid, he's a role model. He ain't *ready* to be a role model. It starts to blow his mind.

"People start coming to that guy and saying, 'No, you don't have to buy dinner—I'll buy it for you. You don't have to make plane reservations. I'll pay your bills for you'—the agent says this. 'I'll watch out for you. All you have to do is get on the court.'

"So what the kid does—he's totally out of reality now, he never looks at his business deals. The agent handles his bills. When he comes into a restaurant, he says, 'I'm Joe Blow from the Pistons—you seat me first.' And it *works*. Until all of a sudden it stops. One day the agent says, 'I got another young guy who's pretty hot. I've got to clean *his* nose. Here, you got to pay your own bills, and by the way, I haven't paid your taxes the last three years.' "

Thomas told Waitzkin that money had corrupted the style of many players. Now, instead of playing to win, they played to fatten their stats.

"A player sits down with a general manager," said Thomas. "He's told, 'You want a raise? You averaged three points, four rebounds. You want a *raise?*'

"Therefore, the player says to himself, I got to get thirteen rebounds a night and fourteen points. So Isiah come driving down the lane. I'm not going to try to block his shot. I'm going to hope he misses so I can get that rebound. When my guy gets beat, I'm not going to help him. I'm going to block out my man and be ready. That's two rebounds.

"I got to get my three steals. I'll get one this time. Doesn't matter if my man got a lay-up—I'm going to try every time until I get a steal. I got my three steals—it doesn't matter that I gave up fourteen points to get them.

"Now when you sit down in the general manager's office, the GM says, 'How can you ask me for a raise? The team only won twenty-two games this season.' You answer, 'Yeah, but *I* averaged twenty points, ten rebounds, and three steals.' "

Team-First Thomas was in a position to be philosophical about money. He'd just moved into what could only be described as a castle in fashionable Bloomfield Hills, and he'd just signed an eight-year, $16-million deal with McCloskey. He was suddenly making almost twice as much as Adrian Dantley, after several years of making only about half Dantley's salary. Dantley hadn't negotiated with McCloskey for that money, though—he'd come to Detroit with a $1 million-plus salary, the result of yearly wars with Utah coach and vice president Frank

Layden. Dantley was a tough negotiator, and Layden had hated dealing with him.

Now Thomas was in the NBA's select circle of wealthy men. Only New York's Patrick Ewing, San Antonio's David Robinson, Chicago's Michael Jordan, and L.A.'s Magic Johnson and Kareem Abdul-Jabbar were in the $3-million range. Next year it would be just Jordan, Robinson, Ewing, and Johnson, since Jabbar was calling it quits. The only reason Jabbar was playing this year was for the money—he'd been swindled by his manager a few years ago, and had stood at the brink of retirement without a penny. But rumor out of L.A. was that Jabbar had reported to fall camp fat and sloppy, and that Laker general manager Jerry West was astonished and mad as hell. Unbeknownst to Thomas, though, one of his prime rivals, Larry Bird, was trying to best Thomas and the members of the Three Million Club. Bird had just skipped the first day of the Celtics' camp in an apparent holdout over his contract. Bird was demanding $4 million or $5 million per year. General manager Jan Volk was said to be apoplectic. The NBA had a strict limit on the total amount each team could pay for players' salaries, and the salary cap this year was $7.2 million. How could Volk give $6 million of that to Bird? McCloskey had only been able to afford Thomas's salary through—in his words—"voodoo economics."

Thomas had to return to the field house, because Daly was still putting them through two-a-day practices. McCloskey needed plenty of exposure to the rookies, so that he could know whom to cut. Also, some of the veterans needed the exercise—Thomas, for example, was getting his butt run into the ground by rookie Michael Williams. And Laimbeer always seemed to report to camp with a puff of blubber. Laimbeer enjoyed drinking a little beer, and he spent his summers on the golf course, instead of working out and learning how to play close to the basket, like other centers. It pissed off McCloskey. But what could he do? Laimbeer wouldn't respond to an ass-chewing. Too independent. Over the summer, assistant coach Dick Versace had tried to teach Laimbeer some low-post moves, but Laimbeer had balked. He'd told Versace, this is what I *will* do, and this is what I *won't* do. He had developed a little running hook, but that was about it. Laimbeer's preference for the long jump shot did have one distinct advantage, though—it kept him out of the congestion under the hoop, where most serious injuries occurred. Laimbeer, at $630,000 a year, was more likely to keep drawing paychecks as a jump-shooter. Not that Laimbeer was desperate for the cash. He had a degree in economics from Notre Dame—as did Adrian Dantley—and he had excellent business connections through his father, a very successful businessman. Laimbeer, in fact, was said to be the only player in the NBA who made less money than his dad.

At the moment, though, Laimbeer was definitely earning his money—he was getting his ass kicked around the court by burly Dave Popson. Popson, who just six years ago had been considered the number one high school player in the country, was fighting to survive the next cut. Within a day or two, McCloskey would eliminate another three or four players, leaving Detroit just one or two over the roster limit. Those one or two players would then join the team for their exhibition games.

Popson felt pretty confident. When camp had first begun, he'd been jumpy with anxiety, but after he'd started playing he'd actually had fun. Basketball was a *game*, after all, and Popson had played for fifteen years without even thinking of money. As soon as he'd gotten some contact, it felt like the same old game, and his adrenaline rose. The same thing had seemed to happen to other players. Some of them, like Isiah and Dennis Rodman, really got carried away. They loved it. The coaches encouraged that attitude. They depended on it. If their players were just in it for money, they were screwed—the players would play it safe and they'd lose. But if the players went at it with pride and joy, they had a team: an excellent team. Thus, even though Chuck Daly knew he was coaching a dozen wealthy men, he did everything he could to deemphasize the money and promote the Just a Game myth. His job security—and his $500,000 salary—depended on it.

Later on, Fred Waitzkin talked with Daly about the conversation on money he'd had with Isiah. Daly looked amused. "You've got this kid," Daly said, "and he makes ten million dollars—whatever. But these guys are no different from the kids I coached at Punxsutawney High School. Because you know what they're interested in? Points scored, rebounds, minutes played. All the basic children's things. It's a children's game, so that's kind of their mentality."

But the following day, just before the next round of cuts, Daly took Michael Williams aside and said, "Mike, you're a good player—you've got the skills to be a million-dollar player. But remember. This is a *business.*" That was all he'd said. What did he mean? Williams wasn't sure. Did it mean he was about to get cut? Had they decided that Kevin Gamble was a better guard?

Williams wouldn't let himself worry. Worry was worse for your game than bad knees. You could think basketball to death—the more you thought about a shot, the more likely you were to miss it. So Williams just assumed that McCloskey knew what Williams knew—that he was as good as *anybody*, even Isiah. Williams was quiet and never squawked about rookie chores like carrying balls or fetching towels. But he knew he was one of the best in the world. You had to think that way. Daly was constantly harping on teamwork, so Williams focused on helping the team—even though he wasn't really a member of it. Williams didn't regret that he was on a team that was deep in talent, particularly at his own position. Depth was what you needed to win, and it was important to Williams that the Pistons win. Even though he wasn't a Piston. Not all the rookies felt that way. Kevin Gamble and Demetrius Gore seemed more worried about their own jobs. You couldn't blame them. They weren't getting as many minutes as Williams, and from the bench, it was harder to believe that this was Just a Game.

After practice, John Salley stood outside the field house in a cold, dismal drizzle, signing autographs for hundreds of kids with shivering hands and blue lips. A reporter hurrying home asked Salley why he was standing in the rain. "I looked out here," said Salley, motioning at the mob of children. "And I saw myself."

"What is there about your team," asked Portland columnist David Kahn, "that you're not happy about?"

Piston assistant coach Dick Versace looked blank. Detroit had just opened their exhibition season by burning the Portland Trail Blazers by 30 points. "I can't think of *anything*," said Versace.

McCloskey was standing behind Versace. "That's the first time I've ever heard him say that," said McCloskey.

"Well, I was asked what's not to like about this team," said Versace.

"I'll tell you what," said McCloskey. "The coaching staff." There were lots of smiles and the locker room was loud. The win was nothing to base a season on, but it was a good omen.

The next day, as McCloskey relaxed in front of a football game in his suite at the Guest Quarters in Portland, the good feeling hung on. "We're not that good and Portland's not that bad," he said. "I'll be surprised if we beat them by thirty any time again this season."

Still, it confirmed McCloskey's belief that a team with the right mix and chemistry could beat a team that looked good in a box score. On paper, Portland was at least as good as Detroit, and had been picked by some experts to dethrone L.A. Portland had three All-Stars—Kiki Vandeweghe, Clyde Drexler, and Steve Johnson—and a center, Kevin Duckworth, who'd averaged 22 points and 9 rebounds since becoming a starter. Their starting backcourt of Drexler and Terry Porter was one of the best in the league. So why did they lose by 30?

Horrible chemistry. Portland's coach, Mike Schuler, was at war with Vandeweghe and Drexler. Kiki had lost his starting position and wanted to be traded, and Clyde refused to practice for Schuler, who specialized in boot camp workouts. So the team was playing half-assed games of three-on-three or four-on-four. The season hadn't started, and Portland was being ripped apart.

Tension on a team was common. Just yesterday, Bill Laimbeer and Darryl Dawkins had gotten tangled up under the basket during practice and had gotten violently pissed off at each other. There was a lot of yelling and fists were cocked. Dawkins, sick of Laimbeer's bitching and blaming, had looked like he'd really wanted a piece of Laimbeer. But the coaches and other players jumped in and nobody had gotten permanently bent out of shape. When you played Coalminer Style, there was going to be a certain amount of rough stuff.

McCloskey wasn't worried about the Dawkins-Laimbeer fight. For one thing, he wasn't even sure that he was going to keep Dawkins. Dawkins had begun at fall camp as a fitness demon, but that had petered out. McCloskey had just made his next to last roster cut, and Dawkins had gotten through it—which was expected, since he had a $300,000 guaranteed salary. But McCloskey had also kept Dave Popson and William Bedford, Dawkins's rivals for the job. The only rookies other than Popson to make the cut were Michael Williams and Fennis Dembo. Kevin Gamble, Demetrius Gore, Mark Plansky, and Craig McMillan were gone. One more player had to be cut, and two had to be cut if Bedford was cleared by his drug treatment program.

"I talked to the league about Bedford," said McCloskey, "and they said that if he got cleared to play, they would give us ten days for him to get in shape, then I'd have to activate him or release him. So I'd have to make a decision on the player that we would keep. Right now, we have fourteen, including Bedford. Say we drop Popson, then we would have thirteen. Then, if Bedford's okay, we'd have to make a decision between Bedford and Dawkins. If I had to choose right now, I'd choose Bedford. Dawkins is in a lot better condition than he's been in the past, but he's still not in good physical condition. He should be fighting for his athletic life now, *punishing* himself. But he's not. After playing a few minutes, it's hard for him to continue."

McCloskey looked sad, and a little bewildered. He still stayed in excellent shape, just as a matter of pride. He'd taken up tennis, the "pussy sport," at the urging of his friend from Penn and Okinawa, Stan Novak—who was now McCloskey's chief scout and closest friend in the franchise. McCloskey had become one of the best senior tennis players in Michigan, and his goal was to be the best in the world in his age group. "Although," he said, "I may have to be one hundred two to make it." He couldn't understand how an athlete could let himself get fat—especially when he was almost broke and had a $300,000 job riding on it.

But McCloskey's problem—too many good players for too few spots—was the problem he'd long dreamed of. Depth, he thought, *was going to win him the Championship*. It was the heart of his strategy.

It was a strategy he'd been forced to adopt. It would have been easier to stick to convention, and build the team around a star center, like Patrick Ewing, Moses Malone, or Akeem Olajuwon. But McCloskey didn't have one, so he'd built a team that didn't really have a central player. Isiah Thomas was McCloskey's star, but the team would have been excellent even without Thomas. Part of the credit for that went to Thomas—he'd sacrificed himself to bring others into the game, and his teammates had improved because of it. Particularly Dumars, who'd become more of a scorer. But most of the credit went to McCloskey, for his constant, gradual upgrading of the franchise through trades and draft picks. Since 1980, he'd made twenty-nine trades. Over the same time, for example, Washington had made eighteen and Denver and Milwaukee had each made seventeen. During four different years, McCloskey had made five trades per year, earning the nickname Trader Jack. He believed that if a trade improved the team 1 percent he should make it. Two seemingly minor trades he'd made had revolutionized the team. In 1982 he'd traded the marginal Steve Hayes for a future second-rounder, and in 1985 he'd let aging guard Terry Tyler go to Sacramento for the right to switch 1986 first-round picks. The 1982 deal became Dennis Rodman. The 1985 deal became John Salley.

McCloskey had also profited greatly from the draft. He'd found excellent players like Dennis Rodman in the second round, and genuine stars, like Joe Dumars, Ricky Pierce, and Kelly Tripucka, late in the first round. McCloskey spent weeks on the road every winter, combing out-of-the-way universities and small colleges.

More than probably any other team in the league, Detroit bore the stamp of its general manager. Most other teams were patterned after their stars. By building a deep, decentralized team, McCloskey had been able to control its style, and to guard his own power within the franchise. "I don't think you can win in the playoffs anymore without depth," said McCloskey, losing interest in the football game as his mind turned to the NBA Finals. "Now you need ten guys who can really play. The days of someone like Boston getting by with their first five are over." During the past few years, McCloskey had designed his team to beat Boston—they had stood between him and the Championship. He'd tried to build a team that was faster, deeper, and tougher. Rick Mahorn had been acquired specifically to negate Kevin McHale. It was no coincidence that McHale hated Mahorn more than any other player in the league.

"You've *gotta* have depth now," McCloskey said, "because the season is so long, and injuries and fatigue are such crucial factors, especially in the playoffs. We were deep last year, and look what happened in the Finals—Mahorn was injured and Thomas was injured and that probably cost us the Championship.

"But we're even deeper this year. I really liked the way Williams played last night"—he'd scored 15 points in 21 minutes.

McCloskey walked over to the TV and snapped it off. "You know," he said, "there are a lot of teams I respect. New York's gonna be good this year. Atlanta's good—they've got Moses now and I hear he's playing like a kid. Even Cleveland—for years that was one team you didn't have to worry too much about—but they're gonna be *good* this year. And there's always that Green Monster from Boston.

"But you know who I think the team to beat is?" He smiled a careful, tight-lipped smile. *"Us."*

Steve Addy was the grand old man of the Detroit Piston beat writers. He was twenty-five. He'd been on the beat for one year.

The veteran Piston beat writers, like Charlie Vincent and Johnette Howard of the *Detroit Free Press,* had become columnists. So now the beat had fallen to beginners, and it was a tough beat to work. There was glamour in it, but a lot of aggravation. Chuck Daly was often condescending, especially to the new reporters, and it was hard to get anything out of the players but mantalk. Rodman was still wary from the Larry Bird fiasco. Isiah Thomas had agreed with Rodman that Bird was overrated because he was white (although sarcastically, some claimed) and had been equally traumatized. Laimbeer was hostile to reporters, and Dantley was polite but icy. Joe Dumars had a sweet, generous personality, but he didn't enjoy interviews, and Vinnie Johnson was friendly but often didn't have much to say. John Salley was funny and the only dependable source of a good quote. Mahorn was dangerous. Nice guy—but catch him in the wrong mood and he'd scream, "Suck my dick!" Didn't matter who was around. That was his stock comeback: Suck my dick.

So Steve Addy, who favored a jaundiced persona—sort of W. C.

Fields as a young pup—wasn't entirely thrilled to be sitting in Dayton, Ohio, ready to watch the Pistons terrorize the miserable Cleveland Cavaliers. It was just another game—one down and a hundred to go. From here on, Addy, who worked for the *Oakland* (Mich.) *Press,* would be working seven days a week until May or June, writing about 1,000 words on each game, plus feature stories and columns. He'd crank out about 150,000 words for the season, the equivalent of about three books the length of *The Great Gatsby.*

He settled in to watch the punishment begin. Cleveland was a Basketball Belt city, but the town's love of the game had been poisoned by the ineptitude of the franchise. Cleveland had been the worst team in the league since its creation in 1970, with an overall .388 won-lost percentage. For years the team had been owned by Ted Stepien, one of the strangest operators ever to bleed the life out of a franchise. Lately, though, Cleveland had gotten new owners and a new general manager, Wayne Embry, who was shrewd and serene. Late last season, Embry had engineered a blockbuster trade, giving Phoenix Mark West, Tyrone Corbin, and excellent guard Kevin Johnson, plus two second-round picks and a first. Embry had gotten star forward Larry Nance, journeyman forward Mike Sanders, and a first-round pick. At first, Cleveland's revamped team had sucked. But Embry hadn't panicked, and neither had his coach, Lenny Wilkens, who'd been hired in part because he was a low-key as Embry. Then, toward the end of the year, the team had begun to play rather well.

Still, Addy thought, Cleveland was Cleveland—the Cadavers. A week ago they had blown out Boston by 41 points, but that was the first exhibition game of the year. A fluke, no doubt.

But then the game started. It hadn't been a fluke. Cleveland was good. Damn good. Their mix and chemistry were superb. They now had two strong inside players, Larry Nance and Brad Daugherty—just enough for power but not enough to clog up the middle. They had a great floor general in little Mark Price, who was pushing Isiah to his limit. Over the summer, Embry had picked up veteran center Tree Rollins as a free agent, and Rollins added age and meanness to the Cav mix, which ran toward young and gentlemanly. The departure of Kevin Johnson had opened up minutes for shooting guard Ron Harper, and he was acting like a kid who'd just seen a chance to make a million bucks.

The Cavs were poised, quiet, and workmanlike. They were unselfish and seemed to really like each other. The one possible flaw in Cleveland's mix was too much youth, but Embry—who had a tremendous belief in the power of strong character—had searched for players who could play beyond their years. Now, as the young Cavs waited patiently on offense and refused to get rattled by Detroit's aggressiveness, it looked as if Embry's search had paid off.

Cleveland beat Detroit 120–102. It was the Pistons' first big loss of the year. Detroit looked thoroughly overmatched. Almost bewildered.

As Addy went to the dressing room to talk to Daly and soak up a little mantalk from the players, he thought, "Jesus—it's not just Atlanta that's going to be tough this year. Cleveland is for real."

In the locker room, Daly was subdued. "Get used to it," Daly said. "They're a good team."

Last summer, Daly had had a dream. He'd dreamed he was watching the 1989 NBA Finals. On television. Detroit wasn't in it. Cleveland was. The dream had seemed very real. After the dream, he'd coined a new name for Cleveland. They were so quiet, but so deadly—he'd begun thinking of them as "the Assassins."

McCloskey was impressed by Cleveland, too. He'd thought they would be good. But he hadn't thought they'd be *this* good. Last year, he'd had a chance to get Larry Nance. When Phoenix had traded center James Edwards to McCloskey, they'd offered him Nance, too. But they had wanted John Salley and Joe Dumars, plus some picks. Too steep. Now Nance was the pivotal player in a trade that had made Cleveland an excellent team. Maybe not picking him up had been a mistake. McCloskey wouldn't know until the season was over.

Shortly after the Cleveland game, McCloskey called Dave Popson into his office. Popson was hopeful. He'd played well against Cleveland, scoring 14 points with 4 rebounds. Dawkins was still fat, and Bedford still hadn't been okayed by the drug clinic. Ever since he'd embraced the Just a Game concept, Popson had played the best basketball of his life.

"We want to keep you," McCloskey told him. Popson felt a surge of joy.

"But we have to let you go." It felt like a door had been slammed against his nose. "I really think you have a chance to play in this league," said McCloskey, "and I tried to work out a trade for you, but it just didn't come together. But if there's ever anything I can do, be sure and call me." He handed Popson a one-way plane ticket to Popson's hometown, Wilkes-Barre, Pennsylvania, which was just up the road from Mahanoy City.

Popson didn't try to argue his case. The league didn't work that way.

Now McCloskey had his team. Thomas, Laimbeer, Mahorn, Dumars, Dantley, Rodman, Salley, Johnson, Edwards, Dawkins, Williams, and

Dembo. The deepest team in the league. But he also had a new worry. He'd built his team to dethrone the Boston Celtics. He had believed he'd accomplished that. But meanwhile, quietly and carefully, someone else had stolen up. The Assassins.

It was going to be a long season.

THREE

"A Bad Start"
The Season Begins

"...BY THE dawn's early light . . . were so gal-lant-ly streaming—"

"Hey, Laimbeer! You're a *dead* man!"

"—the bombs bur-sting in air, gave proof through—"

"Laim-*beer!* Eat shit and *die!*" It was another voice this time, but it came from the same section—down near the Pistons' bench, just behind the stairs that led to the shadowed, moldy basement of Chicago Stadium. Laimbeer stood with his lips tight as the pages of a closed book, staring straight ahead. Laimbeer *liked* the abuse—it helped get him keyed up for the game. But he didn't need too much help with this one, because it was the opening game of the season. Even before the anthem ended, the fans were up and shrieking. It was a high-pitched wail, almost like a dog whistle. The Chicago fans were known as the best fans in the league. Which is to say, they were the most shrill and sadistic. They sat just a few feet from the edge of the court, and every curse and hex knifed straight into the players' ears. The proximity of fans to players was mostly why the home court advantage was more pronounced in basketball than any other sport, often providing an 80–90-percent certainty of victory. It took almost inhuman concentration to ignore the screaming.

Even more than they hurt the visiting team, though, the fans helped the home team. Basketball was the most aerobically demanding sport. Every game called for approximately six miles of wind sprints, about five rounds of boxing or wrestling, and twenty to thirty high jumps. Exhaustion was part of every game. But the fans unleashed a reserve of adrenaline in the home team players that fought this exhaustion, often setting off a "home-court surge" of 8–10 points that won the game. There was something ridiculous, of course, about a player with a $750,000 contract needing *applause* for motivation. But to many of the players, after the opening tip-off, it was Just a Game—and cheering was what had *always* pushed them through the game, just as abuse had always undermined them. But that didn't hold true for Laimbeer—he fed on the abuse. Laimbeer was not physically gifted; he'd gotten to the NBA the hard way, and the abuse told him he finally mattered.

Laimbeer edged into the center circle with Chicago center Bill Cartwright. Laimbeer reached down, touched his toes, sawed up and down a few times, then as referee Jimmy Clark tossed the ball up Laimbeer brought his arms down and shot them into the air to propel his jump. But his feet only raised about ten inches, and Cartwright easily controlled the tip. Laimbeer looked infuriated. Of all the players, Laimbeer was the most emotionally brittle. More than the others, he carried his on-court persona—tense, competitive, belligerent—into the locker room. Some who knew him believed his tightly wired behavior came from his childhood, that his parents—ultrasuccessful members of the southern California executive class—had pushed him too much and praised him too little. He was also, to a degree, a victim of his own body. He'd been fat as a kid, the butt of ridicule, and when he'd finally made the NBA after a stint in Italy, he'd been one of the clumsiest players in the league, suffering from a bad case of what the players called "white man's disease." "He even cheats differently than the black players," a Detroit writer said of Laimbeer. "There are things that are winked at, like pushing with your hips, because everyone does them—they all learned in the same playgrounds. But Bill has his own set of tricks—which aren't as smooth—and they get him into trouble." However distasteful his off-court personality was, though, it translated into a valuable attitude during the game: Bill Laimbeer *hated* to lose.

Laimbeer was still scowling as Chicago brought the ball down. Cartwright ducked into the lane. Laimbeer followed him but Cartwright lowered his shoulder and drove it into Laimbeer's chest. Laimbeer wheezed and teetered backward. Cartwright, seven feet, one inch and quick as a panther, jerked away, took a pass, spun, and popped up an easy jumper. The first points of the season went to Cartwright. Good omen for Chicago. Bulls' GM Jerry Krause, one of McCloskey's prime rivals as an aggressive trader, had just picked up Cartwright in exchange for rebounding demon Charles Oakley. Oakley was a close buddy of Michael Jordan, and when Jordan had found out about the trade, he'd gotten pissed off at Krause. Not only were they friends, but Oakley was Chicago's Badass—he was the enforcer who kept the tough guys off Jordan. Last year during the playoffs, Oakley had marched over to protect Jordan from Rick Mahorn, and had gotten into a hell of a tangle with Mahorn, Detroit's Badass. Chicago coach Doug Collins had jumped on Mahorn, grabbing him around the neck with both hands, and Mahorn had flipped Collins on top of the scorer's table. That's when the bad blood between Chicago and Detroit had begun, and now it was still here. But Jordan no longer had Oakley to protect him. Cartwright was a shooter, not a fighter—in New York, they'd called him Invisi-Bill. Jordan was still pissed off at Krause over the trade, and it was polluting Chicago's chemistry.

It was bad business to have Michael Jordan pissed off. Despite Krause's efforts, Chicago was still a one-man team. But Jordan was glad to be playing again, and several minutes into the first quarter, he bounced in front of Joe Dumars, who was dribbling on the perimeter, looking for an open man. Suddenly Jordan was *behind* Dumars—so fast it looked like a movie special effect—a cut and splice. Jordan batted the ball out of Dumars's hand to Horace Grant and was downcourt almost before Grant got the ball. Grant hook-passed to Jordan, who was a blur, a javelin in midair. Jordan snagged the pass and leaped from almost the free-throw line, floating through the air, then jammed it down with an underhanded scoop as his legs splayed wide. The courtside fans jumped up and the the dog whistle shrieked. Daly looked weary. The season was five minutes old.

A couple of minutes later, Thomas hurried the ball down and zipped a crosscourt pass to Mahorn under the basket. But as soon as the ball was in Mahorn's hands, Jordan shot past and suddenly Mahorn wasn't holding the ball. Jordan flew downcourt with four Piston defenders in front of him. By the time he got to the free-throw line only Laimbeer was still with him. Jordan jolted upward and seemed to freeze in the air as Laimbeer kept moving forward. Laimbeer's hand groped for the ball, but Jordan tucked it under his legs, then windmilled it in a 180-degree arc that ended with a smash through the hoop. Dog whistle. Time-out Detroit. 12–4 Bulls. Daly goose-stepped into the Detroit huddle, his limbs rigid with anger.

But by late in the quarter Jordan was glazed with sweat and Collins took him out and put in some of his subs—Brad Sellers, John Paxson, Charlie Davis: nobodies. Daly countered with Dennis Rodman, John

Salley, Vinnie Johnson, and James Edwards—*his* B-team. His killer B-team. All of McCloskey's work—the trades and the painstaking labor of drafting—became immediately apparent. Detroit's Killer B-Team—to use a jockism—erased the Chicago lead and put the Pistons slightly ahead.

Then: late second quarter—James Edwards anchored himself under the Detroit basket and Bill Cartwright ran down to cover him. Cartwright bounced into Edwards, knocking him back, but Edwards hammered his forearm into Cartwright's kidneys, shoving Cartwright forward. Cartwright fell back into Edwards, leading with his elbow. But Edwards was ready—as Cartwright crashed into him he jerked his knee into Cartwright's ass. Their bodies tangled together and then Cartwright dipped his shoulder and swung it into Edwards's midsection. As Edwards fell back, he flailed his fist at Cartwright's face. Whistle. Foul on Edwards. In the NBA, it was fair to "jockey for position"—but no fists. As Cartwright caught his breath, Isiah Thomas walked up to him, sneered, and put his hands on top of Cartwright's. Cartwright, pissed, pulled his hands away and smacked Thomas's chest, which only came up to about Cartwright's belly button. Thomas gritted his teeth and dove for Cartwright. But before he could get to him, Mahorn was there, his huge hands all over Cartwright. Cartwright, only too happy to mix it up with Thomas, wanted no part of Mahorn. "Hey, fuck you!" Mahorn boomed at Cartwright. Laimbeer swung an arm around Thomas's shoulder and pulled him away. The dog whistle pealed. A fan yelled, "Hey, Mahorn, you're a flaming *ass*-hole!" Daly scowled from the sidelines.

Mahorn came out of the confrontation looking serene, as if he'd shown why he was worth the $800,000 he'd just negotiated out of McCloskey. Cartwright looked jangled. The rest of the Bulls looked uncomfortable, ill at ease, as if the fans were screaming at *them*.

Detroit began to run away with the game. Coalminer Style won it. The tone of the season was set.

John Ciszewski couldn't stand it anymore. For years he'd worked for this moment—the opening of the Pistons' beautiful new stadium—but now he had to get the hell out, and fast. They were hoisting the Pistons' Eastern Conference Championship banner, and part of the ceremony was the screening of the Piston videotape the league was marketing. It was called "Bad Boys," and it had just reached the seventh game of the past year's Finals. Ciszewski—whose name was pronounced Siz-es'-kee—had a tape of that game at home, but he'd never had the guts to watch it. Ciszewski was vice president of corporate sales, one of the small inner circle who ran the Pistons. His job was his life, and he couldn't bear to relive that bitter experience.

Ciszewski, Piston CEO Tom Wilson, and chief financial officer Ron Campbell were all largely anonymous, even to Piston fans. That didn't bother them, because it was the job of the front office to elevate the players to hero status while staying in the background. But, along with McCloskey—who ran the basketball operation while they ran the business side—they were really more "Pistons" than the players were. Tom Wilson put it this way: "Those of us in the front office picture ourselves as long-termers. I've been here for twelve years now. I've seen four or five coaches come and go. Hundreds of players. I feel almost like the head of the FBI, who views the President as a transient. I mean, the President just kind of comes, and four years later there will be another one, but I'm still here. In my own situation, for a few years our team will be based around Isiah, and then it'll be somebody who's just in high school today."

Wilson and his key executives—the Piston brain trust—brought one vital element to the franchise: money. No money—no Pistons. And if there was some money but not really enough, the Pistons would sink to mediocrity. In the modern NBA, it wasn't so much that the good teams got rich, as that the rich teams got good. The wealthy franchises could buy—and keep—the best players. In most cases, excellent teams were the direct result of excellent front offices. The best example was Boston. More than Larry Bird, Bill Russell, or Bob Cousy, general manager Red Auerbach had made the Celtics a dynasty. Bird, Russell, and Cousy had created great teams, but Auerbach had built the franchise that made those teams possible. The franchise always came first. You could build a good franchise out of a bad team, but no one could build a good team out of a bad franchise.

To be a great franchise manager, though, a person had to be married to the franchise, as Ciszewski was. Ciszewski, who had a master's degree in sports administration, hadn't taken a full vacation since he'd started working with the Pistons seven years ago. Over the past three years—as they'd built the new Palace of Auburn Hills and prepared for tonight—he'd only taken a few days off. By now, his emotions were totally linked to the Pistons' fate. Last year, on the night of the sixth game of the Championship Series, when Detroit had lost in the final minute, Ciszewski's father-in-law had been flying in to visit. Ciszewski had been married for seven years, but during that time he'd been chained to his desk, so he'd only met his father-in-law once. He'd wanted to make a good impression, but on game day he'd told his wife, "Your dad's going to either see one happy SOB or one miserable SOB tonight." When they'd lost the game Ciszewski had been in his office, working late selling season tickets to corporations, and he'd felt "like busting up everything in the office." He'd dragged home and had sat on the diving board over his pool for two hours. Finally, his wife and her dad had come out, and the first thing his father-in-law had said was, "Hey, don't worry—it's just a game." *Just a game.* That was the worst thing to say. His wife had given him a nervous look—like, "Please don't commit murder"—but all he'd said was, "It's *not* just a *game.*"

After the Pistons had lost the Championship, Ciszewski had gone back to his work with more gut-churning fervor than ever. He needed the extra emotion, because he could no longer get by on selling season tickets to see the Championship team. Ciszewski felt familiar with the empty, sick feeling he'd gotten after the Pistons lost, because he was one of the front office guys who most often said, "They'll break your heart." But he never said that around customers. His job was to pack the Palace, and to get McCloskey the money he needed to have a winning team.

And he'd done it. Now the "Bad Boys" video was over, so Ciszewski was back in the Palace, standing in the tunnel that led to the locker room, gazing at the packed stands. He'd sold virtually every seat as a season ticket, and he and Wilson had sold all of their 180 luxury suites. Their total revenue for this year would be about $70 million. That was *his* contribution to the team—and if that didn't make him a Piston, nothing did.

The game started. The first visiting-team basket was by Kelly Tripucka. He got a nice round of applause. That was fitting. Tripucka had indirectly helped build the Palace. He'd been drafted the same year that Isiah Thomas had—in part, because he was white. That had been when Tom Wilson and McCloskey had first arrived, and they had been trying to build a good franchise out of a bad team. Part of their strategy was to draft a player to please white Detroit. If considering race as a factor in their image-making had been racist, it was also what virtually every other company in the country did with its advertising and promotion. Tripucka—the White Hope—had been the perfect choice to reform the Pistons' image. He was very good—he'd played better than Isiah their first year—he was the son of a former Detroit Lion football player, and he was good-looking enough to get inundated with X-rated mail and photos from Detroit females. Tripucka had gone along with the promo whole hog. During the *Animal House* craze he'd dressed in a toga, he'd done a parody of Bob Uecker's must-be-the-front-row commercial, and he'd dressed in leather and a ducktail for Punk Night. Tom Wilson's recollection of Tripucka was, "There weren't a dozen guys in the league that would have gone along with this crap, but Kelly was like, 'What the hell, that's stupid, let's do it.' "

So Tripucka got a nice little hand when he scored. But . . . there was something off center about that—cheering when the other team scored. Ciszewski was a little perplexed. Whatever happened to "Eat shit and die" for the visiting team?

Ciszewski had sold most of the tickets to corporations—what regular fan could shell out $10,000 to $40,000 for one season ticket? But they *were* pro-Piston corporations, weren't they? Hard to tell. Whoever they were, they were awfully quiet.

A scrawny, middle-aged black man hustled up to Ciszewski. "Hey, what're you tryin' to do to me?" he rasped. A couple of his front teeth were gone—he looked like Leon Spinks at ninety. It was Leon the Barber, the most famous fan in the NBA, renowned for the vile abuse he heaped on visiting teams. "How can I cuss and say this and that with *her* there?" Leon pointed to an attractive, expensively dressed matron sitting in the courtside seat next to an empty seat—Leon's.

"Leon," said Ciszewski, "believe me—she'll be fine. Just make some noise, okay? Wake this crowd up." Leon looked dubious but trooped back to his seat. He felt miserable. He'd loved Piston games when they'd been downtown, at Cobo Hall, and even when they'd been in the huge Pontiac Silverdome. The Silverdome was a barn, but they'd had unbelievable crowds there. They'd been the first NBA team to draw a million fans in a season, and for the last home game of the 1988 Finals they'd drawn 61,983, which was also an NBA record. The Silverdome fans, many from largely black Pontiac, had been great. John Salley had called them "the crazy carmakers." But the Pistons had been renters at the Silverdome, and here they were owners, which meant greater profits and ultimately more wins. But where were the thirty thousand crazy carmakers? Leon gazed at the quiet throng. *Opera* fans. They'd probably called their friends before the game, Leon thought, to ask what they were wearing. What the hell—somebody had to get them started. He cupped his hands tentatively and tried a mild one: "Hey, Bogues!" Leon yelled at five-foot-three Muggsy Bogues. *"Muggsy,* you pint-sized son of a bitch—go play in a league for black *midgets!"* The woman next to Leon stiffened: Who was this . . . gentleman? Must he be so racist? And heightist? Leon sagged. There was no point in asking for a new seat. He was a permanent fixture behind the visitors' bench. That's where Ciszewski *wanted* him. A long time ago, Leon had sat behind the Detroit bench, but a couple of times the referees had thought Leon's foul remarks were coming from Piston coach Dick Vitale, they'd thrown Vitale out. Leon and Vitale sounded alike. They had the scratchy, larynx-strained voice that was common to basketball coaches, who constantly yelled above the noise of a crowd. Leon coached in the Police Athletic League and worked with kids for the local Parks Department. Before the horrendous 1967 Detroit race riot; Leon Bradley had been a barber, but he'd given it up for community work. He'd pushed the city to convert hundreds of vacant lots into basketball courts, and had helped create a new citywide fanaticism for the game. Now he was a local celebrity, and got national publicity. He was probably the only person ever to earn a favorable profile in *The Wall Street Journal* by screaming profanities and racial slurs.

"Hey, Harter!" Leon yelled at new Charlotte coach Dick Harter—the former Penn coach that McCloskey had once employed as an assistant in Detroit—"You're a goddamn *traitor!* And you're not even a *good* one!" Harter's team was already falling behind.

The lawyers, accountants, stockbrokers, and doctors around Leon chuckled. What refreshing *joie de vivre!* Leon looked bleak. They were laughing at him. John Salley, in for Laimbeer, pulled his huge hands down toward his ears, motioning to the crowd for a little noise. No one responded. Even "the Brow"—a middle-aged man with shaggy eyebrows who was also a famous Piston fan—looked circumspect.

Ciszewski, still standing in the runway—because he was always too nervous to sit during a game—was beginning to panic. He'd packed the stadium, and hauled in all those millions. But he'd packed it with stiffs: mobile corpses. That kind of a crowd could *kill* a team. If you didn't win 90 percent of your home games, you didn't win the Championship. And you didn't win 90 percent of your home games in front of wide-eyed smiling corpses.

My God—what kind of Frankenstein had he created?

"These next three games are going to be barometer games," assistant coach Dick Versace told Drew Sharp, one of the new Piston beat writers, on the day after the win over Charlotte. "After these games, we'll be able to gauge what level we're at right now." It was largely nonsense, of course—the next three games were just a few more in an almost endless season, but the coaches always had to have some reason why the next game or the next week was *crucial.* They had to break the season up that way, because it was just too damn long. The league had made many changes over the years, but one thing they would never budge on was the length of the season. They had one reason for their intransigence. Money. These days the league had a $173-million, three-year deal with CBS, and another lucrative contract with WTBS. The

NBA couldn't pull the money they wanted if they shortened the schedule. None of the teams' front offices wanted to fight NBA Commissioner
David Stern on the issue. Stern was too powerful. Since Stern had taken
over in 1984, overall attendance was up 34 percent, and pro basketball
had been embraced by a young, upscale audience—one greatly valued
by advertisers and promoters. Basketball's appeal to yuppies stemmed in
part from the game's quick pace, which was suited to the younger
generation's shriveled attention span; basketball games were much
shorter than football and much livelier than baseball. But the season
had become a man-killer. This part of the season was especially difficult,
because the games didn't mean as much. Of course, they counted the
same as season-ending games, but nobody's back was against the wall,
so it just wasn't the same. The *real* season was the "second season"—the
long, emotional playoffs. The playoffs determined the World Champion.
The regular season made the franchises money, and it determined who
would get the home-court advantage during playoffs. But that was all.

For Trader Jack McCloskey, though, the regular season served another important function. It gave him a chance to study the team. He
would have from now until the February 23 trade deadline to find the
mix, chemistry, and talent to carry him through the playoffs.

McCloskey had resisted making any major changes over the summer,
because he thought he had the best team in basketball. But after the first
couple of games, he'd begun to wonder. They were playing well, but
they weren't perfect—and it would take perfection to win the Championship. It wasn't easy to pick out the flaw. If anything, it was ball
movement—too slow. But whose fault was that? Hard to tell.

Detroit was heading off to Philadelphia tomorrow for the first of
Versace's "barometer" games. They'd be flying their own plane—
"Roundball One." They were the only team in the league with a plane,
because it cost twice as much as airline flight. But the brain trust thought
the convenience and comfort of the lavishly appointed full-size jet would
help them win a few more games.

Philadelphia hadn't amounted to much since the era of Julius Erving
and Moses Malone, but they'd done a lot of rebuilding around "franchise" forward Charles Barkley. Philly GM John Nash had drafted
shrewdly last summer, picking up little Hersey Hawkins with the sixth
pick instead of gambling on a big man. Philadelphia already had a good
center in Mike Gminski, but it was believed that the Lakers were trying
to lure Gminski with about twice the $700,000 salary Philadelphia could
pay him. L.A. would be allowed by the salary cap rules to pay someone
like Gminski that much when Jabbar retired at the end of the year.
When the salary cap rules had been created in 1983, they were intended

to bring parity to the league by keeping all team salaries at the same level. But some of the franchises, notably the Lakers and Celtics, had already been rich, and were prospering through "pocketbook basketball." The Lakers at the time had a team salary that was about 15 percent more than that of the Celtics and a full 30 percent higher than everyone else's. So the wealthy franchises had insisted on a clause that allowed the rich to get richer. It was a "grandfather clause," which let them keep the players they had at the time. They could keep these players, such as Jabbar, by paying their rising market values, even if that put L.A. over the salary cap limit. Also, when one of these players retired, the team could "roll over" half of his salary to replace him. The clause was one reason it made sense for L.A. to pay the aging Jabbar $3 million this year. He wasn't really worth it, but next year L.A. would have half of his salary—an extra $1.5 million over the salary cap—to hire a replacement. That player's salary could then be increased as his career unfolded. Thus, Kareem Abdul-Jabbar, the Laker's "rolling grandfather," would effectively haunt the rest of the NBA for years to come.

For now, his specter was haunting Philly GM John Nash, and anybody else who had a good center to lose.

After the Philadelphia game, Detroit would play Atlanta. McCloskey had said he was "scared to death" of Atlanta. Like McCloskey, Atlanta GM Stan Kasten had directed his strategies straight at this year—now or never. Kasten had come within one quarter of advancing to the Eastern Finals against Detroit last year, but Larry Bird had killed his dream. Kasten had felt stuck at a plateau, so he'd been the most aggressive GM in the league last summer. He'd let enforcer Tree Rollins go to Cleveland, dumped six-ten Scott Hastings into the expansion draft, traded guard Randy Wittman with a first-round pick to Sacramento for Reggie Theus, and had picked up free agent Moses Malone. "The last hurdle to the Championship may be the toughest," Kasten had recently said. "I don't know how often I'll be this close again—it's time to take our best shot."

The acquisition of Malone, the eighth highest scorer and tenth highest rebounder in NBA history, had been Kasten's golden move. It would become legend if Atlanta won the Championship. Malone had been with the Washington Bullets, but that franchise had been faltering for years, and hadn't wanted to pay Malone's asking price when his $2.1-million contract had expired last summer.

McCloskey had wanted Malone, but Kasten and his player personnel director, Brendan Suhr, had outmaneuvered him. McCloskey hadn't been able to fit Malone under his salary cap without trading James

Edwards, his big center who made $600,000. So Kasten and Suhr had begun negotiating with McCloskey for Edwards, not letting McCloskey know that the player they really wanted was Malone. They did the same thing with Houston. Houston wanted Malone, too, but had to get rid of center Joe Barry Carroll to afford him. Kasten and Suhr had no interest in Carroll, but they told Houston they wanted him. Kasten was presenting great terms to both teams, and tied them down with slow negotiations.

Then Suhr made a surprise call to Malone's agent, Lee Fentress, late on Friday afternoon, August 5. He told Fentress, "Lee, here's what we're gonna do. We're gonna overpay you. We're gonna make you an offer you can't refuse. Four and a half million over three years."

"That's a helluva deal," Fentress had said.

"The problem is, you have one hour to accept it."

Fentress had blanched. "I can't do that," he'd said. "Moses is on his way to the Virgin Islands for a Nike trip."

"We know you have power of attorney," Suhr had said. "If you pass on it, we're signing James Edwards at six o'clock tonight. We've already made the deal."

Forty-five minutes later, Fentress had called back and taken the deal. Then Kasten and Suhr had gone into phase two of their plan, finalizing a deal with Sacramento GM Bill Russell to pick up great scorer Reggie Theus. Russell was in a youth and public relations movement, and was willing to take Wittman, who was no star, but was cheap, white, young, and—unlike Theus—not a prima donna.

Theus, like Malone, was in the tail end of his career, but would probably be good for 20 points a game for the next couple of years. Kasten and Suhr weren't put off by the ages of their two new stars, because they weren't looking toward the future. Besides, they needed maturity in their mix. The oldest of their other players, Dominique Wilkins, was only twenty-eight.

Now they had three All-Stars, and probably more talent than anyone in the league, including the Lakers. If there was a problem, it was most likely to be one of chemistry. Too *many* All-Stars. Not enough fame and fortune to go around. Kasten had acknowledged the problem. "I know there's a potential for trouble," he'd said. "I'll have problems and the coaches will have problems, but without talent I've got no chance at all. I'd rather have talent and then worry about putting it all together and making it work."

McCloskey was skeptical. He feared Atlanta, but thought their chemistry could kill them. He was dubious about "how that group of players will relate to each other."

The other team in the three "barometer" games was Boston. Mc-Closkey's intelligence reports told him that Boston had a problem. A potentially terrible problem. Larry Bird seemed to be having severe mobility trouble. When Bird would feed the ball inside to Kevin McHale or Robert Parish, he'd stay back on defense instead of cutting for an open shot. Strange behavior for Bird. And he must not be following Celtic shots to the basket, because he had only one offensive rebound.

Bird was the Boston franchise. Without him, they wouldn't be Championship caliber. They would miss his skills, and probably more than that, they would miss his obsession. Bird was always the first player to start practicing, was a drill-sergeant team leader, and often won games with little more than amazing willpower. He insisted his teammates stay in shape, and worked out twelve hours a day in the off season, finishing with a six- to twelve-mile run. Like Isiah Thomas, Bird had channeled a tough childhood into a fixation with success.

Bird had grown up in a poverty-laced area of rural Indiana that had a number of hot springs; long ago it had been a resort area, but it had never recovered from the Depression. From age eight, he'd lived with his grandmother, because his mother had been unable to care for him and his four brothers and sisters. Bird's father, an alcoholic, provided little support. When Bird had been sixteen, his father, Joe Bird, by then divorced from his mother, had been arrested for nonpayment of child support. As police had waited in Joe Bird's living room, Joe Bird had phoned his ex-wife from another room. "I want you to hear this," he'd said, and had then pulled the trigger of a shotgun aimed at his head. That kind of trauma had undermined Bird's already shaky self-image. As a teenager, he'd been into drinking, and although he'd played on his high school basketball team, he'd worked hardest on his passing, so that he could feed a more talented teammate. He'd dropped out of Bobby Knight's Indiana University program, and had for a time held a job as a garbageman in his hometown of French Lick. He'd liked that job—it gave him a sense of achievement. Throughout that time, though, he'd kept nurturing an obsession not just with basketball, but with winning. In 1975 he transferred to little Indiana State, and carried that team to the 1979 NCAA championship game, against Magic Johnson's Michigan State. By then, Bird had developed a degree of concentration that was even more pronounced than his skills. Considered slow and not naturally gifted, he hadn't been picked until sixth in the first round of 1978, after players like Purvis Short and Michael Ray Richardson. The pick had been Red Auerbach's last great move as a general manager. The most remarkable thing about Bird's NBA career was that every year he had significantly improved. The improvement was a direct result of little more than practice and work: obsession.

For the Celtics, the bitter irony of Bird's injury—if he *was* injured— was that he'd just signed a deal that would bump his salary to $4.2 million in 1990 and 1991. Bird, who'd apparently known he had a problem, had even implied that the big raise would make him injury-proof. "With the type of money I make now," he'd said, "I can take anything." The salary negotiation with Boston GM Jan Volk, who'd taken over for Red Auerbach, had been horrible for Volk. Bird had come late to fall camp and had blasted Volk publicly, saying he'd been treated "like a rookie." Bird had threatened to leave the franchise if his deadline wasn't met. He'd insulted Volk's negotiating ability, saying that Auerbach could have settled the contract "in about five minutes." But the Celtics had always been known as a tightfisted operation. Furthermore, they now had stockholders to answer to: Volk had spearheaded a drive to take the franchise public, and had raised $40 million. But that money was badly needed. The Celtics were building a new stadium, trying to escape the annual $2-million rent and maintenance fee they paid to the Boston Garden. At the Garden, they got no percentage of the profits from concessions, parking, or sky boxes.

The Boston situation was a stark contrast to that of Tom Wilson and Jack McCloskey in Detroit. Wilson had given McCloskey much more room for generosity than Volk possessed. McCloskey had just completed negotiations with Isiah Thomas, Dennis Rodman, and Rick Mahorn with no antagonism whatsoever. The ease of those negotiations was smoothing the way for the beginning of the Detroit season, while the difficulties with the Bird deal had undermined Boston's early season. The other Celtic players didn't want to see a rich man like Bird threatening to leave over money—after all, wasn't it Just a Game? But that problem would be dwarfed if Bird was injured. That would be a devastating irony—paying all that money, having the team disrupted, and then getting nothing in return.

They were back: scowling James Worthy, owl-eyed, inscrutable Kareem, smiling Magic, whose heart turned to ice at tip-off. They were loping onto the Palace floor, ready for what the sportswriters were calling "Game Eight" of the Championship Series. But things were different now. Detroit was on top.

The Pistons had breezed through their "barometer" games. Joe Dumars, who had made the team as a defender—wisely choosing not to challenge Isiah as the team's scorer—had tossed in 30 points for the win over Philadelphia. Dumars had let "Teacher" Dantley, his best friend, devise a new diet for him, and he was nine pounds lighter and faster on the drive.

Then, Atlanta. The Killer B-Team had won that one. Salley, Rodman, Vinnie Johnson, and James Edwards had vaporized a 13-point Atlanta lead in the fourth quarter, outscoring the Atlanta subs 46–11. So much for Stan Kasten's belief in star power.

On to the Boston Garden—another win. Bird had played and scored 24 points—but something was wrong. He was relying too much on his jump shot, and not rebounding much. Parish and Laimbeer had gotten into a fight, and had been thrown out and fined $1,500 each by the league. After the fight, Atlanta GM Stan Kasten had bitched to the league about Laimbeer and Mahorn. Kasten was still pissed off about a hard foul Mahorn had inflicted on Kasten's new investment, Moses Malone. "What Mahorn did," said Hawks coach Mike Fratello, "was more than an attempt to stop Mo from scoring. He grabbed him and threw him down." The accusations of rough play didn't much bother Daly or McCloskey. It was just Coalminer Style. To win without superstars, that was how you played.

After those three wins, the Pistons had beaten Dallas, San Antonio, and Phoenix for an 8-game season-opening winning streak, one of the longest in NBA history. But then they'd hit Houston—which was in the first flush of exultation following a major trade—and lost a game. Houston had just dumped Rodney McCray, leaving only Akeem Olajuwon and Allen Leavell from the Twin Towers era. McCray, the third pick of the 1983 draft, had been a big disappointment, but mostly he'd been a nagging reminder of better days. Just three years ago, Houston had been in the Championship Series against Boston and was called "the team of the future." Everybody copied their two-center format. But they'd been a victim of bad chemistry—between their two Towers, Olajuwon and Ralph Sampson, and between Sampson and coach Bill Fitch. Good-bye Ralph, hello Joe Barry Carroll. With Carroll, their chemistry had gone totally to hell. "Joe Barely Cares" had almost as much talent as Sampson, but had been the worst kind of influence. Carroll, who's black, didn't want to hang around with the black players, and he didn't want to hang around with the white players, either. He liked to read a lot and use big words. After less than a full season, Carroll was shipped to New Jersey for several nonentities. So now Houston was emphasizing chemistry over talent, and was looking stronger.

After Houston, there had been another win over Charlotte, but then a loss to New York. That bothered McCloskey. New York looked like one of the elite teams, and you couldn't win the title without beating the best. But McCloskey couldn't worry about that now, because the *most* elite team—the World Champion Lakers—were stepping onto the floor of the Palace. Dave Auker, the Pistons' director of sales and a member of the brain trust, blasted the Rolling Stones' "Start Me Up" on the Palace's incredible sound system. The music filled every corner of the plush, purple-upholstered stadium, and had the quality common to music from any superior system: It seemed to be playing in your head, instead of coming from speakers. It was accompanied by stunning, full-color visuals from the scoreboard—a square, four-screen video unit hanging over the middle of the court. The scoreboard, literally as large as a Radio Shack, was the most sophisticated, high-tech scoreboard in America. Tom Wilson had spent months finding its prototype and arranging its design. Auker controlled it from courtside, shouting instructions into a headset. Next to Auker was chief financial officer Ron Campbell, who ran the twenty-four-second clock, and just down the row was CEO Tom Wilson, who was color commentator on local cable TV. The brain trust guys—all young and athletic—loved their courtside jobs. When Auker had gotten the "thirty thousand crazy carmakers" standing and screaming in the Silverdome—which had had a *terrible* sound system—he'd almost felt like he was out there playing.

After the first home game, the brain trust had sat down and mapped out a plan to rouse the crowd. It was vital. The players were bitching— they weren't getting adrenal surges from the crowd. They had their money, but that wasn't enough once the ball went up and it was Just a Game. Consider Dantley, for example—the Laker game had just started and Dantley was gasping for air through a football mouthpiece. In Dallas, Mark Aguirre had pounded his elbow into Dantley's mouth and ripped open Dantley's face, loosening his teeth and breaking his jaw. Now he could only eat pancakes, soup, and eggnog, and he was lightheaded from lack of solid food and from painkillers. What was he supposed to do late in the game when his whole body stung from exhaustion—think about his stock portfolio? No, what he needed was 150-decibel rock 'n' roll and twenty thousand people chanting his name. So that's what the brain trust was trying to provide. Ciszewski had suggested that Auker kill all the public service announcements in crucial situations—go straight for the rock music and get the fans on their feet. Get some good out of their million-dollar scoreboard.

Wilson was all for it. It was exactly what he'd had in mind when they'd first dreamed up the Palace. Wilson, with All-American boy good looks, had had a decent career in Hollywood as a young actor, appearing in about forty TV shows. There he'd fallen in love with slick, highly produced Hollywood entertainment. He was especially impressed by the Walt Disney Company—they'd practically invented the theme-park concept and had developed it almost to a fine art. Wilson thought Disneyland was an incredibly smart entertainment package. Disneyland left nothing to chance—you were forced to have a good time, your every moment jammed with distractions. When Wilson had returned to his hometown of Detroit, after a couple of years in the sales department of the L.A. Lakers, he'd started working with the tiny, amateurish Piston front office, and had imparted some of his entertainment knowledge to the franchise. In the early years, he'd *had* to spoon-feed the fans glitz, because the basketball stunk. Some of his distractions, though, had been pretty lame, almost freak show acts—like Boot—the guy who lit firecrackers in his mouth—or Count Floyd, whose Dracula act ranked among the worst. And once on Halloween he'd staged a costume parade, but only two kids had shown, so he'd just introduced them as the winners of the "older division" and "younger division." But the dog and pony shows had bumped up their gross and stabilized the franchise. As Wilson had ascended in the front office—which had had only about five people, compared to eighty today—he'd developed his own concept of sports presentation. What it amounted to was: Basketball Disneyland. Build a place where the fan was forced to have fun, win or lose. At a Basketball Disneyland, your hot dog wouldn't stick to the bun, your seat would be comfortable, your usher polite, and you'd have good music to listen to and something interesting to watch at all times. You *wouldn't get bored.* You'd feel *good.* Wilson thought that building a Basketball Disneyland was the only way to make the franchise recession-proof. If you had to depend on winning for revenue, you were screwed, because you couldn't always win. Sometimes you couldn't even compete. Wilson had a saying he used almost as much as "They'll break your heart." It was "You're never more than one knee injury out of the toilet." But a Basketball Disneyland could tide you over while you built a good team out of a bad one.

Thus was born the Palace of Auburn Hills—America's ultimate Basketball Disneyland. The place cost $70 million—$30 million more than they'd planned—but there wasn't anything like it in the world. Every detail was exquisite: hardwood floors, marble counters, ankle-deep carpets, polished brass, miles of glass, spacious rooms, cocktail lounges, a fine restaurant, a preternaturally polite staff, space age electronics, and the best possible accommodations for watching basketball. The sight lines and acoustics were faultless, the seats were close to the floor and comfortable, and the four video screens of the scoreboard, as large as those at a cineplex, televised the entire game.

But the high cost had translated into an expensive ticket. And that meant a corporate audience: mobile corpses. What to do?

That was up to Auker. His job was to pump life into the building, and as the Pistons took a lead over the Lakers, he was pulling it off. First, a little "Eye of the Tiger," then some Pointer Sisters—"I'm So Excited." Put some visuals on the scoreboard of Pistons diving for loose balls and making impossible shots while the announcer screams "Ohhhh!" and fans high-five.

It was taking hold. The stockbrokers and doctors and lawyers started to clap along, once they realized they were supposed to, and even stood up a couple of times. Of course, it didn't hurt that Detroit was beating the Lakers—on prime-time network TV too. This was the first regular-season night game on CBS in a decade, testimony to the growing media interest in the Pistons.

But what really seemed to get the crowd going was when PA announcer Ken Calvert, a local disc jockey with a booming voice, made a couple of references to "your Detroit Piston *Bad Boys.*"

The Bad Boy thing stirred them up. Not hard to understand. What was sports, if not a healthy outlet for aggression and anger? At their inception, sports contests had been a form of bloodless, ritualized warfare between neighboring city-states, and nothing had changed that much. Economic competition among cities, which was still fierce as hell, was ritualized in almost every sporting event. CBS was billing this game as "Showtown versus Motown"—just a cute slogan, if you didn't live in Detroit. But if you'd spent the last six years in the Motor City collecting food stamps, while the auto plants recovered from the foreign car invasion that the TV networks and ad agencies in "Showtown" had ballyhooed and glamorized, you might want to see your Bad Boys kick a little Showtown *ass.* There was also a war of style and values between cities that was ritualized in sports. In Detroit, for example, a woman who lived near the Palace was making headlines by bitching about the filth on TV's *Married, With Children.* Here she was a heroine, but in L.A. she was just another ditsy rube. Games like this were a way the rubes could give Gomorrah its comeuppance. Besides any logical reasons for competition, there was just plain bragging-rights—the same thing that would make Mahanoy City want to beat Punxsutawney: My town's better than your town. So it was no wonder that people got a little huffy at sports events, and that "Bad Boys" was just the right button to push.

At the first half horn, Joe Dumars tossed up a fifteen-foot jumper. But the referee waved the shot off—too late. All of a sudden, there was a new noise in the Palace—a deep rolling swell of boos. Some of the accountants and attorneys were even shaking their fists. The call was unjust—almost *litigious*. Leon the Barber looked relieved. His lonely voice wasn't echoing around the stadium. Auker felt better.

Standing by the sidelines, CBS announcer Pat O'Brien, ready for his *At the Half* show, said, "Is Larry there? Is Larry there? What do we start with?" He was about to do a remote interview with Larry Bird.

A crew member said, "Fifteen seconds."

"Am I sweating?" asked O'Brien. Then: "The Detroit Pistons own the Palace of Auburn Hills now, and they own the Lakers in the first half, fifty-two–forty-nine. Hi again, everybody—I'm Pat O'Brien and welcome to another edition of the Prudential *At the Half*. We're sending you out live to a little gym outside Boston, where one Larry Bird has been working out this evening instead of watching the basketball game. And Larry is recuperating from that painful operation removing bone spurs in both of his ankles. Larry—so far, so good, I gather?"

Bird, in a purple sweat suit, appeared on a monitor. "Well, I guess," he drawled. "I'm hopin' in two or three months I can get back and start workin' out and feel good about myself."

O'Brien told Bird that Boston had just lost to Atlanta. "Can Parish and McHale—the so-called thirtysomething crowd—hang in there until you get back?"

"By the time the playoffs roll around," said Bird, "we'll be there."

Behind O'Brien, the Flash and Crash trampoline troupe did bizarre, masochistic stunts. It was part of Tom Wilson's Basketball Disneyland.

After a few minutes, the Pistons came back out and Auker plugged in some music he really liked. It was an obscure instrumental song called "Rock and Roll Part II." It sounded more like classical than rock—it was a rich fusion of organs and synthesizers that started low and arched to a quick crescendo. It was like Lionel Newman sound-track music, the kind you heard when Ben Hur won the chariot race or Gary Cooper rode into the sunset. It was, in short, Generic Hero Music, and Auker had started using it as the Piston theme song. The accountants and attorneys seemed to like it. As the second half started, the fans near the floor were up and yelling, and deeper in the stadium they were chanting "Beat L.A." An hour later, as the game was winding down, they were still pretty rowdy. Magic Johnson was barreling downcourt, about ready to cut the Detroit lead to three with a lay-up. But Dennis Rodman, the most emotional Piston player, was right behind him, and Rodman was revved up for this game. He loved it when the crowd got hot. Rodman ran down Johnson and tapped the ball away. Johnson was pissed. He turned on Byron Scott. "Hey, when I'm out in front, and somebody's coming behind me, tell me! *Tell* me!" Scott nodded and walked off. Sweat was gleaming on his face and neck. The Lakers looked tired. Over the summer, Laker GM Jerry West had added Orlando Woolridge to their bench, but now it looked like that wasn't enough. Jabbar could only play about twenty minutes. McCloskey's intelligence reports out of L.A. had been accurate—Jabbar had a belly puff and was breathless. Before the game, Jabbar had said, "This is a year where I'm being phased out. Pat Riley has to do what he has to do, and I really don't envy him." Good mantalk. But now, sitting on the bench, Jabbar looked edgy and uncomfortable. He wanted to play. His unease was a strain on the team. Bad for chemistry.

. Thomas hit a bank shot with about three minutes left to put Detroit up by 7. L.A. called time. Auker put on "Footloose," then merged it into "Mony Mony."

L.A. was running out of time. They could only win with exotic plays bracketed by time-outs. Color analyst Hubie Brown shouted into his microphone, "Can we get up on the board the number of time-outs left?"

Dave Auker yelled into his headset, " 'Shout.' 'Shout.' 'Shout.' Goddamnit—let's play 'Shout.' " It started blasting through the stadium.

L.A.'s Michael Cooper came out and hit a 3-point shot, but it wasn't enough. Detroit won. The crowd cheered, and then adjourned for the fern and oak cocktail lounges upstairs. Auker felt great. He'd pumped a little noise into the place. Tom Wilson felt great—the Palace was functioning flawlessly, and was making money hand over fist. John Ciszewski felt great—Detroit was 10–2: best record in the league.

Jack McCloskey did not feel great. Not at all. He felt as if his dream of the Championship—his obsession—was not materializing. They'd won 10 of 12. They looked great in the box scores and highlight films. But something was wrong. It was something very subtle. But it was wrong. From McCloskey's perspective—which was very different from that of a fan—Detroit had gotten off to a bad start.

Trader Jack wanted to make some changes. Big changes.

FOUR

"Pull the Trigger"
The Trading Season Starts

A COUPLE OF days after the Laker game, Jack McCloskey went to an Alcoholics Anonymous meeting. It was in a pretty little Catholic church in exclusive Farmington Hills, one of the northern suburbs that had become the Pistons' neighborhood. Tom Wilson's Basketball Disneyland had been strategically situated on the fringes of suburbia—amidst rolling forests, opulent estates, and dots of blue water—where a $100 basketball ticket wouldn't cause apoplexy. The area was home to thousands of auto executives, most of the Piston players, and, once upon a time, Jimmy Hoffa.

McCloskey stuck his head in one of several meeting rooms. A couple of the guys sitting at an oval table recognized him. That hurt. "Hey Jack, come on in—sit down!"

"I'm just here as an observer," McCloskey said. He didn't see William Bedford, so he tried another room.

Same reaction: "Hey—it's Jack McCloskey!"

"Anybody see William Bedford?" McCloskey asked.

"Next room," somebody said.

McCloskey found Bedford and sat next to him. McCloskey could hardly breathe. Everybody in the place was smoking. Guys looked like Hell's Angels. Most of them had pulled up outside in old pickups or rust-eaten junkers. Not Bedford. He had a nice car. But no income.

75

Because he'd been suspended, the Pistons didn't have to pay his $800,000 salary. Now he was living in a plain tract house behind a shopping center, about five miles from Isiah's castle in Bloomfield Hills.

Going to AA meetings was part of Bedford's rehabilitation from cocaine addiction. The recovery program was supervised by a group called ASAP, which had an exclusive contract with the NBA. Over the past four years, fourteen players had gone to the Van Nuys, California, center and then participated in the follow-up program. Bedford, who was twenty-five, square-jaw handsome, and beautifully muscled, had done his six-week stint in Van Nuys, with the Pistons picking up the $500-a-day tab. He had responded well to the highly regimented program, which included a six-thirty wake-up, rigorous workouts, counseling, and group counseling sessions, with only ninety minutes a day of free time. He'd begun the program in a dorm room with no TV or phone, and after a month had moved into a bungalow with a kitchen and living room.

By the end of the six weeks, he had kicked coke. Coke and heroin were the only substances the league banned; there were no sanctions against marijuana, alcohol, or steroids. Of the two banned drugs, only cocaine was a real problem in the NBA, maybe because a coke high mimicked the jock high of athletic heroism: pure adrenal exultation. These days, the NBA had a policy of mandatory treatment whenever there was evidence of drug use. Most treatment, however, was voluntary, and was the result of peer pressure. Bedford's Phoenix teammates had sat him down for a long and painful team meeting and convinced him that he needed treatment. The first time a player was treated he stayed on salary. The second time, salary was suspended, and the third time earned him a minimum two-year ban from the league. The policy, instituted by Commissioner David Stern, had reversed the NBA's image in the late 1970s—when a half-dozen franchises were going broke—as a zoo for rich, dumb junkies.

After the AA meeting, McCloskey made arrangements with Bedford to work out tomorrow. They exercised together almost every day. McCloskey enjoyed Bedford's company, and loved his physical skills. If Bedford could control his desire for cocaine, McCloskey believed, he could be one of the finest centers in the league, making $2 million to $3 million a year. McCloskey had hoped that Bedford would be back on the team by now, as November came to an end, but the ASAP counselors had postponed it. Bedford was supposed to phone in each day, and he'd missed a couple of calls. To them, that meant he wasn't responsible enough to stay drug-free. Bedford was immature. As a kid growing up in Memphis, he'd been a king of the playground—and that's where his development had stopped.

The postponement wasn't bothering the other players. They didn't want Bedford back. When Bedford had practiced with them, he'd screwed around on the perimeter, heaving up thirty-foot jump shots instead of working on the shots he'd get in a game. It seemed contemptuous. Once, he'd been late for practice, and they'd found him in his room, romancing a young woman. That was the kind of behavior the Detroit Pistons didn't tolerate. Almost none of them liked him.

McCloskey did like him. And he had sympathy for him. But he was planning to dump him.

At this point, nobody was untouchable on Trader Jack's team. Not even Isiah. It would take a hell of an offer to pry Isiah away, but no one was exempt. Certainly, no one was exempt because of sentiment.

McCloskey sent out a Telex to every team in the league, telling them Bedford was available. But he didn't get much response. Nobody trusted Bedford. That meant Bedford might have to be brought onto the team. ASAP had just told McCloskey that they were planning on clearing Bedford to play in the very near future. Bedford would have ten days to get in shape, then he'd have to be activated or released. McCloskey wasn't going to release him. Bedford's $800,000 salary was guaranteed, and as soon as he was off the injured-reserve list, chief financial officer Ron Campbell would have to start sending Bedford his checks. It would be crazy to pay that money without giving him a chance to play. But if he came back, McCloskey would have one player too many. That probably meant, good-bye Darryl Dawkins.

McCloskey sent out a Telex on Dawkins, too. McCloskey had definitely decided that if he had to choose between the two of them, he'd take Bedford. Dawkins had picked up on that, and thought he was a goner—probably from the Pistons and maybe from the league. He'd gotten back into fairly decent shape, and had scored 8 points in five minutes in the Dallas game—vintage, low-post Chocolate Thunder. But nobody trusted him, either. Any player who would voluntarily sit out a year—even if his wife *had* committed suicide—was considered suspect by NBA standards. New *Detroit News* beat writer Terry Foster sat down with Dawkins in the locker room and talked with him about leaving the team. Dawkins told Foster, "This is part of the game. I have no bitter feelings about it." Even if Dawkins somehow survived the year, he figured, he'd get picked up in this spring's expansion draft. At the end of the season, McCloskey would have to decide which four of his players he valued least, and he'd have to make them available to the two new teams joining the league. McCloskey could protect eight of his twelve guys from the expansion draft, but four would be up for grabs, and one of those four would be taken. Dawkins thought he'd be one to go. "I don't think Detroit can protect me in the draft," he told Foster. "I think I can play another three or four years, but it won't be here. I would like for it to be here, but I think it'll be somewhere else."

McCloskey had also told the other GM's that Fennis Dembo and Michael Williams were available. If he traded both of them, he'd have room for both Bedford and Dawkins. He probably wouldn't want to keep both big men, though, but in time he might be able to market one of them. The main thing was just to *do something*—stir the kettle— because the team's chemistry was off. They weren't moving the ball quickly enough or often enough, and it was showing up in their scoring. They were getting fewer shots than the league average, and that was dangerous. In Denver, coach Doug Moe had built a whole offensive philosophy out of simply getting as many shots as possible. His reasoning was plain: The team that gets the most shots generally makes the most shots. There was a kernel of brilliance in the strategy, and Moe had won the Coach of the Year award last year employing it. Detroit's lack of field goal attempts was also limiting their number of free throws. Adrian Dantley, who made his living at the free-throw line, was getting almost 30 percent fewer free throws than he'd been getting a year ago. Detroit was still winning games, but they weren't dominating. It was time to find the right player, and then, in the parlance of the NBA, "pull the trigger" on the trade.

Maybe the player they needed was Portland's Steve Johnson. Johnson, an All-Star center in 1987–88, was available, and so was his All-Star teammate, Kiki Vandeweghe. Vandeweghe was *very* available. Portland GM Bucky Buckwalter was dying to move Vandeweghe, and Michael Williams was believed to be one of the players he was most interested in. Buckwalter, like all GMs, was prohibited by the league from talking publicly about players that he coveted. The league called that "tampering"—because it disrupted the other teams—and they could fine a GM who did it up to a million dollars. Therefore, almost all speculation was couched in conditional language: Buckwalter was "rumored to want" Williams, or "thought to be interested" in him. But there was nothing conditional about Buckwalter's desire to unload Kiki Vandeweghe. Vandeweghe, though, had a bad back, and the other GMs, including McCloskey, were leery of him. To help overcome that, Buckwalter was planning to videotape Vandeweghe practicing, and send the tape to interested teams. It was an unusual move, but Buckwalter was desperate.

Vandeweghe was a brilliant scorer, having averaged 26.9 points in

1987. He wasn't as tough as Dantley, but he had the same quick first step and the same mastery at drawing fouls. His .869 free-throw percentage was sixth best in NBA history. Unlike Dantley, who was a great scorer but not a great shooter, Vandeweghe could hit from anywhere, and he'd led the league in three-point percentage in 1987. But Buckwalter thought Vandeweghe was poisoning the Trail Blazer chemistry. Last year he'd lost his starting job to Jerome Kersey, a leaper who made Kiki look sick at rebounding and defense. That wasn't hard to do, though, since Vandeweghe, a $1-million-a-year player, had learned long ago that points meant money and rough stuff meant early retirement. Portland coach Mike Schuler hated that attitude, and had benched Vandeweghe in favor of the $190,000-a-year Kersey. Vandeweghe had come to fall camp pissed off. He thought Buckwalter wanted him gone, and he was ready to go. It came to a head when Vandeweghe and best buddy Clyde Drexler—a prima donna Schuler *really* couldn't stand— went to see the new Trail Blazer owner Paul Allen. Allen, a bearded, thirty-five-year-old computer whiz kid and basketball fan, had taken his two All-Stars out to his driveway, played a game of Horse, and fallen in love. He told them both how valuable they were and not to worry about a thing—thus cutting the balls off Mike Schuler.

Now Buckwalter was stuck in the ego-jam. On paper, he had a great team, with one of the most handsome box scores in the league. In the real world he was screwed—Portland was 11–9 and already 4½ games out of first place. The only way out, Buckwalter felt, was dumping Vandeweghe. But all the GMs were worried about Kiki's injury, his salary, and his age. If any one of the three concerns could be eliminated, Buckwalter thought, Vandeweghe might be marketable. The only one he could mitigate, though, was the back problem, by means of the video.

Buckwalter called McCloskey and sounded him out about Vandeweghe. McCloskey needed a big guard who could shoot, and he thought Vandeweghe could play that position. McCloskey had drafted Fennis Dembo for that role, but Dembo was a little disappointing. Dembo often looked tremendous in practice—he could bull to the hoop and bang—but he kept making mental errors. They were this year's equivalent to Dumb Dennis mistakes: Dumb Dembo's mistakes. When Dembo made them, Laimbeer jumped all over his ass. That wasn't helping the situation, but what could McCloskey do about that? Tell Bill to be nice to the rookies?

Out of necessity, Daly was developing a three-guard rotation— Dumars, Thomas, and Vinnie Johnson—using Dumars and Johnson at both point guard and shooting guard. It was working pretty well. So

McCloskey's need for Vandeweghe wasn't intense. His greater need was for the other available Portland player—Steve Johnson. With the exception of Adrian Dantley, McCloskey didn't have a low-post scorer. Laimbeer hated to play down low, and Rodman, Salley, and Mahorn weren't shooters. Edwards was a mid-post player, and Dawkins could play low post, but was still too lardy to get in the game. Steve Johnson, though, was a genuine low-post player, and was an excellent shooter: His .580 field-goal percentage was third highest in NBA history. At six feet, ten inches and 235, Johnson could play big forward or center. He had a history of knee problems, but was a strong rebounder and was an All-Star center last year. The only reason he wasn't starting was that Buckwalter had lucked into formerly fat, second-round center Kevin Duckworth. Duckworth had come to Portland almost as a throwaway when the Blazers had washed their hands of spacey Walter Berry, a talented kid who was rumored within the NBA to either be on drugs or off on his own natural high. Duckworth had gotten a chance to play when Steve Johnson had been injured, had performed remarkably, and had goosed his salary from $175,000 to $2 million almost overnight. With that much invested, Portland had to make him their center of the future. Johnson had tried to play power forward alongside Duckworth, but they were too similar and fouled the mix. So now Johnson was on the block, and McCloskey was interested.

Buckwalter proposed a trade: Vandeweghe and Johnson for John Salley and Michael Williams. Salley would give Buckwalter a power forward who could work with Duckworth, and Williams would give him a backup for point guard Terry Porter. Buckwalter liked Williams's speed, and he thought Williams could replace some of Vandeweghe's outside shooting.

McCloskey was seriously considering the trade. He thought Michael Williams had star potential, but he didn't need another point guard. John Salley was a more difficult puzzle.

At the moment, Team-First Thomas thought that John Salley was the only thing that stood between the Pistons and greatness. Salley, Thomas thought, was undisciplined and erratic. Sometimes he'd sink into a funk and disappear, and when that happened the Pistons lost their only shot blocker who could run the fast break. Thomas thought Salley was too distracted by his Here's Johnny persona—the friendships with Eddie Murphy and Arsenio Hall, the commercials and promotions, and the desire to be a comedian when he stopped playing.

Salley was of two minds about his offcourt activities. Recently broadcaster Bob Page had asked him if his media interests weren't distracting him, and he'd said, "That's bullshit. Most of the commercials I did were shot during training camp. Then when I started to play well, the Chrysler people started plugging the commercial a whole lot more, so you started seeing me on commercials and television as much as in games. But they were already *done.*'' At other times, though, he admitted that he just couldn't get interested in every game.

McCloskey liked Salley—he considered him a free spirit. But Salley was expendable. McCloskey needed people he could count on, and he couldn't have players like Thomas or Mahorn, who sacrificed their bodies and their glory, thinking Salley could get away with a half-assed effort.

If McCloskey did give up Williams and Salley for Steve Johnson and Kiki Vandeweghe, he'd be giving two healthy, young players for two older players with injury problems. That might work out, though, because McCloskey's main concern was winning the Championship now. Vandeweghe and Johnson could probably help pull that off. But as hungry as he was for the 1989 title, McCloskey couldn't ignore the future. It was his responsibility to make the franchise competitive next year and the year after. A painful responsibility.

McCloskey wasn't going to do anything in a hurry. The Portland offer was on the table, and McCloskey didn't think Buckwalter would pull it away. Things were getting worse at Portland, not better.

Meanwhile, there were other possibilities. In Dallas, Mark Aguirre was in another of his snits. Aguirre had been the Dallas star for years, but the other players had had a bellyful of his ego and moods. In the past, Dallas had been hostage to Aguirre, but now they had the superb Roy Tarpley to take over his minutes. Tarpley had recently volunteered for drug and alcohol treatment, but he appeared to have licked his problem. And there were much more likely prospects for trade than Aguirre. New Jersey star Buck Williams was available for the right price.

Buck Williams was a genuine star—third pick of the 1981 draft, and a three-time All-Star with a 16.9 career scoring average and a 12.2 career rebounding average. Williams was finally fed up with what he considered a very poorly run New Jersey franchise. The Lakers and Celtics had been trying to get him for years, and now Portland was dying to grab him. He carried a $1.5-million salary, and he wasn't young, but for somebody like McCloskey, who was more interested in this year than the future, Williams was very tempting.

Indiana's Herb Williams was also available. So were a lot of people. The trading season had just begun.

Since the L.A. game, Detroit had gone 6–2, for 16–4 record. Best in the league. But the Cavs—the Assassins—were breathing down their necks. Nevertheless. This was no time to panic.

*   *   *

The Pistons were in the Cleveland Cavaliers' stadium, ready to fight for first place. Last night in the Palace, which had again been quiet as a tomb, they'd lost to Milwaukee. It had been their second loss to the Bucks—very disturbing to McCloskey. Milwaukee wasn't a great box-score or highlight-film team, but they had a potent chemistry and were smart as hell—the kind of team that scared McCloskey most. The loss had dropped Detroit into a tie with Cleveland, which had sneaked up from behind. The showdown tonight would mean more than first place—the winner would walk away feeling tough.

Joe Tait, the Cleveland play-by-play announcer, couldn't wait for the game. He disliked the Pistons. Too brutal, too obsessed. He much preferred the style of the Cleveland franchise: more gentlemanly and good-natured. But the Cav franchise hadn't always been that way. Tait, big, black-bearded, and twinkling—sort of Santa Clause as a kid—had announced Cav games for seventeen years, Cleveland Indians' games for sixteen years, and was probably the best known man in Cleveland. But his real source of pride was having survived the Cavs' Ted Stepien era—now synonymous with hare-brained management of a franchise.

"The year that Stepien took over the team," said Tait, "it was Cleveland's turn for the All-Star Game. Right after that, I was in New York, and I got a call asking me to come meet Larry O'Brien, NBA commissioner at the time and a former White House Cabinet member. I thought it was a little strange that he would want some radio announcer to come over, but I went and the secretary ushered me into his office. O'Brien sat me down in a chair by his desk and told his secretary, 'Hold all my calls,' Then, rather than sitting back down behind his desk he came and sat next to me. He leaned over, looked intently at me, and said, 'What in the *hell* is going on in Cleveland?' That was my introduction to the commissioner of the NBA."

Tait had told O'Brien that Stepien was making crazy trades, was grandstanding for the press, harassing his coaches, and that as few as two hundred people were coming to games, half of them with bags over their heads.

"O'Brien just nodded," said Tait, "like—'I thought so.' Then he told me about his visit to Cleveland. He said he'd gone to the All-Star luncheon, and when he'd arrived at the appointed site, he was surrounded by two lines of dancing girls with pom-poms chanting, 'Larry, Larry, we love you, Larry.' Then, looking up at the dais, he saw a three-hundred-pound guy in blue jeans and a T-shirt tearing the top off a beer can with his teeth and swallowing eggs whole." It was the same guy Tom Wilson hired to light firecrackers in his mouth. "Then this guy got down close to O'Brien and he took a powdered-sugar doughnut and popped it into his mouth round-ways and gulped it down. O'Brien said the thing that fascinated him was, there was a little puff of sugar out of the guy's mouth. Like a smoke ring.

"The thing was, Ted thought this was *great.* He thought he was being real . . . *show biz.''*

For a while, Tait had escaped Cleveland and broadcast the New Jersey Nets games. In 1982, the Cavs had played the Nets, and after the game the Cavs' new coach, Chuck Daly—in his first NBA head coaching job—had invited Tait to dinner. As they sat down to eat, Daly had said, "You probably think it's strange for me to invite someone that I don't know to dinner, but I've been working for this team for a month now, and I keep telling people back home what's going on, and nobody *believes* me. So all you gotta do is sit there and listen to me. I just wanted to talk to somebody who's been through it." After that dinner, Stepien had continued to call Daly at six in the morning to describe plays he'd invented, and kept insisting on crazy trades. One he engineered was sending his backup center, Bill Laimbeer, to Detroit. Laimbeer had been playing behind James Edwards, a $700,000-a-year investment Stepien was trying to get as much out of as possible. Laimbeer went to Detroit with excellent strong forward Kenny Carr for seven-foot stiff Paul Mokeski, journeyman forward Phil Hubbard, and a first- and second-round pick. Stepien didn't consider Laimbeer much of a loss. Forty pounds overweight, Laimbeer—then "the Incredible Hulk"—didn't show a sign of having learned anything in Italy, where he'd gone after his mediocre college career. At Notre Dame, Laimbeer had been just another porky white boy and had earned the scorn of tough Notre Dame players like Adrian Dantley.

But Jack McCloskey had seen promise in Laimbeer. McCloskey had devised a complex numerical rating system, and according to his numbers, Laimbeer had great potential. Tom Wilson and John Ciszewski had been thrilled by the trade, because they had hated Laimbeer at Cleveland. Once he'd knocked hell out of Detroit's Terry Tyler, who was one of the nicest guys in the game, and Laimbeer was exceptionally obnoxious, obsessed with winning. Anybody that hateful, they figured, would be of great value.

After the Laimbeer trade, Daly had told Stepien he wouldn't take any more craziness, so Stepien had fired him. He'd replaced Daly with Bill Musselman, one of the most hated men in Cleveland. The animosity for Musselman stemmed from an Ohio State game several years earlier in which Musselman's University of Minnesota team had gang-beaten a popular Ohio boy named Luke Witte, stomping him so badly his career had been ruined. After the beating, it had been rumored in Ohio that Musselman had had his players chant "Kill! Kill! Kill!" every day in practice. So Musselman had not been a popular choice, and the team had ended the season with a 15–67 record and empty stands.

But now the Cleveland stands were full and noisy with fans hungry for first place. Under new ownership and GM Wayne Embry, the franchise had blossomed and now fans were rabid. Cleveland had one of the best home records in the league. "This crowd won't *let* the Cavs lose," said Tait. "There's a crowd psychology that practically turns into mass hypnotism." Once Tait had seen a clinical hypnotist stop a man from bleeding through the power of suggestion, and now he had an almost mystical belief in home-court advantage.

The Cavs' sound system—no match for the Palace's—played "Eye of the Tiger" as the Detroit and Cleveland players ambled onto the floor and touched hands tentatively. After tip-off, Detroit spread their offense, passing back and forth on the perimeter, looking for a way to invade the huge Cleveland interior. Dantley got the ball and tried his usual series of head fakes and shoulder fakes, but Larry Nance waited him out. Dantley tried to pass in to Laimbeer but Ron Harper, the young Cleveland player who'd averaged 22 points as a rookie, batted it to Mark Price. Cleveland walked the ball patiently downcourt. Daly bellowed, "Hands! Hands up!" Cleveland couldn't score and Detroit got the ball back, but there was Harper again, jabbing his hand into the passing lane, knocking the ball to Larry Nance. Nance charged for the basket and jammed it down. The crowd roared and Cleveland was off. Frail Mark Price hit jumpers, Brad Daugherty smashed down dunks, Nance banged past Mahorn to score, and Cleveland hit 12 of its first 17 shots. Detroit still couldn't get inside. Time after time, Dantley stood dribbling at the perimeter, peering in, faking—then finally passing out to the wing. Daly was afraid that Dantley's broken jaw had made him hesitant about charging into the snake pit. Looking haggard, Daly paced the sidelines as the Cleveland lead climbed to 13, then 15, then 19.

In Detroit, Tom Wilson, John Ciszewski, and the rest of the brain trust sat in front of Ciszewski's TV set, getting quieter by the minute. It was ten days before Christmas, and they'd started the evening with gag gifts—Wilson got a bunch of souvenirs of the Detroit Red Wings, his chief rival for the local sports dollar. There had been lots of laughter, then they'd settled in for the game, and now things were getting morbid.

"Jesus," said Ciszewski, "this Cleveland team's for real, isn't it?"

Wilson just raised his eyebrows.

"Well, we didn't do anything to improve ourselves this year," said

Ciszewski. "We've got the same team as last year, and Cleveland's got all these new people they picked up at the end of the year."

"Trust Jack," said Wilson. Wilson and Ciszewski often said that to each other. They were both students of the game, and Wilson had some ambition to become general manager when McCloskey left, so they often talked about how they'd do things. They frequently disagreed with McCloskey's moves. But time and again his maneuvers had paid off, so now their overriding philosophy was "Trust Jack."

But Jack McCloskey, watching the game by himself, was just as worried. He'd built his team to beat the Celtics: Mahorn to outmuscle McHale, Dantley to take advantage of Bird's defensive weakness, and Isiah to outrun Dennis Johnson. But now Nance was outmuscling Mahorn, Ron Harper was shutting off Dantley, and Mark Price was outrunning Isiah. Worse than that, there was something hesitant and stodgy about Detroit's ball movement. Dantley wasn't getting double-teamed when he got the ball, and that was spooky. Boston and L.A. had always doubled Dantley—that was much of his value in the offense. Dantley was still getting his points tonight, but the other players were covered and weren't getting the bail. Salley and Vinnie Johnson were also ineffective. Bad sign. The B-Team had to function well, in the absence of superstars. The emotional distance between Dantley and Isiah was as bad as ever, and that wasn't helping the chemistry.

The Cleveland lead was growing. 25 points. 32 points. Wayne Embry, a huge man who'd been an All-Star center and a successful businessman, stood quietly in the runway leading to the Cavs' locker room, watching his Assassins patiently pick Detroit apart. Embry didn't feel much emotion. To him, it was just another game. But McCloskey was getting emotional. Angry. Frustrated. For the first time this year, they would lose two games in a row. They weren't beating the elite teams— Cleveland, Milwaukee, New York. After tonight, they'd be out of first place. If they never regained it, they'd lose the home-court advantage for the playoffs. Something had to be done.

"If we can get three more buckets," said John Ciszewski, "I can guarantee we've got 'em." Ciszewski was listening to the December 22 Knicks-Pistons game, pacing from counter to door in a Great Stuff store. He was in the suburban Twelve Oaks outlet of Great Stuff, one of the Pistons' new sports paraphernalia boutiques. The first two stores to open—just in time for the holidays—were doing about $20,000-a-day worth of business. Wilson was already projecting a $1-million annual gross. The stores were selling tons of Bad Boys merchandise—

sweatshirts, banners, shot glasses—anything with the skull and cross-bones logo. Isiah Thomas had come to Tom Wilson recently and asked him to downplay the Bad Boys image, because he thought the referees might start to penalize them. Wilson wouldn't do it. For over a decade he'd struggled to give the Pistons an identity in the marketplace, and now he'd found one. He wasn't letting go.

Thirty-eight seconds left. One-point Piston lead. Over the store's radio, Ciszewski could hear the Madison Square Garden crowd howling. Sounded like war—absolute hysteria. Ciszewski was envious. New York was 12–1 at home—their fans had created an almost insurmountable home-court advantage. Hot little guard Mark Jackson got the ball. He was only 5–23 from the field tonight, but New York coach Rick Pitino wanted him to take the crunch shot. He was averaging about 15 points a game and led the Knicks' pressing defense, the key to their excellent record. Most experts—including New York GM Al Bianchi—had told Pitino that pros would refuse to press. And some of Pitino's players were balking. First-round rookie Rod Strickland had been lazing through practice, and Pitino was about ready to get rid of him. He thought he could rely on Jackson as his only viable point guard. Indiana was interested in trading Herb Williams for Strickland, and the better Jackson played, the more likely that trade became.

But McCloskey didn't want to see that trade happen. He was also interested in Herb Williams. Or at least using his interest in Williams as leverage in another trade. The New York trade would kill his flexibility.

Jackson rolled off a pick set by Sidney Green, and drove from left to right across the lane. The Detroit defense collapsed on him—but not entirely, they still had to worry about Patrick Ewing underneath. Jackson leaped into the air and pivoted toward the basket, sending up a high, arching shot.

"Miss!" yelled Ciszewski. He wanted the win—and McCloskey's flexibility.

The ball plummeted straight through the net. Crowd noise hissed madly out of the radio. "Damn!"

Detroit hurried the ball down and fed Dantley. He put up an eighteen-footer from the right corner. No good. In the scramble for the rebound, Gerald Wilkins was fouled and made both his shots. Three-point Knicks lead. Six seconds left.

"I guarantee we're not going to get a good shot," said Ciszewski. No special reason for the belief—just "They'll break your heart."

Isiah got the ball at the 3-point line. He let it fly. It slapped off. Buzzer. Hysteria. The Pistons trudged toward the locker room.

Things were getting worse for Detroit. This was the second loss to New York. Detroit was 18–7—not a great record. They were still in second place. Cleveland was killing everybody. McCloskey wanted to fix Detroit's problem. But what *was* the problem? It wasn't glaring: nobody was in a dismal slump. But some players just weren't contributing. Salley, for one. Daly was getting fed up with him. This was his second year and he was supposed to be improving, but he wasn't playing as well as last year. McCloskey still valued Salley, but he was about ready to put him on the market. If he had to, he might offer Salley for New Jersey All-Star Buck Williams. But he wouldn't start with that offer. First, he'd offer New Jersey GM Harry Weltman some package of lesser players and draft picks, to test the water. Williams might come cheaper than his true value, because he was sick of the beaten-down New Jersey franchise and wanted out. Buck Williams would not be perfect for the Detroit mix. He'd probably want to shoot a lot, his age was a problem, and he wouldn't have Salley's speed. But he would be meaner and more serious than Salley.

There was competition for Buck Williams, though. Harry Weltman had just offered to trade Buck straight-up for Portland's Jerome Kersey, but Portland was hesitant. They were still trying to dump Vandeweghe, and Kersey was their only other dependable small forward.

Maybe a better Detroit trade would be Salley and Vinnie Johnson for Indiana's Herb Williams and John Long. Williams, at six-eleven and 242, could play big forward and center, and had a seven-year scoring average of 15.2 and rebounding average of 7.7. His numbers weren't as high as Buck Williams's, but he'd played almost 25 percent fewer minutes, which at age thirty could be plus. Long was a ten-year veteran who'd played well for Detroit during its Dark Ages, and was the eighth best free-throw shooter in NBA history. But Daly was afraid that Long's best years were gone, and he was reluctant to give up V.J. for him. Losing Salley and Vinnie Johnson would drastically alter the Pistons' chemistry. But Daly had told a *Detroit News* writer, "I think Jack is inclined to think along the lines of, if we can improve our club, we'll do so—whether it disturbs the chemistry or not."

Salley thought he was on his way out. He wasn't happy about it. He loved to clown, but he was very proud and hated to lose. Going to New Jersey or Indiana would be awful. Salley wasn't showing his feelings, though. He'd learned how to hide them behind a joke as a six-foot-seven teenager, when his mother had taken him door to door in Brooklyn as a Jehovah's Witness. Salley's view was "You have to have personality when you're knocking on people's doors at nine-thirty in the morning." So when he'd heard a rumor about being traded for Buck

Williams, he'd just said, "I guess Buck will do my radio show." Good funny mantalk—vintage Salley.

It wasn't really Salley, though, that Indiana GM Donnie Walsh was interested in. Walsh really needed a point guard. The guy he had, Vern Fleming, was a good scorer but only a fair shooter, and he was selfish as hell. Worst trait for the point. Earlier in the year, Walsh had thought he could easily improve his point-guard situation, because he'd had big men to burn. He'd had two centers who'd each been the second pick of their draft, Rik Smits and Steve Stipanovich. He also had forwards Chuck Person, Wayman Tisdale, and Herb Williams. But then Stipanovich, the young starting center, had suffered a career-ending injury and lost his $710,000-a-year job. The shocking loss had prompted coach Jack Ramsay, McCloskey's pal from the old Eastern League, to call it quits. Stipanovich's injury was the last straw for Ramsay. With Stipo gone, Indiana had been unlikely to improve, and Ramsay had had a gutful of snotty Chuck Person, one of the new-breed, kiss-my-ass types that the "players' league" was full of.

The loss of Stipanovich had drastically whittled Walsh's options. Earlier he'd proposed a Wayman Tisdale for Joe Dumars trade to McCloskey, but after the injury that wasn't so desirable. It didn't really matter, though, because McCloskey was in love with Dumars—Joe's flexibility brought a wealth of attributes to the mix. Dumars could play either point or shooting guard, he was as strong on offense as defense, his salary wasn't a burden, and he could get along with both Dantley and Isiah.

Walsh had also been forced to scrub a possible Stipanovich for Terry Porter deal. Porter, Portland's excellent point guard, had a high price tag because he was one player coach Mike Schuler hadn't pissed off with his boot camp practices. Schuler, whose job now seemed to be in jeopardy, continued to spar with Vandeweghe and Drexler. Schuler was also hanging on tightly to rookie power forward Mark Bryant, whom he could have traded for Milwaukee's premiere sixth-man guard, Ricky Pierce.

Now Walsh was considering a three-way deal with New York and Portland. New York's Rod Strickland would go to Indiana, Indiana's Wayman Tisdale would go to Portland, and Portland's Vandeweghe would go to Indiana. But New York GM Al Bianchi had cold feet. He liked Vandeweghe, but didn't know if Mark Jackson could carry the point-guard position by himself. But Walsh was ready to pull the trigger on the trade. The three-way deal made more sense to him than a trade with Dallas that he'd pretty much decided to forget. Dallas's Rick Sund wanted to give Mark Aguirre for Wayman Tisdale, but Walsh just couldn't see the advantage in it. Aguirre and Chuck Person played too similarly; Aguirre wouldn't add much to Walsh's mix. Besides, having Person and Aguirre on the same team might be like having Captain Queeg and Captain Bligh in the same rowboat.

Dallas was hot to get rid of Aguirre, and they were trying to cook something up with Boston's Jan Volk. Volk had no interest in Aguirre, though. If anything, he wanted power forwards Sam Perkins and Detlef Schrempf, who would pick up some of the slack resulting from Larry Bird's absence. But for those two, Dallas wanted Kevin McHale. They thought Volk might let go of him to get a little youth in his "thirty-something" mix and a little room within the salary cap. But Volk was hanging tough. He was looking for a trade, but was afraid to lose his only healthy superstar.

So, the trade waters were muddy. McCloskey wanted to do something. But he wasn't sure what.

The Pistons sat despondently in the visiting team locker room of Madison Square Garden as the New York media crushed in on them. Blood was seeping from a cut over Isiah's eye, there were bloodstains on Laimbeer's wrist, and Mahorn's lip was red and bulging. But the players were making an honest attempt to recite the proper mantalk. "The bottom line is, we didn't put the ball in the hole," said Thomas.

"The bottom line is, we didn't play smart," said Laimbeer.

"You hate to lose like that," said Salley.

Thomas was the nucleus of a crowd of reporters that kept spreading until it engulfed Rick Mahorn's locker. Mahorn had beaten back Patrick Ewing all night, outplaying New York's "monster in the middle." Now Mahorn was in no mood to beat back reporters. "If you're gonna interview," Mahorn boomed, "you better get the fuck out of *my* space."

Mahorn plopped down and yanked off his jersey. "Mike," he said to trainer Mike Abdenour, "get me a couple of Tylenol, will you?"

Abdenour, stocky and muscular, hurried over with the aspirin. "What happened?"

"The motherfucker Ewing elbowed me in the head. Next time I'll fuck *him* up."

"Yeah," said Abdenour, "we'll get that motherfucker next time." Jeff Coplon, a tall, long-haired writer for *Rolling Stone*, jotted down Abdenour's remark. He'd been dispatched on a Bad Boys angle, and figured this was classic Bad Boys. But when Abdenour saw him writing, his face contorted. *"Don't print that,"* he yelled at Coplon. "If you put that in your publication, we'll fuck *you* up next time."

Coplon told Abdenour that he wasn't a beat writer, and that his article wouldn't appear for months. That soothed Abdenour immensely. In pro basketball, months were an eternity. Something that far away defied concern.

But that's not how Jack McCloskey felt. He'd just watched the game on TV, and now he could see the next few months with terrible clarity. They would continue to win most of their games. They would win their first playoff round. Maybe the second. Then they would face a superb team—without the home-court advantage—and they would lose. It would be the end of McCloskey's dream.

Something had to be done.

FIVE

"Homestand"
Looking for Deals

"OUHHH!" AIR gushed out of Joe Dumars, carrying a pink spray of blood from an oozing lip that Patrick Ewing had hammered open in the first quarter. Then, what sounded like "Cock-SUCK!"

Leggy, spidery referee Jimmy Clark shot a hot look at Dumars. "Cocksucker" was one of two words forbidden in NBA games ("motherfucker" was the other). One of the league's refs, who was gay, was particularly sensitive to the word. Clark looked ready to call a technical. But he had to apply some common sense—Joe Dumars just didn't talk like that. Refs weren't supposed to let players' reputations affect their calls, but they did it constantly. Besides, it looked like Dumars, whose hand had just crashed into Gerald Wilkins's knee, was hurt. He was hobbling toward the Detroit bench, his face flashing a quick-cut series of emotions: anger, surprise, frustration, excitement.

Coach Chuck Daly, new assistant coach Brendan Suhr, and trainer Mike Abdenour made a half-moon around Dumars, but their faces were blank, preoccupied. They were at work. Another Knicks game—this one in the Palace. Since the last Knicks game they were only 3–2. Still in second place. Daly was aching for a win.

Dumars lifted his hand off his thigh and offered it to the trainer. "Pull it out," he huffed, pointing to his ring finger. Abdenour, his round,

91 ·

mustachioed face now inquisitive, like a mechanic looking under a hood, gently tugged the finger. "It's not jammed, Joe. Make a fist." Daly and Suhr were stealing glances at the scoreboard. Four minutes left, score tied. It was the first game of a crucial three-game homestand against New York, Washington, and Boston. If the Pistons couldn't take at least two of those three, they'd be in big trouble. Daly thought they already were. He was beginning to think they were suffering from "winner's disease," a blight that hit some team almost every year. As soon as a team got to the Championship level, its players got selfish. Now Dantley was jealous of Rodman. Salley wanted Mahorn's job. Isiah and A.D. were still distant. Vinnie wanted more minutes. Dawkins wanted off the bench. Michael Williams kept his mouth shut, but he was itching to play. It was Daly's job to keep this selfishness from devouring the team, and as he watched Joe Dumars make a fist, he knew his job had just gotten harder. Dumars, Detroit's most unselfish player, had only three knuckles, which meant a hand was broken. Now two starters were down. A week ago, Mahorn's back problem had flared up. But Daly didn't let Dumars's injury get to him. He'd learned not to get too high or too low. Bad for business. Good for heart attacks.

Abdenour double-timed Dumars off the court, Joe's face still ricocheting from one emotion to the next. Daly sat back down, watched Gerald Wilkins sink the foul shot he'd been awarded for breaking Joe Dumars's hand, and murmured to his new assistant coach, "Life without Joe will be interesting." But Brendan Suhr barely heard Daly; his mind was set on getting Patrick Ewing—the monster in the middle—to foul out. Getting rid of Ewing was the best way to beat New York, and the best way for Suhr to prove himself. Suhr was in his first week at Detroit, having just replaced Dick Versace, who'd gotten the head coaching job at Indiana after Jack Ramsay quit. Suhr felt he had to gain the players' confidence right away, or he'd lose them. He knew players were contemptuous of "bullshit coaches," rah-rah guys—especially if they were square little white guys like Suhr. At Atlanta, his last team, he'd had Dominique Wilkins to tell the new guys, like Moses Malone and Reggie Theus, that he knew the game. But here, he had to do his own PR. So he'd linked his immediate fate to showing the players how to foul out Ewing. For a week, he'd drilled them on pulling Ewing away from the basket, then driving at him, which often prompted Ewing to stick out his knee. They'd gotten five fouls on him, but now Ewing, with his tree-stump thighs, was leveraging the 245-pound Laimbeer out of the lane with little more than a twitch of his butt. Ewing hated Laimbeer—a rich white boy with a big mouth. As Laimbeer and Ewing muscled each other, a fan in deck shoes and a monogrammed sweater stood on his courtside seat behind the basket, shouting, "Come over *here*, Patrick! You ain't nothin' to me!" A yuppie by day, a Bad Boy by night. Leon the Barber, in black jeans and black New Balance sneakers, beamed at him.

Dumars and the trainer hurried past the broadcasters on their way to the locker room. Tom Wilson, doing the color commentating for local cable, murmured into his mike, "At first I thought Joe had hurt his thigh, from the way he was holding his hand against it, but now it looks like a jammed finger." Wilson sounded calm, but his belly was roiling: You're never more than one injury out of the toilet.

In the locker room, Dumars could barely sit still. Electric blasts of pain were jolting his arm, and he was still adrenaline-struck from the game. Team doctor Benjamin Paolucci was fingering the break, locating it through "point sensitivity." Every time he brushed his finger over it, Dumars jerked. From the muffled surges of crowd noise, they could tell that the game, down to its last seconds, was still close. "Can you rub something on it," said Dumars, "so that I can get back in?" The doctor shook his head. Abdenour smiled. He *loved* that attitude. He'd been with the team for thirteen years, since the days of the midwinter "Florida injuries."

"Damn, this hurts," said Dumars. "Jesus! I was having a great year!" Abdenour, still focused on following the right order of procedures, didn't feel much empathy. That wasn't his job.

At courtside Tom Wilson, resplendent in a charcoal suit and regimental tie, said, "We've just gotten word that the injury to Joe Dumars is a broken hand." Detroit called time and Wilson killed his microphone. "Shit!" he said.

Dumars, with Abdenour's help, started to get dressed. He was headed for the hospital. "Who's going to tell McCloskey?" asked Dumars.

Abdenour grimaced. "I will."

Seconds were left, the score was tied, and Ewing—seven feet, 240 pounds, three million dollars—stood at the free-throw line, squeaking his hands across his black rubber knee braces. He zeroed in on the hoop. "You ain't jack-shit!" Leon the Barber cried over the crowd's wail. Ewing sank it. His next shot trembled off the hoop, but Charles Oakley banged past Laimbeer to grab it. Oakley scooped the ball out to Mark Jackson, who flipped in a twenty-footer. That was the bitch about defensing the Knicks: Pack the middle and they went outside. Tonight they had nine 3-pointers.

Jack McCloskey, his sharp jaw immobile, watched stoically from fifth-row center court. The Knicks were terrifying. They had the great center, the great rebounder, and the great backcourt man—that was about all it took. More, and your mix got too rich. A runner from the locker room approached. "It's a broken hand, Mr. McCloskey." McCloskey just nodded. He'd known it was a break from the way Abdenour had held Dumars's hand. And he already knew what he was going to do. . . .

Knicks coach Rick Pitino, looking postpubescent but in absolute control—the cherub general—circled his team for a last time-out. "If they flood an area," he said, making eye contact all around, "don't go into that area. Stay with your guy. Now *listen* to me. They're gonna come down on the dribble and try to make a three. If Isiah penetrates, Two and Three go back." He looked up at the scoreboard—16 seconds. "There's a lifetime up there, baby, there's a lifetime up there. *Don't let up!*" They walked slowly onto the floor.

. . . McCloskey was going to call Pace Mannion. Mannion, a CBA player, was at the top of the list of guards to use if Dumars got injured. McCloskey had lists for every disaster. Assuming it *was* a disaster. They would, no doubt, drop some games in the gut of the season because of the injury. But maybe it would help shake up things, get some new combinations on the floor. It would free up minutes for Vinnie Johnson, who was hungry to prove he wasn't washed up at age thirty-two, and it would move Rodman into some shooting-guard minutes, taking him off Dantley's back. It would also give McCloskey a chance to showcase Michael Williams; maybe this would whet New Jersey's appetite for Williams. Fennis Dembo might get some minutes, and if the rich guys saw the rookies diving for loose balls, it might scare them a little. Some of them needed a scare. Adrian Dantley was sulking more all the time, and was in one of his worst slumps since he'd become a Piston. Over the last ten games, he'd averaged 13.4 points on .431 shooting. Dantley thought it was because Daly was giving too many of his minutes to Rodman, and he was pissed off at Daly about it. Year before last, Daly had given Dantley 33 minutes a game, but Rodman had chewed that down to a current 29 minutes. Correspondingly, Dantley's scoring had dropped from 21.5 to 17.3. In Utah, by contrast, he'd averaged 38 minutes and 29 points—if he'd kept that up, he could have become the third highest scorer in NBA history, behind Jabbar and Chamberlain.

"If you look at the games I'm playing since my slump," Dantley had told Terry Foster of the *Detroit News*, "I'm only shooting seven to eight shots a game. I'm not trying to start anything, but it's there in black and white. I don't like it, but that's been my role here. I've accepted this role for three years, and I've never really liked it. But it's a coaching decision."

McCloskey hated to read stuff like that over his morning coffee. The last thing the team needed was another multimillionaire politicking for more glory.

In this morning's *Oakland Press*, acerbic young Steve Addy, the grand old man of the Pistons' beat, had written, "There are a growing number of instances of finger-pointing nowadays. Within the past three weeks, we've seen two veterans, Isiah Thomas and Bill Laimbeer, yell back and forth after a mistake by Thomas. This isn't threatening to destroy all the good things the team has going, at least not yet, but the potential is there." Addy wrote that Dantley was "tired of being just another cog in Isiah's machine," and that "if the small incidents turn into big incidents, GM Jack McCloskey won't waste any time putting on his garden gloves and grabbing his tools."

Just the thing to start the day.

In any case, McCloskey would call Pace Mannion right after the game. And tomorrow maybe he'd try to move ahead with the trade— the big one.

Dave Auker had the fans up and clapping along with "Shout." McCloskey stayed put—he hadn't even noticed the music.

Rodman inbounded to Vinnie Johnson, who was immediately smothered by the Knicks' frantic full-court press. Johnson looked flustered and flipped the ball to Thomas. Thomas faked a drive and squared off for a 3-pointer.

"Isiah!" screamed Rick Pitino.

Thomas sent his shot on a rainbow arc. It clanged against the rim, hopped up to the glass, dropped into a slow, circular slide around the rim, then fell off.

Jack McCloskey winced, then jumped up from his seat. The buzzer sounded. Mark Jackson ran past Pitino, grinning. "We outta here." Pitino didn't smile. He tried never to get too up or too down.

Fifteen minutes after the game ended, McCloskey was in the coaches' room with Daly and assistant coaches Brendan Suhr and Brendan Malone. Daly looked exhausted. They'd lost a couple of days ago in Atlanta, and the loss tonight convinced Daly that New York had the Pistons figured out.

McCloskey was calm, almost upbeat. "I've got two guys who could fill in for Joe. The better one, I think, is Pace Mannion. The other is Ron Rowan. Rowan's a better shooter, but Mannion has NBA experience."

"I had Rowan in some summer leagues," said Brendan Malone. "Good shooter. A shade slow, but I like him."

"But Mannion's got the experience," said Suhr.

"We'll go with whoever you think," said Daly.

A minute later, Pace Mannion, who'd played 206 games in the NBA but was now rotting in the CBA, answered his phone.

"Pace, it's Jack McCloskey of the Pistons. We had an injury tonight to Joe Dumars. How soon can you get out here?"

"Tomorrow." Mannion didn't quibble about terms or worry about deserting the Rockford Lightning. He knew he'd get a ten-day contract, worth about $6,000—a year's salary in the CBA. After Mannion hung up, he tried to go to sleep. He didn't believe in getting too high or too low about basketball. But his resolve eroded. He was on his way back to the League, and he had an unshakable feeling that this time he was going to stay. He couldn't sleep.

When McCloskey got off the phone in the coaches' room, he looked at Chuck Daly and Brendan Suhr and nodded.

"Mannion gonna do us any good?" asked Daly.

"He's just a body," said McCloskey.

"Gotta have bodies," said Daly. Daly asked McCloskey how his trade talks were going. McCloskey had just offered Darryl Dawkins, Michael Williams, and a first-round pick for New Jersey All-Star Buck Williams.

"I'll know more tomorrow."

"Ladies and gentlemen and members of the ensemble!" Will Robinson, the Pistons' last real link to inner-city, black Detroit, strutted into McCloskey's office the morning after the Knicks game, late for the scouting meeting. McCloskey, always tight after an important loss and feeling pressure to cure the team's inertia, groused, "You get caught in fog?"

"I got caught in *everything*. Fog. Snow. Rain. I even got my *feet* wet."

One of two Piston scouts, Robinson was a hard little brick of a man, who was eighty but looked about fifty-five or sixty. He was just in from a ten-day, ten-city scouting tour. Robinson, who was black, was a legend downtown. He had coached a high school state championship team, several city championship teams, was the first black basketball coach at a major college (Illinois State), and was the first black scout in pro football. Robinson had played pro football for fifty dollars a game, when it had been an "outlaw" sport, jammed with college players using fake names.

Now Robinson was on the road five out of every seven days for seven months a year. He rarely saw Detroit's other scout, Stan Novak, McCloskey's old friend from Penn and Okinawa. Novak was gone so much he didn't even bother to live in Detroit. He lived outside Philadelphia, his base for the thirty-one years he'd coached in the CBA and Eastern League.

McCloskey and his two scouts were the oldest scouting team in the NBA, but were probably the best. They'd uncovered Joe Dumars and Dennis Rodman at obscure little schools, had discovered Spud Webb, and had built the deepest team in the league from a series of low draft picks.

"If you're ready," McCloskey said, "let's get going." They sat down at the oval oak table in McCloskey's office. The office, devoid of sports memorabilia, looked like the office of any substantial executive, with modern art, deep carpeting, and a bank of electronics. McCloskey's office was the largest room in a complex of offices just inside the main entrance of the Palace. Across the hall were offices of the business executives, including Tom Wilson, John Ciszewski, and Dave Auker. "Okay," said McCloskey, opening a notebook, "suspect number one—Chucky Brown."

"He's not very tough," said Novak. "I don't like his body."

"If he was in there late," said McCloskey, "we wouldn't take him?"

Novak made a lemon-face and shook his head. Novak was McCloskey's age—just past sixty—but he looked more his age than McCloskey did. Novak was bald, and had a slight paunch from lack of exercise. He had a bionic knee from too much hard tennis and didn't get to play as much as he liked.

"Dyron Nix," said McCloskey.

"Definitely a suspect," said Robinson. "And probably a prospect. Could go in the lottery. Runs, jumps, shoots, dribbles. And *tough*. He plays the shit out of defense, runs like hell, rebounds like hell. He's so good that Don DeVoe, the coach, is in solid now, and they were about to fire him. Nix is better than Dale Ellis at this stage of the game. He's got a better body. Jack, he's everything but white." Robinson knew the NBA favored white players over blacks as a matter of marketing, and he disliked it. But when he'd first come to the University of Michigan, blacks hadn't even been allowed to live on campus. So subtle discrimination didn't get him down that much.

"Is Nix a shooter?" asked McCloskey. McCloskey insisted that players be able to score, even if that wasn't their role.

"Shoot the lights out," said Robinson.

"Then we don't stand a chance of getting him, do we?" asked McCloskey.

"Snowball in hell." The price of success in the NBA was a low draft pick. Last year, the Knicks' Pitino had been under a lot of pressure to let his team ease up at the end of the season, to move into the lottery—

where the Knicks in 1985 had won Ewing. But Pitino, still shocked by
the death of his infant son the prior year, had felt a compulsion to win.

"Mike Smith," said McCloskey. "The BYU kid. I don't like him."

"I don't like him either," said Novak.

"He can shoot the *ball* though," said Robinson.

"But he's so fulla crap, and he's slow," said Novak.

"Now don't start picking him apart." Robinson looked pained.

"I'm not picking him apart," said Novak. "I just say he can't play."

Robinson let it drop. He'd learned long ago to avoid conflict. It had
helped him at Illinois State, where he'd coached headstrong superstar
Doug Collins. Collins had accepted Robinson as a mentor, and now that
he was coaching the Chicago Bulls—and headstrong Michael Jordan—
he was trying to apply Robinson's rules.

"Think we ought to trade away our pick?" asked McCloskey.

"That's a thought," Robinson said hopefully. He wanted to get something of value out of his sacrifices. On a recent trip, he'd forgotten what
his rented car looked like, and waited until the stadium parking lot was
empty to find it. That had happened before—all rent-a-cars looked alike.
Robinson called them "invisible cars."

"Who's available out there?" said Novak.

"Portland's shopping Steve Johnson and Kiki Vandeweghe. But they
want a lot."

"Too much?"

McCloskey shrugged. At this point, he didn't know what "too much"
was. Was Salley and Williams too much? Was Dantley and their first-
round pick too much? The injury to Dumars had made his calculations
tougher.

"What's Portland say about Kiki's back?" asked Robinson.

"That it's fine. Of course," said McCloskey. Trader Jack's first rule of
trading was "Everybody lies."

"So why isn't he driving to the basket?" asked Novak.

"He's not driving?" said Robinson.

"He's not getting any free throws. If he's driving, why isn't he getting
to the line?" Novak turned to McCloskey. "Jack, I wouldn't be too
quick to trade our pick. You know we've found some good suspects on
the bottom." McCloskey didn't argue. For now, McCloskey was going
to keep his pick. New Jersey GM Harry Weltman had called back to turn
down McCloskey's offer of Michael Williams, Darryl Dawkins, and Detroit's first pick for Buck Williams. Weltman wanted Joe Dumars in
place of Michael Williams. That was a much stiffer price.

McCloskey wasn't sure what he would do. But he felt he had to do
something.

*　　*　　*

In the empty Palace, where each bounce of the ball echoed a flat *splat* against the hard floor, Pace Mannion, the Pistons' newest body, shot baskets with injured Rick Mahorn, the baddest of the Bad Boys. Just offcourt, holding a notebook, was Terry Foster, the beat reporter from the *Detroit News*. Foster had just asked Mannion—a gangly, gym-rat-pale kid with unlikely-looking pockets of muscle on his biceps and calves—what he hoped to accomplish.

"I just want to help the team get through this period," said Mannion. "If we win our games, I'll be happy."

Mannion knew that what he was saying was bullshit—the most transparent kind of mantalk—and he knew Foster knew it.

"Pace is like the Equalizer," said Mahorn. "I came, I saw, I kicked ass—I went back to the CBA."

What Mannion was really hoping was to snag a second ten-day contract, then attract enough respect to latch on with a European team. Spain and Italy were paying up to $300,000 a year to American players, tax-free, and there was a lot of talk about a European team soon joining the NBA.

Mahorn looked fluid and strong as he shot, but every time he bent over to pick up the ball he went "Unnnh!" and his body seemed to age about forty years. The generally polite and articulate Mahorn had ripped apart his spine as the Pistons' chief enforcer, and become one of the most hated men in basketball. Mahorn, unlike Laimbeer, didn't like being hated. He spent a lot of time working with kids and going to hospitals. Recently, he'd begun helping a young unwed mother at the request of Leon the Barber. Mahorn had an affinity for pushed-around people because he'd been a fat little kid, living in the shadow of an older brother. His father had left the family early, and Mahorn hadn't had much protection until he'd sprouted from six feet one to six-seven at age sixteen. He'd been too fat to start on his high school basketball team until his senior year. When he'd been traded to Detroit for journeyman Dan Roundfield—one of McCloskey's most remarkable transactions—he'd still been too fat. He'd gone to McCloskey to bitch about not getting enough minutes, and McCloskey had ripped him apart. "I *was* fat," Mahorn said later. "I was two hundred eighty-five pounds, and he told me to do something about it. And I *did*. Jack has this way of getting your attention."

Now Mahorn, at 255, was the soul of the Bad Boys image, which was getting hotter by the week. Tom Wilson's marketing campaign was well received, in part, because it meshed perfectly with the city's self-image:

tough, take-no-prisoners, take-no-shit. Detroit wasn't entirely mortified about its reputation as the nation's murder capital, and this winter's most celebrated local criminal was a high school dean of students who had killed his wife—for calling him "a wimp"—and then kept her in the freezer for three and a half years. On the media front, a local radio station was playing a song entitled "Walk with an Erection." The FCC was pissed, but who cared? Detroit was *bad*.

McCloskey was beginning to worry about the Bad Boys campaign, but he didn't think his team was dirty. As far as dirty went, Atlanta's Kevin Willis was ridiculous, and even beloved Larry Bird was one of the dirtiest players in the league. Bird was always slapping, gouging, and standing on his opponents' sneakers. McCloskey loved Bird. He had the killer instinct. So did Magic Johnson. In Johnson's rookie year, Trader Jack had offered the Lakers any four players on his team for Johnson. They'd turned him down. He'd called back, and offered any six. Turn-down. Then he'd called back, and offered his entire team. Jerry Buss had been called into the negotiation, but Buss had passed. Players like Johnson and Bird were just too rare. They didn't play for money or ego or even glory. They played because they loved to win. Laimbeer, though he had lesser skills, had the same attitude. Whether he was playing darts, negotiating a contract or doing a cross-word puzzle, Laimbeer *had* to win. Laimbeer was a pain in the ass— always bellicose and uptight. But that was okay. It was good for chemistry.

As Mahorn and Mannion left the court, they walked past Darryl Dawkins, who was in the last stages of recovery from yet another injury. A couple of weeks ago, Dawkins had separated his shoulder, and it was still bothering him. During his time off, he'd again begun to puff in the belly and butt. But he was about ready to give it another shot, and when he was ready to return, Mannion would be cut to make room. Dawkins's future, however, was also being shadowed. William Bedford was once again about to come back from his drug rehab routine. When Bedford returned, Dawkins would get the ax.

Mannion and Mahorn paused briefly as they passed Dawkins. "How's the shoulder?" Mannion asked Dawkins.

"It's gettin' lots better."

"Glad to hear it," said Mannion.

Dawkins smiled sweetly, as if he believed what Mannion was saying. Mahorn reached out to Dawkins, slapped his palm, and locked fingers. Mahorn had a guaranteed income of $800,000—this year. He also had a spine that was turning to gravel. Mannion walked on, alone, to get his ankles taped for his return to the NBA.

*   *   *

Tom Wilson, the Pistons' boyish CEO, stood in the tunnel between the locker room and the court with even younger chief financial officer Ron Campbell. It was an hour before the Washington Bullets game, and the stadium was gradually clicking to life. "I told Jack he ought to go after Vandeweghe," said Wilson, whose perfectly aligned face had almost put him over the top in Hollywood.

"Good thing Jack doesn't listen to you," Campbell said. "Kiki's back is gonna blow. Watch Michael Williams tonight. I think Jack believes we can make the Finals with the guys we've got."

Wilson looked dubious.

Just behind them, twenty yards off the floor, a sliding glass door swished open and the tinkling bell sound of ice against crystal echoed in the stadium. The rich folks had arrived. Wilson had been the first stadium-planner ever to put suites only about fifty feet from the floor, and the gamble was paying off exquisitely. The suites' proximity had tripled their value—because what was the point of being a rich guy if you had to bring binoculars? Each of the suites was 360 square feet of pure luxury: a marble bar, a private party area that opened onto an outdoor viewing deck, private bathrooms, kitchen, leather couches, and big-screen TVs. When Oprah Winfrey had filmed in Detroit, she'd wanted to shoot her show in one of the classiest rooms in town and had settled on a Palace suite.

Wilson and Ciszewski had been scared to death when they'd first gone out to sell them. They'd been too deep into the Palace to back out, they were demanding $120,000 a year, and they had 180 of them to get rid of. Bad sales would mean End of Franchise: the Baltimore Pistons, the Cincinnati Pistons. But Lee Iacocca had bought the first and best one, pissing off Ford Motors, and that got the ball rolling. Ciszewski had realized that they were over the top after a conversation with a Rockwell International executive. He'd been trying to soft-pedal the price, but the Rockwell exec had told him, "Hell, we've got executives with ninety-thousand-dollar *expense accounts*. If I get *one contract* from this suite, we're talking ten million."

The money from the suites would soon be a necessity. The latest buzz around the league was that the salary cap would almost double in the next few years to $12 million. Franchises in the smaller markets and those that didn't own stadiums would be choking for breath.

At the other end of the tunnel, just across a narrow hall from the locker room, Jack McCloskey sat at a table in the press room, where reporters and franchise executives were given a preegame meal. This one was typically lavish: choice of game hen or Swiss steak, shrimp cocktail, cauliflower in hollandaise sauce, Caesar salad, black bean soup, hot dinner rolls, and cheesecake with strawberries. McCloskey's food sat to one side, getting cold, as he picked at his shrimp cocktail. He was preoccupied. At the table were Stan Novak, Will Robinson, Piston broadcaster George Blaha, and McCloskey's wife Leslie, an unusually attractive woman who'd been a model when they'd met about twenty years ago in Portland, while McCloskey was coaching the Trail Blazers.

McCloskey had been talking about his days with the Lakers, when Barbra Streisand and Jack Nicholson had sat behind him. "Then we'd come here," Leslie McCloskey had said, "and there was *nobody* sitting behind us. Nobody in our whole section. People would hike over and tell Jack what he ought to do. Not in an abrasive way, just, like, *'Please, anything.'* "

McCloskey had to respond to New Jersey's offer of Buck Williams for Dumars and Dawkins. It wasn't really that complicated. People had been trying to get Dumars for years, and McCloskey would never go for it. When Moses Malone had gone to Washington a few years ago, he'd been offered to McCloskey for Dumars, Laimbeer, and Kelly Tripucka. Malone was at his peak—he was the franchise center all Championship teams *had* to have—but McCloskey wouldn't include Dumars in the deal. Last year, when he'd picked up James Edwards, he'd had the choice of getting both Edwards and star forward Larry Nance for Dumars and Salley, but he'd walked away from it. At the moment, he considered Dumars his most valuable player.

"There are three trade areas right now," said McCloskey, spearing a shrimp but not bringing it to his mouth. "The first is the Championship contender circle—the first tier—which includes us, L.A., the Knicks, Cleveland, Atlanta, and a couple of others. We're all looking for insurance, a deal that, above all, won't have a chance of hurting us, or helping another elite team. Then there's the second tier, the playoff contenders, like Indiana, Portland, or Houston, who can be a little bolder—like we were several years back. Finally, there's the third tier—New Jersey, the Clippers, Sacramento. They're building for the future. The trade matchups tend to be among different tiers, rather than within tiers. That's almost the only way to produce a complementary effect. Most trades have to be good for both teams—otherwise, why do it? But you don't want to help your toughest competition, and you usually don't want to help anyone in your own division. As a rule, most of the people I talk to are out West.

"Like, right now, Jim Peterson will be a free agent next year, so he might be available. The Spurs, I know, are looking for a power forward.

Indiana is looking for a point guard; they like Vern Fleming, but maybe at a different position. Portland is still shopping Vandeweghe and Steve Johnson. We could use Vandeweghe, but . . ."

But his back was probably about to explode. McCloskey had come to a decision. He was going to put Salley on the block. Salley and Detroit's first pick for Buck Williams.

If that didn't work, he might throw in a guard. But it wouldn't be Dumars. Either Vinnie Johnson or Michael Williams.

It was a nerve-wracking decision, but he'd made it, and now it was time to pull the trigger.

Half an hour later, as the lineups were announced, McCloskey, an intense but stoic observer, applauded Vinnie Johnson, who was starting in place of Dumars. Johnson, who at six-two looked like a squashed little pile of muscle next to the other players, came roaring out at the Bullets with leaping passes and blitzkrieg drives to the basket. Coalminer Style. The crowd caught his enthusiasm, started to howl, and Johnson responded with even more abandon. Johnson had grown up in the Brooklyn slums and had idolized Walt Frazier and Willis Reed. He'd never thought about the money they made. He just wanted to *be Frazier*. Now, with a $663,000-a-year salary, he still didn't think much about money. That was why McCloskey had traded for him.

Early in the first quarter, Chuck Daly put Michael Williams in the game. Williams, at 175 pounds, was little more than a long stick of gum next to the other players, who outweighed him by 50 to 100 pounds. But then he got the ball at the top of the key, ran a step, leaped, and seemed to climb all the way to the basket, where he karate-chopped the ball down through the hoop. McCloskey, who'd seen things in Williams no other GM had, grinned.

The Pistons built on an early 10–0 lead, and the game was over practically before it had started. Even Pace Mannion got to play. The Bullets, crippled by their front office maneuvers, were an amorphous, uncentered clump of individuals, as interesting to watch as C-SPAN.

But outside the locker room after the game, McCloskey wasn't particularly happy. Johnson and Williams had both played well. He liked them both. But one of them would have to go.

At the shootaround the morning of the Celtics game, Daly called his players into a group under the basket. "We're gonna work on the zone trap," he rasped in his larynx-grated coach's voice.

"But that's *illegal*," said Laimbeer. Daly ignored the remark, and began running them through a highly choreographed pattern.

"I hate to keep saying it," yelled Daly as they ran, "but if you keep your hands up, there's that much less territory." The rookies and Pace Mannion threw their hands into the air. "Hands! Hands! Hands up, Billy! Hands up, Billy!"

"They're up! They're up! They're up!" bleated Laimbeer.

McCloskey, sitting at the scorer's table, waved scout Will Robinson over. "Where's Dumars?" asked Robinson.

"He had his hand operated on yesterday," said McCloskey.

"He could come and sit. It's his hand that's broken, not his ass."

"Joe's okay. I wanna tell you something. Bedford went back to the center in California this morning."

Robinson was quiet for several moments. "Then I guess that's where he belongs." Robinson, who had made under $25,000 a year most of his life, shook his head. "Feature that. Boy could be makin' six . . . what is it, Jack?"

"Six eighty-seven."

"Six hundred eighty-seven thousand dollars a year. If he just wanted it."

"Well, he oughta want it now," said McCloskey. "He's had to sell his house and his car. We're not paying him, you know."

"Coulda used him against the Green Monster tonight. Anything happening with New Jersey?"

McCloskey shook his head. Weltman had turned down Salley and a draft pick for Buck Williams. McCloskey had sweetened the deal: Salley, Darryl Dawkins, and Michael Williams. Buck Williams had heard about the negotiating, and he thought it was a virtual done-deal. He was practically packing his bags.

On the floor, Daly shouted at Salley, "Don't slide! Which you do all the time, by the way. You want me to work with you on it ten minutes a day?" Salley walked away, scowling. He was starting now in place of Mahorn. He loved to start. Theoretically, the job was now his to try to keep. But he felt like he was losing control of his fate.

Earlier in the morning, Daly had been talking about the difficulty of coaching in a "players' league." "The coach basically has a three-day contract, written in ice," he'd said, "while the player may have a ten-year contract for twenty million dollars. That contract makes him the CEO of his own corporation. You wouldn't go in and scream at the CEO of a corporation, would you? But you've got to. Because while they're tycoons, they're also children worrying about scoring a basket. They're really no different than the children I coached at Punxsutawney High School thirty years ago. They all want to hear the crowd cheer. What you have to do is ignore the fact that they're wealthy men in a serious business, and address them as kids playing a game. Because that's the aspect of their personality that's going to win games. And, ironically, make them rich. That's the quality Jack looks for."

Daly was known as a "players' coach"—he managed to get along with practically everyone. But Daly had a serious problem. Adrian Dantley, his leading scorer, had begun to ignore him. To act as if he *didn't exist*. Dantley would hardly speak to Daly. Daly knew Dantley was hurting inside. Daly had tried to bridge the gap: no go.

That was something Daly couldn't tolerate. A player and coach *had to talk*.

Daly wanted Dantley off the team.

"... And at the other guard ..." The crowd—all those Bad Boy doctors and lawyers—started to get ugly. ". . . in his eighth year . . ." Boos from the balcony and curses from the first few rows. "Danny . . . Ainge!" Through the high, angry sound, the voice of Leon the Barber knifed: "You ain't shit, Ainge!" But where was Ainge? Already huddled amidst his teammates—he'd sneaked out before introduction to avoid the inevitable rain of hostility. Ainge, whose crybaby face made him the most abused player in the game, was actually pretty sensitive. He was a devout Mormon with four kids and a pleasant personality. But he ripped into the Pistons with sadistic glee, popping in rainbow jumpers over the shorter Vinnie Johnson, taking pleasure in Johnson's frustration.

Ainge's Mr. Nasty image had made him rich in Boston; he had deals with Reebok, a local computer company, Citgo gas, and a Mercedes dealership that brought in practically as much as his $625,000 salary. He'd long known that sports was a business. In 1980, Ainge had learned a bitter lesson about the business of sports when the Celtics and Toronto Blue Jays had refused to let him play basketball and baseball at the same time. An ugly court fight had almost ended his athletic career. Despite this experience, once the clock started, it was Just a Game. "When I'm playing," he'd said in the locker room before the game, "it's exactly like it was in high school. Exactly. You just want to win one for Green." Ainge had the "Celtic pride" that Red Auerbach had built a dynasty on, with players like Bob Cousy, John Havlicek, Dave Cowens, Bill Russell, and Larry Bird. Ainge's outlook was exactly the kind of attitude McCloskey was trying to build in Detroit. Team-First Thomas had been talking about it before the game. "You know that when the Celtics step onto the floor that they're feeling the pressure of their tradition," he said. "They *have* to succeed. It's a demand. We're trying to create that demand here."

But it wasn't happening. The Celtics were running up the score. Thomas, who often tried to do too much, wasn't taking his shot, and Laimbeer was getting pushed around by the Celtics' thirty-five-year-old Robert Parish—whom Laimbeer had smashed in the mouth the last time they'd played. At fifth-row center, McCloskey kept swiping his hand over his gunmetal-gray hair. Daly leaned into the court, yelling "Defense!" and "Hands!" It wasn't doing any good. The Pistons seemed sluggish and clumsy. As the half wound down, with the Pistons trailing by 12, Daly put young whippet Michael Williams on Ainge, but Ainge still feathered in his jumpers. When the horn sounded, the Pistons were down 11. As they walked toward the dressing room, the fans started to boo the Pistons. It was the first time this season it had happened. Some of the players had their heads down. Vinnie Johnson held his head up and acted as if he didn't hear the booing. But he did.

Daly stood in front of a chalkboard at the head of a horseshoe of chairs in the locker room, studying a clipboard. McCloskey sat at the far end of the horseshoe. Most of the players were looking at the floor, still sweating.

Daly's face was red. He seemed to be hyperventilating. "Goddamnit, guys," he said, his voice strained, "what'd I tell you when Joe broke his hand?"

No one spoke.

"That we'd have to start earning everything we get from now on! Every bucket! *Every* bucket! We don't have *any* margin for error anymore." As he spoke, his voice jumped in volume. Daly didn't believe in yelling for shock value. It was bullshit, like a coach in a movie. When you did yell, he felt, you'd better be yelling *about* something. And you'd better be right about it. "We don't have *any* margin for error anymore. It's not *there!* I said that the other night, but I guess you weren't listening. Now *listen.* This is a big game. These are the Celtics!" He let his statement hang, as if there were more to say. He stood silently for half a minute, the red still in his face, then started going over technical details.

Isiah Thomas came out of the locker room glaring. Just after the second half started, he slapped the ball out of Ainge's hands and started to run, but got whistled for a foul. He turned his back on referee Jack Madden and said, "Are you fuckin' kiddin' me!"

"You can't swear at me," Madden snapped, and gave Thomas a technical. Thomas's scowl stayed immobile, but he seemed to retreat within himself. After the free throws, he started calling for the ball, ignoring Dantley's waves, and began sinking ten- and twenty-footers. After he hit three in a row, he started skipping and hopping, working to his own rhythm, quickening the pace of the game. About halfway through the quarter, Detroit pulled to within 2, and the fans started stomping. Every time Boston got the ball, Laimbeer churned his forearms into McHale's gut. As McHale angled for a pass, he slipped from the shoves like a man walking on ice. Toward the end of the quarter, McHale yelled at Jack Madden, "Pushing, goddamnit!" Madden ignored him. Vinnie Johnson stole the ball, rocketed off for a lay-up, and Boston called time-out. The score was tied. Boston huddled while Leon the Barber screamed, "Hey, McHale, hey, Great White Hope! Hey, Great White Hope!" A black usher fixed Leon with a dirty look, but Leon kept yelling. McHale didn't acknowledge him; players never did. When Brendan Suhr had been with Atlanta, he'd fined players for responding to Leon. After the time-out, Jim Paxson fouled Vinnie Johnson twice in a row, Johnson made all his free throws, and Detroit was up by 4.

The Pistons got a run of 8 straight early in the fourth, mostly off defense, rebounding and steals—Coalminer ball, fueled by home-court adrenaline. Michael Williams was on fire. He bombed in a jerky lay-up and was back on defense before the ball hit the floor. The generally polite Paxson turned on referee Nolan Fine and snarled, "That's traveling, dickhead." Fine ignored him, and a fan yelled, "Nice mouth, Paxson." Paxson ran back to the other end, yelling at Fine, "Why don't you watch the game?" Fine hit him with a technical and Isiah made the shots. Next time down the floor, Paxson said to Fine, "Gonna watch the game now?" Fine, who apparently knew he missed the traveling call, ignored the insult. Boston was getting stiff and awkward with fatigue. They didn't have the bench for Detroit. At a time-out, the Brow left his seat and ran the perimeter of the floor, his fist aloft, as the crowd screamed.

With 1:59 left and the Pistons up 4, Dantley went to the line. His first shot clanged off the rim. He stepped back, put up an imaginary shot, laughed to himself, and sank the next one. Ainge hurried down the floor, forced up a bad 3-pointer, and watched little Michael Williams float down with the rebound. It was over. McCloskey came out of the stands fast and threw his arm around Brendan Suhr.

After the game, Suhr, McCloskey, and Daly sat in the coaches' room. They were relieved, but emotionally flat. They had survived the three-game homestand, winning two. But something was wrong—and it wasn't the injuries to Mahorn and Dumars. The chemistry was way off. The hardest part of the season was still ahead.

Daly asked McCloskey about the New Jersey deal: Salley, Michael Williams, and Dawkins for Buck Williams.

New Jersey had turned it down. That was the end of it. Forget Buck Williams.

But McCloskey had a new deal in the works. With Dallas. For Dantley.

"Trader Jack" McCloskey, the general manager and architect of the Pistons, built his team on the telephone, through shrewd trades and constant contact with his scouts.

Rookie Dave Popson, from North Carolina, had a good shot at making the team. He had a better attitude than his rival, Darryl Dawkins. But Dawkins had guaranteed money. PHOTOGRAPH COURTESY OF THE UNIVERSITY OF NORTH CAROLINA

Adrian Dantley, the tenth highest scorer in NBA history, was loved by Piston fans. But he wasn't right for Detroit's chemistry. McCloskey's daring and controversial midseason trade shook the NBA—and shook up the Pistons.
PHOTOGRAPH COURTESY OF EINSTEIN PHOTO

ALL PHOTOGRAPHS, UNLESS OTHERWISE NOTED, WERE TAKEN BY THE AUTHOR.

From the beginning, the media spotlight glared on the Pistons. Coach Chuck Daly was ambivalent about the attention—it could tear a team apart. Here, CBS's Hubie Brown with Isiah Thomas.

The luxurious new Palace of Auburn Hills was a financial blessing but attracted a quiet, upscale crowd. Front-office executive Dave Auker used electronic gimmickry to jolt the crowd awake. Seated: Left/right PA announcer Ken Calvert and chief financial officer Ron Campbell.

The most famous and feared fan in the NBA: Leon the Barber. Leon taught the genteel Palace crowd how to be Bad.

Dennis Rodman plays to the crowd. Opponents thought he was a hotdog, but he was the first player the quiet Palace crowd embraced. He's shown here with Washington's Terry Catledge.

McCloskey, Stan Novak (left), and Will Robinson were the oldest scouting team in the NBA. Many thought they were the best.

James Edwards was a prime component of Detroit's Killer B-Team: the back-up center who could score. But Edwards still thought McCloskey would sacrifice him in the expansion draft.

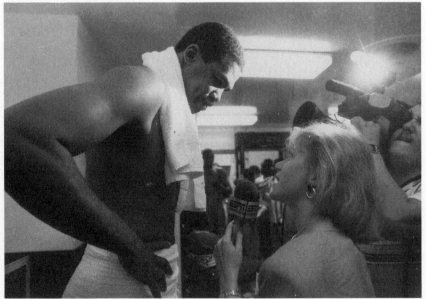

A rare dunk for rookie Fennis Dembo. Dembo went from the cover of *Sports Illustrated* as a collegian to the end of the deep Detroit bench. He wasn't always happy there. The bench fought the starters as hard as their opponents.

Atlanta coach Mike Fratello helped GM Stan Kasten rebuild the Hawks. They gambled big—and lost.

Marketing director Jon Ciszewski surveys the stadium he helped build. Ciszewski was married to his job and helped bring about $70 million to the franchise every year. If that didn't make him a Piston, nothing did.

Rodman jams. In theory, all championship teams had to be centered around strong inside scorers. That was a rule McCloskey rewrote.

Left to right, Will Robinson, Jack McCloskey, and Stan Novak scrutinize the Orlando Classic. Afterward, they exchanged views with other GMs and scouts. But, said McCloskey, "everybody lies."

Dallas player personnel director Rick Sund (left) and Chicago GM Jerry Krause hold a quick conference at the Orlando Classic. Both gambled with big, controversial trades in 1989. Krause's brought him to within two games of the Finals.

Agent Bill Pollack, who represents Dennis Rodman and others, works the Orlando Classic. Fierce negotiating by agents has changed the NBA into a "player's league," where selfishness, egotism, and greed often destroy teams.

Piston CEO Tom Wilson (right) quietly celebrates clinching the division title with publicist Matt Dobek. Wilson, after twelve years of watching his team fail to take the Championship, guarded his feelings. He had a saying about the Pistons: "They'll break your heart."

The team is subdued after clinching the division title in Cleveland. By now, all the title means is home-court advantage during the playoffs. Nothing more.

McCloskey, who stormed Okinawa as a twenty-year-old, prepares for the last game of the first round beneath the Championship banners of the Boston Garden. McCloskey: "It's like waiting for an invasion to start."

One reason Detroit continues to win: The benched players don't sulk. Rick Mahorn cheerleads as Detroit pulls away from Boston.

Lonely in a crowd: McCloskey is the only spectator in Boston Garden who likes what he's seeing. McCloskey built his team specifically to beat the Celtics.

Two of the biggest feats in basketball: beating the Celtics in Boston Garden and going from trade-bait to playoff star. John Salley has just accomplished both.

The morning after: Boston GM Jan Volk fields calls from reporters after Boston's first-round defeat. Volk saw Championship expectations turn to disaster.

Bill Laimbeer and John Salley fight for position among Milwaukee's "Ivory Towers"—Paul Mokeski, Fred Roberts, and Jack Sikma. Milwaukee is the kind of team that scared McCloskey and Daly; the Bucks have good chemistry, strong emotions, and brains.

Jack Sikma, Milwaukee's golden boy, is almost all the Bucks have left after a
string of injuries. Once again, the depth that McCloskey had engineered was the
deciding factor in defeating Milwaukee.

Chuck Daly, after a threat against his life has been turned over to the FBI, tries
to concentrate on the questions of reporters Terry Foster (foreground) and Drew
Sharp.

The difference between fresh legs and starters' legs: Detroit's Killer B-Team has worn Milwaukee out.

Laimbeer hangs on as time runs out for Milwaukee.

MTV's Downtown Julie Brown takes the floor as the Chicago series begins. The mood is festive. It won't last long.

Chicago GM Jerry Krause once hoped to draft John Salley. Krause, almost as active a trader as McCloskey, is still interested in him.

Piston marketing chief John Ciszewski keeps busy during the first game of the Chicago series. It keeps him from getting sick to his stomach from nerves.

Chicago coach Doug Collins gets advice during the game. Collins made Chicago a winner, but he couldn't get along with Michael Jordan or GM Jerry Krause, and he lost his job.

SIX

"The Trade"
McCloskey Pulls the Trigger

MARK AGUIRRE was headed for the door. He was practically running. His Dallas teammates, lacquered with sweat after another numbing defeat, ignored him. Unlike the other exhausted players, Aguirre looked sharp and unruffled in designer clothes—he hadn't played one minute in the game, even though it had been a crucial match with archrival Utah.

Aguirre hadn't played because of "sore ankles." He had warmed up before the game and had looked fine. But just before tip-off, he'd told coach John MacLeod that he wasn't up to it. When his absence was announced over the PA system, the Dallas fans booed and screamed abuse. Some of his teammates had made faces. Aguirre was estranged from virtually the entire team, including the coach, because of his frequent absences, moodiness, and indifference. A few games ago, when he'd been pulled in the vital last minutes, he'd scowled toward MacLeod and the bench and had given them the finger.

After that, he'd said publicly that he wanted to be traded, and he'd listed his favorite teams: Chicago, L.A., and Detroit—his hometown and the two top contenders. The response of the Dallas sportswriters had been: Fine—take a hike.

A reporter intercepted Aguirre as he was stepping out the door. "Are you being traded?" asked the reporter.

"Have a nice day," Aguirre said, and then he was gone.

The situation was ready to explode.

In Detroit, at the same time, Chuck Daly was putting the Pistons through another grueling practice. Since the January 16 win over Boston about two weeks ago, Detroit was 5–2. Not a bad record, but one of the wins had been by one point, another had been in overtime, and they'd lost again to Cleveland. By now, they were 0–8 against Cleveland, Milwaukee, and New York. That was a frightening stat; it worried McCloskey more than anything else about the team. If they couldn't start beating the elite teams they were screwed.

Today's practice was typical—lots of bashing and cursing and T-shirts dark with sweat. Lots of Daly standing at midcourt and yelling over the squeal of gym shoes. Then, suddenly, everything boiled over. Daly and Dantley, who'd hardly been speaking for over a month, were suddenly yelling at each other. All the pent-up anger from the months of tension came spilling out. At one point, according to an observer of the scene, Daly told Dantley, "That's why we're going to trade your butt."

Later on, Daly and Dantley both denied that he'd made that remark.

But the damage was done. Dantley was now an outsider. This situation was also ready to explode.

McCloskey was in close communication with Dallas player personnel director Rick Sund. About a Dantley-Aguirre deal. Last summer, Sund had first contacted McCloskey about Aguirre. He'd also called several other GMs. He wasn't looking for any particular player—he just wanted to be rid of Aguirre. He was sick of Aguirre's temperament and the way it had poisoned his team. Aguirre was a superb box-score player: a two-time All-American, three-time All-Star, first pick of the 1981 draft, with a 24.9 career average. But Sund was desperate to dump him. Coach MacLeod had told Sund that if he didn't trade Aguirre, MacLeod would bench him for the rest of the year. MacLeod had to keep the other players thinking that basketball was Just a Game, something they should play with abandon and generosity, and Aguirre was constantly reinforcing the other perspective: that it was Just a Job, and everyone was entitled to put himself first and take it easy when he felt bad.

With the recent rise of Roy Tarpley, Sund had had less need of Aguirre. But last month, Tarpley had had a drug relapse—he was back in Van Nuys with William Bedford—and Sund *still* wanted to unload Aguirre.

Sund wanted to know if McCloskey would trade Dantley and Salley for Aguirre. McCloskey refused. He wasn't about to pay that much— besides, he was almost certain the offer was just Sund's opening gambit.

They began talking about trading Aguirre and forward Sam Perkins for Dantley and Salley. For McCloskey, that was much more tempting. Perkins had better numbers than Salley: 13.8 career scoring and 7.9 career rebounding averages. But he was a little shorter and a little older than Salley, and unlike Salley he'd probably reached his full potential.

Sund was also still talking to Indiana about Aguirre for Wayman Tisdale, and to Sacramento about Aguirre for Jim Peterson and Rodney McCray. There were not that many teams who could fit Aguirre's $715,000 salary under their caps. Sund had tried to trade Aguirre to the Clippers for journeyman forward Ken Norman, but salary cap considerations had killed the deal. Aguirre could have restructured his contract to make the deal work, but he'd refused to.

For McCloskey, the rationale of a Dantley-Aguirre trade was compelling. "Aguirre is bigger than A.D.," said McCloskey, "and he's about four years younger. He's a more inventive passer, he keeps the ball moving better, and he's a little better rebounder." Detroit might also get the advantage of more fast breaks without Dantley. Sometimes it seemed as if Dantley didn't want to get out on the break—maybe because he got the ball so much more in the half-court game. Still, the choice was agonizing. There was no one on the team McCloskey admired more than Adrian Dantley. There was a lot in Adrian Dantley that reminded McCloskey of himself.

When Adrian Dantley had been a freshman in high school in suburban Washington, D.C., he'd taken a history course from the high school basketball coach. Dantley was flunking and needed a B on an exam to pass. Dantley put his full focus on the test. No one got higher than an 80 on the test except Dantley, who got a 95. The coach was shocked. He knew that Dantley could concentrate on basketball, but thought he'd cheated on the test. So he stood Dantley in front of the class and gave him an oral exam. Dantley got every question right. The coach later told him, "I should never have done that. I should have guessed that you could apply the same discipline to a book that you could to a basketball."

Even in high school, Dantley's game was founded on control and discipline rather than natural grace. When he went to Notre Dame, though, he let himself puff to thirty pounds over his ideal weight, and coach Digger Phelps had suggested he go on a diet. Dantley started eating nothing but vegetables, salad with no dressing, and milk. A couple of weeks into the diet, Dantley—literally starving—had passed out during a game. But he'd waited until a time-out to do it.

When he went pro, as the sixth pick in the 1976 draft, he'd been idealistic and starry-eyed about making a living out of something that was Just a Game. But he was traded after his first year, as part of a business maneuver to raid the ABA, and was traded for James Edwards the next year by a team that needed a center. A year later he was traded again. By then he was markedly less sentimental about "team spirit" and about basketball being Just a Game.

For seven years Dantley played for Utah, averaging a remarkable 29.5 points. He was not a great shooter, but through sheer determination and focus he managed to break free for shots or draw fouls. He was an excellent free-throw shooter—it was one skill that could be mastered through just hard work. Every year, though, Dantley fell further into disfavor. Dantley played with fair to poor teams under Frank Layden, whose joviality thinly disguised his obsession with winning. Under Layden, Dantley developed his reputation for selfishness and aloofness. Dantley did appear to have a me-first attitude, but that might have been a reaction to all the early trades and all the losing seasons. Part of that reputation was also the result of his natural reserve clashing with Layden's bombast. Once, for example, he defended Karl Malone when Layden was giving Malone hell for missing free throws. Right after that, Layden attacked Dantley for "not listening" in the locker room, and fined him thirty dimes—thirty pieces of silver. Layden wanted to suspend him for the season but the owners intervened.

Layden thought Dantley was in the game only for money. To a degree, Layden was right. "If I just wanted to have fun," Dantley had said, "I'd go back to the parks around D.C. I play for the money. Any player who tells you different, he's lying. The money's too good." Dantley had come to believe that there was great hypocrisy in the Just a Game attitude. "If I do something from a business point of view," he said, "I'm selfish. But if the team does something, they're not selfish." There was no doubt, though, that Dantley was infatuated with money. In an airport, he'd sometimes check pay phones for coins. Despite his mercenary traits, however, Dantley played hard every night.

Even before he left Utah, Dantley had become one of the league's biggest enigmas. Utah's Thurl Bailey said of Dantley, "I think, over my years of playing, he is probably the most complex guy I've met, in terms of breaking through his personality and getting to know the real A.D.— which I don't think anybody will ever know."

Dantley has acknowledged that he's difficult to know. "I don't really think of myself as a loner," he's said. "People misinterpret my face. I'm leery of people. I'm always trying to figure them out, decide where they're coming from. I guess I tend to stare right at them instead of smiling."

When Dantley went to Detroit, his primary goal was not more personal glory, but a Championship. He'd won three scoring titles and positioned himself to be one of the leading scorers in NBA history. He'd made six All-Star teams and had been Rookie of the Year. But he'd never been to the NBA Finals. "This is not A.D.'s team," he said on becoming a Piston. "It's Isiah's team. That would have bothered me when I was twenty-seven or twenty-eight years old. But this stage of my career is fascinating in itself. Everybody wants to win. Everybody wants to play well. A lot of times those things don't happen together." When John Salley had joined the team in 1986, Dantley had told him, "The Pistons are Jack McCloskey, Chuck Daly, Isiah, Bill—and then everyone else."

But Dantley never fully reconciled his personal goals with team goals. He never really became part of "Isiah's team." He'd become close friends with the quiet Joe Dumars and had been kind to Salley and Rodman, but he'd never really fit in. For some time, assistant coach Dick Versace had watched over Dantley. Versace had lived nearby and had spent a lot of time with Dantley, listening to him complain about lack of playing time, lack of scoring opportunities, and lack of appreciation. When Versace had left for Indiana, Dantley no longer had an ear within management—and, quite possibly—no longer had a future with Detroit.

There were only three weeks until the trading deadline. Portland GM Bucky Buckwalter was back in touch with McCloskey. Buckwalter was still interested in Michael Williams, and a Williams for Steve Johnson trade was a definite possibility. If McCloskey took the deal, he'd have the post-up scorer he needed. Dawkins was still on the team, but McCloskey was fed up with Dawkins. If Buckwalter could push the deal through, he'd have someone to replace Vandeweghe, and could trade Kiki for a draft pick. The trade would also fit both teams' salary cap situations. Steve Johnson made $715,000, and his high salary was the big reason why most teams weren't interested in him. In Boston, Kevin McHale had said, "I'd give my left nut to get Steve Johnson"—but Boston GM Jan Volk couldn't do it. All his money was tied up in Larry Bird. But McCloskey was in a unique position and could add an expensive player and still stay under the salary cap—when William Bedford had gone back into drug treatment, his $687,000 salary had been subtracted from the cap.

McCloskey wasn't at all convinced, though, that adding another player was the solution. That might increase greed for playing time and make the situation worse. Sometimes, McCloskey believed, the only way to add to a team's strength was to subtract from the team. The player he wanted to subtract was Adrian Dantley.

The chemistry problem with Dantley—both on and off the court—had become too severe. Dantley was up for bids.

A Dantley for Steve Johnson or Dantley for Kiki Vandeweghe trade was fine with Portland. But McCloskey thought he could do better. Kiki's back was a time bomb, and Johnson's knees weren't much more dependable.

McCloskey was beginning to think the best player he could get for Dantley was Mark Aguirre. He liked Aguirre's game, and he thought Aguirre's personality could be dealt with. For one thing, who was to say the Dallas conflicts were Aguirre's fault? McCloskey believed you never really knew a player until he was on your team, so he didn't presume to know Aguirre. And if Aguirre was moody, maybe the Pistons could improve his mood—whether he liked it or not. Isiah, Laimbeer, and Mahorn had twenty-megaton personalities, and would whip Aguirre into line if he became a problem. McCloskey sat down to talk about Aguirre with Dick Motta, who did color on the Pistons' broadcast TV games. Motta had coached Aguirre in Dallas. Motta and Aguirre had hated each other—Motta had made it clear when he was in Dallas that he thought Aguirre was a total pain. But now Motta was telling Mc-Closkey that the Detroit environment would probably cure Aguirre's moodiness. Aguirre wouldn't have as much pressure to star here, and he wouldn't be given as much latitude to sulk. McCloskey also consulted scout Will Robinson, who'd worked with Aguirre at basketball camps. Robinson said he thought Aguirre was largely misunderstood. He was a decent guy who just hadn't found his niche. McCloskey didn't talk to Isiah about the trade, because he thought that if the trade happened, Thomas would get tagged with having engineered it. But Daly talked to Thomas. Isiah said essentially the same thing Motta did. Aguirre would tailor his personality to the Pistons. Or else.

The Pistons were back in Detroit on February 1, practicing for a game against Philadelphia on the third. The mood at the practice was tense, uneasy. Rumors about a possible Dantley-Aguirre deal had leaked out, so the media spotlight had been turned up. Columnists and TV people were here with the beat writers. Dantley was cornered by Shelby Strother, a big guy with a dark droopy mustache who was one of Detroit's best sportswriters—he focused on personality and shunned mantalk. Dantley acted very unemotional about the trade. "They think *I* was trouble and they're gonna trade me for Mark Aguirre?" Dantley said to Strother.

"This is a business," Dantley said. "I learned that a long time ago. You get traded—you just go. That's it. It don't affect me like it used to. When I was twenty-one, first time I got traded, it was different. That was tough. Now, it's just part of the business." Strother didn't buy Dantley's nonchalance. "His face is blank," he wrote. "But the eyes tell on him."

The next evening, Dantley went out and scored 33 points against Philadelphia. After the game, Daly said that "Adrian played clinic basketball out there tonight." Since the blowup at practice, Dantley and Daly had been getting along better. Dantley tended to keep things inside and then smolder, but when he let them burst out he would relax a little. Now Detroit was 29–13, still in second place, but hovering just behind Cleveland. More important to Daly, they seemed to be playing better.

Speculation about the Trade had begun to consume Detroit sports talk, and the media was lining up against it. Former Piston beat writer Charlie Vincent was now the most influential sports columnist in town, and Vincent thought the idea was ludicrous. Vincent wrote, "Why would Jack McCloskey even consider tampering with the Pistons midway through the most successful season in franchise history? Why would he think—for more than a second—of trading Adrian Dantley for Mark Aguirre?"

McCloskey was getting the same advice from everyone he talked to: If it's not broken, don't fix it. Almost no one—except the coaches—thought the Pistons' subtle chemistry imbalance was anything to worry about. The 0–8 record against the elite teams was widely dismissed as an aberration—if it was even noticed.

McCloskey's wife Leslie was against the trade for personal reasons; she'd already suffered through backlash from other trades and didn't want to go through it again. There would probably be death threats, as there had been in the past. After all, this was Detroit—Badass City—where just calling someone a wimp was grounds for murder. Also, if McCloskey made the trade and the Pistons got beaten in the playoffs, McCloskey would probably be branded as the goat. A trade that big, in that situation, could end a job. For McCloskey, at sixty-two, it could even end a career. He could become the Guy Who Traded Away the Title.

The brain trust was against it, too. Chief financial officer Ron Campbell took McCloskey aside and reminded him of two things. First, the Pistons were two games ahead of last year's pace, which had been the best in their history. Second, if it weren't for Cleveland, every sports expert in the country would be raving about the Pistons. McCloskey responded, "That makes sense." Nothing more.

Making the decision even more difficult, Dantley was becoming Mr. Charm. He was smiling at practice—very unusual for him—and trying to warm up. Joe Dumars was coming back from his injury, and that worked in Dantley's favor. Dumars was Dantley's social link to the team. Further confusing the situation, Detroit was playing better all the time. They'd again beaten Chicago—a team that didn't look like it would cause much trouble for Detroit this year—and Daly said after the game the Pistons were playing "as well as we have ever played."

Dumars rejoined the team February 8, two weeks before the trade deadline. At practice, the first thing Dumars did was go off with Michael Williams and reenact the hand-check move that had broken his hand. He didn't want any lingering fear. At practice, Dantley talked easily about the possibility of a trade. Now that it had been in the news for about a week without happening, it seemed less real. Dantley said that he felt positive, that he wanted to stay in Detroit and believed he would.

McCloskey watched the last part of practice. When it ended, Dantley approached him. Very quietly, he told McCloskey that if it were possible, he wanted badly to stay. He told McCloskey that he liked his situation with the team and wanted to help them win the Championship. McCloskey told Dantley that nothing was imminent. "I can't guarantee that you're going to stay here," McCloskey said. "If we get a great deal—somebody that's really going to improve our team—you know we've got to do it." Dantley nodded; he seemed to understand. There were no hard feelings. Nothing personal, just business.

Rick Sund was back in touch. As the trading deadline closed in, he was getting more desperate. His attempt to trade Aguirre to Indiana was dead. Indiana's Donnie Walsh had given him a final no on an Aguirre for Tisdale trade. Walsh was more interested in Dallas's Detlef Schrempf and Sam Perkins. The league's interest in Aguirre seemed to be waning. Too many horror stories about his attitude. Nothing was happening between Sund and Sacramento GM Bill Russell, who'd been talking about taking Aguirre for Jim Peterson and Rodney McCray.

Even so, Sund wasn't ready to pull the trigger on the Aguirre and Perkins for Dantley and Salley deal. He valued Perkins too much. McCloskey made a counteroffer: Dantley for Aguirre, straight up.

That trade, McCloskey believed, could vault his team to the Championship. It would be a remarkable trade because it revolved around a unique and fascinating dynamic: the relationship of Isiah Thomas and Mark Aguirre. That relationship could be the key to an almost perfect team chemistry. The relationship was founded on their having grown up together in a hard and dangerous place. Because of that, they treated each other differently than they did any other player—more generously and with greater understanding. There was an unspoken communication between them. If Aguirre was on the team, he would probably bend over backward to cooperate with Isiah—in part, to show the world the *real* Mark Aguirre, the person only Isiah Thomas had taken the trouble to know. Isiah, for his part, would probably be more unselfish with Aguirre than he'd ever been with another player. Certainly he'd be more unselfish than he'd been with Dantley.

Because, with Aguirre on the team, Isiah Thomas's family would be reunited.

Isiah Thomas came from a complex, ambitious, and tormented family. His father, Isiah II, was a Mississippi man who moved to Chicago after World War II, in which he'd been wounded while serving in a segregated company. He'd learned to read blueprints in trade school on the GI Bill, and become the first black foreman at International Harvester. But when the plant closed he was unable to find another job at that level, partially because it was still an era when blacks were last hired and first fired. For two years he was unemployed. He stayed home, staring out the window and watching television—but only allowing himself to watch educational TV. Thomas later described his father as "a very, very intelligent man," who was "frustrated because he wasn't allowed to use his intelligence." He ended up getting a job as a janitor, and eventually left the family of nine children. The Thomas family wasn't bitter about him leaving; his father was so frustrated, Isiah Thomas said many years later, that if he'd stayed, he "might have done something crazy to us." The family settled into the dirty red-brick ghetto on Chicago's West Wide. While he was still with the family, Isiah's father had once taken the three oldest boys up on a two-story roof. He told them he wanted to see them jump, to see how tough they were, and promised to catch them. The first to jump, Gregory, later recalled, "I jumped and my old man backed up and let me hit the motherfucking ground." The lesson was to trust no one. On the West Side, that was an appropriate lesson.

Isiah's mother, Mary Thomas, began ruling the family with love and anger. She once marched to City Hall and confronted powerful Mayor Richard J. Daley when welfare workers tried to move her family into a housing project. Another time, she stood in the doorway of her house with a shotgun to keep gang members from recruiting her sons.

Virtually all her sons were gifted athletes, as naturally talented as the baby of the family, Isiah Lord Thomas III. The oldest of the sons, Lord Henry Thomas, or "Rat," set a Catholic League scoring record, but was kicked out of school the next day. The family was told it was because of bad grades, but there had been no warnings. Mary Thomas suspected that her son had become too popular in a mostly white school. She picketed the school, but got nowhere. Rat never played basketball again, not even on the playground. He was the first of the sons to let his basketball skills slip away, and the first to turn to drugs, gangs, crime, and pimping.

By the time Isiah was a teenager, one of his brothers had joined a tough gang called the Vice Lords, and two others were pimping and dealing drugs. Isiah was intrigued. But his older brother Larry, who'd been a high school star and had been injured just before a tryout with the Chicago Bulls, confronted him. Larry, who had become a street hustler, told him, "I chose the easy way. I hate myself. Don't do what I'm doing. Somebody has *got* to get the NBA paycheck. Lord Henry failed. Gregory failed. I was *that* close to it and I failed. We owe it to ourselves. *Somebody* has got to get that money."

Isiah redirected his life. He started to channel all of his energy, anger and intelligence into basketball. He began hanging around with another neighborhood kid who had as much natural skill at basketball as he did. That kid was quiet, well behaved, brooding—his reaction to the flamboyant street hustle was to turn within himself. The kid was Mark Aguirre. Aguirre and Thomas were of great help to each other. Now they each had a positive model—someone whose cool didn't come from the street hustle. Every Saturday, Aguirre and Thomas would look for a game, accompanied by their two best friends, Bernard Randolph and Skip Dillard. Randolph was an interesting guy—he had a genius IQ, and once had sat down at a piano and taught himself to play with ease over the course of one evening. Dillard was the classic nice boy caught in the trap of the ghetto. To find a game, they would borrow a pickup from Aguirre's grandfather and cruise the streets, driving for hours to find one that was acceptable. The players had to be big, good, fast, and more interested in playing than fighting. Sometimes, the games got crazy; once, a player got shot and Isiah had to dive under a car. Gunplay wasn't unusual on the West Side. Several times Thomas saw people shot, and was threatened himself a number of times.

Aguirre was also threatened with death at least once, and so was his high school teammate, Eddie Johnson, now with the Phoenix Suns. "I had guns pointed at me two or three times," Johnson once said, "and the only thing that probably stopped them from pulling the trigger was the fact that I was a basketball player and had something going for me."

Aguirre and Thomas didn't think they would ever play professionally. Only occasionally did they fantasize about it. The high school coach of Aguirre, Eddie Johnson, Bernard Randolph, and Skip Dillard drilled into his boys the hard statistics of pro ball: 1 of every 12,759 high school basketball players succeeds in the NBA. Aguirre was a high school star but believed, "I was never going to be a college player or a pro. Basketball just kept us out of trouble. It was really the only fun thing I ever had."

Aguirre's home life was as humble as Isiah's. When Aguirre was recruited by college scouts, he would insist they meet him at school or his coach's house—never his own home. Aguirre decided to go to Chicago's DePaul University, because success there might mean local job opportunities. Dillard and Randolph also went to DePaul. Mary Thomas recommended that her son go to Indiana, in part because Bobby Knight was one of the only college coaches who had not offered her anything under the table.

At college, the personalities of the two buddies became even more divergent. Thomas blossomed at the wholesome Indiana campus, becoming even more outgoing and clean-cut. He met his future wife, Lynn, a delicate, middle-class daughter of a Secret Service agent and a nurse. Increasingly, he funneled his tough ghetto upbringing into an obsession with success at basketball, divorcing his past from his offcourt personality. Offcourt, he cultivated a sophisticated and even refined persona. At one point, he went home and his brother Larry accused, "Why you talkin' like a white boy?"

"Wha' chu tawkin' 'bout?" Isiah said, adopting his native dialect.

"When you're home," Larry Thomas said, "you talk like niggers talk. When you're out there, you learn to speak white talk." But Thomas's father, still separated from his mother, approved of the metamorphosis. His only disappointment was that Isiah wanted to be a basketball player and not a politician.

Aguirre, though, submerged further within himself. In his freshman year, DePaul played for the national championship. But Aguirre still thought basketball was Just a Game, and didn't understand it when people treated DePaul's losing the championship as a tragedy. Aguirre quickly became the team's star, but often angered driven coach Ray Meyer, who expected Aguirre to live and die with DePaul victories and losses. Aguirre gained a reputation for being lazy, withdrawn, and selfish. To a degree, Aguirre *was* lazy, withdrawn, and selfish. What shocked him, though, was the widespread belief that in a basketball player, those traits were practically criminal. His shock hardened into alienation, and his negative traits became more pronounced.

But Aguirre and Thomas stayed close. They saw each other often and talked all the time. By now, they were talking about playing in the NBA together. Their casual childhood fantasy was turning real. Some sportswriters thought it was odd that two men so dissimilar could be so close. What the sportswriters didn't take into account was that their different personalities sprang from the same source. Thomas, traumatized by the ghetto, had reacted by being outgoing—a trait he'd learned to use as a shield. Aguirre had experienced the same trauma, and had shielded himself with introversion. They understood each other perfectly.

In the college draft of 1981, Aguirre was chosen first. Thomas was chosen second. Their good friends Dillard and Randolph, who didn't have the same God-given skills, were chosen in the ninth and tenth rounds. Neither made the NBA.

In the ensuing years, Dillard—the classic nice-boy-in-the-ghetto—became addicted to drugs and was arrested on fifteen counts of armed robbery. Randolph, with the genius IQ, began to commit petty crimes and was put in a mental health institution.

During the same years, Thomas became obsessed with winning an NBA Championship. And Aguirre became the object of tremendous scorn for being moody. Sportswriters still wondered what they had in common.

Now, Jack McCloskey believed, it was time for them to be reunited. It was time for them, once again, to help each other.

Dallas's Rick Sund called McCloskey. He wouldn't make an Aguirre for Dantley deal. The players had similar skills, and Aguirre was four years younger. It just wasn't worth it to Sund. But Sund had a counteroffer: Aguirre for Dantley plus Detroit's first-round pick this year or next.

McCloskey wouldn't go for it. He didn't think the difference in value between the two players was that great. It looked as if the deal was dead. But McCloskey and Sund agreed to talk again at the All-Star Game.

When McCloskey arrived in Houston for the All-Star Game, he was more in a mood for business than pleasure. That was fortunate, because the game itself was a drag. McCloskey was seated in almost the last row of the stadium, behind a guy who had his son in his lap. McCloskey craned to the left and right, but still couldn't get a good look at the court. It didn't matter much, because Isiah was the only Piston on the floor. Even Thomas, who'd made the team all eight years he'd been in the league, had almost missed out. Cleveland's Mark Price had been ahead in the voting until near the deadline.

McCloskey left the game at halftime and never went back. His top priority in Houston was to make the Aguirre-Dantley deal work. He'd met with owner Bill Davidson, and had decided after that meeting to offer Dantley plus a 1991 pick. They'd put the offer to Sund yesterday, and were waiting for his response.

But now Sund was huddling with Indiana's Donnie Walsh about trading Detlef Schrempf or Sam Perkins for Indiana's Wayman Tisdale. If Sund got Tisdale, he'd have someone to take Aguirre's place, whether Aguirre was traded or not. Then Sund would have the option of moving Aguirre in the off-season, when Sund wasn't up against the deadline. Or he could drive a harder bargain with McCloskey.

Back at his hotel, McCloskey was accosted by Dantley's agent, David Falk. Falk wanted to know what was going on. McCloskey told him the same thing he'd told Dantley—that no deal had been made, but that if he had a chance to improve the team, he'd take it. Falk wasn't satisfied with the answer, but there was nothing he could do about it.

Sund got back in touch. He'd spoken with Dallas GM Norm Sonju and owner Donald Carter. They were passing on the offer of Dantley and a 1991 first round pick. The deal was dead.

Jeff Coplon, the *Rolling Stone* writer working on a Bad Boys article, joined the Pistons at the Lakers' Forum for their first game after the All-Star break. Before the game started, Coplon watched Dennis Rodman walk to the spot where he'd thrown up the Dumb Dennis shot that had lost the Championship. He squared off and flipped it up. Swish. He shrugged and walked off.

The game was fast, loud, and hard. The Lakers led by 4 with four minutes left—similar to Game Six of the Championship Series. But this time the Pistons made their shots. They were different now. Losing the Championship had changed them. They were more angry, more obsessed. They outscored L.A. 13–2 in the last two minutes and won going away.

After the game, Jeff Coplon waited outside the showers for Adrian Dantley. Dantley was taking forever; he usually did—he was as deliberate in the shower as he was at basketball. Finally, Coplon got tired of waiting, and told Dantley they could talk tomorrow. That was fine with Dantley. Because Dantley didn't think he would be on the team tomorrow. He didn't have any inside information. It was just a feeling.

After he dressed, Dantley approached Harry Hutt, who directed the Pistons' radio and TV operations and was a member of the brain trust. Dantley shook Hutt's hand and told him he'd enjoyed working with him. Hutt was confused. He asked Dantley what he was talking about. "I know I'm gone," said Dantley.

At that moment, just before midnight, Jack McCloskey was on the phone with Dallas. They'd changed their minds. They had decided to accept the offer of Dantley and a 1991 pick. As Dantley headed out of the Forum, McCloskey closed the deal.

Dantley went back to the team's hotel in Marina del Rey and went straight to bed. He slept well.

Dantley's phone woke him at seven-fifteen the next morning. It was McCloskey. He wanted to come to Dantley's room right away. Dantley knew what he wanted.

McCloskey was there almost immediately. He got straight to the point. Fifteen minutes ago, he'd completed a conference call with Dallas and a league representative. The call had finalized the trade. Dantley didn't look angry. He looked very, very sad. "You've been instrumental in our success," McCloskey said. "And you've handled yourself very well through all of this." McCloskey got out of the room as quickly as he could.

McCloskey felt as if he'd just made the deal that would win the Championship. And he felt like hell.

Later, McCloskey would say, "It was a calculated risk. I knew that from the beginning. The bomb may go off in your face. But you look at it this way and that, and you analyze it from every angle. You do your homework, and you don't let public opinion enter into it. You just agonize over it.

"Then, after all that, you just pick up the gun. You pick up the gun and pull the damn trigger."

"Shit!" John Salley had just been told about the trade. His eyes were tight and his brow was creased in anger. "How could they trade the Teacher?"

Salley hurried up to Dantley's room. Dumars was already there. For most of the morning, players buzzed in and out. Some of them, like Laimbeer, were people Dantley had never been close to. But now that he was leaving, he was one of them. At least, for the rest of the morning.

Salley ran into Isiah in the hotel's hallway. "Zeke," said Salley, using Isiah's nickname, "we got your boy Aguirre. You'd better be ready to handle it." Thomas was shocked. He had mixed feelings. He was happy about Aguirre coming to the team; it would be good for him and it would be good for Aguirre. But by now he'd learned to value winning more than friendship, and he wasn't sure they'd win with Aguirre.

Things were different from when they'd been kids. Back then, you'd rather lose with your buddies than win with strangers. Not anymore.

Vinnie Johnson was told about the trade, and for a moment he looked stunned. But not heartbroken. It could have been he. Just a few weeks ago he'd been slumping and people had been saying he was over the hill. Great morale booster. He'd been up for bids and had known it. But then Dumars had broken his hand and Johnson had gotten a starting job and big minutes. He'd averaged almost 20 points a game during Dumars's absence and had seen the light in Daly's eyes click back on. Now that a big trade had come without him being part of it, he had a little security. "This happens to me just about every year," said Johnson. "A.D. is a great guy. We'll miss him. But he's been traded before. He knows how it is."

Dantley went to the front entrance of the hotel to catch a cab. He was headed for the airport, carrying his own bag. Shelby Strother, the columnist who didn't go for mantalk, was with him, and so was John Salley. "It's a cold business," said Salley.

Later, when McCloskey would hear about the "cold business" remark, he would get angry. "That borders on stupidity," he would say. "He should try coal mining. That's a cold business."

Strother asked Dantley for a comment. "I have something to say," said Dantley, almost whispering, "but not right now. Please. I can't talk right now." For an instant, it appeared to Strother as if tears welled in Dantley's eyes. But Dantley seemed to fight them down. "Just a business," he murmured to Strother.

Strother asked if he'd expected it. "Yeah, I knew," said Dantley. "But nobody ever told me. You kidding? Why would they tell me? I've been expecting this for a while, but when it happened I was still shocked. Jack called me this morning and told me he was coming to my room to talk. I knew then what had happened."

Darryl Dawkins came by. He shook hands with Dantley and said a few quiet words. Dawkins was almost certain that he was on the way out, too.

"I wanted the ring," Dantley said to Strother, peering impatiently for his cab. "Last year we came real close."

One of the Piston flight attendants walked through the lobby. "We'll miss you Adrian," she shouted. "Real bad."

"Yeah, me too," said Dantley.

Strother said something about Aguirre's style of basketball compared to Dantley's. For the first time, Dantley looked angry. "No matter what *anybody* says, this ain't got *nuthin'* to do with basketball." Dantley's mouth twisted into a sneer.

Dantley's cab pulled up. He handed his luggage to the driver. He got in the cab, stared straight ahead, and was gone.

Inside the lobby, Joe Dumars stared at a newspaper. He held it over his face like a shield.

They took a bus to Loyola Marymount University to practice. The bus was deathly still. In the gym, Daly told them to pair off and shoot free throws. Dumars, by habit, headed off to a side basket, then realized Dantley wasn't there to shoot with him. He turned around. Salley ran over to join him. No one spoke.

It was hell back in Detroit. The phone lines at the Palace were on fire with irate fans. The response to the Trade wasn't mixed—it was 100 percent negative. John Ciszewski, whose people were taking the calls, went to Tom Wilson. "Hey, would you mind talking to the guys," Ciszewski said, "and telling them what our company line is? We can't have guys taking calls and saying, 'Yeah, I know Aguirre's a trouble-maker, but we'll be okay.' And they can't say, 'Well, Isiah and A.D. weren't talking, so it's for the best.' "

Wilson agreed. They called in the season ticket sales people, and told them to stress Aguirre's youth, and that the Pistons were now 1–9 against the elite teams. And most of all: Trust Jack. Remind people that McCloskey had made controversial trades in the past—like Greg Kelser for Vinnie Johnson, or Kelly Tripucka for Adrian Dantley—which had worked out extremely well.

But Ciszewski didn't feel too buoyant himself. If the trade had happened a month ago, when they were playing badly, it would have been different. But now. . . . How did he sell *this?* That morning, Ciszewski's wife had dropped their daughter off at school, and the principal had run out to the car. "Why did they make that *trade?*" the principal had demanded. Not too heartwarming.

The Detroit media was already buzzing about the Mavericks' reaction. Jubilation! They were doing everything but throwing a ticker tape parade. James Donaldson, Dallas's big center, had said, "There was a night and day difference in practice today." Sam Perkins said, "Today should be an all-day party. I will never understand Mark. Maybe he has a chemical imbalance." Influential columnist Randy Galloway simply wrote, "Good riddance."

McCloskey, who was still with the team out West, talked to Isiah Thomas and Rick Mahorn about integrating Aguirre into the squad. He wanted them to explain to Aguirre what being a Piston meant. So that night, Mahorn, Thomas, Laimbeer, and Vinnie Johnson took Aguirre to dinner.

They were all blunt. Team-First Thomas told Aguirre, "You were a star in Dallas. Here in Detroit, our ninth man on the squad is as popular as you were in Dallas." Thomas told him he'd have to play hard and unselfishly, or "someone's going to be on your ass."

Laimbeer told Aguirre, "If you weren't a friend of Isiah's, I wouldn't even talk to you. All the things I've heard and read about you have been bad." But Laimbeer said that since Isiah had asked him to give Aguirre a chance, he would.

Mahorn told Aguirre that he'd help him on defense, but he expected that help back. If it didn't come, "I'll be hollering at Chuck to get you out of the game."

Vinnie Johnson told Aguirre he'd better be ready to get pulled from the game in the crunch minutes—like Johnson usually was—because Daly always went with defense at the end. "It's nothing personal, it's just how we win."

Aguirre didn't act put off. He knew his reputation.

The next day, when practice started, the team seemed happy and friendly. The morbid feeling from yesterday was gone for almost everyone but Dumars. Dantley was gone—so what? It was Just a Job. The media was there in force, charting Aguirre's first practice as a Piston. They shot him lacing up his sneakers—for his first moment on the floor as a Piston, and stretching his legs—his first stretch as a Piston. At one point, they looked ready to follow him into the bathroom, to record his first pee as a Piston.

The other players didn't pay any attention. Over by the scorer's table, Mahorn picked up a huge black Hefty bag. "Hey, Dawkins," he yelled, "I found your mama's underpants." Everybody laughed, but for some of them, it hid tension. A few players were still counting the days until the February 23 trade deadline. Five and a half days. Salley was still worried. Michael Williams was still rumored to be going to Portland for Steve Johnson. Fennis Dembo knew he was just a pawn. Dawkins felt he was already halfway off the team. The other day he'd missed a flight, and the coaches had made a big deal out of it. Bad sign. If you were playing really well and missed a flight, it was like, hey, big deal, no problem. But they'd made him run laps—like a rookie. No doubt about it: He was gone.

They started to scrimmage. Isiah warned Aguirre that they scrimmaged hard, but Aguirre wasn't worried. He was an inside player and was accustomed to a lot of contact. But then Michael Williams rammed into the lane and Laimbeer stepped in front of him—bam!—it made a sick, quick fleshy sound, like someone hurling a wad of hamburger against a wall. Williams collapsed. He lay on the floor with his limbs splayed in strange angles. Trainer Mike Abdenour ran up, alarmed at the dreamy look in Williams's eyes. Aguirre stopped smiling as they carted Williams off. Aguirre got in the scrimmage, and suddenly Rodman was in his face, keeping him from getting any shots. Every time Rodman would devil Aguirre, Aguirre would say "good defense" and smile. But pretty soon he was huffing for air and his chest was fluttering. He saw an opening in the lane and darted into it. But Mahorn charged toward him, Coalminer Style; Aguirre pulled up—too late. Mahorn smashed into Aguirre's chest and face and Aguirre crumpled to the floor. For a second, he was just a big pile of meat. Then he stirred and began to take a more human shape. He wasn't smiling anymore. Isiah walked over. "Welcome to the Pistons," he said.

Isiah Thomas sat in a plush hotel in downtown Denver, looking out a huge, square picture window at the city. He was talking about his son with *Rolling Stone* writer Jeff Coplon, who also had a young son. Coplon found Isiah extremely bright and genuinely friendly. But there also seemed to be a detached side to Thomas—part of him was always watching, never participating. Coplon thought maybe that came from reinventing his identity. You didn't go from ghetto boy to wealthy young god without losing part of yourself.

Midwinter's early nightfall was shadowing the room. With another guy, someone less famous, Coplon would have suggested going out for dinner. But he'd never felt comfortable going out with celebrities, so he picked up his stuff and prepared to leave. Thomas gazed out the big square of glass as the city lights blinked on. He looked lost. In here, he was trapped by the walls, and out there he was trapped by his fame. Coplon felt bad for him—as bad as you could feel for a rich young god.

Thomas was reluctant to pal around every night with Aguirre. Aguirre had to get to know the other guys. Besides, they weren't just friends now. They were business associates. Thomas was on Aguirre's ass all the time now, and it was a strain. Thomas was also absorbing a lot of criticism for the Trade. Adrian Dantley's mother had been the most outspoken. She'd told the press, "You shouldn't blame Jack McCloskey. He's not the one. It's that little con artist you've got up there. When his royal highness wants something, he gets it."

Thomas looked at Coplon. "So," Isiah said plaintively, "what do I do *now?*"

At last, he and Aguirre had been reunited. In the NBA. This was what they had long ago dreamed about. But this wasn't like the dream.

*   *   *

Over the next few days, the league's GMs scrambled to nail down their deals. The most ambitious was a four-way trade involving Portland, Indiana, Atlanta, and Milwaukee. It was the latest version of the three-way deal Portland's Bucky Buckwalter had cooked up to get rid of Kiki Vandeweghe. In the trade, Indiana's Herb Williams would go to Atlanta for a first-round pick; then Indiana would give the pick to Portland for Vandeweghe; then Portland would trade the pick plus forward Mark Bryant to Milwaukee for Ricky Pierce. That would give Portland its perimeter shooter, Atlanta would get a forward to replace injured Kevin Willis, and Milwaukee would inject some youth into its aging mix. After that deal went through, Indiana's Donnie Walsh planned to trade Vandeweghe to the Knicks for Rod Strickland, to give Indiana the guard it needed.

But Vandeweghe queered it. He wanted to go to New York, but was afraid he'd get stuck in Indiana, so he told Donnie Walsh, "I don't know how my back will take to the weather in Indianapolis." It was outrageous. Every GM in the league was pissed. If players started directing trades, there would be chaos.

The busted deal set off a flurry of patch-up trades. Donnie Walsh traded Wayman Tisdale to Sacramento for six-foot-ten LaSalle Thompson and guard Randy Wittman. Then Walsh traded Herb Williams to Dallas for Detlef Schrempf. After all that, Walsh still didn't have a premiere point guard, but at least he'd rearranged his chemistry. "We had seven or eight first-round picks," said Walsh, "and they just didn't work together. The chemistry wasn't what it should have been." To make room for the new players, Walsh waived veteran guard John Long, who'd been with Detroit in the grim years.

In Boston, GM Jan Volk pulled the trigger on a Danny Ainge trade. Volk needed some immediate help up front because of Bird's injury, so he went after Joe Kleine and Ed Pinckney of Sacramento. Volk was also getting some much-needed youth.

Finally, Bucky Buckwalter dumped Kiki Vandeweghe. Shipped him to New York. For a first-round pick. Three and a half years ago, Portland had traded almost half its team for Vandeweghe: All-Stars Calvin Natt and Fat Lever, with Wayne Cooper and two draft picks that became Blair Rasmussen and Otis Smith. Now, they were getting one pick for him. Black day in Portland.

In Dallas, Rick Sund was trying frantically to get rid of one more player. Adrian Dantley. Dantley had refused to report. He wanted to get his contract extended. The holdout was fossilizing and causing great bitterness. Sund was willing to trade Dantley for just a first-round pick. But no one would take the deal.

*   *   *

Twelve hours until the trading deadline. Darryl Dawkins was still on the team. Daly held a practice and Dawkins played well. He'd lost weight again and was showing some of the moves of the Chocolate Thunder of old.

Dawkins saw Jack McCloskey walk through the tunnel leading to the court. He knew he was gone. McCloskey sat down with Dawkins. He told Dawkins they were releasing him to make room for John Long, the veteran guard Indiana had just released. McCloskey wanted Long as an insurance policy in case Dumars, Thomas, or Johnson got hurt. McCloskey liked the way Long handled himself. He hadn't bitched when Indiana had cut him loose, and he hadn't burned his bridges when McCloskey had dumped him two and a half years ago.

Dawkins took the ax well. He didn't burn his bridges.

On the way out of the stadium, he talked to beat writer Steve Addy. Dawkins seemed pretty calm for a guy who had probably just worn an NBA uniform for the last time—and who had almost nothing to show for a fourteen-year career. "What do you want me to do," he said to Addy, "cry?" He smiled broadly and headed out the door.

Rick Mahorn rolled downcourt, his huge shoulders heaving as he ran. At midcourt, little Cleveland guard Mark Price jogged toward Mahorn, then slowed up to let Mahorn pass. Suddenly, *crack!* Mahorn's elbow shot out and exploded against Price's temple. Price dropped into a crouch, his hand on his head. The fans in Cleveland's Richfield Coliseum howled. Price struggled up and found his way to the bench. He kept touching his head, then checking his hand for blood. He had a serious concussion. After the game, the examining physician would tell Price that if the blow had been one inch lower, it could have killed him. At the bench, Price kicked a chair and screamed, "For gosh sakes!" For Price, those were hard words. The Cleveland fans were still wailing. They wanted blood.

The Cavs were already ahead. Now they were off on an emotional surge that buried Detroit. The Pistons looked hopeless against them. Totally overmatched.

Cleveland won by 16. As it ended, Cleveland GM Wayne Embry stood in the tunnel leading to the locker room, nodding his head, as if to say, "Yes—right on schedule."

Mark Aguirre played a great game. 28 points. Good passing. Solid defense. The Pistons were stronger than ever. And it didn't mean a damn thing. Cleveland was unbeatable.

SEVEN

"Turning Point"
Detroit Versus Cleveland

"ROD THORN can kiss . . . my . . . ass!" hissed Rick Mahorn in low, dangerous tones. It was a voice different from the epiglottal blast Mahorn leveled against petty annoyances. Quieter. Scarier.

Mahorn had just heard that Thorn, the NBA's chief of police, had fined him $5,000 for driving his elbow into Mark Price's temple three days ago. Now, Mahorn's fines for the season came to $15,000. A *lot* of money. Rick Mahorn made $800,000 a year—but most of that was just hieroglyphics in his accountant's ledgers. Mahorn had grown up in a small apartment with his mother, brother, and two sisters, and he knew damn well how much money fifteen thousand bucks was: a *lot*.

"Thorn's biased. He's narrow-minded about the situation," said Mahorn, leaning against his locker as the other players began drifting in for the crucial March 3 Cleveland game. "I don't care *what* he thinks about me. 'Cause I feel the same about him."

Steve Addy and Terry Foster were standing in front of Mahorn taking notes. "Think it'll effect the way you play?" asked Foster.

"If he don't like the way we play, then I don't *care*," said Mahorn. "There was a situation where Bill Cartwright hit him"—Mahorn pointed across the locker room at Isiah Thomas—"and he gets five stitches. *No* one's gonna get us to stop playing our style of basketball."

145

From the weight room came Tone Loc's "Funky Cold Medina." Someone was trying to rap along with it—it sounded like Laimbeer. "A Caucasian," said Mahorn, looking toward the weight room, "trying to be cool." He shook his head.

"Wanna see the Money Dance?" asked James Edwards, whose locker was next to Mahorn's. Edwards did an up-and-back two-step shuffle, then jabbed out his right elbow and chanted "Five-*thou!*"

Mahorn stood in front of the reporters and began earnestly adjusting his balls, offering everyone in the vicinity a healthy dose of penis envy, and perhaps preparing for the rage he'd soon be prime target of. His hand made a giant lump in his crotch.

"You Bob Probert?" said one of the reporters, referring to a local hockey star who'd tried to sneak cocaine across the Canadian border in his jock.

"That's right," said Mahorn. "This is how I get my coke through Customs. Me and my man Probert. Only difference, they see a *brother* with a wad down there, they don't think nothin' 'bout it." Mahorn, thoughtful now, screwed up his face, "I can understand him telling the cops somebody else put it in the *car*. But who could've stuck it down by his *balls?* A big guy like that?"

The small ball boy came in with a stack of thick white towels. "Cleveland got a *bomb threat*," he said, excited enough to break the ball boys' primary rule—Keep your mouth shut. Several of the players looked at him—a big moment in his career. Emboldened, he continued, "And Lenny Wilkens got a *death* threat. They're out in their bus now, ridin' around."

"Horn threatened 'em," shouted someone from the weight room.

"*Fuh*-que!"shouted Mahorn, using the ghetto inflection. "I sent a bomb threat to *Thorn*."

Isiah Thomas—diplomatically silent, as usual—threw an approving glance at Mahorn. There was Mahorn, on the verge of getting the hell beat out of him in payback, $5,000 lighter, and minutes away from the most important game yet—Thomas considered it the first must-win game of the season. With all that, Mahorn was keeping everybody not just loose, but pissed off, too. Fans never understood the value of something like that. Most general managers didn't, either.

But Steve Addy wasn't impressed. He'd originally written that the elbow to Price had been tough luck, a little bump. Then he'd seen videotape from a better perspective and had felt like a fool. He was sick of the Bad Boys angle. He decided, on the spot, never to use "Bad Boys" again. "Hell," he thought, "let somebody else sell their T-shirts."

*   *   *

Out on the court, Spencer Haywood grabbed Leon the Barber by his ball-bat-thin bicep. "Come on, man—you've gotta *coach* us." Tom Wilson, as part of his Basketball Disneyland concept, had organized an "NBA Legends" game before the Cleveland game, and Haywood (19.2-point career scoring average) was there with Dave Bing (20.3), Walt Bellamy (20.1), Bailey Howell (18.7), Lou Hudson (20.2), and former Pistons Willie Norwood, Archie Clark, Eddie Miles, Bob Quick, Tom Van Arsdale, and Jim Davis. The former players had entered the stadium unnoticed. By the standards of most careers, they were young men—not figures from ancient history—but nothing evaporated faster than athletic fame. Nor had most of them come away from the game with much to show for it. Stars like Bob Cousy had made only $25,000 a year, and Wilt Chamberlain had only made $100,000 a year—while the competitive Bill Russell had made $100,001. All-Stars like Bellamy and Howell had made much less, hardly more than mailmen or house painters. It hadn't been until players like Haywood and Lou Hudson had left the NBA for the ABA that salaries had started to rocket. Back then, the Just a Game myth hadn't been a myth at all—basketball had barely qualified as a business. Virtually all the players in the Legends game—who now were circling Leon the Barber for pregame strategy—still had to work. Bing had become a multimillionaire from his Detroit steel business, and Bailey Howell had a good job with Converse. But most of them—men who would have made $2 million a year if they'd been born fifteen years later—labored at mid-level jobs in government bureaucracy or business. Haywood had a good job and was a community hero, but he'd put most of his basketball fortune up his nose; he was one of the NBA's early cocaine casualties. Walt Bellamy, who'd averaged 31.6 points as a rookie in 1962, had seen the big money coming. It had been close enough to taste. But he'd retired in 1975. He'd wanted to stay in basketball, but there were hardly any black coaches or executives at that time, so now he worked for the Census Bureau.

Leon sent his players out and they did a remarkably good job, hitting their jumpers and protecting the ball, as Leon watched in silence. But from behind the bench, fans started screaming, "Hey, Leon, you're overcoaching!" and, "Get a *job*, Leon." Leon burrowed into his red sweatshirt, pulled his baseball cap down, and when he got a chance he disappeared into the stands.

From the runway, the Pistons watched the end of the Legends game, shifting nervously and tugging at tight spots in their uniforms. They were 4½ games behind Cleveland. If they lost tonight, they'd be 5½ out of first with 28 games to go. Even if the Cavs lost *half* their remaining games, Detroit would have to win 21 of 28 to take the division title. And it wasn't likely the Cavs would blow half their games. Right now, the Cavs were 43–12. They were 28–1 when they'd held their opponents below 100 points. They were 39–1 when they led going into the fourth quarter and held their opponent's field goal percentage under .500. They were 20–2 at home. They hadn't had a serious long-term injury all year. They were young, unselfish, quiet, and good-natured. Daly still called them the Assassins.

In the hall, just behind the runway, a gurney from a hospital sat waiting, white butcher paper stretched over its mattress. Laimbeer was at the head of the line in the runway, smirking at a private thought. Just behind him stood Isiah, looking distracted, lost in his own world, happy.

At the introductions, Auker plugged in the Generic Hero Music and cranked the volume all the way up. The deep, funereal organ matched the dark brooding noise that began rolling down from the stands. The noise built, until it became big, dull waves of sound pounding onto the court. Security man Dave Behnke stood in front of Lenny Wilkens, his eyes darting around the crowd. Behnke had a strategy; if somebody deep in the stands tried to shoot Lenny Wilkens, Behnke would fall on the coach and try to get to cover. If somebody close up tried to get at Wilkens, Behnke would leave the coach and go for the assailant. Either way, he was screwed. He just hoped nothing happened, because there was no practical way to protect someone in a stadium. Auker segued into "Eye of the Tiger" as they took the floor, and a fan yelled, "Hey, Price, you're a goddamn sissy! You're a goddamn *sissy!*" Behnke scanned for the source of the yell. It was just Leon. Lenny Wilkens knelt quietly by the bench, in front of Price. Price had tried to warm up before the game, but to Wilkens it had looked like Price was walking on ice. So Wilkens had pulled him from the lineup. Price sat on the bench in street clothes, his eyes distant and floating in water.

Darnell Valentine started in place of Price, but within four minutes he'd committed two turnovers, allowing Detroit to stay even. Wilkens called time and stood in front of Valentine with a clipboard, talking to him in his high-pitched, controlled voice, as if Valentine were a student struggling with a math problem. "Just show a little patience as you go through that screen," Wilkens said. "That's all you need to do." Valentine nodded, stretching his legs by pulling on the toe of his basketball shoe. Most of the players had a thick ridge of muscle running down the front of their thighs, but Valentine—who probably had the strongest legs in the NBA—had a corresponding ridge in back. When Valentine had been at Portland, he and coach Jack Ramsay, a fitness demon, had often crossed the Coastal Range—by bicycle—to visit Ramsay's beachfront home. Valentine had twice the strength of Price, but only half the shot. With Price out, Detroit was able to sag off Valentine and pound on Daugherty and Nance under the hoop.

After the time-out, Laimbeer slapped up against Daugherty under the basket so hard that it sounded like a wet towel smacking cement. Referee Dick Bavetta blew his whistle and pointed at Laimbeer. Leon the Barber jumped out of his seat and advanced on the court, pointing at Daugherty and screaming, "It's *his* goddamn fault!" The crowd blasted out an angry wall of noise onto the court. Leon stood just behind Mark Price, ranting. Price seemed to wince, as if the noise were banging into his head.

Rodman and Vinnie Johnson came in, popping with nervous energy. As soon as Johnson got the ball, he drove down the key, leaped into the air—bringing his defenders up with him—then flipped the ball backward over his head to Laimbeer, who planted firmly and threw in a perfect rainbow jumper, his eighth point of the quarter. Laimbeer also had 5 rebounds. It was the kind of game Laimbeer loved: angry, noisy, and important. The early-season games didn't count less in the standings, but to the elite teams, they were just the preliminaries. How a team performed *now*, when the chips were down, would determine who'd win the Championship.

Laimbeer's shot tied the game as the quarter waned. But then Cleveland plodded downcourt, passed the ball patiently until a percentage shot opened up, and hit it. During the quarter break, as the crowd still seethed, Lenny Wilkens talked quietly to his team and laughed.

Just after the second quarter started, John Williams, Cleveland's important backup big forward, slammed onto the court and came up limping. Cleveland trainer Gary Briggs ran out, then called for an assistant with an ice pack. As they helped Williams to the locker room, a murmur ran through the crowd: Could this be the long-awaited Cleveland injury? The core of Jack McCloskey's strategy had been to build the deepest team in the league, since injuries were almost inevitable. That depth had powered Detroit past its own string of injuries early in the year, and it was still helping—Salley was out with a cracked ankle, but Detroit still had a strong front line. Detroit's depth, however, wouldn't win them the Championship unless the other top teams started to suffer injuries. Now it was finally March—when the games really began to matter—and fatigue and wear often touched off a rash of injuries. So far, Cleveland had been immune. Maybe, because of their youth, they'd stay that way. The odds were against it.

Tree Rollins came in for Williams, hushing the crowd. Rollins was

Cleveland's only terrorist, at seven-one and 240 pounds. His biceps and shoulders looked like they were made out of pig iron. Cleveland GM Wayne Embry had picked up Rollins as an unrestricted free agent last summer, covering Rollins's million-dollar salary despite his career scoring average of 6.9. Rollins couldn't shoot and didn't even try, but he was definitely a son of a bitch under the hoop and balanced the sweetness of guys like Daugherty and Ehlo and Price—the Good Boys. As soon as Rollins got in the game, there was a blur of arms and fists under the basket—with Rollins in the middle of it—and when it ended with a whistle four guys were holding their noses or rubbing their eyes. The score was still tied.

Next time down, Rollins and Mahorn got tangled up, and suddenly Mahorn collapsed—his arms and legs flew off into inhuman angles and he became just a pile of flesh on the floor. Mahorn held his right eye as trainer Mike Abdenour rushed out. For long moments, Mahorn didn't move. Rollins had speared his huge, hard finger into Mahorn's eye, which was now dripping water. In the first quarter, Rollins had smashed his elbow into Mahorn's head, in a move obviously intended as a payback for Price. It had looked like that was the end of it. But now Mahorn was down again. Abdenour helped Mahorn to the locker room, where Dr. Paolucci examined the eye. Mahorn had a scratched cornea, a serious injury. It could permanently impair his vision. But he wanted to stay in the game.

The first half was ending. With one second left, Isiah Thomas heaved up a shot from the corner. No good. But Thomas thought he'd been hacked. He ran toward referee Tommy Nunez screaming. Nunez hit Thomas with a technical.

Thomas's eyes expanded and hardened. Thomas got in Nunez's face and said, "Fuck you!" Nunez walked away. The horn blared. Detroit up 4. 12 lead changes.

Daly led Detroit off the court stoically, as he did in every situation. But those close enough to see his eyes saw worry so acute it looked like pain. If the Pistons couldn't beat Cleveland in the Palace, without Price playing, they probably couldn't ever beat them. And if the Pistons didn't win tonight, they almost certainly wouldn't be able to knock Cleveland out of first place, which meant no home-court advantage in the playoffs. Without that, Detroit was screwed.

The Pistons were flat when they came back out after the half. They seemed to be overwhelmed. Cleveland was so powerful, so controlled. A bomb threat hadn't rattled them. Mahorn hadn't rattled them. Leon the Barber hadn't rattled them. Three times this season Detroit had tried to find Cleveland's weak spot and had failed. Now they were beginning to fail again. Detroit lost its 4-point lead and then slipped to 3 behind, as the Cavs, with their unspectacular system of hard work and patience, began to take control. The intimidating broil of noise from the stands got softer, then came only in spurts. The fans seemed short on faith, too aware of the Pistons' legacy of failure: "They'll break your heart."

Then, with 6:51 in the quarter, something happened that seemed very strange. Daly was sitting quietly on the bench, saddled with a technical foul; if he got another, he'd be gone. Laimbeer and big Larry Nance were muscling under the boards and suddenly there was pushing and cursing and hot red eyes and players rushing toward the two of them. Daly and Wilkens ran onto the floor to keep the skirmish from getting bloody. The coaches helped pull the players apart, but then referee Tommy Nunez announced that the foul was on Laimbeer and Daly exploded. "How could you do that!" he screamed at Nunez. It was suicidal. Daly was gone in a flash. He stalked off the court. The bitter, low, loud sound started flooding down from the stands again. Laimbeer was galvanized—his jaw was clamped and he moved in stiff, robotic jerks—Daly had gotten kicked out for *him*. Isiah Thomas also looked spurred, as if *he* were the one Daly had sacrificed himself for. Mahorn, at the bench, was standing, furious, screaming. Rodman was scowling.

There they were. Biggest game of the year. No coach. Down by 1. Assistant coach Brendan Suhr gathered the team around. Suhr, who'd only head-coached in the NBA a couple of times in his life, felt fine. No nerves. For one thing, he was certain Daly had gotten thrown out on purpose, to light a fire. Daly was too shrewd to piss away their season's first must-win game on a temper tantrum. Suhr knew the players would be watching him for panic so he was nonchalant. The players were already keyed up by the ejection—Suhr wanted to channel that energy. He put Vinnie Johnson in, and left him in even though Johnson traveled ten seconds after entering the game—an adrenaline turnover. Suhr didn't believe in what he called "the golf approach" to coaching— "you're only as good as your last shot." Suhr thought that if a player was good enough to get in, he was good enough to stay in. Johnson rewarded the faith—he scored 6 points in the last half of the quarter and led Detroit to a 5-point lead. The crowd was rumbling again and Auker got them clapping to "Mony, Mony."

Fourth quarter. Auker blasted Generic Hero Music, the crowd screamed, and Rodman was jumping around like a dog in a cage. But Cleveland kept passing and passing and Craig Ehlo made three straight baskets to wipe out the lead. Craig Ehlo was pure Cleveland: blond, calm, and God-fearing. A milk commercial. His only problem was that he couldn't shoot worth a damn. But within Lenny Wilkens's controlled system, even Ehlo could be an Assassin.

Suhr called time. "All right," said Suhr, "they've scored six in a row; we have to stop them right *now*." Suhr wanted to start getting the ball to Aguirre. It was only Aguirre's eighth game with Detroit, and Suhr thought Aguirre was still "in his infancy" with the Detroit system. But Aguirre was a pure shooter, much more than Dantley had been, and if the Trade was going to work, it had better work now.

"I don't need any help on Nance," said Rodman.

"Then let's come back off Valentine," Laimbeer said, "and trap Daugherty."

"Get a good shot," said Suhr, and he sent them back out. He'd told them to run play number 15, a high pick-and-roll they usually ran for Vinnie Johnson. This time, though, Isiah would be the target. It might be enough to throw Cleveland off.

It worked. Thomas scored two quick baskets. But as they built a small lead, Steve Addy began to be aware of something out of the ordinary. Every few minutes the phone closest to the bench would ring, and PR director Matt Dobek, who sat behind the phone, would pick it up. Midway through the fourth quarter, Dobek got off the phone and yelled to Suhr, "Don't leave Vinnie in too long."

"Jesus Christ," thought Addy, "he's relaying messages from Daly." Daly must be in the coaches' room, Addy thought, watching on TV and phoning in instructions.

On the floor, Rodman was smothering Nance, whirling his arms so fast that they left an after-image. Tommy Nunez blew his whistle and pointed at Rodman. Rodman looked up, shocked. "That's *so* bullshit," he said, but he covered his mouth, and Nunez let it pass.

Detroit called time, and, sure enough, the phone rang again. Dobek passed the receiver in to Isiah Thomas. Thomas crouched down in the middle of the huddle and Mike Abdenour stood in front of him.

There were five minutes left, and it was anybody's game—Detroit up 4. Time to put in the crunch team. Laimbeer was an easy choice—his jumper was on and he was clawing Daugherty to death. Aguirre—yes, he could score. Rodman for defense. Thomas for his desperation to win. But: Johnson or Dumars? Dumars hadn't made a shot all night. Johnson was 6 for 10 and had ice water in his veins at crunch time. Johnson was the obvious choice. But Suhr—and Daly—decided to go with Dumars. He hadn't been playing particularly well, and he needed to feel their faith in him. There was only one time you could show that faith: when *everything* was on the line. Suhr put his hand on Dumars's shoulder. "Joe, you're one of our best guys. You're going to be in there as long as you keep playing good defense." Dumars nodded his head one time. Suhr called a play for Dumars and sent them out. Ken Calvert shouted, "Ladies and gentlemen, let's welcome back *your . . . Detroit . . . Pistons!"* The stadium rocked. Auker put on a quick blast of Generic Hero Music.

Dumars curled around the free-throw line and immediately hit a flawless fourteen-foot jumper. Calvert yelled, "Joe Duuuumars!" Within a minute, Dumars drew a foul from Nance, hit both his shots, and then Isiah stole the ball and rifled it to Dumars for a quick lay-up. Again: "Joe Duuumars!"

Lenny Wilkens was up now, but not pacing, just watching. Cleveland worked the ball, took their time, then found Ehlo for an easy lay-up. Wilkens nodded calmly. Detroit by 5—three minutes left. The Palace shook with noise. Leon the Barber screamed, "Hey, Price, you sissy, whattaya gonna do in the playoffs? Gonna get your *period* again?" Dumars hit another long jumper but then Daugherty scored. Detroit's shot missed and Rodman tipped the ball up to try to control it, tipped it up again—fought off a mob of Cav rebounders—up again, and finally the ball sailed out of bounds. Rodman dived after it, crashing Coalminer-Style into the Cleveland bench. Tommy Nunez pointed toward the Cleveland end. Rodman picked himself up and snarled, "You're an *ass*hole," at Nunez. Nunez gave no sign of hearing. Then Ron Harper scored. Detroit by 3; 1:39 left.

Jack McCloskey, who was in Asheville, North Carolina, to scout a college player, stood by a pay phone, nervous and frustrated. He was trying to call the coaches' room, to find out the score. But the line was busy.

Thomas, Rodman, Laimbeer, and Dumars took the floor. So did Mahorn, his eye full of blood.

Dumars scored again. So did Cleveland's Hot Rod Williams. Detroit by 3, 25 seconds. Hot Rod Williams got the ball again, and worked toward the hoop. He got within a foot of it. He had a percentage shot. Lenny Wilkens, his arms folded, his lips twisted into his lemon-face, silently mouthed, "Go." Williams shot. The ball bounced off the front of the rim. Laimbeer grabbed it and was immediately fouled.

Laimbeer stood at the free-throw line. On the bench, John Salley folded his hands and seemed to be praying. The Palace was silent. Laimbeer took a deep breath, blew out, and swished his shot. Then—deep breath, blow, swish. It was over. Leon the Barber erupted from his seat. Jack McCloskey dialed the coaches' room again. Busy. Auker put on "Shout" and got the rhythmical clapping going. As time elapsed, Auker segued into "Celebration," and Laimbeer led the team off the court.

He'd scored 24 with 14 rebounds. Wearing a dead face, holding his chin up, he gave the smallest ball-boy a high-five as he stepped into the tunnel.

Later in the year, when Chuck Daly was asked about a turning point in the season, he singled out one game. This one.

About ten minutes after the game ended, Bill Laimbeer returned to the floor as the guest on George Blaha's postgame show. A couple of thousand people clotted in the front row seats for the show, cheering when Laimbeer walked out with a white towel around his neck, making a weak reverberating sound in the emptiness of the Palace. Laimbeer sat down and launched into a diatribe against Rod Thorn. He said that Thorn was picking on the Pistons, holding them to a higher standard of behavior than the rest of the league. The more Laimbeer talked, the more worked up he got and the more the fans cheered. "You have to understand," Laimbeer said, "that this is from a man who *despises* our team—for whatever reasons." Boos. "He's trying to *dictate* how we play." Louder boos. "From now on, it's the Detroit Pistons against the *world*!" Big cheer.

As Laimbeer walked back to the locker room, he passed Cavalier play-by-play man Joe Tait, whom he knew from his days in Cleveland. "How'd you like that?" Laimbeer said.

"Just fine, Bill," said Tait. "I live on a farm. I know all about horseshit." Laimbeer laughed.

When Laimbeer got back to the locker room, Steve Addy was in the players-only hall with Brendan Suhr. Addy was agitated. He felt that he ought to cover the phone-call situation, but he didn't want to. If he did, it would probably be his ass. It wasn't the kind of story the team would want to see.

Nevertheless, he asked Suhr about it. "I don't know," said Suhr, "you'll have to ask Matt about that."

Addy found Matt Dobek. He asked him about the calls. "Chuck was just calling to find out what was going on in the game," said Dobek, with his usual curt, rapid-fire delivery. Addy thought the answer was pretty lame. Daly was obviously watching the game on TV.

"Well," said Addy, "what about the phone going in the huddle to Isiah?"

"I don't know what you're talking about."

Addy explained what he'd seen but Dobek wouldn't budge. "But I'll tell you," said Dobek, "if you print that, you and I are going to have a problem."

"Why?" said Addy.

"What do you mean, why? I'm not going to tell you what to write, Steve—you can do whatever you want. But if you write it, you'll fuck yourself, okay?"

That was all Dobek would say. Addy stepped into the public hallway that circled the arena floor. He leaned against the hard concrete wall, feeling miserable. He had to come to a decision, fast. His deadline was zooming up; the other writers were already tapping away at their computers in the press room. He didn't want to commit professional suicide. This wasn't Watergate. If he made a big stink, he might blow himself out of a dream job—watching NBA basketball at courtside, for money. On the other hand, if he turned his head the first time he saw something sticky, wouldn't that make him a shill? Just as Addy was taking a deep breath, Brendan Suhr came out of the players-only hallway.

"You have a puzzled look on your face, Steve," said Suhr.

"Yeah," said Addy. Suhr walked on past. Addy decided to write the story.

Addy checked with Daly before he started writing. Daly, of course, wasn't happy about it. But nothing could ruin how Daly felt. It was too early to tell, but this—he hoped—was the turning point.

Two days later, Cleveland beat writer Terry Pluto sat at his courtside seat, watching as the Sunday after-church crowd began to dot Cleveland's Richfield Coliseum. "Atlanta scares hell out of me," said Pluto, one of the more prominent NBA writers and author of several books. "Everybody talks about all the problems they're having and, look, they're fifteen games over five hundred and they're eight-and-two in the last ten. It'll be Atlanta in the Finals, or Cleveland. *Not* Detroit." Pluto couldn't stand the Pistons. He thought they were violent and arrogant. He'd recently written, "They have been warned and warned by the league to clean up their act, yet nothing changes. They just smirk and write the checks. Who cares? It's time for the NBA to do whatever it must to stop the Pistons." He didn't even like the Piston fans—too bloodthirsty, especially compared to the Cleveland fans. Though Cleveland, like Detroit, was a Rust Belt, beer-and-bratwurst town, Cleveland's stadium was even more rural than Detroit's, and it attracted a country-club crowd that was polite, middle-American, and short-sleeved: in other words, pretty drab. Today's crowd was especially introverted; it was a Sunday crowd, the least likely to provide a home-court advantage. Sunday crowds had too many kids who were bored with the game and too many parents watching their kids.

Soon the national anthem started, and the announcer invited the crowd to sing along. They *did*. They even put their hands over their hearts.

Price came out looking much more human than he had Friday in Detroit, when he'd looked like the Undead. His eyes held focus and had lost some of their gloss. Price wanted badly to play, since they would be going up against the Milwaukee Bucks, who were just a couple of games behind Detroit and were looking better by the week. Big game. After this, Cleveland took off on a long West Coast trip that GM Wayne Embry was hoping would lock up the title.

The game got off to a lousy start for Cleveland. Cavs' star center Brad Daugherty drove into seven-foot Jack Sikma under the basket and they both went down. Daugherty came up slowly and walked to the bench as if his left shoe had a large rock in it. "He's really hurting," Cleveland announcer Joe Tait murmured into his microphone as the crowd went dead. "Very decidedly." Was this the big Cleveland injury? If so, it was bad news for Cleveland. Daugherty was the heart of the team. He was what's known as a "true center"—he had arms that hung halfway to his knees, a butt that was about two feet long and two feet wide, and he moved in that loping, stuck-in-the-mud way common to true centers. The first pick of the 1986 draft, Daugherty was the element Wayne Embry had built his team around.

Even without Daugherty, though, Cleveland hit from inside and outside, and wouldn't let Milwaukee anywhere near the hoop. They led by 10 at the quarter and 5 at the half, and had reduced Jack Sikma to wandering aimlessly around the floor muttering, "Fuck. Fuck. Fuck." Lenny Wilkens was smiling and Wayne Embry, standing in the runway, felt confident. But then, fourth quarter. Milwaukee was one of the smartest, most disciplined teams in the league, with excellent mix and chemistry, and they figured out a way to choke off Cleveland's offense. Mark Price, still shell-shocked, didn't have the strength to break the chokehold. For the first nine minutes of the quarter, Cleveland scored only 5 points. Six times, Cleveland ran down the 24-second clock and had to take a bad shot. That bothered Embry. It was a sign of immaturity. Embry had gambled in putting together a very young team: He'd tried to find kids with enough character to play beyond their years. But Embry wasn't too worried. He still believed in his strategy. Besides, they hadn't lost in Cleveland in twenty-two straight games.

Toward the end, with the score tied, Price brought the ball down and started to set up the play. Suddenly, a whistle. Referee Darrell Garretson, who looked like Robert Duvall, called illegal defense. "We were trapping!" yelled Milwaukee coach Del Harris. Garretson looked right through him. "We were trapping the *ball!*" Harris spread his arms wide in supplication. The crowd didn't make fun of him, and he kept it up. But Garretson walked away. "Shit," Harris cried, flopping his arms to his sides. Larry Nance made the free throw and Cleveland had a 3-point edge. The crowd finally made a little noise, and the stadium's audio department plugged in a tired little tape of "Da-duh-da-da-ta-da-Charge!"—with no graphics. The Coliseum was definitely not a Basketball Disneyland. At a moment like this, Cleveland needed that.

Daugherty was back in, but he was wobbling. Price still had scrambled brains and it showed. Milwaukee's Ricky Pierce drove past Price for a lay-up. Then Pierce hit a jumper. Cleveland—the Assassins—looked vulnerable for virtually the first time all season. They tried to fight back, but something was gone and they didn't even know it was missing yet.

Just before the end, announcer Joe Tait said, "They're teetering on the brink of their first back-to-back loss in a *long* time. Not the way to start a long road trip."

As the horn sounded, Wayne Embry turned his back to the floor and began a heavy-footed trudge to the locker room. Embry hated to lose. But he wasn't particularly upset.

He didn't know what was ahead.

EIGHT

"Crunch Time"
The Race Gets Hot

"H**E'S** *HOOKIN'* 'em, goddamnit!" Denver coach Doug Moe barked at referee Ed Rush in his fried-larynx coach's voice. In front of Moe, Badass Rick Mahorn was pinning down pink-cheeked Blair Rasmussen with a machine-gun volley of elbows. Moe looked wild-eyed at Rush, then at referee Ed Mihalak. "Shit, fellas!" he wailed. Moe's center, who was big but baby-faced and blow-dried, was getting chewed to bits in front of his eyes.

"Welcome to the *East,* Moe," screamed Leon the Barber. "Tell your troubles to Curly."

Rasmussen edged away from Mahorn, but found himself wedged against Laimbeer, who shrugged him off like a nuisance. Rasmussen sidestepped. Straight into the massive, puff-pillow butt of Mark Aguirre. Trapped. A prisoner. Dribbling on the perimeter, Denver star Fat Lever gave up on working the ball inside and heaved up a jumper. It clanged off the rim and Mahorn was suddenly glued to it. Moe sat down, breathing out, "Lookit-that-shit," in one long sigh.

On the other side of the stadium, Jack McCloskey's eyes were on fire. He virtually never smiled during a Piston game, but when he felt good his eyes took on a hot glint. The team he'd envisioned for years—a team almost perfect in its mix, chemistry, and talent—was coming to life before his eyes. And it was mostly because of Aguirre.

158

After the Pistons had won a few games with Aguirre, Detroit fans had decided they loved him—confirming the theory of Tom Wilson that it was victory they paid to see, not players. But all that most fans noticed, when they scanned box scores or watched highlight film on TV, was that Aguirre was scoring about 18 to 20 points a night, and had a beautiful, God-given shot. McCloskey saw much more. He saw the extra pass. When Dantley had been on the team, there hadn't been enough searching for the man with the best shot. There had been more of a feeling of "If I pass off, I'll never get it back." It had resulted in a shooting percentage that was maybe 1 percent or 2 percent lower than it should have been. Fans didn't notice that slight drop-off, but it meant scoring 2 or 3 fewer points per game—often the margin of victory. Aguirre also made their passing game zippier, because he had an excellent baseball-throw pass. His passing hadn't shown up that much in Dallas, because there hadn't been that many people to pass to.

Another thing Aguirre was adding was an extra 1 or 2 rebounds per night. More important, his help on the boards allowed the real rebounders—Mahorn, Laimbeer, Salley, and Rodman—to cover a little more of the floor. Aguirre added some real pounds to the front line— that was obvious right now, as he laid body all over seven-foot Blair Rasmussen.

Then there was, of course, his shooting. Dantley had been a scorer, but not a pure shooter. Dantley had needed more help and better position to score, which sometimes pulled other shooters out of position. Aguirre could shoot from anywhere, including the 3-point line; at the moment, his 3-point accuracy was 10–23, the best on the team.

Most important, though, were the intangibles. Ever since that first day, when Mahorn had knocked Aguirre on his ass and had said, "Welcome to the Pistons," Aguirre had been a real honor student. He seemed painfully aware of his ugly rep and acted desperate to prove that it had been the Mavericks who'd been jerks, not he. In the Pistons locker room, he was sticky-sweet to Mahorn and Laimbeer. He was given to singing out, "Oh, Rickeeee?" and then laying some compliment on Mahorn. It was sucking up, of course, but Mahorn deserved it—he was the one who bullied the bullies and kept them safe. Aguirre was also Mr. Nice Guy with Chuck Daly. It was the opposite of Dantley's behavior toward Daly and it had a soothing effect on the whole team. When Dantley had refused to talk to Daly, being on the team had been like living with two parents on the verge of divorce.

Probably the most important intangible was the emotional state of Isiah. Thomas's frame of mind was of critical importance, because he was still the one player who was as desperate for the Championship as

McCloskey. The brilliant strategy of the Trade—in emotional terms—was that Aguirre's victories would be Isiah's victories, and vice versa. That strategy was playing out perfectly. Aguirre was one of the few people on earth Isiah didn't mind stepping out of the spotlight for. And when Aguirre stepped into the spotlight, his standard line was "I owe it all to my man Isiah—Mr. Assister." That proved what a *misunderstood guy* Mark Aguirre had been, and pulled Isiah back into the spotlight—a mutual benefit. Isiah was now more unselfish than he'd been with Dantley on the floor, and Aguirre seemed happiest when he made Isiah look good. They were always looking out for each other.

At the present moment, for example—Isiah had just smacked into Denver's Michael Adams, who at about five-ten and 165 pounds was even smaller than Thomas. But Adams, a third-round pick and former CBA player, was on the verge of stardom, and wasn't about to let *anybody* push him around. He *liked* fame and fortune. So he'd gotten pointedly pissed off and was going after Thomas. Over Mark Aguirre's dead body: Aguirre threw himself at Adams. Then Mahorn stepped up, and Adams wanted a piece of *him*. What a joke—a guy built along the lines of a chickadee going after Badass Rick. Dennis Rodman fell back laughing.

Detroit held a nice lead and the Killer B-Team was running the Denver subs like dogs. The Pistons, McCloskey thought, were playing better than any other team he'd ever coached or put together. McCloskey was having a hell of a good time.

When the half ended, McCloskey was relaxed enough to watch most of the halftime show; tonight it was a contortionist in a body suit and gold lamé shower cap whose gig was to stuff himself inside a glass box about the size of a microwave oven. It was a great geek act—a box full of human meat—one of the best Basketball Disneyland sideshows Tom Wilson had ever come up with. McCloskey's only worry, as he watched the snake-bodied contortionist coil up in the box, was that their win the night before in Miami had drained them. They hadn't gotten in until 2:00 A.M. It had only been three days since the blockbuster win over Cleveland, and the hectic, intense last month of the regular season was sure to begin destroying certain teams. Somebody *always* folded during the season's crunch time. Who would it be? Cleveland, maybe. They hadn't been through a title fight before. Their kids might freak out. Maybe New York—Vandeweghe seemed to be mucking up their chemistry, and when the battle got hotter, that flaw would stick out more. Pitino was already worried; he'd just been quoted as saying, "Chemistry is more important in basketball than any other sport. Bad chemistry gets coaches fired and players traded." Maybe the team to fall would be

L.A.—their bench wasn't very good, partly because Orlando Woolridge was too much of a hot dog to accept a bench role. Also, Kareem was still bloated and stone-legged, and time was running out for him to get in shape. McCloskey didn't think Detroit would be one of the teams to collapse in the crunch. He'd built this team with the long season and the playoffs in mind. Detroit was deep, had a good mix of experience and youth, was desperate to win, and finally had the right chemistry. Theoretically, that was enough. Theoretically.

"I just hope our legs can hold up tonight," said McCloskey, as the contortionist folded his last remaining limb into the box. "Actually, we're the traveling team tonight. They were here last night sleeping, while we were dragging home from Miami." The contortionist's assistant closed the lid, and began pivoting the box in a circle, so that everyone could see the contortionist's face squashed against the side of the box. It drew a mixture of cheers and groans. "But we've *still* got the home-court advantage. The *fans* are the home-court advantage. You know, Denver's a very good team, but they've lost seventeen of their last eighteen road games." McCloskey never thought it was odd that a player on the cusp of either making $500,000 a year—or coaching junior college—would need applause to become fully motivated. To him, that was quite understandable, probably because he was a former player. That empathy, more than his successful track record, was what made many of the players respect his authority and accept his decisions. Laimbeer sauntered out of the runway and stood near McCloskey, watching the contortionist. They didn't say much to each other.

In the second half, the Detroit front line continued to hammer Denver's big people into the ground. Denver had some good-sized players—Wayne Cooper was six-ten, Rasmussen was seven feet and 250, and Dan Schayes was six-eleven and 245—but even good, big western teams seemed weak and intimidated when they ventured into the Basketball Belt. When clean-cut Blair Rasmussen had walked onto the court, Mahorn had given him a frightening smile, as if to say, "So young, so fresh; let's eat!" Even his name was pussy. Blair? An NBA center named Blair? Now Mahorn was on his way to a 19-rebound, 19-point night. McCloskey was thrilled to see Mahorn playing so well. He didn't think they could win the Championship without him.

In the fourth quarter, Denver got to within 4 points. Isiah was nervous. This was no time of year to be screwing away big leads and losing games. He decided to take control. Auker put on the Generic Hero Music as Isiah walked onto the floor after a time-out, and the Palace got loud as hell. From behind the bench, a fan made fun of Doug Moe's green sport coat: "Nice jacket, babe! Original color, babe! Put on a tie and siddown, Moe!" Isiah stood at the top of the key, dribbling, dribbling, dribbling—then a high arcing shot: net. He ran back on defense, forced a turnover, got the ball in the corner and made another perfect jump shot. Moe called time, Auker put on "Shout," it got even louder, and then Isiah came out and hit a jumper, then a drive, and suddenly the game was a blowout. By the last minute, Detroit had 129 points, just 1 point short of the total needed for every ticket holder to get a free Buddy's pizza. The fans were chanting, "Pee-zuh! Pee-zuh!" Denver ball. John Long, Michael Williams, and Fennis Dembo came in. Laimbeer yelled, "Foul them right away!" They made the foul, Denver missed the free throw, and Detroit rebounded. "Pee-zuh! Pee-zuh!" Ten seconds left.

Moe looked disgusted. He jumped up and waved his players off their men. "Back off!" he yelled. "Let 'em have their goddamn pizza!" A long pass sailed down to Williams. Over his head. The crowd moaned. McCloskey looked ecstatic.

Then McCloskey hurried home to watch Santa Clara play Loyola Marymount at midnight on cable. Will Robinson was at the game, and McCloskey wanted to get double coverage of a kid named Hank Gathers. He was just a junior, and last year he'd only averaged 8.5 points. Definitely a suspect, not a prospect. It would have been more fun, of course, to hang around the Palace and celebrate. Finally having this good of a team was something worth celebrating. But maybe in two years Hank Gathers would be of some small value. When you ran the franchise, you had to think like that.

At practice the next day, John Salley, still out of uniform because of his cracked ankle, stepped onto the floor to take a few shots. Mahorn burned a Mean Mahorn grin into Salley and yelled, "Yo! Spider! Get your lame fuckin' ass off the floor! This is for players only."

Salley grinned uncomfortably. For once, he didn't have a comeback.

"Don't strain yourself, John," singsonged Laimbeer. "We're doin' okay without ya. We got Jim-Bob now." Jim Rowinski, the CBA player McCloskey had picked up to take Salley's place, smiled shyly and looked at the floor. Laimbeer called him Jim-Bob because his sweet, unassuming personality was reminiscent of TV's Jim-Bob Walton.

At the mention of Rowinski, James Edwards went, "Arrrgghh!" Rowinski brightened; the growl was his trademark. It signified that Rowinski was an animal, the strongest guy on the team. He had a Schwarzenegger body and could bench-press 420 pounds. He much preferred "Arrrgghh" to "Jim-Bob," but he wasn't bitching either way.

He was just glad to be in the NBA instead of Topeka, Kansas, where he'd been playing his ass off in the CBA to catch somebody's attention. The year before, he'd been in Italy, pulling down $90,000 a year, about ten times what Topeka paid—but nobody scouted Italy. In 1984, Rowinski had been a late third-round pick by Frank Layden of Utah, but Layden had made him the last cut during preseason. Layden had dumped him in favor of Billy Paultz, "the Whopper," a blubber-gutted veteran who'd come to camp with guaranteed money. A bad career blow. Rowinski *knew* he could play at the NBA level; he just had to get inside the NBA bubble. Getting in was a lot harder than staying in. Right now, Rowinski had to hope that Salley's injury would be serious enough to warrant his getting another ten-day contract. In that length of time, he might impress some other team. Of course, it was blasphemous to admit you wanted another player to remain injured, but who was kidding whom? Rowinski didn't owe Salley anything. Just like the Whopper hadn't owed Rowinski anything.

Before Salley had a chance to take many shots, trainer Mike Abdenour hustled him off the floor. Abdenour knew Salley's ego was taking a beating, but Adbenour didn't want Salley to aggravate the crack in his ankle.

"Go shoot a commercial, John!" Laimbeer yelled. "You're better at that." Salley was only averaging 5 rebounds and 23 minutes per game, the same as last year, but was scoring less and blocking fewer shots. Some of the guys—notably Laimbeer, Mahorn, and Thomas—were getting fed up with him. They thought he was concentrating more on being a media star than winning the Championship. How could they ask Aguirre to sacrifice himself if Salley, at the locker next door, was more interested in dicking around with the media people than playing? McCloskey seemed to have had enough of Salley, too. There'd been talk all winter of Salley getting shipped out, maybe to Indiana with Michael Williams, for Herb Williams and John Long. Or maybe to Portland, with Michael Williams for Kiki Vandeweghe and Steve Johnson. Or maybe to New Jersey, straight up for Buck Williams. None of the trades had materialized, but Salley had the message: Don't buy a house.

It was a short practice. They had another game tomorrow. Against Seattle, the team the coaches called Atlanta West. Daly was really afraid of Seattle's trapping defense, so he'd been drilling them on it. When he felt as if they'd figured it out, he broke up practice and headed for the coaches' room. On the way, he ran into Steve Addy and pulled him aside. Addy knew he was about to catch hell.

After Addy had seen the phone being passed into the huddle during the Cleveland game, he'd called NBA headquarters in New York to see if that was against the rules. The NBA executive he'd talked to had told him it was, and had pumped him for information. Addy wouldn't tell him anything other than what he was preparing to publish. Addy told them it wasn't his job to tattle on the team. So the league officials had called other people who'd seen the incident, and one of them spilled his guts. The league then started a full investigation. Daly was pissed.

"You tried to get me in trouble with the league," Daly said to Addy.

It was hard not to be intimidated by Daly. He'd spent his career laying down the law to huge, famous millionaires, and he knew how to turn on the power.

"I just wrote a story," Addy protested, looking up at Daly. "I did my job, I followed my story."

"Naw, you tried to get me in trouble. You tried to fuck me with the league." Now Daly was being threatened with a fine of up to $5,000. Like the players, he made a small fortune, $500,000 a year. But he'd started at $3,600 a year, and those memories were still too vivid.

But after a few minutes, Daly relented. He had a big ego, but he didn't have the undiluted arrogance that most of the players did—probably because his $3,600 a year had come at the same age most of them had gotten their first million. He even gave Addy an interview about Aguirre. "He's losing weight," Daly told him, "and his attitude is *good*. We just have to muddle through it. Hopefully, he's picking up on what we're doing. We run a lot of sets, more than most teams." Defense, though, was still a problem. "I'd love to see Mark be a better defensive player. Work, that's all it is. Anybody could play defense. Even you writers could play it—if you wanted to *work*. I swear, you could make anybody a decent defensive player if they're willing to spend the time. But he'll get better. Hell, he's going to be sitting if he doesn't work defensively."

Addy liked Daly. It was easy enough to piss Daly off, but he didn't keep you in the doghouse forever. Addy wouldn't fare quite so well, though, with PR director Matt Dobek, who'd apparently relayed most of the messages. For the next three games, Addy's seat would be moved from its regular spot behind the Piston bench to the row of out-of-town writers behind the visiting bench.

Addy went on into the locker room. Most of the players had left. John Salley caught Addy's eye and quietly said, "Hey rookie, c'mere." Salley had started calling Addy "rookie" last year, when he'd first covered the Pistons.

Salley ducked his head inside his locker, so it wouldn't be obvious he was talking to Addy. Salley told Addy that some of the players were nervous about talking to him, because of the phone-call story. They apparently felt that Addy had violated protocol by not just sticking to play-by-play and mantalk.

"Well," said Addy, "they know that I've treated them fairly and accurately. I'm not worried."

"Well, I just thought I'd tell you."

"Thanks a lot, John. I appreciate it." Addy had recently ripped Salley to shreds in a column. He'd accused him of being more of a showman than a player. After that column, some of the other players had taken Addy aside and told him they agreed. Now *they* were pissed. Writing about rich twenty-five-year-old gods was not the world's easiest beat.

One of the ball boys came over to Jim Rowinski. "Mr. McCloskey wants to see you upstairs," he said. Rowinski, who had gym-rat pallor, seemed to grow more chalky.

Brendan Suhr stood at the blackboard under the locker room's television, writing down last-minute reminders before the Seattle game: "Look for a long pass at the beginning of each quarter." "Watch for trap after free throws." "Worst free-throw shooters—Lister, McMillan, Polynice, McDaniel." The players were warming up on the court. In a few minutes, they'd come in and watch an "edit"—a video that showed each of Seattle's primary plays. Each player already had a written report on the team, and they'd watched videotape that morning after their shootaround.

Suhr was worried that the guys were getting complacent. They were playing well and they knew it. "But you can't try to get guys up for games," he said, as his chalk made staccato pecks. "There's no rah-rah speech here. That doesn't work at this level. What you try to do is stress to them from the first day of training camp that to be a successful player you have to be self-motivated. That's the only true form of motivation. For most of these guys, that's more important than money. Most of them have guaranteed contracts. What they're playing for—or should be, if they really want to win—is that ring. That pride. That sense of being a World Champion."

Suhr thought that Seattle was a dangerous team to be complacent about. "Seattle has fabulous talent. That's why we call them Atlanta West, because Atlanta probably has the most talent in the East, along with New York. Next to the Lakers, Seattle probably has the most talent in the West. *Great* athletes. Very good coaching. They have a chance to win fifty games."

There was another reason to take this game very seriously: If they were ever going to catch Cleveland, it had to be now, during the Cavs' long road trip.

When the game started, there was no sign of complacency. Detroit raced to an 8-point lead and Laimbeer came to the bench at a time-out bellowing, "Don't let up! Don't let up! Don't even give 'em *one shot.*" His face was drawn and rigid. Auker put "Bad to the Bone" on, and flashed the Pistons' Trivia question on the scoreboard: "What NBA executive was selected by Seattle in the expansion draft of 1967?" Announcer Ken Calvert boomed the answer: "Rod Thorn." The crowd hissed and whistled.

When they took the floor, Detroit's improved passing game bewildered Seattle. The ball didn't loft and then slap into the other player's hands—it shot in a straight line, like a javelin out of a cannon, and then suddenly was part of the other player's body, with no apparent reception. Even Seattle star Dale Ellis, whose body looked like it had been sculpted out of bronze, seemed befuddled. The lead kept building and Detroit's momentum got so heavy that they started getting the benefit of the doubt from the refs. Toward the end of the half, Rodman grabbed a rebound and dribbled downcourt, punching his fist into the air. Then he walked a good two steps and started dribbling again. No call. The crowd went crazy. Seattle called time and Laimbeer came to the bench choking down a smile; when he got there he buried his head in a towel and guffawed. Detroit had a 15-point lead and the game, for all practical purposes, was over. From here on, it was just entertainment: Basketball Disneyland. The high point came when Roger the Chimp did the Celebrity Free-Throw Shot. The whole Detroit team watched. Even Daly. Later on, Daly even put Jim Rowinski in the game. McCloskey had given him another ten-day contract. Rowinski looked happy, as if he believed everything in the world could change within ten days. He was right. In the NBA, it could.

Two nights later, Cleveland GM Wayne Embry left his seat late in the game during the Pacific Ten tournament in L.A. to see how the Cavs were doing. They were playing across town, against the Clippers, but Embry had decided he should scout the Pac-Ten rather than watch his own team. That was his job.

So far, it hadn't been a great road trip. They'd beaten Sacramento, a team that had only won 16 games, but they'd lost to Golden State last night. It had been an ugly, exhausting dogfight, with 19 lead changes and 17 ties, and Warrior Mitch Richmond had sunk a 3-pointer with 27 seconds left to win it.

But that was just one game. And tonight: easy pickings. The Clippers. Worst team in the West, and probably in all of basketball. The Clippers, a pathetically run franchise, were 12–49, 30½ games out of first. Embry wasn't worried about the Golden State loss. What the hell. Those things happened, Embry thought, to young teams. When young players found themselves in a difficult situation—like playing eleven out of seventeen games on the road—they let themselves off the hook too easily. Players on experienced teams, like Detroit or Milwaukee, weren't so quick with excuses.

Embry called a number back in Cleveland to find out the score.

Odd news. Bad news. Cleveland had lost again. To the *Clippers*.

That was something else young teams did, Embry thought, as he trudged back to his seat. They let up on weak teams.

Embry was disappointed. But not shocked. And not worried. It was just one more game.

Jack McCloskey sat at dinner with Laker GM Jerry West and Dallas player personnel director Rick Sund. They were all in L.A. for the last weekend of the Pacific Ten tournament. They were talking about the players they liked—UCLA's Pooh Richardson, Stanford's Todd Lichti, and Arizona's Sean Elliott. But none of those guys would be available to McCloskey, West, or Sund. That was the price of success. Sund had the only possible chance to get into the lottery, but his team was starting to look strong again. With Dantley finally playing, Sund had a renewed sense of hope. Roy Tarpley would soon come off suspension for drug use, and James Donaldson—Sund's seven-two, 280-pound center, was having his best year ever. Donaldson was sixth in the league in rebounds, with a 10.8 average. With Donaldson's heft—his thighs were almost as thick as garbage cans—he seemed indestructible. Sund had gotten Donaldson in 1985 for cheap, boosting Sund's stature in his franchise. All Sund had given was Kurt Nimphius, a stringy white center whom Sund had dumped after Nimphius's only good year, when he had some market value. Even after Nimphius had settled back into mediocrity, though, McCloskey had picked him up in exchange for a first- and second-round pick. All the GMs were suckers for big men. Even McCloskey.

After awhile, the conversation turned to the Trade. Dallas was playing much better with Dantley, McCloskey thought. Their frontcourt game was more versatile.

"That may be," said Sund, "but I think you guys just won the NBA Championship."

Jerry West looked up. *"Everybody's* saying Detroit is gonna win it. But we're still where we are." McCloskey knew what "where we are" meant: on top, with the title. "You've got to beat us first," said West.

They went back for the evening session. Sund had to leave in the middle of the game to see how Dallas was doing.

When he came back to his seat, he seemed wobbly. James Donaldson had gone down with a knee injury. It looked like it might be serious.

There was virtually no one to replace Donaldson. The backup center was Bill Wennington, who was averaging about 4 points a game. The strong point of Wennington's game was waving a towel on the bench. Behind Wennington was Uwe Blab, whose legs seemed to be made out of wood. If Donaldson stayed out, Dallas was doomed—another victim of lack of depth. Sund now had better reason to watch the college game. Maybe now he'd be in the lottery. But it was almost impossible to concentrate.

The next morning, McCloskey went to the airport to fly to Atlanta. He was going to see the Atlantic Coast Conference tournament and take a look at guys like Danny Ferry and J. R. Reid. It would take a monster trade to move high enough to draft either of them, and with his team playing like it was, McCloskey wasn't inclined to make that move. But the season was far from over, and McCloskey was holding his team to the highest expectations. If they didn't win the Championship—or, more important, play well enough to win it—there would be major changes.

But even if McCloskey couldn't draft a blue-chip player, there were still guys in the ACC worth looking at. Like North Carolina State's Chucky Brown and North Carolina's Jeff Lebo. Will Robinson liked Chucky Brown. Robinson had graduated Brown from "suspect" to "prospect." Brown would probably be a second-round pick, but some excellent players always slipped to the second round. In 1986 alone, for example, the second round had included Mark Price, Kevin Duckworth, Johnny Newman, Jeff Hornacek, Larry Krystkowiak—and Dennis Rodman. A case could be made that the strongest franchises were those that made the shrewdest second-round picks. Almost anybody could choose a first-round player. The second round was where a team could gain an edge.

While McCloskey was waiting for his flight, Rick Sund walked up. He was on the same flight. "Boy, I just got some bad news from Donaldson," said Sund. "He's out. For the season."

The season's crunch time had just claimed its first victim. Dallas, which had pushed the Lakers to the seventh game in the past year's Western Finals, was gone. There was one less team to beat.

*   *   *

Two days later, McCloskey was back in Detroit, sitting in the Palace dining room before the March 12 Washington game, pushing his food around on his plate. As usual, the Pistons were serving a sumptuous feast to the franchise executives and the press: choice of prime rib or baked salmon, new potatoes and green beans, garlic bread, pasta salad, creamed peas with pearl onions, a salad bar, and choice of cherry pie à la mode or chocolate cake, with coffee and soft drinks. But McCloskey wasn't interested in food. He sat impassively before his plate, muttering, "First place by the end of the night. *First* place. First!" George Blaha and McCloskey's wife Leslie sat on either side of him, but they both left him alone.

Cleveland was playing Portland now, and the Cavs were less than one full game ahead of Detroit. Day after tomorrow, Cleveland would go against the powerful and beautifully mixed Utah team. The goal of first place, so remote just ten days ago, was now so close that McCloskey could smell it.

But—one hour later: Isiah Thomas slammed into rock-hard Charles Jones and collapsed to the floor. He lay on his stomach, both legs in the air behind him, bent at the knee, waving in unison. His face was taut with pain. Brendan Suhr jumped off the bench, crying, "Oh, shit!" Mike Abdenour leaped up and ran to Thomas. Daly stood watching. He turned his back and said, "God *damn* it!"

From his seat, Jack McCloskey watched in horror. Was this as close to the goal as they would ever get? He repeated to himself, over and over, "Don't let it be serious. Don't let it be serious."

Tom Wilson, sitting at the press table, was stunned. In a moment of illogic, he blamed himself. One of his most constant quotes around the office was "In this business, you're never more than one knee injury away from taking a dive financially." As he watched Thomas writhe, he said to himself, "You should have shut up. It's your own fault." Wilson felt as if the Pistons' legacy of failure had once again caught up with them: "They'll break your heart." He was thinking, "There goes first place. There goes the playoffs. The season's over."

A deathly hush settled over the Palace. Even when Isiah struggled up, and limped off on Abdenour's arm, Dave Auker didn't try to play any music. It wouldn't be appropriate. Besides, he didn't feel like it.

NINE

"We're Number One"
Detroit Becomes the Target

"WHY AM I the way that I am?"
Jack McCloskey locked his fingers behind his neck and slanted back in
his office chair. He was in a reflective mood. He felt that the season—and
maybe his entire career—had just shifted. Detroit was back in first. It
was Tuesday, two days after the Washington game—another victory.
Cleveland had beaten Portland on Sunday, but last night Cleveland had
lost again, to Utah. A 15-point loss—a real ass-kicking. Maybe things
had shifted for good. Or maybe this was just a brief window of happiness. There was no way to know.

Now they were everyone's target, both on the court and off. Every
team would be gunning for Detroit, and the team's media and business
activities would intensify. The potshots had already begun. Today a
banner headline trumpeted the accusation of a local black leader: PISTONS
DESERTED DETROIT. But even that crisis—the kind that would have managers
of most businesses foaming with rage and fear—bothered McCloskey
very little.

"Why am I the way that I am?

"There was the time NASA was looking to take civilians up in the
Shuttle. In the *Challenger*. I made formal application, and we had tons of
correspondence back and forth for a couple of years. I *begged* them to let
me go. But they decided to send someone in education. I told them, 'I

am in education—it's a big part of what I do.' But they finally said, no, we want to send a teacher, it's not going to happen. I remember Tom Wilson's wife Linda, who was my secretary at the time, coming in with that letter. She was almost in tears.

"Now I guess there's some sort of deal where you can go up for a fee? Maybe I ought to do that. Get a bunch of sponsors together. Wear a Pistons logo. They'd say, 'There goes one of the Bad Boys. The baddest one of all. 'Cause he may not *come back.'*

"I guess that doesn't explain *why* I'm the way I am. I dunno. It's just—I'm that way. The baddest dude of all."

McCloskey was laughing when the phone rang. It was Rod Thorn. Thorn wanted to know about a skirmish in one of their recent games. "Yeah," said McCloskey, "I didn't see that tape. . . . I saw it, but from a different angle. . . . Well, you know, Gentle James. . . . Fifteen hundred, huh? Okay. Okay. . . . You're right—Boston would be dangerous. Very dangerous. . . . Yeah. Okay. . . . Rod—don't call me anymore, okay? Right. 'Bye."

"He only has one tape of it," McCloskey explained, "where the shoving takes place. But one of the officials says there were some punches thrown, and I didn't see that from my angle. He'll get another tape of it somewhere. He also says Chuck is going to get fined fifteen hundred for the phone-call thing." McCloskey shrugged: no big deal.

McCloskey was getting ready for a lunch meeting with Oscar Feldman, one of the team's owners and its chief counsel, to talk about giving Laimbeer and Dumars more money. Both were underpaid by the extravagant standards of the NBA. Laimbeer's $630,000 was considerably less than the salaries of several centers who weren't as good, such as Joe Barry Carroll ($1.4 million), Dan Schayes ($1 million), Ralph Sampson ($1.9 million), Kevin Duckworth ($2 million), Alton Lister ($1.1 million), and Bill Cartwright ($1.2 million). Dumars made $400,000 but was better than guards who made more: for example, Gerald Wilkins ($625,000), Terry Tyler ($560,000), and Vern Fleming ($507,000).

McCloskey didn't have to offer the money, but it was obvious now that William Bedford wasn't coming back this year, so his salary could be cannibalized. "Joe's and Bill's salaries are not commensurate with their stature, with some of the recent signings that have taken place. So I wanted to push them up, and add a year or two onto Bill's contract, so they would feel comfortable. I think it's *good business* to make sure your players feel comfortable." It also helped deflect the specter of free agency. The market was going crazy. Bird's $6-million-per-year deal was just the tip of the iceberg. With players like Wayman Tisdale making $1 million, Otis Thorpe making $1.1 million, and Buck Williams making $1.3 million, who could say what Joe Dumars might command on the open market in a couple of years? Better to wrap him up now.

McCloskey had spoken to Laimbeer and Dumars about it, and, as he'd expected, he'd gotten two very different responses. "I said to Joe, 'I want to do something with your contract this year.' And he said, 'You don't have to tell me that. You don't have to worry about me playing hard or not playing hard—because I'm going to play the same.' I said the same thing to Laimbeer, and he said, 'Well, I think it's *time* we got to talking about that.' "

The phone rang again. It was a TV station needing a statement on today's crisis—a series of accusations about the Pistons leveled by the Reverend Jim Holley, president of the Detroit chapter of Jesse Jackson's Operation PUSH. The Reverend Mr. Holley had charged, with great media fanfare, that the Pistons were promoting "plantation basketball"—exploiting black athletes "for the amusement of upscale whites." Holley was calling the Pistons "a racist organization," and chastising them for moving from the predominately black inner-city to the mostly white suburbs. He was also angry about Piston ticket prices, which had the highest average in the NBA at $23.11. "They have completely taken the team away from Detroit young people," said Holley. He was calling for a boycott of all Piston advertisers.

McCloskey wasn't worried. The Reverend Mr. Holley had a tough sell on his hands. How was he going to get people up in arms over poor Isiah Thomas, who made $2 million a year and lived in his castle in Bloomfield Hills? Or James Edwards, who made $800,000 and owned macadamia orchards in Hawaii? These were *not* men who had to sing spirituals to get through the day. McCloskey's business was probably the most thoroughly integrated in the city of Detroit, and it was the black players—not the white executives like McCloskey and Tom Wilson—who were getting wealthy.

"One time at Wake Forest," said McCloskey, "I was the first coach that had two black starters in the Atlantic Coast Conference, and I used to get letters from rednecks using the word 'nigger-lover,' and letters from blacks saying that I wasn't playing the black kids enough. I got three or four more black guys each year, and I remember a writer from Richmond saying, 'You've got X number of blacks on the team, you know.' And I said, 'Is that right? Who are they?' He named them off and I said, 'Damn—you're right! I've never counted them.' "

When McCloskey and Tom Wilson had first taken over the franchise and had decided to move it from downtown to Pontiac, they'd locked horns with Detroit's black mayor, Coleman Young. Young was a serious manipulator, who made the Reverend Jim Holley look like a punk. If

Young decided to join forces with Holley, the battle might get bloody. But that wasn't likely. Young was neck deep in an ugly paternity rap, and had his hands full.

On the other side of the hall, in the business offices, Tom Wilson was getting ready to haul out his biggest gun against Holley: Isiah Thomas. Isiah would squash Holley like a bug. Nobody in Detroit could resist Isiah. Isiah was still ghetto-tough, but he'd focused that part of himself strictly into basketball. Off the court, wearing his thousand-dollar suits and high-beam smile, he was the young gentleman—and just what Wilson needed to blow Holley away. "Isiah gets brought into everything," said Wilson, sitting in the red leather chair by his glossy redwood desk. "Isiah's kind of an unofficial spokesman, because he's very articulate and he's well known. Whatever he says has clout, so he's the guy news people go to." Thomas was so good at his young gentleman routine that Wilson thought Thomas might have a future in politics. "Isiah's very political. He has a lot of deep cares, but he's not going to come out and say, I'm a this, or I'm a that. But I can see him going in that direction if he chooses to. He also has an acting career, I think, if he wants it. He has free rein to do whatever Isiah Thomas wants to do."

Which, right now, was to go out and squash the Reverend Jim like a bug.

Wilson thought all of Holley's charges were just headline hype. "We never did draw in Detroit," said Wilson. "Rightly or wrongly, there are a lot of folks who just won't go to downtown Detroit. And until recently, we had a five-dollar ticket, but no one would buy it. Nobody wants to sit in the cheap seats.

"The news people I talk to are saying, you know, this guy's going to be running for office and this is his issue, and if the Pistons were sixteen and forty-three now, instead of forty-three and sixteen, he'd have to find another target.

"I guess that's the price of being number one."

John Ciszewski came in from his adjacent office, and he and Wilson started talking about the old days when nobody bitched about their ticket prices. Because they practically had to give them away.

"It was like, you'd leave two Piston tickets on the windshield of your car for somebody to take, and you'd come back and there'd be four more," said Ciszewski.

"Remember triskaidekaphobia?" said Wilson.

"Right—the fear of having only thirteen people in the stadium."

"Remember when we'd have crowds of three thousand," said Wilson, "and we couldn't figure out why so *many* came, since there was no *reason* to? It wasn't good basketball and it wasn't even fun."

"And *coooold*!"

"Yeah—I remember the scoring crew sitting there with mukluks on and big hoods over their heads. And none of the players wanted to go in the game because they couldn't break a sweat. And remember those huge kerosene heaters? Kicking out flames, trying to heat the stands?"

"The stink, I remember," laughed Ciszewski. "The *smog*."

"And you'd get a buildup of condensation, and it would freeze on the ceiling. Then we'd get some heat from a crowd, and it'd melt and rain in the arena."

"Remember the rodeo?"

"Yeah," said Wilson. "On the other side of that big curtain. All that dust! The players were slipping in it! A guy would be ready to shoot a free throw and you'd hear, 'Maaahh!' "

"And the next day Charlie Vincent writes, 'The game wasn't the only thing that smelled.' You *knew* that was coming."

"But we had great promos back then," said Wilson.

"You bet. Like Boot."

"Boot! The guy who could light off firecrackers in his mouth! And Crazy George—he lived with you for a while, didn't he?"

"Crazy George the dribbler! Crazy could dribble ten basketballs at a time. He was like Ed Sullivan gone bad, 'cause he couldn't do plates. We *worked* with him on that, too. He was the kids' role model. They liked Lanier, but they loved Crazy."

"And who could forget the Classy Chassis?" said Wilson.

"I wish I could."

"Boy, those girls—what a dance team. Some of them were terrific-looking, and some of them were . . ." Wilson strained to be diplomatic.

"Wholesome," said Ciszewski.

"Wholesome. And some of them were straight from the red-light district. You could've gotten herpes just sitting next to them."

"Linda Blair!"

"Linda Blair—after the Exorcist was done with her! She'd do those dance routines and we kept expecting her head to spin around! Oh boy, wow."

"Remember the night the high school prelims outsold the Pistons?" said Ciszewski.

"Swartz Creek High School."

"And the time we had Punk Night?"

"Who *was* that—Marques Johnson?—that called us a bunch of punks? So next morning you come in my office and say, 'Hey, Tom, let's have a Punk Night and let people with chains and leather in for half price.' And we had Tripucka do a commercial in shades and a black leather jacket, with his hair greased back. We got on CNN with that, didn't we?"

"Yeah," said Ciszewski. "Letterman, too. You know, maybe we oughta have a Bad Boys night, where everybody wears black."

Wilson drifted off for a moment. "That reminds me," he said. "Jack doesn't want us to do any more Rod Thorn questions on Pistons Trivia."

Ciszewski sagged. Thorn's nemesis, Rick Mahorn, was one of Ciszewski's favorite people. Mahorn could always be counted on to visit a school or hospital, so long as it was kept quiet—he didn't want to sully his Badass Rick reputation. "Does this mean we can't introduce the team as Your Detroit Piston Bad Boys?"

"Don't even ask."

Again, Ciszewski looked disappointed. But not that disappointed. His company—a company he identified with totally—had gotten blasted as racist, capitalist pigs on the front page of the morning paper. But they were in *first place*. Nothing could spoil a day like this.

The following day—the ides of March—the buzzards came home to roost on the Cleveland Cavaliers' stadium.

Every year on March 15 the region's flock of turkey buzzards migrated to Hinckley, Ohio, near the Cavs' stadium. It was a sign of spring. The hardwood forest surrounding the stadium was alive with the ugly hiss of buzzards.

One more omen: Michael Jordan was in town with a new plan to destroy the Cavs.

Inside the stadium, Lenny Wilkens sat pensively in his office, working on a way to stop Jordan's new scheme. Jordan had cooked it up with coach Doug Collins. The plan was for Jordan to play point guard. It would give him more opportunity to cash in on his body's magical abilities, and spread his attack to the other players. Wilkens wasn't sure how he would try to stop Jordan, but he wasn't terribly worried. There was no way a one-man team should be able to beat a team with the mix and chemistry Cleveland had. Then again, nothing worried Wilkens too much. Not even slipping out of first place.

"I tell the players, you have to be concerned with what we do, without looking over your shoulders worrying about the other teams. You take care of what you can control. When we play Detroit again, okay, then we have a chance to do something. But we can't affect who they play, so why worry about it. Right?" Wilkens smiled his little puckered-lip half-smile.

"We didn't play consistently well on our road trip, but that's not the end of the season. When we finish the season, I want to finish it strong. So, all right, we had a slump. Every team has one, and we just got ours now. The thing to do is come out of it and refocus."

Wilkens thought his team would beat Detroit when—and if—they met in the playoffs. He knew McCloskey and Daly thought they could beat his team in a series, but he thought they were wrong. "I think that Detroit's defense has a little more experience, yes. I don't buy the fact that they'll beat us in the seven-game series. I just don't *buy* that. I don't think they have a better bench than we do. I don't think they're better than us as a whole.

"And I think we'll prove that."

Wilkens seemed confident, not boastful. Cleveland GM Wayne Embry had carefully chosen a coach who was as quiet, cautious, and controlled as himself. Wilkens smiled his little oval smile and went back to picking apart Michael Jordan's new strategy.

A few hours later, Michael Jordan began playing point guard in the NBA. He was brilliant, knifing through the defense to add a new dimension to the Chicago attack. Jordan scored 28 points and made 12 assists. But Cleveland murdered Chicago. They were still the Assassins. The season's crunch time was here, and the Assassins—calm and controlled—were deadly in the crunch. Now the day's omens—the buzzards and the ides of March—seemed silly superstition. But they were real. Michael Jordan would be back.

It was St. Patrick's Day, March 17, and Larry Bird was supposed to be in uniform for the Piston-Celtic game. He wasn't. Bird had just run the floor in practice but his aching feet had made him plod to a halt. "It's killing me," he said. "Even when I'm running straight ahead." Now it looked like Bird wouldn't be back until just before playoffs. If that happened, though, Boston would be dangerous. They would probably be in seventh or eighth place, and face Cleveland or Detroit. But with Bird playing, they'd be much better than their record and would make the normally easy first round into hell. For now, it was important to beat them to undercut their confidence. You didn't want them coming at you in the first round thinking, "Hell, we just beat these guys *without* Larry."

Auker started the game with "Bad to the Bone," which got drowned by crowd noise. But seconds later Kevin McHale sank a jumper, just as Brendan Suhr was yelling, "Hands up." The crowd went dead.

"He's gonna shoot all night, for Christ's sake!" shouted Daly. "It's gonna be a looong night." The two Brendans were wearing green ties, but Daly had on a no-bullshit dark tie and a black silk suit.

Aguirre got the ball at the other end and put up a soft hook. It didn't fall. He ran back downcourt saying, "Fuck! Fuck!" to no one in particular.

Daly called time and scowled at the starters. "We're not workin' like we used to. It just doesn't *happen* when you don't work. *Set the screen.*" He sent them back out, but they only stayed even. Daly looked down the bench and said, "Dennis. Get Rick." Rodman tried to look blank, but his happiness shined through. He stripped off his sweat suit as he giant-stepped to the scorer's table, and tucked in his shirt, as he always did, on his way to center court. Soon Edwards and Vinnie Johnson were in, facing Celtic starters who were already starting to soak through their jerseys. But the game stayed close and Daly called time again. Beating his clipboard against the heel of his hand, he bellowed, "It doesn't happen *automatically* at home! Put a *body* on somebody! Play *basketball*. Shit, that's what we get paid to do!" Edwards and Johnson looked pained, serious. They had less job security than any of the other prominent players—they were old men, in their early thirties.

When Edwards hit the floor, he almost immediately fouled Parish under the hoop. He blurted, "Oh, shit!" and cast a nervous look at Daly. Daly stared back. Next time down, as a shot went up, Edwards leaned over and drove his shoulder into Parish's chest, making the huge, iron-muscled Parish go "Ooooph" and lurch backward. Edwards got the rebound and passed to Johnson. Johnson sprinted toward the hoop, stopped so quickly it looked like he'd hit a wall, and flicked up a perfect jumper. He stared after the ball as it sailed through the net, and seemed to drift into a daydream.

"Hey, Great White Dope!" yelled Leon the Barber at McHale, "you're not jack shit without Bird."

Vinnie Johnson was in a trance. Daly had seen it coming and kept calling play number 15, a screen-and-roll that generally got V.J. a jump shot. Even after Boston started double-teaming Johnson, he kept scoring. He was in the zone of altered consciousness. He hadn't drifted into the graceful dance that Isiah Thomas did when Thomas found the zone, but Johnson had a more perfect shot than Thomas would ever have. With two minutes left in the game and Detroit up by 8, Daly took Johnson out. As he returned to the bench, every player stood up and slapped his hands. He had 30 points on 12 for 20 shooting.

With one minute left, the phone in front of Dobek rang. He picked it up and jammed his finger into his other ear. It was McCloskey, out scouting in Tucson. Detroit was up by 9 points; the game was over. Fans were leaving. But McCloskey stayed on the line until the horn sounded. Then he hung up immediately. As Dobek hung up, Daly led the team off the floor. Daly looked tired, and even more apprehensive than he had before the game. Now it was time for Detroit to go on its road trip. Everywhere they went, the other team would be keyed up, ready to show its fans that it could beat Number One.

McCloskey sat in the press room of the Seattle Coliseum with Chuck Daly and Brendan Suhr. In an hour they'd play the SuperSonics, the pivotal opponent on their road trip. McCloskey wanted to talk to his two coaches about John Salley.

"I think we've got to try to build his confidence back up," said McCloskey as he pushed a can of Diet Coke around the table. Suhr and Daly agreed. "He says he's not hurting anymore. I think he just needs some encouragement." The message, in part, was: Lay off the kid. Salley was a favorite target of Daly, because Daly was never positive if Salley was giving all he had to give. Salley seemed to take the bitching well. His college coach had once told him that he shouldn't worry about a coach yelling at him—he should worry when the coach *stopped* yelling. But beneath his Here's Johnny persona, Salley was pretty sensitive, and some of the criticism undercut the almost irrational confidence that a pro athlete had to have. So it was time to back off a little, and use the carrot instead of the stick.

They'd been playing superbly without Salley, which was one reason for his discomfort. Since Salley had cracked his ankle on February 22, Detroit was 13–2. On this road trip, they'd beaten Charlotte and Utah, to pull 2 games ahead of Cleveland. In the Utah win—a brutal, exhausting game that went into two overtimes—Salley hadn't scored. McCloskey wanted Salley to get plenty of playing time, even if he was rusty. These games were absolutely crucial, but it was even more important that all nine of their key players get in sync. If Detroit was going to win the Championship, it would be because of their depth.

Daly and Suhr left for the locker room. McCloskey, who was in Seattle to scout the NCAA Final Four tournament, finished his Coke. "I was thrilled with that Utah win," he said. "The guys are really starting to show their confidence. Utah was the most physical game I've seen all year—guys were really bopping each other. Looked like the Super Bowl. When Karl Malone is the smallest guy in the opposing front line, you've *got* to be physical. 'Cause Malone is a *bull*."

Beating Utah on the road was tremendously reassuring to McCloskey, because he thought Utah was the team Detroit would probably be facing in the NBA Finals—if Detroit could get past the Assassins. Utah was 4½ games behind L.A., but McCloskey thought they were better than L.A. Better mix of talent, and stronger. Beating Utah away from home also reassured McCloskey that Detroit had developed great mental strength. Now that the season's crunch time had hit, and now that they were number one again, psychological factors would be especially important. From here on out, pressure and battle fatigue would be tearing at them. If they lost their focus for even a couple of games, the other teams would rip them to shreds, and the Assassins would sweep past.

McCloskey pushed away his unfinished Coke and headed for his seat in the small Seattle stadium. Seattle GM Bob Whitsitt was pushing for a new arena, but local politics was holding him back. The stadium was not just small, but low-tech—when the game started, the cheap little scoreboard flashed on a crude silhouette of two hands clapping and said, "Clap. Clap." The fans ignored it. Detroit jumped off to an 8-point lead, playing in the desperate, obsessed style that Daly and McCloskey insisted on. Thomas was electric in the backcourt, running the fast little Sedale Threatt so hard that Threatt started to get a crazy look in his eyes. Finally, Threatt chopped Thomas on the arm and the ball jolted away. "Thomas just lost *hold* of it," Seattle announcer Bob Blackburn shouted into his mike.

Thomas ran up to referee Dick Bavetta and cried, "He hit my *arm!*" His face had the high-cheeked hysterical look that it took on when he felt he was getting screwed. Bavetta shook his head and turned away. Thomas ran back downcourt, but some of his steam seemed to be gone. The game was young, but it was already 11:00 P.M. back in Detroit. The Seattle bench was up, applauding. They had a safe playoff spot, but to them, this was a big game.

Seattle began to pull away. Mahorn struggled to hold the Seattle momentum down, pushing seven-foot, 240-pound Alton Lister out of the paint, but Lister, who had thighs thick and solid as sacks of concrete, fought back fiercely. At one point, Mahorn tried a short jumper, but Lister smashed the ball back down at Mahorn so hard that Mahorn looked shocked and dizzy. Xavier McDaniel swept the ball up, raced downcourt, and jammed. The scordboard made some squishy hisses that were supposed to be laser sounds and said, "Gettin' Hot." Thomas kept trying to speed up the Detroit offense but the rest of the players were dragging, and Seattle got farther and farther ahead. Just before the half, Seattle was up by 23. With 7 seconds left, there was a scuffle for a rebound, and all of a sudden Mahorn was heaving his open hands into the shoulders of seven-foot Olden Polynice. Polynice bounced away from the shove and stuck his chest in Mahorn's face. "C'mon, asshole!" Polynice yelled. Mahorn hauled off to swing, but Laimbeer caught his

fist. The half ended with an angry clot of players bunched around Polynice. Seattle GM Bob Whitsitt felt a twinge of admiration. The Pistons
were getting their butts kicked, but they'd contrived a fight at the most
opportune moment to pull Seattle's attention away from the game.
Whitsitt just hoped it didn't work.

In the locker room, Daly was pissed. "Any guy that quits won't play
the rest of the night!" he said. "Play hard—or I'm not gonna use you."

"If any of you guys quit," Thomas said, "I'm personally going to kick
your butt." He looked as if he meant it.

Laimbeer came out of the locker room with his face grim and rigid.
As soon as he got the ball, he charged the hoop and scored over Lister.
A minute later he made another low-post move—a rare event for him—
and scored again. Then he hit two consecutive 3-pointers. Then Aguirre
hit two straight 3-pointers. With all that, Detroit was still down 17. The
Piston defenders—exhausted but obsessed—began throwing themselves
after every ball, forcing turnovers and making almost impossible steals.
McCloskey was impressed. They were still way behind, but *they didn't
know they were doomed.* Salley came in and made an offensive foul. He
looked disgusted, and glanced over at Daly. Daly looked disgusted, too,
but he left Salley in.

Daly made an offensive change, having Dumars and Thomas run
straight at Seattle's big men, and they started scoring and picking up
fouls. Dumars and Thomas scored 10 straight, while the defense choked
Seattle off completely, and by the end of the third quarter the lead was
down to 7.

The lead stayed at 8 until eight minutes were left, then Thomas
missed a shot and Salley went after the ball as if his career depended on
it. He grabbed it and seemed to choke it as he leaped toward the hoop.
He brought the ball over his head then crashed it down through the rim,
looking angry and relieved at the same time, shoving it down so hard it
bounced six feet when it hit the floor. It was Salley's first basket in
almost six weeks. Daly called time and Mahorn came to the bench with
his forearm resting on Salley's neck, patting him affectionately on the
head. Daly got in the middle of them and said, "No offensive fouls!" He
started to look at Salley but looked back to his clipboard. "Billy, go
around like this"—Daly sketched a line on his slate. They broke up.

"Everybody, hands up!" yelled Salley as they took the floor.

"Everybody, hands up," echoed Daly. His voice was hoarse.

Thomas drove on massive Alton Lister and whipped by him for a
lay-up. Next time down, he did exactly the same thing. The lead was 4.
Then Dumars knifed in at six-foot-nine Derrick McKey and sailed past.
A minute later, Dumars lowered his head deep in the perimeter and

charged forward—this time McKey sagged off him, trying to block his route. Dumars stopped suddenly, and threw in a gently curving 3-pointer. Tie game. Seattle wanted time-out. Less than two minutes left. "Box out now," Daly said in the huddle. He looked at his clipboard and fell silent. For fifteen seconds he said nothing. Then Isiah started to trace a play on the board and Daly watched silently, nodding.

"Five seconds to get it over the line," said Mike Abdenour. Laimbeer's eyes were wide and intense. Salley was still in the game—his face was a blank.

They took the court and Laimbeer lifted a long jumper. It made a twang on the rim and hopped off at a crazy angle. Salley crouched slightly and exploded upward, his long arm twelve feet in the air. His fingertips found the ball and he nudged it to Dumars. Dumars shot it back to Salley and three Seattle defenders converged on him. Salley sprang off his toes and shot, but as he was letting go McKey tapped Salley's hands. Salley's arms flew off in different directions as he pantomimed a terrible blow. The whistle blew and he got his foul. He stood at the free-throw line, the first time he'd been there since February, shifting from one foot to the other, looking at the hoop, then at the floor, then at the hoop again. He wiped his palms on his shorts. He inhaled—shot—it dropped. He exhaled. Detroit by 1. 53 seconds. Salley spun the ball in his hands and squeezed it. His eyes fastened on the rim as the crowd behind the basket screamed and waved. He inhaled—shot—it dropped. His face stayed blank. McCloskey applauded.

Seattle ball. It went to Dale Ellis, third in the league in scoring with a 27.6 average. Ellis darted toward the hoop with Rodman in front of him. Whistle. Foul on Rodman. Rodman's mouth bent into a pained smile. It was his sixth foul, and he kept smiling as he walked to the bench. Ellis stepped confidently to the line, the crowd hushed, and he sank the first shot. Ellis was shooting .823 from the line. Detroit was up 1. 25 seconds. Ellis bounced the ball once, eyed the hoop, shot. Missed. Detroit grabbed the rebound and called time.

"They're gonna trap," Daly yelled over the crowd. "Horn, be ready to shoot. Keep the floor spread. Billy—in the middle. Move the ball."

"They got no time-outs," yelled Brendan Suhr.

With the inbounds pass, Detroit started whipping the ball in a wide box. Ellis and Lister dived after it, but they couldn't get it. The clock ran down. The fans at courtside screamed, "Foul! Foul!" But no one fouled. With 3 seconds left, Thomas tossed in an easy jumper. At the horn, Laimbeer threw his arms up in his Rocky pose, grinned and kept grinning. He ran up to Thomas and embraced him as if they'd just won the Championship.

McCloskey hurried down to the locker room, and ran into the team in the hallway. He slapped players on the back and shook hands. "I don't know if we'll ever again have two wins like the last two," he said to a small loose group of players. "I can't tell you how good I feel about the way you guys are playing." They beamed, but seemed vaguely uncomfortable. Even at a moment like this, McCloskey scared them.

In the locker room, Laimbeer yelled, *"Never quit! Never quit!"*

Isiah Thomas, who was going to watch the University of Michigan in the Final Four tomorrow, indulged in a burst of college spirit: "We're number one," he said, half kidding.

"We're number-*fucking*-one!" boomed Mahorn.

McCloskey sat down at a table just outside the locker room. "This is what I call a Remember Day," he said, his voice still husky with excitement. "There are certain things that you do in certain games that you don't want to ever forget. They should be remembered."

He was quiet for a moment, then said, "That was *great*. The guys are so mentally tough now."

Brendan Suhr walked up and McCloskey shook his hand. "I was just saying the guys are really mentally tough now," said McCloskey.

"They'd better be tough," said Suhr.

"How'd Cleveland do tonight?"

"They won," said Suhr. "So did Atlanta."

"You're right," said McCloskey. "They'd better be tough."

Sweat cut glossy vertical lines in Adrian Dantley's face. It dropped off his cheeks like tears. He had just had another fine game for Dallas. He'd scored 24 points, bringing his career total to well over 22,000—tenth highest in NBA history. But Dantley looked sad.

Dallas had lost again, but that wasn't why Dantley looked so bleak. For all practical purposes, Dallas's season was over; the loss was just one more log on the fire. Dantley was depressed because he was talking about Detroit. Alone in a dingy locker room in a strange town, he was remembering how his kids had gone to school right down the street from where he'd lived. And how he'd known everyone on a first-name basis. And he was remembering how the Pistons almost always seemed to win. His family was packing now, preparing to join him in Dallas. He was living in a hotel, and would stay there for the rest of the season. He hated that. He didn't like having to eat in restaurants, and he missed his wife and kids. Once again, he was a stranger wherever he went. He felt awkward and unsure in Dallas's offensive system.

"It feels like I'm starting all over again," he said softly. "It feels like the exhibition season. It's hard. I've been around a long time, and I'm kind of set in my own ways. And the team here—I only played two games before Donaldson tore his knee up." The Dallas offense was geared more toward him scoring than the Detroit system had been— "but it doesn't mean a thing if you don't win games." Dallas was not going to be winning many more games. Meanwhile, Detroit was charging toward a possible Championship.

"You don't like to get traded in the middle of a season," said Dantley, pulling off his shoes. "You don't like to get traded, period." Dantley said he didn't feel any bitterness toward McCloskey. "If I saw Jack, I feel like I could talk to him. I respect him. He's good at his job. It was a funny trade, though." His voice got even softer. "If I ever saw Jack, I would be nice to him."

He tugged off his socks and looked at his feet. "This trade wasn't a basketball trade. But I don't want to talk about the Pistons. . . . 'Cause I'm not a Piston no more."

There was pain all over Dantley's face. He was as desperate for the Championship as any of his former teammates. Recently, he'd returned to the Palace for Dallas's only game of the year there. Just before the game had started, he had gone up to Isiah Thomas, touched Thomas's hands, and had said something in Thomas's ear. The fans had cheered at the apparent reconciliation.

Dantley had said: "I'll never forgive you for what you did to me."

TEN

"On the Road"
The Fight for the
Home-Court Advantage

CARTWRIGHT! WHAT a son of a bitch he'd turned out to be! Nice guy, very bright, but he'd become a GM's delight: a son of a bitch under the boards. After nine years of being the wimpy Invisi-Bill in New York—where he'd lost his job and his chance for big long-term money to Patrick Ewing—Cartwright was now a born-again Badass. Chicago GM Terry Krause had given Cartwright a starting position and a fat contract, and Cartwright was hanging on to his big minutes and big money with bloody claws. It wasn't all just Cartwright's personal predilection, though. The Chicago fans would accept no less. Chicago was the biggest market in the Basketball Belt, but for years the team had been getting its butt kicked around the league and the fans were sick of it. Besides, they missed Charles Oakley, the player Krause had given up for Cartwright. Oakley had once pulled down 35 rebounds in a game, and—more important—he'd been the beat cop who'd kept Saint Michael free from harm. Cartwright knew the fans expected him to kick ass. More to the point, he knew Krause expected it.

So, when Cartwright got the ball and saw a little room under the basket in the first quarter of the April 7 Detroit game, he heaved his muscle into it. He beat Edwards, who was also about seven-one and 250, because for all his size Cartwright was quick as a cat. Now directly under the hoop, Cartwright pushed off from his toes, swinging the ball up with him, but—whoosh!—little Isiah Thomas jetted into the general vicinity of Cartwright's belly button and swatted the ball away. Then everything happened in a blur.

Cartwright's arm came flying in a windmill over his shoulder and cracked Thomas in the back of the head, knocking him downward and forward. Thomas stutter-stepped away from the blow—and came up *pissed*. Twice this season Cartwright had cut Thomas open with his hands and elbows, gouging slits under Isiah's eyes that had needed eleven stitches to close. As far as Thomas was concerned, this was more of the same, and he was *very* pissed. As Thomas came up, he karate-chopped Cartwright with the back of his arm, bouncing away from Cartwright with the force of the swing. Cartwright, his dark, intense eyes glowing with rage, leaped after Thomas. Thomas planted his feet and launched an explosive left uppercut with the full weight of his body. Thomas's knuckles crashed into the bottom of Cartwright's jaw—bone on bone—but Cartwright kept coming. Thomas landed another punch as Cartwright descended on him, knocking Thomas—sixty-five pounds lighter—flat on his ass. Cartwright kept coming. The other players froze for a fraction of a second, but Isiah's pal Aguirre jumped into Cartwright's blur of arms and smashed Cartwright back—away from Thomas—with a brutal jab to the throat, which was as close to Cartwright's face as he could reach. Cartwright reeled back and James Edwards rushed in from behind and caught Cartwright's right arm, which Cartwright was cocking for an assault on Aguirre. Aguirre waded forward and grabbed at Cartwright's other arm, breaking up Cartwright's momentum and rhythm. Dennis Rodman jumped into the nucleus of the fight. For a moment things started to slow down. But then Thomas threw himself back into Cartwright, and got knocked flat again. Thomas bounced off the floor and Cartwright catapulted out of the mob and grabbed Thomas around the neck with both hands. The Piston bench emptied. That meant an automatic league fine of $500 per player. Laimbeer and Mahorn flew in a huge wall of flesh at Cartwright, slamming into him hard enough to break Thomas away. Thomas was knocked to the floor again and Laimbeer and Mahorn grabbed Isiah's torso and yanked him out from under the growing pile of players. Salley leaned over the top of Thomas to scrape off anybody who was hanging on. As they retreated, Jordan walked behind them with his back to them, ensuring their safe withdrawal. Cartwright, now sandwiched between Rick Mahorn and meaty Chicago forward Horace Grant, was still lunging toward Thomas and yelling like a pro wrestler. Thomas, with Laimbeer's arm around him, stared blankly at Cartwright, slack-jawed, his eyes filmed over.

Thomas and Cartwright were ejected. Thomas walked down the steep, narrow stairs of Chicago Stadium into the moldy visiting-team locker room. He sat on a hard plank bench. As his adrenaline subsided, he began to feel a throb beat into his left hand, the one he'd smashed into Cartwright's jaw. After a few minutes, he asked the ball boy to bring him an ice bag. The Chicago team doctor ducked into the room and asked to see Thomas's hand, but Thomas refused. He was afraid there would be bad news and he didn't want to hear it.

They took a bus to O'Hare Airport and boarded Roundball One right after the game—another win, which gave them a paper-thin 1½-game edge over Cleveland. They had 9 games left, 2 against Cleveland.

Thomas's hand ached during the entire flight. When they touched down at 2:00 A.M., Thomas and trainer Mike Abdenour headed for Harper-Grace Hospital, where they met Dr. Eugene Horrell, who'd treated Joe Dumars's broken hand. To begin his diagnosis, Dr. Horrell pinched Thomas's hand. A jolt of pain ripped through Thomas's arm. As the hand was X-rayed, Thomas kept trying to convince himself it didn't really hurt. The playoffs were three weeks away.

The X rays confirmed that the hand was broken. Thomas had fractured his second metacarpal, the bone above the palm that attaches to the first knuckle of the index finger. Dr. Horrell told Thomas that he'd have to put the hand in a cast, and that Thomas would be out for up to eight weeks. Thomas didn't believe him. "You can put a cast on my hand," he said, "but I'm playing against Cleveland on Wednesday."

Horrell looked at him doubtfully. "Am I going to die if I play?" asked Thomas.

"No."

"Then I'm playing." He couldn't believe a sore hand could keep him out eight weeks.

Horrell pinched the hand again. This time, Thomas believed him.

Jack McCloskey was in a dead sleep in his room at the Waterfront Hotel in Portsmouth, Virginia. He was attending the first of the year's two biggest showcase tournaments for college players. It was 3:00 A.M. The phone rang.

Mike Abdenour was on the line. "I've got some good news and some bad news," said Abdenour. "The good news, obviously, is that we won the Chicago game."

Obviously. McCloskey had known that for hours. He also knew that Abdenour wouldn't call at 3:00 A.M. because of good news.

"The bad news," said Abdenour, "is that Isiah has a break in his left hand and will probably be out two to three weeks. Dr. Horrell says it could be more. But Isiah wants to play and doesn't think it's that serious."

The call was over quickly. McCloskey was shaken. He felt as if there was no justice in the world. The year before last they'd missed the NBA Finals because of one bad pass, and last year Isiah and Mahorn had been crippled for the last game of the Finals. "You only get so many chances," he thought to himself. It especially hurt that it had happened during a fight, instead of during play. That damn Bad Boy gimmick was starting to haunt them. Now every team had to show the Pistons how tough they were.

In a matter of minutes McCloskey was trying to sort out the damage and solve it. But how? Ennis Whatley? Right now, Ennis Whatley was at the top of McCloskey's list of point guards to bring in if disaster struck. Whatley was living in the Washington, D.C., area, not playing for anyone—availability was no problem. The six-three guard had had a couple of decent years in the NBA—in 1984 and 1987 he'd averaged about 8.5 points, and his rookie year he'd averaged 8.2 assists. He was an excellent ball-handler and had once been a bright prospect, as the thirteenth pick in the first round. But he wasn't much of a shooter and had been waived by several teams. The year before, he'd played for the Mississippi Jets in the CBA. He was, in short, a body.

McCloskey tried to go back to sleep. It was gut-wrenching to be away from the team at a time like this, but this last scouting trip of the year was crucial—not to the team, but to the franchise. As he lay in bed, he kept thinking about Isiah Thomas. And Ennis Whatley. And John Long—thank God for John Long.

McCloskey did not want to lose the home-court advantage to Cleveland. Cleveland was 35–3 at home: almost unbeatable.

After several hours, as the sun began to clear the darkness, McCloskey fell asleep.

"See number twenty-three there," said Will Robinson. He pointed out a thick-muscled white kid to Jack McCloskey as they sat in a high school gym in Orlando, Florida, two days after the Thomas injury. "He reminds me of a player I won the state championship with against Cazzie Russell of Pontiac, who hadn't lost a game all year. I told him, whenever we get the ball, you go *away* from it. Won the *state championship* that way." McCloskey grinned. He loved Robinson's war stories, the older the better. Robinson, at eighty-two, was by far the oldest man in the gym, but McCloskey thought he had the best eye for young talent of anybody there. Which was saying a lot—the best basketball men in the world were crowded into a small, steep waterfall of bleachers, study-ing the kids they'd be gambling their future on in the 1989 draft. They'd just seen most of them in Portsmouth, and were here at the Orlando All-Star Classic for one last look. Just in front of McCloskey, Robinson, and Stan Novak was Bill Russell, now GM of Sacramento, and a few feet from Russell was L.A. GM Jerry West. Russell was bleating out bursts of high-pitched laughter as he talked with his scouts, while West examined the players on the floor with a cold, analytical stare. They'd both been superstars, but only West still radiated superstar arrogance. Chicago's gregarious Jerry Krause was working the room, feeling out what he could get for his lottery pick, as Cleveland's Wayne Embry, huge and solemn, watched from the highest row in the gym. The players were practicing now for games on Friday, but they knew the practices were as closely scrutinized as the games, and it showed in their brittle, overanx-ious movement. Once in a while, the players who weren't in action would steal looks at the bleachers, trying to figure out who the GMs were. It wasn't too hard. A few of them, like Denver's Pete Babcock and Seattle's Bob Whitsitt, were young, between thirty-five and forty-five. But the majority were in their fifties, were tall former players, were wearing several hundred bucks worth of excruciatingly casual sports-wear, and were gaping at the floor. Almost all of them, with the excep-tion of L.A.'s West and Boston's Jan Volk, had been working many years toward a goal they would never achieve—the Championship. Detroit's front office team was easy to spot. It was by far the oldest, and had been working—in vain—the longest.

McCloskey had arranged earlier in the morning to have Mike Abde-nour call him at 1:00 P.M. tomorrow, right after Abdenour and Isiah Thomas saw Dr. Horrell again. McCloskey had to make up his mind soon about Ennis Whatley. He was still jumpy and upset about the injury, but he knew that Thomas would play as soon as humanly pos-sible. Thomas had an ungodly ability to endure pain, and he was as obsessed with the Championship as McCloskey was. McCloskey had just called Thomas, and had cautioned him to follow Horrell's lead. Sportswriters often accused management of pressuring players to come back from injuries too quickly, but that was just headline hype. GMs put the franchise first, so they had to use their players as long-term assets. It was usually the players, with their Just a Game fervor, who came back too soon.

On the floor, a powerful kid with muscles wrapped around his arms like thick ropes got the ball at the perimeter, hesitated, then drove to the basket. "That's Dyron Nix," said Stan Novak. Novak had his program tucked under the arm of his sport shirt; he knew all the players by face.

He'd been following them around the country since they'd been freshmen. "He could have taken the perimeter shot," Novak said to McCloskey. "He's probably reluctant. I'd have been more impressed if he'd put it up."

McCloskey, lost in thought, didn't respond; then he turned suddenly to Novak and nodded briskly. "Have you talked to Nix?" he asked.

"Not really, Jack."

Dyron Nix had a million-dollar problem. He had the stats and the body to be a first-round pick, which meant guaranteed money at about $250,000 to $400,000 annually for several years. But he had horrible word-of-mouth among the basketball men. The story on him was that he was lazy and selfish. He'd started his senior year at the University of Tennessee as a golden boy, a king of the playground, with comparisons to Dale Ellis and Bernard King. He'd averaged 22 points as a junior and had led his conference in rebounding as a sophomore. Tennessee had won 11 of its first 12 games this year, Nix had built a 20-plus scoring average, and the scouts and agents had been coming out of the woodwork. But Tennessee started losing, and Nix got the blame. He was quoted as saying, "If you don't give me the ball, you don't win in this league." Everybody thought he had the gleam of NBA money in his eyes, and didn't give a damn about anything else. His coach benched him, and the GMs around the league started telling each other that they were no longer interested—but this time, they weren't bullshitting. They already had plenty of arrogant young millionaires on their hands. NBA chief scout Marty Blake issued a statement on Nix: "The guy is a great talent," he said. "If I had his ability, I'd make a million a year. It's up to him." In other words: Head Case. Kiss of death. After awhile, the scouts stopped visiting and the agents trickled away.

Now Nix was making a last stab at rehabilitating his reputation. Before practice he'd said, "No, I *don't* have a bad attitude. *Yes,* I want to play *basketball.*" He denied the quote "If you don't give me the ball . . ." and he said he "never *once* whined or showed disgust" about getting benched.

But McCloskey wasn't too impressed by what players said. "You always hear the right answers," he said, straining against the hard bleacher. "Occasionally you can tell something, if the guy is bordering on being obnoxious, but usually you don't question him. You just rely on your talents of observing character—how does he react out on the court, and how is he with his teammates and coaches?" Last week in Portsmouth, McCloskey had been very impressed with the character of an obscure little guard named Tim Hardaway. During a time-out, Hardaway had gathered his team around him and said, "Defense! Defense!

Defense!" Just those three words. But the three words had told Mc-Closkey more about the kid than he'd have learned by listening to him spout an hour of mantalk. While everybody else had been worrying about running up their own numbers, Hardaway had been trying to *win the damn game*. McCloskey wasn't the only one who'd noticed. Hardaway won the tournament's MVP award, and had probably moved up from the second round to the first. He had, in other words, gone from the league minimum $100,000 salary—none of it guaranteed—to guaranteed money of $250,000–$400,000 for several years. And his gain hadn't just been in his first contract, but probably over his entire career. Second-round picks tended to get cut, because the team had no investment in them. They tended to end up teaching gym and talking about their four glorious weeks in an NBA summer league.

"When it comes time to zero in on five or six guys," said McCloskey, "we'll get some more information. We may hire a professional investigator. Once when we did that, we found out that a guy had been involved in purchasing some drugs. So we didn't get involved with him."

"What do you think of Horton, Jack?" asked Novak.

"Seems to be having trouble getting his shot in the crowd," McCloskey said. "He doesn't have the bounce to jump over people. He has to muscle to do it, and I don't know if he's big enough to get away with it in our league. I don't think so." At Iowa, Ed Horton had been considered a real bruiser at six-eight and 235—but here, for the first time in his life, he was among his physical peers. None of the players had ever been a face in the crowd before, and it was shocking to them. Besides stiffer competition, they were playing for the first time with a 24-second shot clock instead of a 45-second clock, with a 3-point line that was four feet farther out, and with no zone defense. So they all looked a little shell-shocked.

Except for Stacey King. The big Oklahoma center was cruising around the hoop like it was the basket over his garage, having fun and acting like a king of the playground. Though about 80 percent of the players who would constitute the 1989 first round were in this gym, King was the only possible number one pick who was here. "A lot of people think that it isn't that smart for the top four or five players to come here," said Novak. "Because they have too much to lose and not enough to gain. But I think King made a smart move. It's not clear-cut who the number one or two pick will be, like it was last year with Danny Manning. The top pick could be King, or it could be Sean Elliott, Danny Ferry, Pervis Ellison, or Glen Rice. And whoever it is, it'll mean millions of dollars in that first contract. King's putting it on the line, and I think it'll pay off for him."

"But it's all academic, as far as we're concerned," said Robinson. "Very few of these guys are gonna be around when we pick." He looked sad. In a real sense, he was being punished for his skill and hard work by the draft system, which rewarded the badly run franchises.

"Pat Durham might be there when we pick," said Novak.

Robinson's eyes zeroed in on the stringy forward. They'd stopped running the floor now and were being tested for their vertical leap. Durham crouched beneath a pole with an ascending series of horizontal slats attached near the top. The goal was to touch the highest possible slat. Durham jumped, and scored a 32-inch vertical leap. His jump was ordinary by NBA standards, but it was bolstered by the fact that Durham, standing flat-footed, could reach 8 feet, 9 inches into the air. When a 32-inch jump was added to that, his hand was 11 feet, 5 inches off the ground—not bad. Durham was able to reach so high flat-footed because he had a long "wingspan"—the length of his outspread arms. The average person has a wingspan that's about the same as his or her height. But NBA players commonly have wingspans that exceed their heights by up to half a foot. In other words, long arms. Wingspan was something the scouts had to know, since a player's real height wasn't where the top of his head was, but where the tip of his hand was.

It was Villanova guard Doug West's turn to jump. "West might be there when we pick," Novak said to Robinson. West crouched, jumped, and batted the slats at 11 feet, 6 inches—an inch higher than Durham, even though he was an inch shorter.

Anthony Cook, a six-nine forward from Arizona, took his position under the bar, took a breath, coiled, then exploded upward. He looked as if the floor had suddenly flexed and heaved him, and he kept going and going until he swatted the slats at 12 feet, 1 inch. His body recoiled as he hit the floor, then he looked to see how he'd done. 37-inch vertical leap. Best of the day. His 12-foot, 1-inch jump would be the highest of any player in the tournament. One of his buddies slapped his hands and he sauntered off. The gazes of several GMs followed him.

"Cook will be there when we pick," Novak said to Robinson. Novak knew there was no way in hell Cook would be there, unless McCloskey traded up.

"Get the hell out," said Robinson, jabbing his elbow into Novak's ribs.

"Take it easy, Coach," said McCloskey. He looked at Robinson and Novak like a father warning his sons. McCloskey had a lot on his mind—specifically, the Cleveland game tomorrow night.

Right now, they were 3 games ahead of Cleveland, after a win last night against Milwaukee. But in the battle for home-court advantage in the playoffs, their lead was really just 2 games, because in the event of a tie, Cleveland got the nod, since they were leading in the season-long head-to-head competition. So if they lost against Cleveland tomorrow, their real lead would only be 1 game, with 6 left to play. They'd be locked into a dogfight finale. It would be a battle, McCloskey believed, that they had better win. Cleveland had kicked their butts all year, and if Detroit had to face Cleveland in the playoffs, Cleveland would be excruciatingly hard to beat without the home-court advantage. McCloskey was guessing that they'd face Cleveland in the Eastern Finals, and that it would go to the seventh game. He wanted that game to be in the Palace. With Auker at the control board and Leon the Barber behind the Cleveland bench. Cleveland was 35–3 at their Coliseum, but Detroit was 33–4 in the Palace.

There was also the West to worry about. McCloskey was convinced Detroit would have won the Championship last year with the home-court advantage, and he wanted to be certain they had it this year. At the moment, they had a fairly safe lead over L.A. in won-lost percentage, but it wasn't L.A. that scared McCloskey. It was Utah. They were huge and powerful, and their mix was extraordinary: They had speed with John Stockton, defense with Mark Eaton, scoring with Karl Malone, and bench strength with Thurl Bailey.

But Utah was next month's nightmare. For tonight: Cleveland. Without Isiah.

Wayne Embry, GM of the Cleveland Cavaliers, negotiated his six-foot-eight, 300-pound body into an easy chair one buttock at a time. Embry was making a brief stop in the lobby of Orlando's Buena Vista Palace Hotel, where all the GMs and players were staying, before catching the Detroit-Cleveland game at a sports bar. Around him, vacationers in Mickey Mouse T-shirts were disembarking for Disney World, about a mile away, looking relaxed and happy. Embry fit right in. His face was calm and content, giving no hint that he was a GM on his way to a career-shaking game. "It's just another game," said Embry. They all said that—standard mantalk. But Embry *meant* it. That was the philosophical foundation of his franchise: It isn't whether you win or lose, but how you play the game. Players at other franchises would laugh their asses off at that. But nobody in Cleveland laughed at Wayne Embry. The six feet, eight inches and 300 pounds helped, and so did the fact that he'd been a five-time All-Star and premier NBA butt-kicker. But most of his credibility came straight from management success. He'd built Milwaukee into one of the best franchises in the league, and now he'd done it with Cleveland. "I think our players will play the best they can," he said. No emphasis, no dramatics. "They'll want to win the game. I can guarantee you that Lenny Wilkens will not say, 'Guys, we've got to win this game.' My guess is, he'll say 'Fellas, this is when it's fun. Go out and do the best you can and have fun doing it.' The fans or press might view this as a must-win situation for us, but we don't. That's not our agenda." Nor was Embry preoccupied, as the Cleveland press was, with the notion that Cleveland had peaked a month ago, and now wasn't prepared for the playoffs. "If you have to prepare a team for the playoffs," he said, gazing out the window at water splashing peacefully into a fountain, "then you've got the wrong team. If you have to prepare a player mentally for the playoffs, then you've got the wrong player." Embry wasn't paying much attention to who his first-round opponent would be. "It could be Chicago. Or Philadelphia, Atlanta, or Milwaukee, or it could be Boston. It doesn't matter. If you want to win the Championship, you've got to beat them all." He wasn't even too concerned about losing the home-court advantage. "If you think you'll automatically win at home, you're wrong. You just try to go out on your own floor with the attitude that, we damn well better win because we want to satisfy the people that support us." One thing that did worry him, though, was Detroit's experience. "There's no substitute for experience. You have to have gone through it at least once to understand the level of intensity in the playoffs." He'd worked hard as hell to find players who had the character to overcome inexperience, and he thought he'd found them in people like Price and Daugherty—the Good Boys. But time would tell.

Embry hoisted himself out of the chair—first one leg, then the other, then a mighty two-handed heave as the torso lifted off. He disappeared into the happy, slow-moving crowd.

On the far side of the hotel's grotto, between its two swimming pools, Bob Ferry, GM of the Washington Bullets, sat musing over a very different set of concerns. His team was playing too *well*. It looked like they might squeak into the playoffs and miss the lottery. That had special meaning for Ferry, because his son, Duke star Danny Ferry, would be in the lottery, and Ferry was dying to get a crack at him. Ferry wouldn't admit to a desire to see his team lose a few games and sink back into lottery position. That was thought-crime in the NBA. You were supposed to want to win every game, no matter how badly it screwed you in the long run. The ethic was ridiculous, of course, particularly for GMs, whose responsibilities were long-term. It was the reigning code of honor, though, and nobody challenged it.

But Ferry edged toward heresy by predicting that his team would blow it. "I still think we'll be a lottery team," said Ferry, a huge guy, naked from the waist up, with a chest about the size of a sheet of plywood. "I don't think we can catch Boston because they've got a much easier schedule than us."

Ferry was already satisfied with the season. He'd let go of Moses Malone and Manute Bol to rebuild the team, and had started from scratch with a bunch of no-names like forty-third pick Dave Feitl and disappointing Mark Alarie. At the beginning of the season, he'd thought they'd be lucky to win 25 games, and had issued disaster warnings to the fans. But coach Wes Unseld had made his pack of strays as feisty and nasty as he'd been in his playing days, and now they were knocking more talented teams flat. It showed how much chemistry and mix could do. They were hovering around the .500 level, and had already won more games than they ever had with Million Dollar Moses. But enough was enough. Ferry had already had his thrill of victory for the year—watching Danny lead Duke into the NCAA championship game—and the best thing now would be to build some future into the franchise. What Ferry needed was height. The only guy he had over six-nine was seven-one Feitl, and Feitl had a vertical leap that lifted him to about seven-two. Ferry needed somebody about the size of, say, Danny Ferry.

To get that, though, his team would have to put together a good losing streak. And that was something Bob Ferry couldn't hope for. At least not out loud. Ferry squinted into the white glare of sun and rubbed half a bottle of suntan lotion onto his huge chest. It was early evening, an hour before the Detroit-Cleveland game, but Florida's spring sun was still high and burning.

Jack McCloskey settled into his table at the sports bar with Will Robinson, Stan Novak, and his wife Leslie. The Detroit-Cleveland game was just starting as they ordered some food. There were a half-dozen screens showing various games, and everywhere he looked there were basketball men—Bob Zuffelato of the Bucks, Bob Whitsitt of Seattle, Dave Checketts and Scott Layden of Utah, and Bob Weinhauer of Philadelphia. Wayne Embry was downstairs.

Vinnie Johnson, starting in place of Isiah, was on fire, and he led Detroit to an early lead. But Mark Price started hitting perimeter jumpers and 3-pointers and as the half neared it was very close. McCloskey couldn't tell exactly what the score was because it was too noisy to hear the announcer, and the bar was picking up a straight satellite feed so the score wasn't flashed onto the screen. Not knowing the score had McCloskey doubly nervous. But then, just before the half, he saw something that made his muscles unknot. Isiah Thomas, wearing a black orthopedic splint on his hand, entered the game. McCloskey knew that the doctor had allowed Thomas to suit up, but he'd had no idea that Thomas would try to play. It gave McCloskey a warm feeling to see Isiah out there, catching hardball passes that must hurt like hell—it was reassuring to see how completely Thomas shared his obsession. To McCloskey, it wasn't just another game, and it wasn't to Thomas, either. Isiah's appearance gave the Pistons a lift. As the game wore on, they started to pull away. Toward the end, though, McCloskey still wasn't sure how big the lead was. Then Cleveland made a run. McCloskey kept thinking, "Jesus, how close *are* they?" But then he saw Lenny Wilkens put in Chris Dudley, one of his scrubs. He breathed out a heavy sigh. Then Fennis Dembo came in. McCloskey knew it was over.

Without any numbers being flashed on the screen, McCloskey knew the crucial statistics: They were 3½ games ahead of Cleveland, and 2½ ahead in the fight for the home-court advantage. There were 6 games left, including games in Cleveland and New York, where they hadn't won all year. Detroit had won 22 out of their last 24 games—the best indication yet of the importance of the Trade. They had won 17 games in a row at home. They were 58–18, 40 games over .500 for the first time in franchise history.

Clearly, this was the best team McCloskey had ever been associated with. It had a good shot at winning more games than all but six or seven teams in NBA history.

But nothing was certain. Not at all. With Isiah hurt, they could easily lose the home-court advantage to Cleveland next week, and if that happened . . .

McCloskey wished he were home.

ELEVEN

"It'll Never Be Over" The Season Ends

THE MORNING after the Cleveland game came with a hard, cheerful glint of sun. McCloskey met Novak and Robinson early and drove their "invisible" rent-a-car to the high school gym. The grass was glossy with dew and the wetness cooled the breeze. But as they settled into the bleachers, the gym began to collect a steamy heat. They didn't talk about the Cleveland game. They didn't even talk about the race against Cleveland for the division title, which would be settled within a week. That was for the fans to talk about. They had to worry about the franchise, not the team.

On the floor, Ricky Blanton, a six-foot-seven forward who'd been a butt-kicking rebounder and power scorer at Louisiana State, drove toward the hoop with one of the muscle moves that had terrorized the Southeastern Conference. He hit Stacey King like a bug thumping a windshield. He picked himself up, his eyes rattling around his head. "Blanton's a bastard size," said Will Robinson, trying to lie back on the bleachers. "He doesn't really have the body for an NBA front line, and he can't play the backcourt, doesn't have the quickness."

Tim Hardaway, the little guard that McCloskey had come to like at Portsmouth, got the ball at the perimeter and floated up a knuckleball—it had almost no rotation. The ball plopped through the net and Hardaway watched without expression, skipping backward. "He seems to be part of the ball," said Robinson. McCloskey beamed approval at Hardaway. He had no need for another guard, so there was no point in trying to hide how he felt from the other GMs. A few feet away, standing on the floor by the door, NBA scout Marty Blake said, "Hardaway can *play* in this league. Most definitely." Blake, a fairly small guy with thick glasses and hair that seemed to have a mind of its own, looked happy. He'd organized the tournament, and loved to see his unheralded players do well. "Feelin' good, Marty?" asked Bill Russell.

Blake nodded vigorously. "I like the hotel," he said. "The towels are so fluffy I'm going to have a hard time getting my suitcase closed." Russell bleated out a laugh. McCloskey smiled. He'd had a good night. For the first time in this long, difficult season, the Pistons had a strong hold on first place. There were only six games left, and one was with Cleveland. Win that one, and they'd probably have a lock on first.

Though the win over Cleveland—and Isiah's appearance—had helped McCloskey relax, he still kept his eyes glued to the game. He'd been scouting some of these players for years, but he'd never seen them play against top competition. He'd scouted Rick Mahorn at this tournament, and also Dumars, Rodman, and Salley. Salley, in fact, had been the MVP of the tournament in 1986, much to McCloskey's disgust. McCloskey had had the twelfth pick that year, and thought he'd be able to get Salley with it, because Salley had had a mediocre senior year. But most of that hope had evaporated with Salley's play in the tournament. It had been a deep draft, though. The first to go had been Daugherty, then Len Bias, Chris Washburn, Chuck Person, Kenny Walker, William Bedford, and Roy Tarpley. It had been a bad year for druggies: Bias, Washburn, Bedford, and Tarpley. The eighth pick had been Ron Harper, but then Chicago's Jerry Krause had screwed up and had taken seven-foot Brad Sellers—GMs were always suckers for height. Johnny Dawkins had gone eleventh, and that had left not only Salley but John Williams, who was stronger than Salley and also a better scorer. McCloskey had been building defense, though, and wanted speed and shot-blocking, so he'd taken Salley. Had it been a smart move? Hard to tell. Salley had been available for trade most of the year. And the night before, Daly hadn't put him in until the last minute. With Fennis Dembo. Obviously, Daly was fed up.

An agent came over and huddled with McCloskey. He had some anonymous player who was serving time in the CBA. After he'd left, McCloskey turned to Stan Novak. "He was looking for guaranteed money for next fall," he said, shaking his head. Novak rolled his eyes. "I told him he could come to fall camp and we'd take a look."

A local sportswriter leaned over and asked Will Robinson if many of the players had picked agents yet.

Robinson shook his head. "The agents are picking them," he said.

Agent Bill Pollak sat in the lobby of the Buena Vista Palace, watching the commerce carnival unfold. Besides sunburned parents in Mickey Mouse T-shirts, the lobby featured two general types: huge, graceful postadolescents, mostly black, and sharp-looking guys sporting booth-tans, hundred-dollar slacks, and bright knit shirts. At the moment, one of them was hard on the heels of head-case Dyron Nix, taking two steps to Nix's one, saying, "Dyron, if I could . . . Dyron . . . Dyron . . ."

"Just a sec, man," said Nix, stepping into an elevator. "Gotta go see my man."

"Great talking to you, Dyron." The elevator door clamped shut and the guy—a "lobby rat," an agent who worked the lobby for clients—started stalking another kid. Pollak, president of Professional Management Associates, watched the scene with a mix of horror and amusement on his face. A major trial of two sports agents convicted of bribery had just concluded yesterday, and Pollak, an attorney, was sensitive about the integrity of his profession. "Some of these guys are running around after anybody who'll talk to them," he said. "We'd rather represent a few players who have the character and attitude that we like to work with. We don't do a shotgun approach." Pollak, who represented Dennis Rodman, Chris Mullin, Charles Oakley, and about a dozen others, had worked in the Carter White House, negotiating with Iran for the release of United States hostages. So he was used to a little higher road than many of the agents. "Agents scout players just like the teams scout players," he said. "An attorney has only his time and expertise to sell, and I don't have time to help players who don't want to help themselves. We look for players who really want to work hard at this." But it was hard to tell who was serious. "You've heard all the answers before, so it's a question of really looking into the eyes to find out where he's truly coming from. The words themselves—we've heard them all a thousand times." Learning to spout the right kind of mantalk, in fact, was part of what Pollak worked on with his clients. "We will prepare a player to be interviewed by an NBA team; they know it and we know it."

Pollak wasn't recruiting any players in Orlando. He'd come to Florida over the weekend to see Florida State senior George McCloud. He'd stopped in Orlando because that week it was the epicenter of world basketball. McCloud, an excellent two-guard who was a possible lottery pick, had called about a week ago in a panic. He'd been scheduled to play in Orlando, but he'd screwed up his ankle and couldn't make the knife-sharp lateral cuts pro players had to. He was afraid his dreams of fame and fortune, which had seemed so imminent, had suddenly become illusion. Pollak was surprised that McCloud had called, because he wasn't a client. Pollak had previously talked to McCloud, but then McCloud had been squired up to Boston by agent Bob Woolf to meet Bird—Larry, to McCloud—and get a taste of a $4-million life-style. Pollak had figured that that was probably the end of that—but McCloud had called, apparently feeling he could trust Pollak with sensitive information. Pollak had gotten McCloud a good specialist and physical therapist, and the injury had turned out to be minor. So over the past weekend, Pollak had gone to see McCloud, had met his family, and signed him. The signing wasn't just gratitude. McCloud knew Pollak had just gotten the very ordinary Rony Seikaly $800,000 annually over five years from the local Miami Heat franchise.

The McCloud signing meant big money to Pollak's agency. If McCloud went anywhere from number six to number eight, he'd be in for about $650,000 per year. But with the salary cap going up in August, that figure could escalate to anywhere from $750,000 to $900,000. If Pollak got the usual 4–5 percent commission, his take would be somewhere around $30,000 to $45,000 per year for several years. With that figure multiplied by about fifteen players, Pollak had a good thing going. Of course, some of his players, like seventy-fifth pick Chris Dudley, made less, but guys like Chris Mullin—whose contract was expiring— were gold mines.

Pollak also had an inside line on Illinois junior Nick Anderson. Anderson was eligible for early entry into the draft, but Pollak had just advised him to stay in school. Pollak believed in education. He also believed Anderson would be a lottery pick as a senior.

Pollak had to go up to his room to take a call from Italy. One of his players, John Fox, was playing for an Italian team that had just lost a big game at the end of the season. The owner had decided to fine each player $4,000 and make them practice for a month as punishment. "John Fox will be home next week," declared Pollak. "He'll be fishing in Pennsylvania, and he'll get his money. I'm going to let the owner know in no uncertain terms that he does not have the right to fine the player—the player will receive 100 percent of his money. And I'll tell him that if there *is* a problem, the player will not be back next year. Though I'd rather not play that trump card."

As Pollak headed for the elevator, he ran into Jack McCloskey, who was on his way to the tennis court in white shorts and a white knit shirt. "Good game against Cleveland," said Pollak.

"Thanks, Bill." They shook hands, for no particular reason. Earlier in the year, during the negotiation of Rodman's contract, they'd been adversaries. But now McCloskey's gain was Pollak's gain. Pollak also negotiated Rodman's endorsements, and endorsements could be substantial for a player on a Championship team.

One of the lobby rats caught sight of McCloskey and scurried over, but McCloskey saw him coming and ducked out the door.

Twenty miles north of Disney World was the real world. It was old Orlando, the Orlando that had never been touched by the amusement park boom. Little cement-block houses, shaped like mobile homes, squatted in sandy, weedy yards that sloped down to streets that had no sidewalks or gutters. It was Darryl Dawkins's old neighborhood. And his agent's current neighborhood.

The Reverend W. D. Judge, who had an office in a one-story concrete-block apartment house, sat behind his desk. His eyes were heavy with age and his movements were slow and in right angles, like an automaton in Disney World. The Reverend Mr. Judge had lived in this neighborhood for thirty years, serving as the pastor of the Antioch Baptist Church. When he'd first taken his position, he'd met Darryl Dawkins's grandmother, the woman who'd raised Dawkins. "She was a beautiful woman. The church only had 'bout seven or eight members and the only money I would get would be mebbe five or six dollars a week, but ever day at noon I would be at Darryl's grandmother's house and they'd have a special tray set out for the preacher. She would say, 'Reverend, don't leave, because I am cooking now.' I wasn't *going* to leave, because I wanted to *eat*. Darryl and his two brothers would be out in the yard playin' basketball with a barrel hoop nailed on a piece of board, fussin' and fightin'. Dribbling on the *sand*—it's amazing what the black man can do! Darryl was extra large. When Darryl was in high school he was the most sought after player in the country. Every agent, every NBA team in the country was trying to get to Darryl. I wanted Darryl to go to college, but because of the economic condition of his family, Darryl made a decision to go pro. It was not a *wise* decision. Because if you look at what Darryl has today, he was not able to protect himself financially—because of immaturity, and college would have helped that, from an educational point of view."

The Reverend Mr. Judge had become Dawkins's first agent in 1975. "He wanted me, his pastor, to be his agent. I am Darryl's spiritual father. I love Darryl and Darryl loves me. I strongly recommended that he not sign with the Seventy-sixers. I wanted every pro team to make an offer and then a decision would be made. I was overruled by the family. They thought the Seventy-sixers were offering enough."

Judge had gradually faded out of Dawkins's professional life, but had reentered it the previous year, when Dawkins's wife had committed suicide. "Darryl went into a shell, and called me and told me he needed me, and I immediately flew to New Jersey." It was shortly thereafter that he began negotiating with McCloskey. But now those days were over. Dawkins was no longer a Piston, and never again would be. Judge didn't think McCloskey had been fair with Dawkins, but that was blood under the bridge. Judge's current concern was Dawkins himself. Judge had made the deal with the Italian team, but he was no longer Dawkins's agent.

"I am a praying preacher. I have been guided by the Holy *Spirit*, and you would be surprised in the manner God uses me. The contract I wrote up for the Italian team was done through prayer and meditation. I was up at three o'clock in the morning, communing with God and sitting and talking with God, and as the Lord would reveal things to me I would make notes. I didn't do it for the commission, I did it because of my love and concern for Darryl."

The Reverend Mr. Judge sighed deeply. He wished he were still Dawkins's agent. He leaned back in his desk chair. "Darryl is still my son. I am Darryl's spiritual father."

Nonetheless, Dawkins was on his own now. Far from home.

It was just hours before tournament time—the end of the week—but Atlanta Hawk GM Stan Kasten had only recently arrived in Orlando. Kasten was also GM of the Atlanta Braves, Ted Turner's other sports franchise, and Kasten had his hands full. Even so, Kasten had built one of the teams McCloskey feared most—and one that Detroit would probably soon have to beat to make the Finals. At the moment, Kasten was sitting on a couch in the lobby of the hotel, wearing Bermuda shorts and a short-sleeved shirt. Scratching his mostly bald head, bemusement on his face, he looked sort of like a miniature Joe Garagiola, and not like one of the most powerful executives in sports.

Kasten had dramatically rebuilt his team, and now it was time for the payoff. But they were 11 games out of first place, and the press and fans were howling. Kasten found it ridiculous. For one thing, they were 11 back in the Central Division, possibly the best division in NBA history. Five out of the Central's six teams were poised to win 50 games, and Detroit was on the verge of winning 60. Atlanta was 48–29—a hell of a record—with a 5-game winning streak. "Last night," said Kasten, "we were a game behind the Knicks, and they're supposed to be having this *magical* season. We lead the Eastern Conference in injuries this year and we're still playing six hundred ball. So they're ready to execute us all—not just fire us—we have to be *executed*. That's what sports is like. It's one thing to be in business and try to build up a customer base, but in this business I've got twenty-six teams of very bright people trying to beat my brains out, so I think if you're over five hundred you're ahead of the game. It's unfair, but it's not going to change."

Kasten had been criticized for putting together a great box-score and highlight-film team—a team of superstars—without enough concern for the mix and chemistry. But Kasten's team, which he'd built to be a strong playoff team, was now peaking at the right time, and Kasten felt that his approach had been vindicated. "The first thing you have to worry about is talent," he said. "Chemistry is second. All I know is, if I have the talent, then I can put it all together and see how the guys get along and see how the flow is offensively and defensively. If I don't have the talent, I don't have a chance at all on this level, because talent is where it starts."

Kasten's biggest worry was going into the playoffs without the injured Kevin Willis. "We don't have our tough guy. Our force. But we've played better lately and we still have the talent to win the Championship. Although Detroit is really good. We've won in New York, Chicago, Cleveland, Utah, Phoenix, and L.A. But Detroit's the team to beat. They're playing the best and they look the best. They're the most confident and they're playing that way."

Kasten thought that a lot of Detroit's strength could be traced directly to McCloskey. "I've voted for Jack McCloskey for Executive of the Year for four of the last five years. He really hasn't gotten the recognition he deserves. Especially when you consider they won sixteen games the year before he came. I don't know how bad you have to be to win sixteen games. I mean, Miami has already won fourteen, so think about it. Everything they've got is because of Jack. Every time I call somewhere, Jack has just called them."

Kasten was keyed up about tomorrow night's game with Milwaukee, the team Atlanta would most likely face in the first round of the playoffs. Right now, his team was tied with Milwaukee in a fight for the home-court advantage. "I'll know more about where we are after that game," he said. "I'll feel a lot better if we have the home-court advantage. But nothing is automatic. Right now, it's about as tight as it can be."

Jerry West wandered by in a short-sleeved dress shirt on his way to the tournament. Kasten didn't see him and he didn't see Kasten. But it didn't matter. Jerry West wasn't particularly sociable. He didn't have to be. He'd been a king of the playground since he was a child, and now he was king of the strongest, richest, most glamorous franchise in basketball and possibly in all of sports: the L.A. Lakers.

But Jerry West wasn't acting like a man in the deep folds of prosperity. He was acting more like a man who was headed for a fall—and knew it.

Jerry West sat in the plush orange seats of the brand-new Orlando Arena, home of the Orlando Magic. The stadium featured a trick scoreboard, sky suites, a concert-class sound system, VIP booths, Lycra Girls, and instant-replay monitors. Basketball Disneyland. West was in a courtside section that had been set aside for the most powerful men in basketball: Jack McCloskey, Stan Kasten, Wayne Embry, Indiana's Donnie Walsh, Dallas's Rick Sund, Boston's K. C. Jones and Jan Volk, Washington's Bob Ferry, Portland's Bucky Buckwalter, Sacramento's Bill Russell, and others. Nowhere on earth was there such a gathering of basketball luminaries. But when fans seeking autographs ventured into this special section, the one man they headed for was Jerry West. Not home team GM Pat Williams—they didn't even recognize him. Not even Hall of Famers Bill Russell or K. C. Jones or five-time All-Star Wayne Embry. They wanted West. He radiated celebrity. He signed with prickly disdain, not looking at the fans or even the paper he was signing. Jerry West looked distracted and unhappy. He had problems.

His team was headed for its sixth Championship series of the 1980s. But what did the 1990s hold? Jabbar would be gone. Magic Johnson would soon be gone. James Worthy and Byron Scott were very good, but Jabbar and Johnson were the franchise. Before the game started, West talked about his dilemma. "An awful lot of our time the last four years has gone into finding someone to take Kareem's place, and it simply hasn't been possible. There aren't that many centers out there, so you just have to hope that through trade or free agency you'll be able to come up with a center. But we're not going to find someone like him. We're going to have to settle for something less. We'll try to make a bid for a player, but it's probably not going to be successful. But I really don't want to talk about it, because it's nobody else's business." West grimaced. The subject of Jabbar was painful. For one thing, West acted as if he were still pissed off at Jabbar for coming into fall camp out of shape. It had screwed up the team's momentum, and they had never entirely recovered. "We'd never seen him quite like that," said West, "and it's taken its toll. He looked heavier than he'd ever been, and he labored through training camp."

With the playoffs around the corner, West was worried that his biggest move of the year, picking up free agent Orlando Woolridge, wasn't working. West had gotten Woolridge, who had a 17.9 career scoring average, "to come in and give us some offense off the bench, which we were missing. Unfortunately, it hasn't turned out that way. He just has not been able to fit in with what we do. We were asking him to be more of a bench player, but he's more of a starting player. He needs minutes to be productive and it's not a role he's been able to handle that well." Around the league, people were questioning Woolridge's desire to play—they said the only reason he'd wanted to play in L.A. was to be close to his rehab center. Whatever the problem, picking him up had not been West's finest move as a GM.

A basketball writer sat down next to West and asked, "If you make it to the Finals, what's your best guess as to who you'll face?"

"I really don't like to presume anything," said West. "I think the best team in the East is Detroit. Period."

"Do they scare you more than Cleveland?"

"I told you, I'm not going to talk about something I don't know about. Okay?"

"Do you think Detroit is more physical than L.A.?"

"Listen, I don't know if Detroit is more physical than L.A. Obviously, everyone thinks they are. Maybe they are." The writer thanked West and beat a hasty retreat.

All around West were general managers with big problems. Donnie Walsh's Indiana team was entering its fifth lottery in five years. Bucky Buckwalter's Portland Trail Blazers had been picked by some experts early in the season to dethrone the Lakers, but they'd failed miserably and the local press was calling for Buckwalter's head. Rick Sund's Dallas Mavericks had almost beaten L.A. the year before, but now they were 8 games under .500. Dallas had suffered injury, dissension, and drug problems, and now might never recover. Stan Kasten had gambled big and now stood to lose big. Wayne Embry had seen Cleveland fall from 5 games up on Detroit to 4 behind since March. Even Jack McCloskey was entering the playoffs with his biggest star wearing a plastic hand. As the game began, all the GMs looked stoic and serious. But Jerry West looked miserable. The Lakers had been "the Team of the Eighties." But the 1980s were ending.

Home! At last! Time to drive a stake through Cleveland's heart. The Pistons had already won 58 games, but Cleveland was still coming at them, like a monster that refused to die. Tomorrow night they'd play in

Cleveland—in the House of Horrors, where they hadn't won all year. A win would clinch the title, but a loss might cause all hell to break loose.

McCloskey sat at the scorer's table in the Palace, watching the end of practice and scrutinizing the players he'd have to trade in order to get one of the top draftees he'd seen in Orlando. There were probably four fairly good draftees he could get without moving up—but anybody else would cost him a player. The least disruptive thing would be to stand pat and take whoever was left at the bottom of the draft. But most of those players were suspects, not prospects.

Even the four he liked would be gambles. "Hubert Henderson from Southwest Missouri State is interesting," said McCloskey. "He's six-ten but plays more like a small forward. He's a decent shooter. He's on the lean side, but he's got a brain, and the body we could build up. Jeff Sanders of Georgia Southern is a six-nine power forward who wasn't very impressive in Orlando, but we've got tapes on him that we'll show the coaches. Another guy would be Roy Marble—if he'd slip down to us we'd grab him in a second. The fourth player we're interested in is John Hudson; he's a great leaper. Those are the four players that I think we'll see down at our pick."

There were much more impressive picks, of course—Anthony Cook, the kid with the great vertical leap, had been tantalizing. But everyone else had noticed him, too, so now it would probably cost McCloskey a player to move high enough to get him.

This summer, though, would be a difficult time for McCloskey to make a trade. The expansion draft was coming up, and it would deplete McCloskey's roster. The two new expansion teams, the Minnesota Timberwolves and Orlando Magic, would get to pick one player from each team. For free—no reimbursement. Each team was allowed to protect eight of its players from the raid. Most teams only had eight valuable players, so it wouldn't really cut into their muscle. But for McCloskey, the expansion draft would be painful, because he'd built a nine-man rotation. His starting five—Laimbeer, Mahorn, Thomas, Dumars, and Aguirre—depended heavily on the Killer B-Team: Rodman, Salley, Edwards, and Johnson. It wouldn't be too painful to leave the other three players unprotected—Dembo, Williams, and Long were good, but weren't essential to the mix. But where would McCloskey find his fourth victim? He'd have to make that decision during the playoffs. He dreaded it.

On the floor, Daly was yelling at John Salley. Tomorrow night in Cleveland, Salley would have to help stop Brad Daugherty for Detroit to win. "When Daugherty gets going," Daly said, shuffling his feet toward the basket and holding an imaginary ball, "he's hard to stop. So you've gotta *box out.*" Salley looked at Daly with the slightest knit in his brow. Since the Cleveland game last week, when he'd gone in with Fennis Dembo in the last minute, Salley had known he was on Daly's black list. Even more disturbing, he'd had a long talk with Isiah Thomas, and Thomas had told him, in words cats and dogs would understand, that he was in *trouble.* Thomas had told Salley that he was carrying the Here's Johnny role too far, and it was ruining him. It was time, Thomas said, to get serious. It had been sobering. You didn't want to hear that kind of talk from Isiah, because Isiah took any disruption to the team as a personal insult. It was bad business to be on the wrong side of Thomas, because he had tremendous power on the team. It wasn't that McCloskey and Daly took orders from Thomas—that's what the out-of-town press had said during the Dantley trade and it made good stories, but it was bullshit. The reality was that McCloskey and Daly had built their team around Thomas and trusted him implicitly—*that* was the source of his power. So Salley had taken Thomas's words to heart.

Over the weekend, Salley had had a good game in New York—where the Pistons had lost again. After the game, Terry Foster had talked to Daly about Salley. "It's amazing what being benched does to a guy," said Daly. "I think it sent a wake-up call. You see, I don't care *who* plays. I am not going to put a guy in at the expense of someone who's doing the job. But it's amazing how a guy responds. Whoever comes to play will get in."

Salley had tried to downplay the benching. "I haven't been able to jump off my right leg and I'm right-handed," he'd told Foster. "I sat out and now I'm able to do more things. I'm playing hard and my head is back in it. I sat and waited. Now it's my turn." He even finished off with classic mantalk: "I'm just happy to be winning." Of course, they'd just lost, but Salley was still a little new at mantalk.

Practice broke up and Daly was the first off the floor, pausing briefly to supply product to Terry Foster and Charlie Vincent, who'd just been speculating about the players McCloskey would leave unprotected in the expansion draft. They'd quickly come up with Dembo, Williams and Long, then had lapsed into a long silence. Daly told Foster and Vincent that he was rooting for Rodman in the voting for Defensive Player of the Year, which was coming up soon. The writers pointed out that Rodman might also win the award for top field goal percentage. Daly didn't have much to say about that. He shrugged his shoulders, sending a ripple through his black-and-gray velvet sweat suit—the kind you'd rush to the dry cleaners if you ever actually sweated in it.

PR director Matt Dobek walked by and spotted Will Robinson, who was sitting next to McCloskey. "Looks like you got some sun in Florida," Dobek said.

"I did," said Robinson, "but no one can tell."

Under the basket, Salley was talking about his weekend. "Went to the disco last night," he said. "Saw this girl. Thirty-six–twenty-four–thirty-six. Five-eleven. I'm like, 'How old are you, baby?' She goes, 'Six-teeeen.' Later, baby! Jesus! Mr. Statutory Rape. What I need. It was ridiculous. I'm trying to get to my car, but there's this limo in the way. How many people in Detroit have limos? It had to be somebody. But it didn't have shit for a sound system. Not like Dennis's car—it's all speakers in the back. It's like, take down the top and have a block party."

In the runway leading to the locker room, ESPN's Larry Burnett was trying to get an interview with Rick Mahorn. But Mahorn was giving him the Badass Rick treatment. "You said I had a big ass!" Mahorn boomed, standing close to Burnett to emphasize their size difference.

"I didn't say that," Burnett protested.

Laimbeer, coming off the court spinning a ball, said, "It was Karl Malone who said you had a big ass."

"Yeah," said Mahorn, pointing at Burnett, "and he *reported* it."

"You do have a big ass," said Laimbeer, walking past.

"I know where you live," Mahorn said to Burnett. "Up there in Connecticut. You think I can't send people up?" He was doing the Mean Mahorn grin now. He felt good. Daly had just said that Mahorn was playing the best basketball of his career. When people speculated about who'd go in the expansion draft, or who'd get traded to move up in the college draft, his name was never mentioned. He wasn't just a force on the court, but was the team's rudder of confidence and good humor. In twenty-four hours, they would be in ultrahostile Cleveland, putting a 3½-game lead on the line against the team with the best home-court record in the league. If they lost, their lead would be down to 2½. Really, though, the lead would be just 1½ games, since Cleveland would win the home-court advantage if they tied. It would be an incredible irony to win 60 games and still not have the home-court advantage, but bitter irony was the Pistons' legacy: "They'll break your heart." As they loped into the locker room, most of the players seemed all too aware of the importance of the next day's game. But not Mahorn. He clipped on the ESPN mike and started talking about the "fashion statement" he was trying to make with the blue, long-legged nylon girdle that descended beneath his game shorts. He looked radiant with self-confidence.

He had no idea that his value to the franchise had just peaked, and would never again be as high.

*   *   *

Chuck Daly stood on the still floor of the Cleveland Cavaliers' stadium. His voice made an odd, hollow sound in the shadows of the empty coliseum, as if it were coming from deep inside him. His players had gone downstairs after their shootaround. He was alone.

"Sometimes I wake up when I'm having this dream. I dream that I'm in college, and it's the final exam of my last class, but I haven't studied. It's all I need to graduate. But I know I can't pass that test. So I won't graduate. It'll never be over.

"That's kind of how I feel about the basketball season. It'll never be over. It won't be over until I pick up the paper and read that we've won the title. Even then . . .

"You know, Cleveland still feels strongly that they're a better club than we are. They really, truly believe . . ." He drifted off, as if he'd gone back into the dream. The stadium was silent.

Joe Tait, the Cleveland radio announcer, sat in the basement of Cleveland's Richfield Coliseum with an old friend who was in town for the Detroit game. Tait arranged the meticulous box score that he keeps throughout each game and talked about the playoffs.

"Being in the playoffs is just like making love," he said. "The more you do it, the better you get. The more the Cavs play in the playoffs, the more they get used to getting beaten up and beaten back, and the more they get used to giving it back. You ever see a playoff game?" His friend shook his head. "The intensity level—in the stands, on the floor—it's all different. Magnified!" he boomed in his rich, deep announcer's voice. "Regular-season games give you some degree of experience, but they're not the same as NBA playoff basketball. *Nothing* is."

"What was it like around here when you guys slipped out of first place?" asked Tait's friend, who'd known him in college. "Was it a letdown?"

"No. The Cavs were already having problems. The first half of the season really favored us—we were forty-three and twelve with no injuries. Then the schedule got tougher and Price got his concussion from Mahorn. Then Nance had so much pain in his ankle that they finally had to sit him out. On top of that, none of these guys had ever played on a team that was the fastest gun in the West. Every time we came to town the media was standing in rows at the airport, and then they'd come to the hotel. The other team was always *dying* to beat us because we were number one. It took its toll. A *real* toll."

"How you guys gonna do against the Knicks?" Tait's friend was presuming Cleveland would automatically advance past Chicago, since they'd beaten them every game all season. Michael Jordan had just scored seven consecutive triple-doubles in his new role as point guard, but the Bulls were still a one-man team.

"Oh, we'd beat the Knicks," said Tait. "Because we have the home-court advantage. We can't beat them there, but they can't beat us here." Tait was the NBA veteran who had an almost mystical belief in the home-court advantage. He thought that something along the lines of mass hypnotism occurred, empowering the home team and disabling the visitors.

"But I don't think we're going to be facing New York," said Tait, looking up from his stats. "I think Philadelphia is going to eliminate the Knicks in the first round. New York is in a terrible state of affairs right now. The Knicks were just super, and their coach opens his big mouth and says, 'I'd really rather be coaching in college.' And then somebody reveals that Pitino has an agent out scouting for college jobs. . . .'" Tait's voice tailed off. He loved basketball and hated the politics that surrounded it. He was silent for a moment, absorbed in his box score. Suddenly: "And *then*! And then, they go out and get Kiki *Van*deweghe. Now you've got players who had been getting X amount of minutes sitting on the bench because of Kiki, and you've disrupted the whole chemistry of the team. Absolutely *disrupted* it!"

"Know what I heard?" said Tait's friend. "A sports reporter said Al Bianchi picked up Kiki just to piss Pitino off."

Tait looked dubious. He hadn't been exposed to that kind of craziness for a long time—not since the Ted Stepien era.

Tait's buddy cut to the chase. "So. You guys gonna win it all this year, or what?"

Tait put down his notebook and leaned back in his desk chair. At an angle, his face was almost lost in his black bush of beard. "I knew from *day one* that we were *not* going to win the Championship," he said.

His friend looked surprised. "Why not?"

"Because," said Tait, "this team is not good enough." Tait's friend looked expectant, as if there were more to say. But of course there wasn't.

McCloskey bounded onto the Cleveland floor wearing his game face—the pleasure-aggression mask—as the stands began to come alive with movement and noise. "Boy, were the players *loose* coming over here!" he said. "Their attitude is, we've still got three more shots to win it at home, so the pressure's on Cleveland. Laimbeer said if he got anywhere near the ball, he was going to shoot it, and Isiah and Joe said they were, too." McCloskey scanned the stadium. It had seemed so state-of-the-art when it had been built in the 1970s, but now it fell far short of being a Basketball Disneyland. He spotted his seat and took the steps two at a time toward it. Typical of visiting-team seats, it was nothing special—no VIP box. He'd be sitting just up from the runway where Wayne Embry paced during games. But when McCloskey got to his seat, he felt a shudder of apprehension. Sitting next to him was this huge greasy biker, with forearms the size of Christmas hams and a long red beard. He looked mean as hell. McCloskey settled in next to him— trying to maintain his anonymity.

A few minutes later, Mahorn and Laimbeer were introduced, and the biker started spewing the most remarkable combinations of obsceni- ties—he was like a thesaurus of dirty words. But he didn't stand out that much because the stadium was vibrating with screams. The Cleveland fans did not forgive Mahorn for Price's concussion, and they didn't forgive Laimbeer for existing. Detroit was relaxed, though, almost ca- sual, and they hit 10 of their first 12 shots for a 14–2 lead. Suddenly: quiet. A sullen stillness.

Then little Mark Price drove along the curve of the 3-point line. Laimbeer leaped in front of him and splayed his feet wide. Price tripped over Laimbeer's outside foot and smashed into the floor. For several seconds he lay dead-flat. The crowd moaned. Referee Bill Oakes blew his whistle and shot his arm at Laimbeer. Laimbeer threw his arms up and his mouth went into a huge O. The crowd's moan climbed the scale and settled into a sharp, high bark. Laimbeer acted out his footwork for Oakes, but Oakes wheeled around and walked away. The biker next to McCloskey screamed, "Laimbeer, you motherfucker!" His face was pink and wet and the muscles on his arms were knotted in spasm. McClos- key's eyes darted around the immediate area—he was thinking, "Jesus, if I'm going to get into a brawl with this guy, I'm going to need *space*." At close range, he figured, the guy would put a bear hug on him and that would be that. Price walked to the free-throw line and made one of his two shots, but then Laimbeer got his hands on the ball and, sure enough, he heaved it up. It dropped. Laimbeer looked surprised, happy. 18–3. Lenny Wilkens jumped off the bench and called time. As Laim- beer walked off the floor, Isiah pounded his back.

Wilkens quietly went over several technical points, talking mostly to Price and Daugherty—the Good Boys. Cleveland came out of their hud- dle looking calm and began executing crisply and hitting their shots, ripping away most of Detroit's lead.

Just before the quarter ended, there was a pileup on the floor, a writhing snake's-nest of limbs, punctuated here and there by quick, slashing forearms and the blur of huge sneakers being used as clubs. The massive bodies of Mahorn and Laimbeer were part of it, and so were the thick, exaggerated arms and legs of Tree Rollins. Rollins came out of it swinging at Laimbeer, and was hit with a technical. Laimbeer stepped to the line as the crowd spent its fury. Laimbeer made his shot and raised his index finger at the crowd. It looked like he was giving them the finger, and they howled. From the far side of the stadium, half the crowd started chanting a blurred, ear-shattering trio of syllables. As it got louder, it became clear: "Laim-beer *sucks!* Laim-beer *sucks.*" Then the other side of the stadium picked it up in arrhythmic counterpoint: "Laimb-*sucks*-beer-Laim-*beer*-sucks-Laim . . ." As the halftime horn was about to sound, Thomas tried to call time-out. As he signaled, Craig Ehlo ran in and tried to steal the ball. Thomas pulled it away; then they were swinging at each other, Isiah protecting his broken hand as best he could. The horn blared. They separated. 53–49 Detroit. Laimbeer and Thomas led the team through the tunnel where Embry liked to pace, as fans overhead snarled and cursed. Thomas and Laimbeer looked completely at peace. Cleveland, using the same tunnel, looked frazzled.

Cleveland hit first in the second half, cutting the lead to 2. On the bench, where he'd spent most of his time since the hand injury, Isiah Thomas had a feeling that Cleveland was ready to make an adrenaline-fired rush—the dreaded home-court surge. But then Dumars hit a jumper, and next time down Dumars swished a 3-pointer, a perfect shot that pierced the heart of the basket. Dumars skipped backward after the shot, and he could feel himself sliding into the zone of altered consciousness. It wasn't really a happy feeling, because there wasn't much emotion attached to it—emotion would break it up. It was a nonthinking, peaceful feeling—the Zen of basketball—and Dumars let himself sink deeply into it. Dumars started hitting everything. The distance of the shot and rhythm of the game didn't make any difference. He was in his own world. He hit a driving lay-up, another 3-pointer, and followed it with a perfect shot from the top of the key. He came downcourt next time and faked a jumper, took one long leap toward the basket with the ball over his head, changed to an underhanded shot halfway there, flipped it up, kept driving toward the hoop as it bounced off the rim, and tapped it in. All with a blank face. He hit from the left corner, Cleveland couldn't convert, and Dumars hit again from the same spot on the left. Next time down, he went to the other corner and made another 3-pointer. It was his seventeenth straight point. Cleveland was far behind; they looked dazed. Rodman threw his fist into the air.

A Cleveland fan who'd recognized McCloskey turned to him and yelled, "Hey, McCloskey, how come you don't have your guys just play basketball and quit hotdogging?" The huge biker swiveled on McCloskey.

But McCloskey couldn't resist. "Would you like to have Rodman on your team?"

"I guess," said the guy.

"There you are, then."

Now the biker had McCloskey locked in a stare. "I *thought* it was you!" he said.

McCloskey thought, "Oh, Jesus, here it comes."

But the guy slapped McCloskey on the leg. "Hell of a team!" he said, and went back to screaming profanities.

Cleveland struggled to keep up, but their timing was jangled and they kept turning it over under the basket—a sign of frayed nerves. The team that early in the season had seemed so fearless—and *was* so fearless— now looked unsure of itself. Lenny Wilkens stood by the bench with his pained, sour-lemon look, rarely raising his voice. If he was desperate to win, he didn't show it. And neither did his players. They knew that if they didn't win the Championship this year, they might next year, or the year after. Wayne Embry had purposely built a young team. He wanted the franchise to prosper for many years. One bright day, their time would come.

But Detroit was desperate to win. McCloskey had built a championship team for *this* year. He wanted in *now*. The team's looseness didn't reflect a lack of desperation. It was part of the plan.

Dumars was still in "the zone." His movements were a dance. He'd tied a team record with 24 points in the third quarter, and he would set a record with 30 points after the half, for a game total of 42. Most impressive to McCloskey, he had no turnovers. He'd also end up with 11 assists and 3 steals. Even Daly was in awe.

Toward the end, Cleveland put "Eye of the Tiger" on the sound system. But it sounded like the music was coming out of overhead speakers, instead of playing inside your head, like it did at the Palace. The crowd didn't respond. As Detroit built a wall of points, the fans started jamming the aisles. A couple of players on the Cleveland bench turned around and watched the fans leave. It became deathly still.

In this silence, amidst total hostility, the Detroit Pistons had won the division title.

After it was over, they sat in the locker room and talked quietly. There was no celebration. The division title meant home-court advantage. Nothing more.

*   *   *

Jack McCloskey arrived at his office the next morning singing "Happy Days Are Here Again." He'd gone to bed with the song running through his mind and it was still there when he woke up.

Nancy Maas smacked his shoulder and said, "If you feel that good, you ought to buy us lunch."

"Fine," he said. She watched with surprise as he disappeared into his office.

Next door, chief financial officer Ron Campbell was punching numbers into his calculator. He was smiling. "The season starts *now*," he said.

He explained. "What you have now is a period of playing games with *very* little expense. You don't pay your players. Players are paid all their salary during the regular season and now they don't get another nickle from us. All our traveling expenses are picked up by the NBA. Our building rental is less than ten percent of the gate, or about thirty thousand to forty thousand dollars a game." And that money still stayed in the Bill Davidson empire. "The NBA gets fifty percent of our gate for playoff games, but that still leaves about two hundred fifty thousand per game for us. For the games not on CBS, we will show them on cable and net a hundred thousand per game. We'll make another fifteen thousand on radio. Bill Davidson Enterprises gets the concession, and they'll get about seventy-five thousand per game from that, about twenty-five thousand of it from novelties. We'll park about seventy-five hundred cars at five dollars each, so there's another fifty-five thousand per game."

Campbell looked up from his calculator. "When the Red Wings got knocked out in the first round of the playoffs, Jacques Demers got on TV and said something like 'I publicly apologize to my owner for not winning, because I've cost him millions and millions of dollars.' And he's exactly right. If we were to get knocked out by Boston in the first round—which isn't going to happen because Bird's not going to play—it will cost us two million dollars over the next two months. And then the dominoes start falling. All of a sudden your T-shirts are not as attractive, and your season tickets aren't such a hot item anymore—you'd probably lose about twenty percent of your ticket holders.

"And then you have to consider what you *could* have earned. If we win the Championship, it would mean millions on top of millions. The NBA Championship would mean adding three million dollars directly to the bottom line this year. And then the ripple effect starts in the *right* direction, in terms of season tickets and T-shirts and TV and the rest of it."

Campbell was excited—as a businessman, and as a fan. To him, basketball—at the world-class level—was a business and a sport. It was as much one as the other. To try to separate them would be more than ridiculous. It would be impossible.

Just moments after Campbell's happy assessment, Jack McCloskey sat in his office looking at videotape. Of Larry Bird. His information network had just reported that Bird was ready to play.

McCloskey wasn't singing anymore.

TWELVE

"The Franchise"
The Boston Series

ALONE ON the fractured, jagged parquet floor of Boston Garden, Larry Bird stripped down to a gray, sleeveless "Celtics Pride" T-shirt, while the rest of his team screwed around in the locker room. The morning paper had described him as woefully out of condition, but he had the kind of body a million health-club devotees would kill for: washboard stomach, hard-packed shoulders and weight-room thighs—a manufactured body. At the hoop, just off the floor, a ball boy in a green sport shirt and Celtics cap stood ready to rebound.

Bird began to shoot 3-pointers. In hypnotic cadence, he caught every ball with his hand straight up and fingers spread, planted his right foot pointing at the basket, flexed his knees, stared at the rim, jumped, released, and snapped his upper wrist in follow-through.

The ball boy grabbed each shot just after it had made the quick, hollow sound of ripping the net, and fired it back at Bird with a two-handed chest pass.

Again and again, it was exactly the same: Plant—flex—release—follow—rip. "Nice shot, Larry."

Plant—flex—release—follow—rip. "Nice shot."

Plant—flex—release—follow—rip. "Nice."

Plant—flex—release—follow—rip. "Nice shot."

"Shut the fuck up. Okay?"

Plant—flex—release—follow—rip.

The ball boy took no offense. The people close to the Celtics were used to the hard-ass side of Bird. Bird, like Isiah Thomas, had so successfully reinvented himself as an American hero—a king of the playground—that his dark, poverty-forged hardness was now practically invisible, at least in public. All the nightmares of Bird's youth—the alcoholic father who'd killed himself, Bird's own drinking, and his stunted hopes for his future—had been channeled into an obsession with basketball. The obsession had given Bird incredible success and an apple-pie image. But in the gym he didn't need the image—just the obsession.

People began to trickle onto the floor. One of the first was WTBS's Rick Barry, here to cover the third game of the Detroit-Boston series, which had essentially been decided the minute Larry Bird had said he wouldn't play in the first two games. Detroit had won both, and only needed one more in the best-of-five match.

Barry, in a fleece jacket and sneakers, still had the boyish looks and quickness he'd had as a twelve-time All-Star. He walked into Bird's field of vision and said, "Hi, Larry, glad you're feeling better." Bird flicked his eyes to the sidelines, offering scant acknowledgment of Barry's existence. Bird could still afford that arrogance. Probably. A week before, it had appeared that his playing days might be over—forever. His injured heels—after a moderate workout—had suddenly begun to puff and inflame for reasons no one could explain. But then the swelling had begun to subside. "Haven't lost your stroke," said Barry.

Bird looked annoyed. "Damn right," he said, his eyes fixed on the hoop.

The other players began to wander up from the Garden's basement, which was full of mice and smelled like mold and backed-up toilets. Kevin McHale took over the basket at the other end of the floor, and Joe Kleine, the Celtics' new 270-pound bump-and-grind center, joined Bird. Red Auerbach ambled over to the sidelines, mouthing a lit cigar and watching Bird shoot. Soon Auerbach was flanked by former coach K. C. Jones and general manager Jan Volk. They talked quietly as Bird ignored them: plant—flex—release—follow—rip.

"Know where we are?" asked Auerbach. "Just one or two players away from where we were." His volume rose to where Bird could hear. "Take Michael Jordan away from Chicago. Take Magic Johnson away from L.A. Where would they be?" Bird didn't glance over.

"Tell me about it," said Volk. Volk picked at the buttons on the sleeves of his suit. Of medium height, the only man in the stadium wearing a suit, Volk stuck out like a sore thumb. It had been a bitter year for him. He'd started the season thinking Championship. He and Auerbach had put together a team that was not only a fantastic box-score team—Bird, McHale, Parish, Ainge, Dennis Johnson—but also a team with great chemistry. Mostly, though, it was a team with Larry Bird: the "franchise."

But things had quickly soured. First, Volk had gotten into the contract war with Bird, who'd wanted $4 million—about twice the average superstar salary. Volk had finally caved in to the demand, since Bird was the Celtic franchise. Then Volk found out Bird could barely run. After that, there had been a ruinous string of injuries to other players, including McHale, Ainge, Johnson, and Parish. Suddenly his box score was ugly—Lewis? Acres? Upshaw?—and his chemistry was shot to hell, mostly owing to the loss of the obsessed Larry Bird. Bird was happy to crack the whip and keep the peace; he was clearly top stud, and his trickle-down obsession was the core of the Celtic chemistry.

So what did Volk do now? Rebuild, or cross off the year to bad luck? Volk didn't like to believe in luck. It was bad luck to believe in bad luck.

"Bet me," Bird said suddenly to Kleine. "First guy to hit three straight three-pointers." Kleine, with a big square face and shoebox jaw, nodded slowly.

Kleine went first. He'd only attempted one 3-pointer in his career—missed it. But as Bird eyeballed him, he made his first shot. "That's one," said Bird.

Kleine shot again. "That's two," said Bird.

Kleine unfolded for his third shot—"Miss!" Bird yelled. The shot banged off the rim. Bird snorted. "I don't even need to practice," he said. The ball boy who'd been rebounding Bird's 3-pointers for the past twenty minutes looked away. An assistant coach walked up to Kleine and pointed to the floor, showing Kleine a flaw in his footwork. Bird planted, flexed, released, followed, and the ball ripped the net. He shot again, and it missed. Kleine was still looking at the floor. Bird shot, and it swished. "That's one," said Bird.

"I heard another one, Larry," Kleine said.

Bird looked at Kleine like he was crazy. "Nawww."

Bird shot again. "That's two," he said. He shot again, and it circled the rim and fell through. Kleine looked over at Volk as if he were searching for a witness. Volk gave Kleine a tiny shrug, as if to say, don't push it. "I win," Bird crowed.

Volk smiled at Bird. Even though Volk was heir to the throne of Auerbach—the most powerful autocrat in NBA history—Volk needed to have a good relationship with Bird. The league had changed since Auerbach's era. These days, even Auerbach needed to make nice with Bird. For a GM, there were many dangers in building a team around one franchise superstar. Losing the superstar to injury—and losing games— was just one of them.

As soon as the first of the Pistons began to appear on the floor, the Celtics scattered. No handshakes. No joking. To hell with "sportsmanship." The Celtics hated the Pistons. The Pistons were displacing them as the East's greatest team. Even beyond that, there was poisoned blood. Parish and Laimbeer often tangled violently, and had gotten into fistfights. Kevin McHale couldn't stand Mahorn, the player McCloskey had acquired to negate McHale. A couple of years before, Mahorn had stepped on McHale's broken foot—purposely, McHale thought. McHale considered it "the most bush league thing that's been done to me." When it happened, McHale told Mahorn, "My foot will get better. But you'll still be six feet seven and fat, and I'm going to go at you." None of the Boston players liked Dennis Rodman's theatrics. Red Auerbach couldn't stand Jack McCloskey. And there was always the Bird's-great-because-he's-white disaster.

John Salley was the first Piston on the floor. "Can't see in here," he said. "Too much shit up there blockin' the light." He glanced up at the ceiling, where row after row of Championship banners hung. No team had ever dominated its sport the way the Boston Celtics had, not even the New York Yankees or Green Bay Packers. In the forty-two years of the NBA's existence, Boston had won sixteen Championships. They'd won eight consecutively, a record that may never be equaled by any other sports franchise.

The game wouldn't start for eight more hours, but Salley was wearing his thousand-yard stare. He was still fighting for his life on the team. Ever since his long talk with Isiah, he'd tried to change his outlook, and to change the way the management looked at him. It wasn't easy, because Salley's Here's Johnny image ran deep. But he was sick of all the trade talk—Salley to New Jersey for Buck Williams, Salley to Indiana for Wayman Tisdale. He'd rather go to *hell* than New Jersey. Hell was a better franchise. Salley couldn't stand losing, no matter what anyone thought.

In the first playoff game, Salley had been tremendous. He'd blocked 6 shots, triggered a second-quarter defensive stand that limited the Celtics to 4 baskets, and had gotten 7 rebounds, 3 on offense. Daly had left him in at crunch time, when Boston was only 3 behind, and he'd blocked a shot by McHale and then gotten an offensive rebound to win the game. Boston's game plan had been to blanket the Piston guards and force Salley and Rodman to shoot. It had backfired. Rodman had sunk 4 of 4 and went 2 for 2 at the line, and Salley had scored 15 points on 7 for 9 shooting. After the game, Salley had dished out a little mantalk on his game-saving blocked shot. He'd said he was "lucky" and "in the right place at the right time." But it had felt great to have the reporters asking about something substantive, and not just sniffing around for one-liners. He wanted it to happen again. Soon. It better happen again—or he'd be hearing from Trader Jack.

McCloskey and Daly emerged from the basement. Daly joined the players while McCloskey stood looking at the ceiling. All those banners! They represented a tradition that could carry a franchise indefinitely. Even if the team started losing, the Boston franchise had the name and cash to withstand it and forge ahead. The basketball decisions Volk and Auerbach had been making the last few years were questionable; they'd assembled the best five-man squad in the business, centered around a single "franchise" player. But they hadn't built depth, and their young/ old mix was deplorable. All their top players were getting old, and that had a lot to do with why they were spending so much time in the hospital. So it was quite possible that a long drought was imminent. But the business decisions of Volk, who was a lawyer, had been brilliant. Selling stock in the franchise had provided a puffy cushion of $47 million, which could bring in new stars when the salary cap rose. And building a new arena—a project Volk was spearheading—would position the franchise properly in Yuppieville. There, the team could be the vital hub of a galaxy of entertainment enterprises. But even as the franchise migrated, it would carry the tokens of its tradition—the banners, and even the parquet floor.

McCloskey studied the floor. What an astonishing piece of shit! It had ragged corners of parquet jutting up almost a quarter-inch, and faded dead spots that sucked a ball like quicksand. McCloskey pressed the toe of his shoe against a jag of wood. "This place sure brings back memories," he said in a hollow voice. "I'll never forget the game we lost here year before last, that kept us out of the NBA Finals. The bad-pass game. We had that game *cold*. And we made a poor play and Bird made a spectacular play. It was one of the most difficult losses I've ever experienced. Just being here, after experiences like that, makes you . . . uncomfortable." His eyes were drawn again to the ceiling—involuntarily.

"I remember the time Parish hit Laimbeer three times, and the referee, Jess Kersey, was looking directly at them. Kersey claimed he didn't *see* it. Ridiculous! There was a camera right behind him. When we got back to Detroit, I showed the film at the Silverdome. Kersey's mistake, I think, was that he thought Laimbeer was going to retaliate, and then he could throw them both out. He didn't want to throw just one of them out, because of the importance of the game. So he just ignored the thing. I think he was suspended for several games."

Despite the beginning of the playoffs, McCloskey was preoccupied with the college draft. He'd spent the last few days looking at tapes of college players with Will Robinson and Stan Novak. Frustrating. It was shocking how few kids had the skills, body, and mind to play in the NBA. One flaw meant disqualification. And all but ten or fifteen players had major flaws. But McCloskey knew that somewhere in the vast collection of flawed players was a kid who had what it took to overcome his flaw—a Dennis Rodman, for example. Or a John Salley—maybe.

It was hard, during the playoffs, for McCloskey to concentrate on the draft. "But you have to stay a jump ahead to protect the franchise. We just finished planning our 1989 exhibition season, and we're just starting our 1990 exhibition season. We're also finalizing arrangements for the 1989 summer camp and starting plans for the '90 camp."

At the same time, McCloskey was looking ahead to the next playoff round, when they'd face Milwaukee or Atlanta. "Coaches and GMs say they don't look ahead to the next opponent," he said. "But they do." Atlanta had more wins than Milwaukee, and was a team of superstars. But McCloskey was more afraid of Milwaukee. They had the brains, he thought—a legacy of Don Nelson—and the chemistry. McCloskey would take that any day over a great box-score team like Atlanta. Even scarier was the Team Out West. Particularly: the Old Man. "It's playoff time and the Lakers are ready to go," he said. "A month ago they were winning a lot of games, but I wasn't that impressed. They weren't playing defense like they can. But against Portland the other day they put the pressure on and got the feet going. And Kareem! It's his swan song and he's playing better than he has any time during the year. A *lot* better."

Utah had just lost its first two games to Golden State, and McCloskey was pissed off about it. It meant Utah was finished; nobody recovered from a wound like that in a five-game series. He'd been counting on Utah to soften up L.A. in the Western Finals. He loved the thought of Eaton and Malone torturing Kareem and Worthy the week before his team tangled with them. But now that wouldn't happen. The Lakers would be fresh and bloodthirsty.

McCloskey looked into the stands on the other side of the court. All the Celtics had gone now. Except one. Watching with his hands folded, blowing cigar smoke in the direction of the banners overhead, sat Red

Auerbach. He was glaring at the Pistons as their sneakers squeaked across the floor.

"Red's upset with us because we're starting to displace the Celtics," McCloskey said, failing to conceal his smile. "They were top dog for a loooong time. It's a natural thing for him to resent our success."

McCloskey joined Daly at midcourt, and Red Auerbach pulled his cigar out of his mouth and started telling columnist Charlie Vincent why he hated the Pistons. "You really want to know what I think," he said. "I'll tell ya. I think that guys making millions of dollars who try to pick up another ten cents with this Bad Boys crap are strictly *bush league.* We won a lot of Championships," he said, waving his cigar at the flags overhead, "and we didn't resort to minor league crappy things like that—the image and the T-shirts and all that crap."

"You're not objecting to T-shirts?" asked Vincent.

"It's the image I'm talking about. When people talk to them about it, they laugh—'Ha ha we're doing it just to make money. We're not really like that.' Well, who are they kidding?"

Auerbach's gravelly, cigar-burned voice lowered in contempt. "*Sure* they're that way. Otherwise, they wouldn't have been able to market it.

"But *mark my words*; it's going to backfire. After a while, the games will be called a little closer, and they'll have problems, because they're used to doing certain things and getting away with them."

"I know you don't want to name names," said Vincent, fishing, "but they didn't have this image in 1980."

"I wasn't interested in them in 1980."

"When did you become interested? When they became a playoff team?"

"I'm not interested in them today, either. Why should I give a shit about them? There *is* some obligation you have for kids, and to have a kid go around saying 'I'll win and be famous, vicious, dirty and bad'— that's no image for kids."

Rick Barry was attracted by Auerbach's throat-grated diatribe, and he sauntered over. He was part of the media now, and had come to value straight talk over mantalk. "What do you think about this Bad Boy business, Rick?" Auerbach said.

"Well," Barry shrugged, "it's working for them. Some teams get so wrapped up in the image thing that instead of just going out and playing, they let the image affect them."

"I think the image is going to *hurt* 'em in the playoffs," said Auerbach.

"Well," Barry said, "the officials are human. They read and hear all this stuff. They have to be looking for—"

"If they blindside guys now," Auerbach interrupted, "they're going to throw them outta the fucking ball game."

"Especially if they give a shot like Mahorn gave Price," said Barry. "Totally uncalled for. The one thing I do respect about Mahorn and Laimbeer, though—and this is something that's never been brought up—they'll accept the banging back, as long as it's not anything really dirty. But I can't accept the cheap stuff, because you've got guys making a living that can't take those kinds of chances."

Auerbach looked into the distance. "Over the history of the NBA," he said, "we've had a lot of bad guys. Eventually, they get them. Rick, you remember way back, you always had a couple of vicious guys and somehow or another they always got it. Because you can't intimidate everybody. What goes around comes around. Whoever it may be—Detroit or anybody—if you take cheap shots, there's always going to be a guy to take a cheap shot at you. I'd like to see these guys"—he pointed his cigar at the Pistons—"go after Karl Malone. Or Ewing. Their whole attitude would change. There's always somebody bigger and stronger—I don't give a shit who you are."

"You see the *Rolling Stone* piece?" asked Vincent.

"I'm not on their subscription list," Barry said.

"I saw that," said Auerbach. "You think that's good for the city of Detroit? I live in a city with as much violence as Detroit—Washington—and something like that, Christ, you don't *need* to steam them up that much! But you," he said to Vincent, "you write for Detroit, so *you're* not going to call a spade a spade. You got to tone it down, play it their way."

Vincent nodded slowly. He'd just come back from the Kentucky Derby and was tanned and relaxed, in no mood to get defensive about his journalistic objectivity. "Before Mahorn came to Detroit," Vincent said, "when he played for Washington, we thought he was an asshole. Isiah jumped up one time and Mahorn hit him on top of the head—he hit *Isiah*. So we thought he was an asshole. But now," said Vincent, "he's *our* asshole. And it's a little different."

Auerbach smiled for the first time. The corners of his mouth raised outside the O of his cigar, and his eyes crinkled. That kind of loyalty to the franchise was something he understood.

The Pistons finished their shootaround at noon and headed back down to their dirty little locker room in the basement.

They had to descend through a cramped concrete stairwell. "When are they gonna tear this building down?" Aguirre said.

"Nevvah," said Salley. "It's his-taw-ric."

As they turned a corner, the ceiling lowered even more. "Watch your head," said Dumars.

"Will," said Laimbeer to five-eight Will Robinson, "watch your feet. Mark," Laimbeer said to Aguirre, "watch your sides."

"Bill," said Aguirre, "watch your mouth."

"Not playing tonight," boomed the Celtic PA announcer as he finished his introductions, "Larry B-i-i-i-rd!" The crowd clapped. But that was it. They just clapped. Bird, in a checkered cardigan sweater and open shirt, bobbed up from his seat at the end of the bench, ducked his head once, and sat quickly down, looking mildly perturbed. He was used to more. But so were the fans.

Bird's doctor had said in the paper that morning that Bird's heels were healthy enough for him to play, and as the crowd had filed in, that's what everyone had been buzzing about. As they'd lolled about the beer gardens in the lobby, it was obvious many of them were nursing soft-focus images of Bird making a grand entrance and leading the Celts to a quick pair of wins in the Garden, as he had hundreds of times before. After that, according to the buzz—the series would be 2–2, and Bird's supernatural powers would take over to provide another legend in Celtic history. So when Bird had emerged from the basement in a sweater, a malicious torpor had settled over the crowd.

There was nothing in the Garden's audiovisual facilities to provide an artificial gaiety. Auerbach liked his basketball straight. Unlike the new arenas, such as the Palace, lean years hadn't been factored into the Garden's physical plant. The Garden just had a tinny, whiny organ and a scoreboard with nothing but numbers on it. Boston Garden was strictly a peanuts and popcorn place, a steep banking pit filled with cheap plastic seats, sitting over a train station. It had been built as a miniature version of Madison Square Garden. Mice and roaches infested the building and the upscale crowd seemed out of place—practically every other guy looked like the short yuppie on *thirtysomething*: red-haired, pug-nosed, well-barbered, and loud-mouthed. Everybody seemed to be in a bad mood, as if they'd just paid thirty dollars to park, which many of them had. Before the game even started, a red-haired guy with a seat just behind the basket started taking out his anger on Mahorn. "Hey, Rick," he yelled. "*I'll* give *you* an elbow." He grabbed the inside of his elbow and shot his fist into the air. Mahorn looked through him.

McCloskey settled into his seat a few rows up from the floor. "Know what this building reminds me of?" he said. "In this situation? It reminds me of sitting in your landing craft before an invasion, with the battle wagons throwing in sixteen-inchers. Waiting. In both situations you've got the same feeling: Let's get out of here alive."

The game started with noise and brutality—it was finally playoff time; every move was magnified, and every move was contested. With Detroit up 2, Aguirre got the ball in the corner. In front of him was McHale, the great defender. Aguirre started to drive, stopped, lurched, then jetted—he was suddenly near the basket as McHale backpedaled furiously. He jump-hooked and scored. McCloskey clapped his hands together; he clapped hard, but just one time. His face lit up. Now he had not only Mahorn to punish McHale, but Aguirre to drive him crazy and draw fouls. It didn't matter that the combined attack was overkill this year. McCloskey had to worry about next year—Bird would be back.

At the other end, Mahorn bulled McHale out of the way for a rebound, then passed to Thomas, who got it to Aguirre, now downcourt in the corner. McHale's giraffe legs churned down the floor and he barricaded Aguirre from the hoop. Aguirre hesitated, then darted hard at McHale—daring him to a quickness duel—and McHale's knees buckled like a drunk's. Aguirre pulled up and feathered in a jump shot. McHale's sides were working like a bellows and his face now had a slick coat of sweat.

It was time for the Killer B-Team. Johnson, Salley, Edwards, and Rodman came in, looking excited and adrenaline-struck. The Boston starters stayed on the floor. As soon as Mahorn sat down at the end of the bench, the red-haired guy yelled, "Take a seat, you fuckin' thug!" Mahorn looked over at him and puckered a kiss.

The B-Team started running the Celtics into the ground, keeping the score even, but into the second quarter they also started making their dumb B-Team mistakes. Vinnie Johnson stood nailed to the floor as his man drove around him and scored. Daly turned away in disgust. "You can't stand there and watch 'em go to the basket!" he yelled—to the bench, to nobody. But then V.J. sunk a high, weightless jumper and part of the glare crumbled off Daly's face. Next possession, V.J. brought the ball down and waited for the defense to set up; as soon as it did, he called a play. "Way to call it, Fifteen!" yelled Mahorn. Johnson faked to his right and shot. It swished. "Fuckin' V.J.'s not afraid to call his own play." Mahorn laughed. His laugh was full and from the gut.

"Mahorn! Know what's funny?" yelled the red-haired guy. "Your fuckin' face!" Mahorn smiled sweetly and blew another kiss. Mahorn was happy. For the first time in his career he was reasonably secure. In many ways, he was the heart of the Pistons, both in the locker room and on the floor. There were never any trade rumors about Rick Mahorn.

When Boston got the ball, they worked it to Ed Pinckney, the six-nine muscleman whom Volk had gotten in the Ainge trade. Pinckney cannonballed toward the basket, ramming the ball as he went. Isiah jumped in and got his right hand on the ball. Pinckney kept pushing and Thomas, playing Coalminer Style, wouldn't let go. Suddenly, Thomas felt a sick little rip in his shoulder—in that brief moment, he could almost hear it. When he came down, his shoulder hurt like hell. He made an instantaneous decision to keep playing. It was player's instinct. It was also ghetto instinct.

By halfway through the third quarter, with the game still close, Thomas knew something was terribly wrong. His shoulder felt rubbery and on fire, and his shots were shaky and off target. But he hid the injury from trainer Mike Abdenour and Dr. Ben Paolucci. Instinct. Besides, even with a broken hand and a burning shoulder he could do things most players wouldn't try. With the quarter waning, he brought the ball downcourt. Two Celtics came at him hard and he lost his balance, falling in the direction of the ball. But he turned his fall into one long dribble, leaping after the ball and finally catching up to it and pulling it in to his body. Suddenly he was in total control of it as Laimbeer knifed straight toward the basket. Isiah launched a perfect flyball pass, Laimbeer caught it and laid it up and . . . out. Thomas put his hands on his hips and his face turned to stone.

Daly put the B-Team back in. Salley was a mad blur of action—fighting for his life!—and Rodman was pulling in rebounds as if his arms could stretch like rubber. With the quarter ending and the score still close, Rodman tapped away a defensive rebound and latched onto it himself. He dribbled over the halfcourt line, got cut off, spun to his left to keep going, hit another clump of Celtics and went 360 degrees to slip through them, drove to the hoop, jumped from almost the free-throw line, hung in the air—kept gliding—and . . . *jam!* Vinnie Johnson, sitting next to Mahorn at the end of the bench, slapped his own face. "NBA action," he cried. "It's fan-fucking-tastic."

Mahorn smirked at the red-haired guy who'd been tormenting him and said, "Take that, asshole."

The quarter ended with the organist playing the theme song from *Entertainment Tonight*. It was a real upbeat, swinging arrangement. McCloskey didn't notice the music—all he noticed was the fragile 2-point lead. If Boston stole this one, Bird might suit up for the next one. And if that happened . . . They'd better win this one.

The fourth quarter started with V.J. drilling a long turnaround jumper, then skipping backward downcourt. "He's on," said Steve Addy. Johnson had already scored almost 20 points. At the other end, Dennis Johnson slipped away from V.J. to fire a pass to Brian Shaw. Shaw jumped up and hit a short bank shot. It looked like a good play to the fans, who gave Shaw a nice cheer. But Daly exploded. "Goddamnit,

Vinnie," he yelled, "did you see . . ." His voice trailed off. A minute later, V.J. dribbled downcourt and traveled. "Zeke!" yelled Daly, "get Vinnie." The expansion draft was less than two months away, and Johnson knew he was a potential exile. This was no time to screw up in front of McCloskey. As Johnson and Thomas met at midcourt both of their faces were full of hurt.

But Thomas's shots, as his shoulder began to freeze with pain, were clumsy and amateurish. Daly pulled his superstar. He didn't need him. Vinnie Johnson might not be good enough for McCloskey to keep on the team, but he was good enough to win the most crucial game of the season. Besides, John Salley was kicking ass all over the floor.

Salley and Johnson led Detroit on a 10–0 run midway through the fourth quarter that deflated the gasping Celtic starters. Boston needed some fresh legs. They didn't have them. The crowd was getting surly. As Detroit stepped to the foul line, a Coke can shot out from the crowd behind the basket, and the forty-year-old Celtic ball boy said to the security cop at the end of the Detroit bench, "Watch those people!"

"Watch who?" yelled the cop, the heel of his hand on his gun. "What the *fuck*! I'm gonna watch *everybody*? Right!"

"Hey," said Mahorn. "I saw the guy who did it. It was that motherfucker with red hair." The cop nodded and waded into the crowd. Mahorn unleashed his Badass Rick grin.

As the game clock ran down, time seemed to accelerate—instead of slowing like it usually did at the end of a game. Detroit's lead was ballooning and Boston wasn't calling desperation time-outs. The Celtics just didn't have the manpower for the last-minute heroics. McHale was exhausted. Dennis Johnson's ankle hurt. Kevin Gamble was out. Jim Paxson was out. Parish's arm was numb with tendonitis. Danny Ainge, with his 3-point capability, was in Sacramento. And Bird was on the bench, his face set in a grim mask.

As it ended, Boston fans surrounded the Detroit bench. A guy in a black suit yelled, "You'll always be a bunch of *losers*! You lost last year and you'll lose this year!" Next to him an old man with an umbrella screamed, "Hey, Isiah, don't blow it like last year!" A teenager grabbed his own throat and shouted, "You guys *choke*! Don't choke like last year!" In the stands, the fans surrounding McCloskey began to chant, "L-A! L-A! L-A!"

When the horn sounded, the organist broke into a cocktail version of "Thanks for the Memories." A lively, jazzy version.

Before Salley could get to the locker room, a TV reporter intercepted him and hooked him to a mike. Salley had shot 5 of 7 for 14 points, with 6 rebounds. Daly had just told the reporter that Salley had made up for the whole year during the Boston series. As the white TV lights flicked on, Salley looked very happy. "I was nervous about being a Piston this summer," Salley said idly as the reporter adjusted his sound level. "Now I can go out and buy a house."

Just before the interview started, McCloskey walked by and saw Salley. "Way to go, John!" he said, his mouth curling up, with one hand on Salley's shoulder and the other shaking Salley's hand.

Salley suddenly looked ecstatic.

So did McCloskey. His B-Team had won the game. In the Garden.

Isiah Thomas sat in the training room with Dr. Ben Paolucci. In the adjacent locker room, the players were feeling good, but not great. Still ahead was Milwaukee or Atlanta, and Chicago or New York, and finally the Lakers. But Thomas was miserable. Dr. Paolucci had just told him that his shoulder injury, which Thomas had admitted to after the game, might be a torn rotator cuff. Thomas wasn't sure what that meant. All he knew was Bears quarterback Jim McMahon had suffered one. It had almost ended his career.

Thomas went back to the hotel and sat in his room alone, ice on his shoulder. The other players went to a bar across the street to celebrate— without alcohol. Thomas's shoulder hurt too much for him to go.

He tried to move his arm. Pain hit the shoulder like an ice pick. He put the ice back on. He tried to order dessert from room service, but the kitchen was closed.

He tried to go to sleep. But it was very hard.

The morning after: Celtic GM Jan Volk looked small behind his desk. Part of it was the piles of memorabilia on and around the desk—trophies, a minihoop with a ball jammed into it, a row of "NBA Finals" caps, sports magazines, a basketball shoe, and reams of paperwork and telephone messages. But part of it was also the situation: for the first time in thirty-two years, Boston had been eliminated in the first round. That was enough to shrink the body language of any GM.

Volk, in his shirtsleeves and a yellow paisley tie—looking a lot like the lawyer that he is—was spending the day taking calls from reporters. Their theme: What the hell happened? He was trying to put the best possible face on the season, talking about how the young players had gotten more experience, but it was still a painful postmortem. It was especially painful that this ugly fate had fallen on the Celtics—God's Team, or, at least in Irish-Catholic Boston, the Pope's.

"A short-term failure that might be expected by some teams," said Volk, "is just not tolerated here. It's the end of the world." He tried to grin.

Though the fans were still in a state of shock, Volk had seen the hellish finale coming months ago. After Bird's injury, Volk had readjusted his expectations. "It permitted us to focus on long-term goals." It gave Volk the impetus to make the Ainge trade. After years of the same starting lineup, the team had sacrificed some of its box-score luster to gain some youth, strength, and depth. The injury had also opened minutes for rookie Brian Shaw and second-year man Reggie Lewis, and Shaw and Lewis had established themselves as the team's future.

Even so, it was impossible for Volk not to play What If? What if Bird hadn't gotten hurt? "We would have proceeded towards one of the best, if not the best, record in the division. And the Championship." And that led naturally to the ultimate What If? What if burly Len Bias—the number two pick in the 1986 draft, behind Brad Daugherty—had not died of a cocaine overdose? "We would still have Reggie Lewis and Brian Shaw, along with Len Bias," said Volk. "There is no question that we would have been a much better team. We will never recoup that loss. I hate to put it in such an asset/chattel-oriented way—it isn't like you suffered a loss at a factory and can just put on another shift. There is no way to make it back."

Volk looked out his Boston Garden window, remembering how he'd heard about Bias's death. "I got a call very early in the morning from a reporter at a TV station. He said he'd heard a rumor and hoped it wasn't true—or was a cruel joke—that Len Bias had been rushed to the hospital. I said that I hadn't heard anything. He called me back fifteen minutes later and said he'd gotten hold of Len Bias's agent, and that when he'd asked about Len Bias the agent hung up. So I called the agent and found out that Len had been rushed to the hospital, but learned nothing more than that. I called Red, and by the time I got hold of him, he'd already found out that Len had died.

"Talk about a kick in the stomach. It was gut-wrenching. But we can't let it hurt us any more than it already has. I can sit here and speculate how we could have won the 1987 Championship, or the 1988 Championship, or how we could be contending right now. But it just wouldn't do any *good*. It's *gone*."

Maybe Volk's drafting of Bias had been bad luck. But there had been rumors of Bias using drugs—though the rumors were shadowy and unconfirmed. So maybe it hadn't been bad luck, but bad management.

No matter. Bias was gone. But he wasn't forgotten. Bias would have been a "franchise" player. He would have greatly decreased Volk's dependence on his other "franchise," Larry Bird. At this moment, that would have been of great value. Because right now, Larry Bird was on the other side of town, blasting hell out of the Boston Celtics.

*　　*　　*

Larry Bird, in baggy cotton shorts and a loose practice jersey, had been shooting by himself at Hellenic College, in the little gym where the Celtics work out in suburban Brookline. Several of his teammates had stopped by to clean out their lockers, and Bird had asked each of them to play with him. No one would.

When he was done, Bird tossed down his ball and started talking to a small group of reporters. He was pissed off. The team had let him down. "To get this going again," he said, "everyone's got to give one hundred percent. We never had to worry about guys not giving the effort three, four, or five years ago. But we have that now. Not only this year—I'm talking last year and the year before that. This has been going on for three years now.

"We can turn it around if we want to, but if guys don't want to, nothing's going to be able to do it. It's all minor things, really. We have to set picks, help on defense and give the extra effort. Guys have to *want* to do it.

"The coaches, the players—everybody *knows* who misses their assignments. Everybody on the *team* knows. The fans don't, but the players do. And when it's the same guys doing it over and over, what are you gonna do?"

The few writers there tried to get Bird to name names. He wouldn't. Later, after Bird had finished, they speculated briefly on who he was talking about. Dennis Johnson's name came up. So did McHale's. So did Parish's.

"We can harp and bitch all day *long*," Bird continued, "*but* if you guys see someone not hustling, *that's* who you should write about. This year, we always had the excuse—Larry's not here. Larry usually does this, Larry can do that. In the back of your mind, you've got sort of an excuse to lose.

"All I know is our guys kept talking about *Detroit.* 'Their guards shoot a good percentage; Detroit packs down low so Kevin and Robert can't shoot well.' What I see is, Detroit gets very good picks. Detroit works together on the defensive end. They clog the middle and make you beat them from the outside. Those are the things the Celtics *used* to do. You'll never be able to beat teams that do it. The last couple of years, we haven't done that. We worry about yourself getting off picks—instead of helping someone else out.

"That's what I've seen all year."

The reporters stood in a half-moon around Bird, pointing their cassette recorders at him. Normally, they just jotted down pieces of a player's remarks in their notebooks, to save the trouble of transcribing. But for Bird, they made verbatim tapes. It was important. He was, after all, the franchise.

That afternoon, back in Detroit, Isiah Thomas met again with Dr. Paolucci. His shoulder still hurt like hell.

Dr. Paolucci examined the shoulder again, and then made some calls. A torn rotator cuff was still a distinct possibility. X rays were needed, as well as an examination by an orthopedic specialist.

After making the arrangements, Dr. Paolucci talked to McCloskey about the injury, and its possible consequences.

As McCloskey talked to Paolucci, he held his panic in check. For one thing, the injury might not be as serious as everyone feared. For another, they could probably get by without Thomas. He was a great player—a superstar—probably the most valuable player on the team. But he wasn't the franchise.

Assistant coach Brendan Suhr diagrams the "Jordan Rules," a complex set of double and triple teams. The rules, said Chuck Daly, boiled down to: "When Jordan goes to the bathroom, we go with him."

McCloskey and Stan Novak wait for the second Chicago game to begin. If they lose again tonight, they're finished. The two old friends are trying to talk about anything but the Bulls.

The Brow whips the Palace crowd into a frenzy. The days of quiet are over. The Pistons are fighting for their lives and the fans respond.

Isiah Thomas has just won game two against the Bulls almost single-handedly. But he's mad as hell. One-man teams don't win Championships. He wants help.

Thomas is trying to get Michael Jordan to think like a point guard, worrying about distributing shots, instead of like a shooting guard. When Jordan concentrates on just shooting, he's virtually impossible to stop.

Jordan sorts his tickets before game three. Bill Cartwright wants a pair. "Not those, man," says Jordan. "Those are for Oprah."

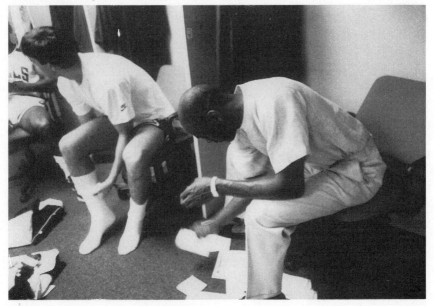

John Salley puts in the overtime that saved his job and helped Detroit win the Chicago series. Salley is sick of people thinking he's just a clown.

The lowest moment of the season. McCloskey and his wife, Leslie, watch helplessly as Chicago pulls ahead in game three. Now Detroit will have to win three out of four to survive.

Steve Addy, the toughest reporter on the Pistons beat: "Why should I care if they win? They're not going to cut me in on a playoff share."

After Daly and McCloskey went to work on the referees through the press, Jordan stopped getting the calls he was accustomed to.

Bill Laimbeer's elbow puts Scottie Pippen out of the game. It's the turning point of the series.

Tom Wilson congratulates John Long at the end of the Chicago series. Wilson had always tried not to get too close to the players—it made it too hard when they were let go.

A greatly relieved McCloskey in the small, dark locker room in Chicago Stadium. At right, team doctor Ben Paolucci.

The Worst Boys—Rick Mahorn and Bill Laimbeer—celebrate another Eastern Conference title. But this time, that's not enough.

Mahorn played well in the Chicago series—well enough, he thought, to merit some job security.

For a few moments after winning the conference title in Chicago, McCloskey is preoccupied. He is thinking about all the players who'd helped bring the franchise to this moment: Kelly Tripucka, Terry Tyler, Ron Lee, Phil Hubbard, Kent Benson.

McCloskey and Vinnie Johnson talk just before the Finals begin. They've both waited a long time for this moment. They don't want to blow it.

"Do you feel any nostalgia?" Kareem: "No."

As usual, Isiah Thomas got cut up during the Finals. But nothing was going to stop him from playing. He was obsessed.

After the Los Angeles Lakers fall behind in the series, the Laker players are calling coach Pat Riley a "madman."

Just before the last game of the Finals, McCloskey meets briefly with Los Angeles Raiders boss Al Davis, the man who gave the Pistons their Bad Boys nickname.

By the last game, the burden of winning has fallen to James Worthy. But, by himself, he just can't do it.

After the final game, Kareem Abdul-Jabbar hangs it up.

McCloskey and Isiah Thomas mount their float in the victory parade. McCloskey is still trying to work a deal to save Mahorn from the expansion draft.

Chuck Daly and Piston owner Bill Davidson atop their float

McCloskey and Will Robinson, as the parade begins. McCloskey is waiting for a call from Minnesota about Mahorn. He's offered them an excellent deal.

John Salley, with his "sweep" broom, leads the crowd in a Bad Boys chant. Salley finally has job security.

McCloskey is on the phone with Minnesota, trying to keep Mahorn. Assistant coach Brendan Malone, from the float up ahead, sees McCloskey smiling. "My God," Malone thinks, "he's done it."

The deal with Minnesota fizzles, and McCloskey's attention goes back to the parade. At this moment, he could have been elected mayor of Detroit. A few hours later, when the loss of Mahorn is announced, his popularity will plummet.

Laimbeer, Daly, and trainer Mike Adenour address a huge downtown crowd at the end of the parade. This is one of the last happy moments of the celebration.

Back in the Palace after the parade, McCloskey listens grimly as Mahorn thanks him for his help. In a few minutes, McCloskey must tell Mahorn that he's no longer a Piston.

Isiah Thomas, reacting to the loss of Mahorn, tells President George Bush and Piston owner Bill Davidson, ''Say good-bye to the Bad Boys.''

THIRTEEN

"Just a Game"
The Milwaukee Series

"**T**ALK WITH you? After the shit you said on me!" Rick Mahorn jumped out of his locker room chair into his terrorist-forward stance: elbows out, fists close together, neck muscles fanning like a cobra's, biceps popping. "On the motherfuckin' *air* you said it!"

"I was just, you know, I was just"—one of Detroit's most prominent TV sports reporters stood tentatively before Mahorn, craning his neck, wearing a smile as thin as string—"doin' my *job*, man." Which meant, in the quiet aftermath of the Boston series, concocting drama.

"Fine. Now I'll do *my* job. On your *ass.*"

The reporter coughed up a little one-of-the-guys laugh. But he wasn't one of the guys. None of the reporters were. To be one of the guys, a reporter would have to stick to transcribing straight mantalk and jockisms, but they were all too busy trying to be Howard Cosell to do that. They always had to find a hero, and they always had to find a goat. And if they contributed to squeezing some semiliterate young man out of his $600,000-a-year position—so that he could go teach gym in his hometown junior college—they were just *doing their job.*

The TV reporter, now standing in front of Mahorn with his long shotgun mike pointing down—waiting—had said on the air yesterday that Mahorn, who'd only averaged 2.6 points in the Boston series, should wake up or McCloskey would make him meat for the expansion draft. It was the first time anyone had floated that notion, and Mahorn was pissed.

"Okay, man," said Mahorn, "I'll do your interview."

The reporter's mike sprang back to attention.

"But first do something for me."

"Name it." The other reporters, who had been watching the little melodrama, began to drift off.

"Suck my dick!" Mahorn boomed.

The mike dropped. "Oh, mannnn," whined the reporter, his stringy little smile back.

"Fuck you, man," said Mahorn, using the ghetto enunciation: *Fuh-cueman.* He started stripping off his practice shorts. "You took your shot at me. Now suck my snake!" He flashed his Badass Rick grin. "G'wan—do it!" Mahorn thrust his pelvis forward. "Speak into the mike!"

The reporter—this *star,* this man who was the pride of his family and the envy of his friends—turned his face away. But he didn't leave. The players had the power and there was nothing he could do about it.

"Look, I'll make it easy on you," said Mahorn, enjoying himself more and more. The reporter's face swung back to Mahorn, and he brought his mike back up. "There," said Mahorn, coating himself with baby powder, "smooth as silk." The other reporters were laughing now, lapping up the locker room humor, happy to be in on the joke. Even if, indirectly, they were its butt.

"You're cold, Horn," said the reporter.

Mahorn relented, and did the interview. For one thing, he genuinely liked most reporters, and they liked him; he was a blowhard, but at least he didn't walk past you as if you didn't exist, as many of the players did. Besides, he *had* to deal with the press. They had the power.

Over at his corner locker, Isiah Thomas ignored the hubbub. Thomas didn't approve of letting go in front of the press; he hadn't ever since the Bird Disaster. Besides, he had a lot on his mind. Such as, the end of his career.

When Isiah Thomas had tried to stop the Celtics' Ed Pinckney from dribbling to the basket two days ago in Boston, it had been like reaching out to stop a train. Pinckney, at six-nine and 215, had torn right through Thomas's thin, wispy arm.

Dr. Paolucci's initial assessment—that it might be a torn rotator cuff—had scared hell out of Thomas. But X rays that Paolucci had ordered yesterday had, for the most part, ruled out that diagnosis. There was still some chance of it, though. The X rays didn't absolutely prove that the rotator cuff was intact. Thomas had seen orthopedic specialist Robert Teitge, and Teitge thought Thomas had just hyperextended the shoulder, at the point where the collarbone and shoulder blade connect to the arm. If that was the case, Paolucci had said, Thomas would be out just a week to ten days. *If* that was the case. . . .

For now, all Thomas could do was keep ice on it, take some medication, and hope that it quickly started to improve. If it didn't respond over the next twenty-four hours, that would be a bad sign.

Outside the locker room, columnist Charlie Vincent was playing GM, doing a postmortem on Cleveland. Cleveland—Daly's nightmare—was dead already—beaten at the buzzer by Michael Jordan. Where had Cav GM Wayne Embry screwed up? He had put together a hell of a group, but one thing he couldn't do was teach them how to be older. "I think Cleveland's on the same path the Pistons were on three years ago," said Vincent, "when Detroit lost to Boston in the Eastern Finals and then to L.A. for the Championship. That *prepared* them for this year. I thought Brad Daugherty looked a little uncertain when he shot those free throws late in the game. The knowledge is that, if you fuck up right now, it's the end of the season."

Maybe Embry should have stirred more veterans into the mix. Vincent was at practice to do a column on Rodman, and one of the things Rodman had just told him was how the veteran Dantley had helped him gain experience beyond his years. "He'd do things I couldn't comprehend," Rodman had said, "and make moves that I couldn't make a move to. He'd psych me out. I knew I had to use my head and I had to move my feet and gradually it came to me. I just had to ask myself, 'Do you want to work hard to stop that guy?' And I knew that if I could stop him, I could stop anybody in the league." Rodman missed Dantley, just like Salley and Dumars did, and it was that kind of intangible that could derail a team during the hyperemotional playoff period. It wouldn't show up in the box scores, but it might surface in the team's chemistry, and be fatal.

Vincent thought that Atlanta, which was struggling to beat Milwaukee and earn the right to play Detroit, was a classic victim of fouled chemistry. Stan Kasten had thrown the dice last summer and assembled a great box-score team, and one designed to win playoff games. But during the season the chemistry hadn't clicked, and now the playoffs were here and Atlanta was tied with Milwaukee 2–2.

"If Atlanta loses," said Vincent, "I bet they'll tear that ball club apart.

If I was their general manager, I'd sure make some changes. They thought Theus would help, but he really hasn't. Malone is old. Dominique has been a great offensive player but I've never seen him as a real force, a real leader. If I was Kasten, I don't think anybody would be untouchable. I think Kasten . . ."

"*Fuh*-cue! *Fuh*-cue!" A reporter in the press room was doing Rick Mahorn.

"That's the honky Rick Mahorn," said Vincent. "No, I think Kasten is doing too many things, trying to run the Braves *and* the Hawks."

Steve Addy wandered by. "I think Chicago might beat New York," he said.

"Nooooo," said Vincent. "They don't have a prayer. They're a one-man team."

"They beat 'em three out of five in the regular season."

"Only way Chicago could win is if Jordan goes twenty-two for twenty-five at the line, like he did against Cleveland. You know, I guess they have to call the games closely and I guess they have to protect Jordan, but I really can't see him going to the line again like that. If he does, Chicago will be in it at the end, and if they're in it, Jordan can do anything in the last couple of minutes. But I say New York in five."

"They *can't stop Jordan*," said Addy. "They've *never* shown any signs of shutting him down."

Vincent shook his head slowly. "S-O-L. Shit outta luck. Except if Jordan goes to the line twenty-five times."

"You think the NBA would let New York get beat?" said another reporter. "A market of that size?"

"You think they want it won by somebody going to the line twenty-five times, stopping all the action?" said Vincent.

"Who thinks Isiah will play against Milwaukee?" somebody asked.

Steve Addy, the resident cynic, snorted and raised one of his cheeks. "I'm not going to say they exaggerate his injuries," said Addy. "But let's put it this way; it's good theater for them to make his injuries look as bad as possible. Then, when he takes the court: It's a miracle! He's back! Another Isiah miracle, brought to you by the Detroit Pistons." Addy extended his forefinger, and stabbed it toward his open mouth.

From the locker room, someone boomed, "Suuuuck it, white bitch!" But it wasn't Mahorn. Mahorn was quiet. Someone had just sent him a dozen dead roses. It appeared to be a threat.

A couple of days later, on Sunday, May 7, Jack McCloskey sat in the den of his lakeside condo, watching the last game of the Milwaukee-

Atlanta series. It was hard to sit still, because both teams were frightening. McCloskey was rooting for Atlanta. Practically every other Piston fan in Detroit was, of course, rooting against Atlanta. Atlanta was, in fan idiom, "awesome." They had one of the league's ultimate fan-appeal teams, with Moses, Dominique, Reggie Theus, and Spud Webb—a team tailor-made for great newspaper stats and TV visuals. But what did fans know? Milwaukee didn't look like much in a box score, but they had chemistry, intelligence, and emotion, and that scared hell out of Mc-Closkey. Also, they didn't depend on just one "franchise" player, the way Boston did.

Right now, Larry Krystkowiak, the Bucks' handsome, young power forward, was sitting on the bench with a banged-up hand, but Fred Roberts was taking his place and was running circles around Moses Malone. God! Fred Roberts—a classic NBA garbageman—making a fool of Million Dollar Moses! You couldn't buy desire—no matter how often GMs tried to do it. You had to find it.

Roberts was leading his team to a 7-point advantage with just a few minutes left. Sharing the glory was Paul Mokeski—which was also a hoot. Mokeski wasn't much more than a bouncer. It showed how much chemistry meant; Milwaukee was winning—in Atlanta—without stars. But then Atlanta exploded, the way a great box-score team can. Doc Rivers hit a 3, then even Moses hit a 3. In the last half-minute, Dominique Wilkins had a chance to tie it, but he missed his shot. So much for superstars. Milwaukee coach Del Harris left the court on the verge of weeping, his arms in the air. Atlanta coach Mike Fratello jammed his hands into his pockets and stalked off the floor.

"So what's Atlanta gonna do now?" said McCloskey. "Shake up the whole team? That's a team that won over fifty games. Strong finish. Some awful good personnel on that team. Now Stan Kasten's got some decisions to make." If Kasten did decide to shake things up, McCloskey wanted to be around for the rummage sale. Bad chemistry sometimes meant big bargains. Maybe somebody like Theus would be available. Or even Wilkins.

Del Harris came on the screen. "A lotta prayers were answered on that one," he said, his voice trembling. A tear slipped down his check and he wiped at it, sniffling. "We knew we could win but . . ." He halted, choking and exhaling. "Lot of emotion . . ." he managed to say, "in our locker room . . . right now."

It was frightening. Good chemistry and strong emotion. Add luck, and you had a nightmare.

*   *   *

The next day, as the layoff dragged on, Steve Addy got a call from Mike Bencsik, one of the city-side reporters at the *Oakland Press*. Bencsik had just been talking to one of his sources in federal law enforcement. "Hey," said Bencsik, "I heard about this letter—it's a death threat. It's to Chuck Daly. How can I get hold of him?"

"Call the Palace," said Addy. "You gotta try to get him if you're gonna run it." Bencsik couldn't reach Daly at the stadium, so he tried his home number. Daly's wife answered. Daly wasn't there, and because of the nature of the letter, Bencsik didn't want to tell her why he was calling. She hung up on him—he got the impression she was still pissed off about Addy breaking the coaching-by-phone story.

While Bencsik tried to track down Daly, Addy called Piston PR director Matt Dobek. When Daly had gotten the letter a couple of days earlier, he'd given a copy to Dobek and McCloskey. McCloskey had notified the FBI; he'd gotten death threats himself before—usually after trades—and generally took them seriously. Dobek and McCloskey had agreed that the best thing to do was keep it quiet. They didn't want to inflame things or create a copycat situation. So when Addy called Dobek, Dobek was shocked to learn the story had leaked.

Bencsik, meanwhile, called the local FBI office, and talked to an agent named John Anthony. Anthony told him the letter was postmarked from Cleveland, and that it had been written in block letters—an attempt at anonymity—which made Anthony take it more seriously than most hate mail. Anthony told Bencsik that it didn't seem like just a crackpot letter. The only positive part of the situation, Anthony said, was that Cleveland wouldn't be facing Detroit in the playoffs. "The nature of the threat," Anthony said, "was in reference to the Pistons playing the Cavaliers. With Cleveland eliminated, we hope that nullifies the threat. But we are taking it seriously."

Addy knew Daly wouldn't like the story—who would?—but his attitude was, "It's news, so what the hell." It wouldn't improve his access to Daly, but he couldn't worry about that. He knew, having already landed on Daly's blacklist over the reach-out-and-coach-someone story, that Daly and Dobek might resent him, but they probably wouldn't try to limit his access.

It hadn't always been that way with the Pistons. Before the current front office regime, when Scotty Robertson had been coach, a young reporter named Jay Mariotti had written a story critical of Robertson for the *Detroit News*. The editors had tagged a bloodthirsty, circulation-hyping headline on it, along the lines of ROBERTSON SHOULD GET THE HELL OUT. And Robertson had cut Mariotti off cold. No more interviews, no cooperation—don't bother to ask. The PR head at the time hadn't intervened, and there was even some evidence that they were planting stories in the other papers, just to chip Mariotti off at the knees. Mariotti got taken off the beat, and eventually moved on to bigger things in Denver. But Daly didn't work like that. One of the things reporters said about Piston press relations was, "Isiah acts nice, but he doesn't like us; Daly doesn't always act nice, but he likes us." So Addy wrote the story.

Daly marched out ahead of the players after practice the next day. His movements, almost always double-timed, were faster and stiffer. To Addy, Daly looked pissed.

The reporters formed a semicircle around Daly as he leaned against the wall. "What's your reaction to the death threat, Chuck?" asked Terry Foster.

"Who printed that, anyway?" said Daly. He damn well knows who printed it, Addy thought. Daly looked at Addy. "Your paper?"

"Yep," said Addy.

"I'm not paying any attention to it," said Daly. "There's nothing to talk about. I don't even know why I gave it to Jack. It's not the first time I've received them, and it won't be the last. Players get them all the time. When I was in Philadelphia, it seemed like Julius Erving got one every series."

"What are you gonna do about it?"

"Wear hats and dark glasses. Anybody want to talk about basketball?"

"You surprised to see Milwaukee kick butt?"

"I'd picked Atlanta. But Milwaukee is very tough. Everybody's tough. Especially in our division. I've been called the Prince of Pessimism, but you know what a pessimist is? A pessimist is just an optimist with experience." The print reporters scribbled madly—good quote. Maybe even a wire service quote. "Just as I told you guys—and none of you would listen—three of the top seven teams lost in the first round, *with* a home-court advantage. Utah. Cleveland. Atlanta. If you go in not concerned about your opponent, especially in the second round, you're even dumber than I thought. Cleveland was the best team in the league on February twenty-eighth. Now they're out of the playoffs." Daly shuddered slightly. "Scary," he said softly.

"But Chuck, you're like thirty and three in the last two months. How can some team expect to beat you four times?"

"Milwaukee beat us four out of six in the regular season. They averaged a hundred eighty points to our one-oh-two. Ricky Pierce has a twenty-three-point average against us, on sixty-percent shooting." Daly clamped his lips; letting go of Pierce in 1983 was probably McCloskey's worst mistake. "Ricky Pierce *owns* us," Daly said.

"That's ironic," said Charlie Vincent, "since you used to own him." Everyone laughed. Except Daly, who smiled stiffly. The layoff period was getting to him. He didn't like seeing his players beat hell out of each other every day in practice. He was worried that his players would get involved with all the personal problems that they shut out on game days. He was afraid they were losing conditioning and shooting touch. He didn't like seeing them badgered by the press, when there was nothing to report. And there was the annoyance of having a psychopath waiting to blow his brains out.

"Will Joe guard Pierce?"

"That's one of the keys to the series—our guard rotation, based on Pierce coming into the game. When Vinnie comes in, it could be a problem. But Vinnie has a groin pull. He woke up with it this morning."

Confusion flooded Terry Foster's face. "He . . . *woke up* . . . with it?"

Daly swallowed a smile. "Hey, that's what he said."

"Woke up with it."

"Like I said, he woke up this morning with a groin pull. I don't know what that means." The reporters were laughing again.

"Whoa," said Foster, "we can't write that." Daly shrugged.

"Have you had a chance to ask Fratello about Milwaukee?"

"Not really. I put a couple of calls in—not to talk about the Bucks, but just to talk in general."

"He could use a friend right now, huh?"

The reporters thought Fratello's head was on the chopping block. Kasten had to blame somebody—or Ted Turner might blame him. But Daly wanted no reminder of coaches' mortality. "He's doing *fine*," Daly said. For the first time that day, he shifted into his quiet, confident Daddy Rich voice. "Mike's doin' *fi-i-i-ine*." He did it so well that no one thought to ask how he could know.

After Daly adjourned to the coaches room, the reporters—a few more than there had been for the Boston series, including a small, blond woman from *USA Today* and a guy from ESPN—trooped into the locker room. Brendan Suhr was at the table in the middle of the room, picking at a platter of Greek salad and pizza. "Brendan," asked Charlie Vincent, "when you were at Atlanta, did you get the idea that Stan Kasten was trying to do too many things at once?"

"Well," said Suhr, staring at an olive, remembering perhaps his painted-over parking space, "I really wouldn't know. He's very talented, obviously."

Columnist Mitch Albom started to write the quote in his palm-sized notebook, then stopped abruptly. "Very . . . talented . . . obviously," said Albom, looking at Suhr over the top of his glasses. Albom was the closest thing Detroit had to a poet-sportswriter—he'd been recognized as America's best sports columnist three years in a row—and he wasn't much given to mantalk. "How sincere!" said Albom.

Suhr, keeping a long face, picked up a napkin from the table and wiped away an imaginary tear. "The Atlanta Hawks," he said wistfully, "where are they now?"

"They're very talented—obviously," said Albom.

A loud, ugly scream came from the adjacent weight room. James Edwards, a pack of ice strapped to his ankle, burst into the locker room. He had somehow poked Mahorn in the eye. "Laimbeer started it," shouted Edwards to Brendan Suhr, as if Suhr—at five-eight, and 160—was going to wade in and break things up.

Matt Dobek hustled out of the weight room. "He's really *pissed*," said Dobek, his eyes wide. "He lost his contact lens."

"Laimbeer started it!" said Edwards.

"He's really pissed off," Dobek repeated to Suhr. Neither of them moved an inch toward the weight room.

The reporters paid little attention. Deadlines were looming; they still had hundreds of column inches to kill and wouldn't have an actual basketball game to write about until tomorrow. A few of them clotted around Aguirre; they all wanted exclusives, but felt much more comfortable in groups. "Is this the most fun you've ever had playing basketball?" someone asked.

"Yes." Aguirre nodded several times, to pad out his response.

"How come?"

"It's just that, everyone's playing tough basketball and everybody's pulling the same rope."

"Was it different in Dallas?"

"Well, I really, I mean, I've talked about that. I don't even want to talk about that. I really don't. I'm done with that."

"How is it different for you when the game's fun?"

Aguirre looked thoughtful. "If you enjoy what you're doing," he said, "then you have fun at it. Anybody's job—you can be a surgeon in the hospital and don't necessarily like the surroundings, or you can be a surgeon in another hospital and you like the surroundings, and it's a lot more comfortable to do it."

"Does basketball seem more like a game than a business now?"

"It's always been a game. I play it as a game. In college, I played it as a game. That's how I play it—as a game."

"When you were in college, what did you major in?"

"Communications." The reporters nodded, to pad out his answer.

Game day. At last. McCloskey took the steps two at a time as he sailed down from the front office to the stadium floor. Now he could see if his playoff strategies worked against a team that had beaten them all season. He'd find out if Aguirre could push them over the top. He'd find out if Salley's resurgence was for real. He'd find out if the chemistry and mix were perfect. It had to be, because from here on, they'd be facing the NBA's finest teams. He'd find out if the bench—his major contribution to the team—could win games in the playoffs the way it had in the regular season. Historically, the playoffs had been a first-five contest. Boston had been winning that way for years. But McCloskey didn't have a Championship-caliber first five, so he'd have to change history.

He could also get down to the business of building next year's team. Win or lose, he had to protect the franchise. He was going to soon have to make up his mind on who to dump into the expansion draft, and it would be a difficult, painful decision. And if the team didn't perform the way he expected—like the *best team in the world*—he would have to make decisions that would be even more painful.

But it felt great to be back in action. He shook hands with everyone he met as he hurried toward the locker room. "Were you disappointed to see Milwaukee beat Atlanta?" a reporter asked him.

"Naw—I'd rather face Milwaukee."

"But a week ago you said you'd rather face Atlanta."

"People change," said McCloskey.

Leon the Barber was whistling along with the Generic Hero Music as the players took the floor. In front of him, a kid selling Cokes walked by; he was tall and lithe and graceful and bore such a striking resemblance to Isiah Thomas that Leon did a double-take. A moment later Isiah wandered onto the floor, ready to start the game—another Isiah miracle, brought to you by the Detroit Pistons. He caught sight of the kid and looked at him oddly: There but for the grace of a jump shot.

The Pistons came out vibrating with pent-up energy. Aguirre was particularly hyper. He was driving past Fred Roberts with so many millisecond fakes that Roberts's eyes looked like marbles in a jar. Aguirre was dancing to his special, internal rhythm—the Superstar

Dance—hitting high, soft jumpers and twisting toward the hoop with moves he made up as he went along. Milwaukee managed to stay close, though. Then, halfway through the first quarter, Ricky Pierce stripped off his jacket and took the floor with a cold-serious look in his eyes. Six years before, McCloskey had exiled him to the Clippers, and Ricky Pierce was *still pissed*. Having McCloskey give up on him was bad enough—but going to the Clippers: Jesus! The franchise was a disaster. He'd only lasted a year there before the Clipper office had made one of the worst trades in league history, letting him, Terry Cummings, and Craig Hodges go in exchange for Junior Bridgeman, Marques Johnson, and Harvey Catchings. Now he and Cummings were stars and Hodges was one of the best 3-point shooters in the NBA. The three guys San Diego got were out of the league.

Part of the blame for McCloskey trading Pierce to the Clippers, though, belonged to former coach Scotty Robertson. Robertson had believed in the old boot-camp system—treating rookies like dogs, humiliating them, and not letting them play. So McCloskey hadn't had a good chance to evaluate Pierce during the season. And he hadn't seen him much during the preseason either, because Pierce's agent, Lance Lechnick, had held him out of camp while he'd hammered for more money. Lechnick thought all his kids were Hall of Famers. In this case, he'd hurt his client.

But Pierce didn't blame his agent—he blamed Detroit. Pierce had a big ego—he was probably the best sixth man in the NBA, was movie-star handsome, and was married to the lead singer of the Fifth Dimension. He wanted *revenge*. Just before the game, Pierce had said, "I want to *hurt* the Pistons. Bad." Now he had his chance.

He started making good on it. He got the ball at the 3-point line—Dumars knifed out toward him but he ducked under Dumars and drove straight at Mahorn. Pierce pulled up, jumped, and Mahorn jumped. But Pierce just kept rising and rising as Mahorn hit the apogee of his leap and started back down. Pierce snapped his wrists and the ball flew in a perfect line through the net. Pierce skipped downcourt, hopping every few steps to burn off adrenaline. For the next ten minutes he kept doing exactly the same thing—jolting to a halt for jumpers, piling up 15 points for a 13-point Milwaukee lead. Dumars tried to stop him but couldn't—for one thing, Pierce was too big. Pierce had biceps like thighs and shoulders so massive his head seemed to sit on them like a basketball on a refrigerator, and he was "a big six-four"—which meant that he was six-four without lying about it. Salley and Rodman tried to contain him, but a guard whose jump shot is falling is almost impossible to stop—his attack area is just too large. As Pierce picked apart the Piston defense,

Daly—surrounded by an extra squad of security—kept mopping his hand over his eyes, as if to wipe away what he was seeing.

But Pierce *had* to score for Milwaukee to stay in it. Terry Cummings, Milwaukee's highest scorer, was out with a sprained ankle and Paul Pressey, its leader in assists and steals, had been injured for over a month. With them gone, the rest of Milwaukee's bench was fast food for the Killer B-Team.

Just before the end of the half, a rested Laimbeer came in wearing his desperate, joyless scowl, and started tangling arms and legs with big Jack Sikma. Sikma shrugged away from Laimbeer, so Laimbeer took a step to the side and started wrapping himself up with little Jay Humphries. Humphries looked horrified and motioned to referee Tommy Nunez. Nunez stared at Humphries blankly and turned away. Leon the Barber stood and pointed at Humphries. "Welcome to the Palace, you little chickenshit," he screamed. Leon's dignified neighbor, who was wearing a black velvet jacket and a lot of gold jewelry, nodded quietly in agreement. Laimbeer kept pinballing around the court, body-bumping every Buck he was near, throwing Milwaukee into disarray. But Pierce's damage had been done. At the half, Milwaukee led by 9. McCloskey hurried to the locker room—so recently the site of so much laughter—looking like he'd just swallowed something very hot.

As he left the floor, McCloskey walked by John Ciszewski, who was clutching a two-way radio and frantically scratching at his face. "Fracas!" Ciszewski muttered. "We need a little *fracas* to get 'em going. How many times have you seen Milwaukee guys on their rear ends? None. None! They're coming into the lane like they owned it. The *last* time we played these guys, Pierce got knocked on his rear end, and he stopped coming into the lane." Ciszewski was almost sick with worry. Losing the first game—and with it the home-court advantage—would be a disaster. It would supercharge Milwaukee's emotion, and if Milwaukee also won the second game in Detroit, the series would be all but over.

Ciszewski didn't even want to think what losing in the second round would do to the franchise. It was a seven-game series, but nobody *ever* recovered after losing the first two at home. It would be a bitch to sell season tickets after that kind of debacle, and the blow to the business could ignite a downward spiral they might never recover from. It was beginning to look as if the salary cap would increase by almost $2 million in August, and if that happened, the money-making franchises would beef up their teams, while the poorer franchises declined. It was grow or die.

As the second half started, Dave Auker went straight into "Mony, Mony"—it was early in the game to use up such a guaranteed crowd-hyper, but this was no time to screw around. The crowd responded, and the team took the floor with courtside fans chanting "Kick-some-*ass*! Kick-some-*ass*!" The Milwaukee players picked up on the hostility, and seemed to tighten a little. A couple of minutes into the half, Sikma missed a free throw—a good sign of raw nerves; Sikma had led the league in free-throw percentage. Mahorn came down with Sikma's miss, his legs spread wide, and rammed his elbow into Fred Roberts's gut. Roberts sucked in some breath, turned to referee Dick Bavetta, and yelled, "Hey! What the hell! Elbow!" But by that time, Bavetta was streaking downcourt. Milwaukee started fumbling the ball and the fans got even more carnivorous. Milwaukee tried to counter the physical assault with their huge, all-white front line—Fred Roberts (six-ten), Sikma (seven feet), Paul Mokeski (seven feet), Randy Breuer (seven-three), and Larry Krystkowiak (six-ten). But their Ivory Towers didn't have the badness to push Laimbeer, Mahorn, Salley, and Rodman out of the way. They were easy to market in a lily-white town like Milwaukee, but they had too much of what the players called "white man's disease"—no speed and no leap.

The Milwaukee lead continued to erode until two minutes into the fourth quarter, when Vinnie Johnson caught a fireball pass from Laimbeer and drilled a 3-pointer to put Detroit ahead for the first time since tip-off. Laimbeer's arms V'd into his Rocky pose and they stayed up—up, up. For endless moments they stayed there, and his face was demonic, possessed. He and the front line had pulled Detroit back with brute force—the guards were only shooting about 30 percent. The fans screamed. Dembo, Williams, and Mahorn came off the bench with their fists in the air. Auker put on Generic Hero Music. Leon the Barber twirled his jacket over his head.

But Pierce kept nailing jumpers. His form was textbook-perfect, and the game stayed close as the end approached. But then Rodman and Sikma went up for a rebound, and Rodman grabbed Sikma's elbows from behind so that he couldn't reach for the ball. The ball came down on Sikma's back, and Sikma rocked one of his elbows back toward Rodman's face. Rodman ducked it and drove his open hand—no fist, no ejection—into Sikma's face. Referee Tommy Nunez jumped in and pushed Rodman away, calling a foul on him, but the skirmish seemed to drain the Bucks. Two minutes later, Ricky Pierce ran by Milwaukee coach Del Harris and blurted, "Take me out!"

Veteran star Sidney Moncrief came in with two minutes left, but Moncrief's legs were tracked with surgery scars and his jump was flat and painful to watch. Moncrief tried to go against Salley and Rodman for a rebound but he looked like he was jumping in hip boots. "Damn!"

said Harris, "they're killing us on the boards!" But Rodman lost the ball—Dumb Dennis—and Milwaukee got a shot. It was off, but Moncrief was exactly where he was supposed to be; he jerked a few inches upward and tipped the ball in. Milwaukee by 1. Moncrief hobbled back to the bench and settled onto the floor, spreading his leg out flat, moving like an old man who'd just felt his hip snap in two. Pierce went back in even though he was spent. Del Harris didn't have the bench to do anything else.

Laimbeer hit from the top of the key. Detroit by 1. Pierce back in. 51 seconds. Pierce drove on Rodman. They collided. Rodman bounced backward. Foul on Rodman. Dumb Dennis. Rodman fell to his hands and knees, pounding the floor and making strange noises. Daly held his arms over his chest and glared at Rodman. McCloskey, his face immobile, stared at the clock. 42 seconds. Two free throws for Milwaukee, the best free-throw team in the league. Pierce stepped to the line. The crowd shrieked, and the section behind the basket—in Pierce's field of vision—waved black Bad Boy handkerchiefs. "Hey Ricky Retardo," yelled Leon the Barber, "Airball! Airball!" Soon the whole stadium was sing-songing "Airball." Pierce dribbled and flexed his knees. He put it up and it clanged off the back of the rim—too much force: an adrenaline miss. Del Harris worked his tongue against his cheeks. Larry Krystkowiak bit his towel. Pierce took a deep breath—held it—and shot. The ball went up and laid on the flat back of the rim. It almost came to a dead stop. Then it rolled off. Laimbeer grabbed it and held it like a father holding his child at the edge of a cliff. The game was out of reach. Dave Auker put on "Celebration," and slumped in his seat.

The following day, as practice concluded, Jack McCloskey sat at courtside with Stan Novak, his oldest and probably closest friend in the franchise. They didn't say much. Occasionally, McCloskey would murmur something about how badly Detroit had played. "I'd like to think it was because of the layoff," he said.

Novak held a copy of "Game Notes," and kept running his finger down the Milwaukee roster: Roberts, Mokeski, Humphries—a bunch of stiffs. "A lot of it's coaching, Jack," he said. "Nellie rubbed off on Del. I noticed he even used some of the same signals."

Part of McCloskey's job was to provide ballast to the team, and part of Novak's job was to provide ballast to McCloskey. "Don't worry," Novak said confidently, "things will change."

"I know they will." Trader Jack snorted a short laugh. "One way or another. I know they will."

In front of McCloskey, on the floor, a handful of reporters clustered around John Salley. Anchorman Scott Wahle spotted PR director Matt Dobek and said, "Hey, Matt, what's the deal? Nobody's talking."

"John," said Dobek, "is that true?"

"That's what they said," Salley said. "Hey—that gives them more of Sal-Sal. Tell 'em to be happy."

"Be happy," said Dobek, as he hurried off to the locker room to find out what was going on.

"How did you get elected spokesman?" a reporter asked Salley.

"They said, you're gonna talk anyway, Salley—you might as well go ahead and do it. Everybody else is just gonna stay away from everything that doesn't have anything to do with basketball."

Salley got some dirty looks. "You don't think *this* has anything to do with basketball?" said Wahle. Meaning: "Who do you think invented you guys as Culture Gods, if not the media?"

But a star never backs down: "No," said Salley. "At least not anything to do with *winning* at basketball." He smiled, though, and granted eye contact.

"It's going to be a long series if you do all the talking," said Wahle.

"Hey, that's cool," said Salley. "I'll get more ads. They'll say, 'Ooh! This man can speak *English.*'"

"If you're going to be the designated talker," said Wahle, "give us some good stuff. Tell us Milwaukee's a bunch of chumps, it's sweep time. Something we can sink our teeth into."

"I'll take you to a steak dinner if you want something to sink your teeth into. Everybody to Sizzler, let's go!"

"You see Harris after they won the Atlanta series? He was in tears. How's that kind of emotion play a role?"

"*Most* of it is emotion," said Salley. "We play with emotion. We play with the pride of Pistons, as opposed to guys sometimes playing just to get paid. It's an honor for each of us to be a Piston. It's an honor for us to win, not just for our own glory, but for the city of Detroit."

Salley beamed. Even Future Mayor Isiah Thomas couldn't have spouted better mantalk.

"You did good," said a reporter.

"I did *well*," corrected Salley. "Very well."

McCloskey got up from the stands, and walked upstairs to the front office to call Bill Musselman, the coach of the new Minnesota Timberwolves. He wanted to trade one of his players plus his draft pick for Musselman's draft pick, which would be the tenth selection. McCloskey would probably have to offer a player he really liked—like Michael Williams—but it would be worth it. Stan Novak and Will Robinson had been combing the country for months, sitting through games at hundreds of little jerkwater colleges, trying to find that one overlooked player who'd be at the bottom of the draft. But none had materialized. If McCloskey was going to get a player who could help, he'd have to move up.

But Musselman wouldn't go for it. Bad PR. A franchise just getting started needed all the hype it could get, and one thing to ignite public interest would be its first draft pick. If that pick was in the dregs instead of near the top, the fans might feel cheated out of their first NBA experience. It didn't matter that Michael Williams might be better than anyone the Timberwolves might draft—Williams was a known commodity. A high draft pick would be a mystery man, a dream. To a new franchise, dreams were important. That was all they had to sell.

McCloskey understood. For years, the only thing he'd had to sell was a dream. But his fans had long ago paid cash for the dream, and now they were demanding to see it come true.

Del Harris threw his clipboard to the floor, and even over the racket of the Palace crowd, it clapped out a sharp *whap!* that made Larry Krystkowiak wince. "We're just pissin' it away!" Harris cried. Again Krystkowiak winced; he was a sweet-mannered young man, bright and conscientious—a coach's dream—who was not given to histrionics. Krystkowiak was on the bench, a white towel over his legs, watching the hapless Milwaukee bench squander the slim lead that he and the starters had gained. Krystkowiak had been throwing himself into Mahorn and Laimbeer—which was like throwing yourself onto a grenade—managing to pile up 7 points and 8 rebounds in the first quarter. But the sacrifice showed—sweat was still dripping off Krystkowiak's slender nose several minutes after he'd sat down.

The game stayed close into the third quarter, but the Milwaukee starters were starting to wheeze and drag. "Milwaukee is really a patched-together team," Greg Kelser shouted into his microphone. "Del Harris is doin' it with mirrors."

"Not a pretty sight," said George Blaha. "But you keep looking at the scoreboard, and they're right in it."

A minute later, Mahorn and Krystkowiak went up for a rebound. Krystkowiak came down with the ball, but Mahorn came down with Krystkowiak's' *head*—he had his neck in an armlock as they both hit the floor. Mahorn could have broken Krystkowiak's neck with one quick twist, and he looked pissed off enough to do it. But he let go. Krystkowiak backed away as Mahorn sneered and wiggled his fingers at him. Mahorn got a foul, but the damage was done. Krystkowiak missed his free throw, then retreated to the bench, his face red and confused. For several minutes he sat twisting his neck, as sweat rained onto his jacket. He looked shocked—they didn't play that way in Shelby, Montana, where Krystkowiak had grown up. Krystkowiak wasn't built for beatings—he was only big in the areas where muscles could be cultivated; he had a work-built body, not a God-given one. From an aesthetic standpoint, his physique went well with his 1963 haircut and Peace Corps wholesome looks. But it didn't scare anybody.

As the third quarter wound down, Laimbeer tangled with little Jay Humphries and push-popped him in the chest. Del Harris jumped up and yelled to referee Jack Madden, "He hit Jay! He hit the shit out of him! Couldn't you see that!" Madden called a technical on Harris, and Laimbeer hit the shot to put Detroit up 8.

In the fourth quarter, John Salley took over. Every time Milwaukee would mount a charge, Salley would come screaming out of nowhere to block a shot, grab a rebound, or make a basket. Salley had 16 points in the quarter, making virtually all of his attempts. Salley felt untouchable, exalted. He was finally in the zone of altered consciousness. Now he knew how guys like Vinnie and Isiah felt.

Milwaukee fought to keep up, mostly on the strength of Pierce and Krystkowiak. Krystkowiak's performance—he'd finish with 22 points and 13 rebounds—was the finest of his career. After several years of struggling to stay in the league, he was suddenly on the verge of stardom—and a star's money. By this time next year, he'd be rich.

But with Milwaukee threatening to get back in the game, Salley scored twice in a row, and put the game away. Rodman ran up to Salley at midcourt and embraced him.

McCloskey watched with great satisfaction. He'd resisted the great temptation to trade Salley. Now it was paying off—right on schedule.

Again, Detroit had moved to a strong playoff advantage over a team that had almost everything Detroit had—except for a killer attitude and a Killer B-Team. For those two attributes, the Piston fans could thank Trader Jack. Not that any of them would, of course. Only a few of them were even vaguely aware of it. To them, it was box scores and highlight film: Just a Game.

McCloskey found his seat at center court in Milwaukee's Bradley Center. The fans around him knew who he was, and were mildly hostile. He was, after all, not just the architect of a team, but the architect of the vicious Bad Boys. With half their starters out with injuries, they weren't inclined to feel generous.

McCloskey settled into his seat as the action started. Then, seconds into the game, Larry Krystkowiak was running down the floor, with Laimbeer at his heels. They were close together under the Milwaukee basket. Suddenly Krystkowiak was flying. He was shooting forward, out of control, his arms and legs exploding into odd, twisted angles. Laimbeer pulled away from him as Krystkowiak crashed onto the floor. Krystkowiak was screaming even before he hit.

The referee blew his whistle and pointed at Laimbeer.

Krystkowiak was still crying out in pain, writhing on the floor. The fans around McCloskey were shrieking, and glaring at him.

Krystkowiak had ripped apart half the ligaments in his knee. It was the end of the game for him. It was the end of the season. In all probability, it was the end of his career. The big money, it appeared, was now lost forever. But maybe he could coach junior college in Shelby, Montana.

Del Harris ran onto the floor. As he passed Laimbeer he yelled something at him. Harris was hit with a technical. Daly heard the remark, lurched toward Harris, and had to be restrained by his players.

The game, for all practical purposes, was over. So was the series. Milwaukee could barely field a team.

Even from the stands, McCloskey could see that Krystkowiak's injury was devastating. He *hated* to see that happen. He felt sorry for Krystkowiak. But he didn't feel sorry for Milwaukee. He'd built a bench, and they hadn't. He was glad. He tried not to show it.

The fans around McCloskey were furious, and the stadium was rocking with the release of anger. Everywhere you looked, fans were letting go of their emotions and blowing off steam. They could afford to. To them, it was Just a Game. McCloskey kept his mouth shut.

Larry Krystkowiak, strapped into a stretcher and wheeled into an ambulance, had already begun to absolve Laimbeer of blame. His leg, he said, had "just exploded." Not placing blame was more than just Krystkowiak's generous nature. It was more than just mantalk. To Krystkowiak—and to McCloskey—this wasn't a game. This was business. And keeping your mouth shut was good business.

FOURTEEN

"Dreams of a Lifetime"
The Chicago Series, Part One

ARC LIGHTS dazzled hot and white
in the hallway outside the Pistons' locker room as a beautiful black girl
in a see-through white petticoat and long black ruffled pantaloons
preened for a video camera. "We're rolling," said a guy behind the
cameraman. "Four, three, two, one"—he pointed at the girl.

"Hey!" she chanted, "this is Downtown Julie Brown at the Palace of
Auburn Hills with the Detroit Piston *Baaad* Boys! It's MTV's NBA Sunday and we're . . ." Downtown Julie Brown, who considered herself "a
superstar," snipped off the end of her sentence. "Cameraman," she said,
her voice an octave lower, "I'm sorry, I don't know your name."

"Davey," said the little blond guy holding the camera.

"Davey. Can I see some *happy faces* back there, Davey?" She smiled,
but tapped the steel-tipped toe of her cowboy boot. "Some energy?"
She had an English accent, so it came out, "in-a-gee."

James Edwards slipped past, a white towel around his neck, not
making eye contact, and she chirped, "Gawd! He must be big."

"Seven feet," said Davey.

"Seven *feet*! I didn't know one of them *grew* seven feet," she leered,
spreading her arms and staring wide-eyed at the space between them.
Davey blushed. A makeup woman raked at the MTV veejay's towering
Christmas tree of hair, then Brown did her intro again and pushed her

face into the camera and said, "Now *stay right there* while I slip into something more comfortable." She pranced through the locker room door and the director quietly said, "Cut."

Steve Addy, watching with a sick look from a few feet away as he waited for the postpractice interviews, was almost hyperventilating. "They gonna do a *video*? Shit! Any team that does a video is *screwed*."

Through the tunnel, from out on the floor, came the hollow echoes of the last few practice balls rattling the hoop. Williams and Dembo stood patiently, waiting for Dumars and Johnson to stop shooting so they could rack the balls and wheel them to the locker room. A couple of rows into the stands, McCloskey watched his players finish up and talked softly about the upcoming Eastern Finals. They'd be facing the Bulls in another best-of-seven match. Jordan had done it again. His 40 points and 10 assists in yesterday's sixth game had kept the Bulls close to the Knicks, and then at the end he'd buried them. The media had preordained that the Pistons would beat the Bulls, because Detroit had won all six regular-season games. Daly kept ranting to everyone that the playoffs were a whole different world, but no one really believed it. Except McCloskey. McCloskey was almost as scared as Daly, mostly because of Michael Jordan. "At least one team in the Finals will have a super-superstar on it," he predicted. "Because those are the guys that get it done. You can't overestimate their danger." McCloskey, though, feared that his players didn't realize the threat—they were too loose, too happy. They'd beaten Boston, a team that didn't have its "franchise" player. And they'd beaten Milwaukee, a team that didn't have the kind of bench McCloskey had built. So they figured they could stomp a one-man team like Chicago. That kind of figuring, McCloskey thought, could be fatal.

Downtown Julie Brown suddenly materialized on-court and, spotting McCloskey as the sole spectator in the stands, turned and wiggled her butt at him—it was sort of a no-hands wave and was one of her trademarks. She'd changed into a baggy Pistons jersey and baseball cap, cocked to one side, suggesting "tomboy," or, more to the point with her red-gloss lips and Lycra pants, "jailbait." "Who's *she*?" asked McCloskey.

"With MTV," said a ball boy.

"What's that?"

"Music television. Music videos."

McCloskey nodded. "Gotta go through a lot of carnivals to get to the top," he said. His thoughts darted back to the team. The college draft was looming and McCloskey had been talking with Elgin Baylor, GM of the Clippers, about trading a veteran for Baylor's lottery pick. Baylor already had plenty of young stars from the draft, including Danny Manning, because the Clippers were such god-awful losers. So he was in a unique position to let go of another high draftee for someone who'd give him a little stability and brains. The Clippers, under flaky owner Donald Sterling, were dying for stability and brains. "Elgin knows that if he can get a blend of a veteran player with the young people they have, they're on the verge of being a very good team," said McCloskey. But giving up a veteran right now would be hard as hell for McCloskey, mostly because of the expansion draft. McCloskey could only protect nine players, and that meant he might lose one of his most valuable veterans, someone like Vinnie Johnson or James Edwards, or maybe even Mahorn or Aguirre. After that piece of legalized theft, courtesy of the market-hungry league, McCloskey probably wouldn't have a veteran to spare. Of course, the high-draft player he might acquire—someone like sharp-shooter Glen Rice—might have more skills than the veteran he'd lose. But what would it do to the mix? At the moment, McCloskey had the right mix of youth and experience, and upsetting it might dump his house of cards.

A few yards away, Salley and Edwards were waiting to do an MTV promo. "When's this gonna be on?" Salley asked Downtown Julie Brown, now seated in the stands and thrusting her breasts (she called them her "good parts") against Rick Mahorn's thick shoulders.

"Sunday."

"Sunday! Nobody watches MTV on Sunday. You only watch that shit when you don't have nuthin' to do." Edwards laughed. He was the team's best straight man, which was very valuable, and he was also its only true center, which was even more valuable. It would be terrible to lose him. But maybe necessary.

There was a lot more on McCloskey's mind, though, than moving up in the college draft, or even surviving the expansion draft. As far as McCloskey was concerned, this was his last, best chance with this group of players. They'd finally won the home-court advantage throughout the playoffs—"it's what we played all season for." With that advantage, there would be no excuse for not winning the Championship. For the past two years, this team had been achingly close to winning it all. But something had gone wrong—Isiah's bad pass against Boston, then Rodman's Dumb Dennis shot against the Lakers. "So you have to ask yourself," said McCloskey, standing now, anxious to go play tennis and burn off some anxiety, "can this particular team *play* better? Or is it time to . . . dismantle? To start over?"

Dennis Rodman took his turn with Julie Brown. Before the camera rolled she sidled up to him and said, "I heard you grew eight inches.

Overnight!'' Davey, current victim of penis envy, was blushing again, and Rodman looked sheepish. "I grew eight inches in a *year,*" Rodman said.

"Still," she replied, nodding, "not bad." But Rodman didn't seem to hear her. In the parking lot outside, a radio station was giving away $1 to $5,000 to everybody who drove by, creating a tremendous racket. But that wasn't what had distracted Rodman. He was watching Mc-Closkey leave. McCloskey made him nervous. Then he found Julie Brown and got back to the more pleasant aspects of being rich, young, and famous.

At practice the next day—the day before Chicago came to town—Tom Wilson sat with McCloskey, quietly watching the players run through drills, the squeak of their sneakers amplified by the vast arena, which was even more plush in its emptiness. Wilson was antsy. Normally, the practices were rough and loud, full of muscle slapping into muscle, grunts, curses, glares. Now everyone was cordial and a little slow. Granted, the coaches had pulled in the reins to avoid injuries. But Wilson didn't see the look he wanted in the players' eyes. And their body language wasn't right. They weren't ready.

The coaches, on the other hand, seemed immaculately prepared. They'd flown to Chicago to scout the Bulls-Knicks series, and had analyzed a catalog of Chicago plays. They were working through each of them now with the players, first at little more than a walk, then at full speed. Daly was worried about the long layoff between series. If they came out as flat as they did against Milwaukee, they'd get their butts kicked. He had considered hauling the whole team back to Windsor for two-a-day practices. Hopefully, that would snap them back into the bloodthirsty feeling of fall camp. He'd talked the idea over with former Philadelphia coach Billy Cunningham. Cunningham, whose 1983 team had endured long layoffs to win the Championship in just thirteen games (almost fulfilling Moses Malone's famous "Fo', Fo', Fo' " prediction), had talked him out of it. If Daly could just keep his team's concentration and motivation, Cunningham had said, he'd be allright. All Daly could do now was hope that the Bad Boy spirit—the desperation to win, which McCloskey had combed the league to find—was in full force. Even if it was, though, Detroit would be up against an equally tough-minded Chicago team. Bulls' coach Doug Collins preached that "the mind is everything," and he'd just pushed his team past two opponents who should have beaten them.

Daly, in a fancy red-and-gray warm-up suit with yards of braiding and piping—he looked like George Jetson as costumed by Pierre Cardin—was standing at halfcourt with the guards. In his burnt-larynx coach's rasp, he exhorted them to be careful about Craig Hodges and Scottie Pippen shooting from the wings. "They made *nineteen* threes against New York and Cleveland," Daly squawked. "Nine*teen*." Dumars nodded slowly and Isiah cupped his elbow in his hand, impassive. If the Bad Boy spirit was in force, it wasn't apparent to Tom Wilson.

"You know," Wilson said to McCloskey, "we may need to lose one to get people to listen again."

McCloskey caught Wilson in his eye, held him there, clamped his lips together, and nodded.

After practice, ABC News reporter Dick Schaap, who specialized in sports features, went to work on a story about Joe Dumars. "Joe Dumars," Schaap had said during practice, "is not going to put asses in seats in front of the TV. But Michael Jordan is, and Joe's got to guard him." Schaap had considered a story on Laimbeer—"that rare breed, a white basketball player"—but he considered the quiet Dumars a more offbeat angle. As the players drifted through the tunnel toward the locker room, Schaap corralled stars to appear in his piece. Dumars stood silently to one side. "I'm going to get Isiah to give me a couple of comments first, okay?" Schaap said to Dumars. "I just did it with Laimbeer, and he accused you of just about everything but being white."

"That sounds about right," said Dumars.

When it was time for Dumars, they sat on folding chairs facing each other under the basket, Dumars in silk warm-ups and Schaap in a plain navy blazer. The interview was low-key, chocked with fewer jockisms than usual, centering on the defensive strategies of Dumars, whom Jordan had acknowledged as his toughest defender. The hardest part about guarding Jordan, Dumars told Schaap, was that "since he has such huge hands, he never has to slow down to gather the ball in. Whatever he wants to do, he takes the ball with him. He just scoops it up and goes." Not much of a revelation, but at least it wasn't just mantalk.

After the interview, Schaap and Dumars began talking about Cajun food, because of Dumars's Louisiana upbringing, and Dumars became much more animated. Unlike many of the players, who were estranged from the harsh environments of their childhoods, Dumars loved going home to little Natchitoches every summer. Dumars was very close with his family, which had been stable and loving throughout his youth— accounting, in part, for Dumars's sweet personality. But there hadn't been anything easy about Dumars's youth; he'd shared a bedroom with six brothers while his father had worked eighteen-hour days, and he'd learned to play basketball on a homemade basket illuminated by the neon of an all-night liquor store. There was still hardship in the Dumars family. Dumars's father had recently lost both legs to diabetes, and this season he'd had three heart attacks. Now Dumars called home after every game, no matter how late it was. He'd already decided what he would do if he won a Championship ring—he was going to give it to his father.

As Schaap walked off the court, Brendan Suhr did some press-stroking, telling Schaap how much he liked his Sunday morning ESPN show, which featured a panel of sportswriters. "Looks like you guys have lots of fun," Suhr said. "You toss it around really well. I was watching Mike Lupica on it the other day. Reminded me of the time in Atlanta when he came into our huddle. Fratello was trying to diagram plays, so I said, 'Can I help you?' He said, 'No.' No! So I got kind of pissed off and he did too, for a while. But the hell of it is, he was the only guy in the huddle who was paying attention."

Suhr looked relaxed—for a coach. A couple of players, dressed now in street clothes, looked at him quizzically. But they shrugged: What the hell—if even the coaches could keep from freaking out, so much the better. They'd beaten Chicago *six straight*. It was in the bag.

From outside the Bulls' locker room came the sound of the Palace crowd—a muffled wall of white noise—as Michael Jordan pulled his tailored game shorts, 2½ inches longer than normal, over the blue North Carolina gym shorts he wore underneath. Even in repose, his skinny legs were all sinew; they looked like pulled taffy. In the midst of standard jocktalk with reporters—"How do you feel?" "Worried about Dumars?"—Jordan stopped suddenly and looked up. "Know what?" he said casually. "We're gonna win. I bet you. The first game is the easiest to get, because they don't know what to expect." A few of Jordan's teammates glanced over. They looked shocked. The other Bulls didn't treat Jordan like an icon, as the media did, but when he talked they listened.

Minutes later, tip-off. Mahorn versus Bill Cartwright—the center Bulls' GM Jerry Krause had gambled on, and alienated Jordan over. Cartwright drew ugly noises from the fans; they were still pissed off about the Cartwright-Thomas fight. How dare he break Isiah's fist with his jaw? When the ball went up it was bobbled four times before Mahorn finally controlled it. The Pistons' timing was off. A few moments later, Isiah shot an airball. Dumars, veiling a look of shock, tried to grab the ball but it went out of bounds. Daly clapped his hands fiercely and yelled, "C'mon! Let's *go*!" But Detroit was moving too carefully. Chicago wasn't. As soon as 265-pound Dave Corzine hit the floor, he staked out a place under the basket, and when Mahorn backed in toward him, Corzine hammered the heels of both hands into Mahorn's kidneys. Mahorn didn't yield, but he straightened suddenly and looked stunned. With 3:37 left in the quarter and Chicago up 11, Thomas stole the ball and streaked downcourt. For the first time, Detroit seemed to come alive. But Horace Grant knifed in and jabbed the ball away. Referee Joe Crawford hit Grant with a foul, and suddenly Jordan was in Crawford's face. "He didn't get nuthin' but *ball*," Jordan yelled.

"He got 'em," said Crawford, turning away. By the time the confrontation was over, the Pistons had cooled off again. "They're too loose, George," Greg Kelser said to George Blaha. "They're not bumping."

McCloskey kept waiting for somebody to go on a streak—he thought Dumars might—but it didn't happen.

With Chicago up 16, Detroit called time. The Piston guards, the core of their offense, hadn't scored. Daly madly scribbled plays designed to ignite them. But as Daly X'd and O'd, Mahorn, and then Aguirre, started watching the scoreboard as Dave Auker played a tape of Jordan beating Cleveland at the buzzer. After a moment, even Brendan Malone—*coach* Malone—was watching. As the tape ended, they all slowly cranked their heads back down to Daly's chalkboard. Aguirre was thinking that it had been the worst quarter Detroit had played since he'd arrived.

It got worse. Chicago started the second quarter by continuing a 25–2 run. McCloskey sat grimly in his seat, his hands folded, just a few rows above a stone-faced Downtown Julie Brown, who was sitting in NBA Commissioner David Stern's seat. The highlight of the quarter was when Julie Brown did the Celebrity Free-Throw Shoot. She backed onto the court in stretch cycling shorts, pointing, for some reason, at her ass. Then she did her trademark butt-wave, clanged a few shots off the rim, and took her seat to thunder, the only real noise of the quarter. Auker was doing his best to dump some adrenaline onto the floor, but as the lead grew from 16 to 24 points, rigor mortis set in. Laimbeer, usually the heart of the team's anger, was slow and heavy. With 5:25 left in the half, Laimbeer traveled—his third turnover in four minutes—and he pounded the ball onto the floor, again and again. Then he took position under the basket. Cartwright backed into him; they muscled for territory, and Cartwright swung his head back and raked it across Laimbeer's face. Laimbeer stood there, wincing and scowling. But it wasn't anger, just frustration. Leon the Barber yelled, "Bring back Rowinski!" It was getting ugly. Daly pulled Laimbeer for Mahorn, who walked slowly onto the court rolling his eyes. He paused briefly to tap Laimbeer's hands, and said, "What is this shit?" Head scout Stan Novak felt his fear physically—his arms ached.

In the third quarter, it started to change. Dumars picked up Jordan sooner, and suddenly Jordan, who'd scored 14 in the first quarter, couldn't get shots. Aguirre, Mahorn, and Laimbeer began pushing and elbow-popping, and by 5:32 Detroit was within 7. Jordan got the ball on the next possession and began one of his drives to the hoop—the kind that no other player in the history of the game has consistently attempted. He darted toward the basket, faked, fell to his left, recovered, fell to his right to avoid the collapsing defense, regained his balance, then ducked under four hands in front of his eyes and chest and exploded upward. He hung there—hung some more—and finally flipped the ball up on his way down. But it rimmed the hoop and slid back out. The law of averages was taking over.

Just before the end of the third, Jordan got the ball down low and scrambled toward the basket, his loose trunks flapping against his skinny thighs. But suddenly Laimbeer and Salley were jammed up against him, and then Thomas came hard from out of nowhere to scoop an overhand arc from the top of Jordan's nose down to the ball. Jordan got off a shot, but it bumped out and Laimbeer grabbed the rebound. Aguirre got the ball at the Detroit end just inside the free-throw line, and drove into four Chicago defenders, anchored underneath by big Dave Corzine, whose pasty white arms were high over his head. Aguirre weaved in, then dropped to the left of Corzine, twisting backward and throwing the ball up with his left hand as he collapsed onto the floor. He sprawled on his back with his feet curled over his head as the ball banked in. It was the kind of shot Jordan made.

The B-Team defense continued to hound Chicago in the fourth. Rodman blocked the much taller Corzine, then Salley stuffed Jordan to help bring Detroit to within 4. Next time down for Chicago, Pippen got the ball at the top of the key, but then stood there helplessly as three Pistons surrounded him. The longer he stood there, waving the ball, the more his face contorted, until pretty soon it was all balled up like a wad of paper. Shortly after that, Jordan got his first foul of the game—testimony to either his exquisite body control or being the game's biggest piece of money. Two minutes left—Bulls by 5. McCloskey sat tight-mouthed just above the floor and Daly stood on the sidelines, his arms X'd over his blue paisley tie. Detroit had the ball; Thomas sped downcourt. He dribbled into the right corner, faked a drive to the hoop, and tossed it out to Laimbeer, who was alone at the 3-point line. Laimbeer, so often paralyzed at crunch time, took the shot. The ball bounced straight back, and seven players went up for it, including Mahorn. As Mahorn came down without the ball, he got brushed on the hip by Jordan. Mahorn lost his balance and came careening out of the pack. Referee Tommy Nunez saw Mahorn go dancing by—Mean Mahorn, who must have suffered a hell of a smack to go dancing by like that—and blew his whistle. He pointed at Jordan. Jordan started bitching and Mahorn started clapping. Mahorn went to the line, his face happy and calm, and sank both shots. It was a moment for Mahorn to savor—he wanted to be on McCloskey's protected list. The lead was down to 3.

It stayed at 3 for the next minute. Then, with 56 seconds left, Vinnie Johnson drove to the hoop and dished off at the last second to Mahorn, who was right under the basket, alone. Mahorn went up—his chance to be the hero. But Jordan flew crosscourt and swatted Mahorn's hands. The shot missed. Mahorn danced up and down in anger. He had his Mean Mahorn grin on as he stepped to the line. The grin faded, but his face stayed tight. The first shot was long—an adrenaline miss. Mahorn stood stoically as the crowd moaned. The second shot went up—and did exactly the same thing. Daly cried, "Oh, no!" and grabbed his head. Scottie Pippen leaped up for the rebound. Mahorn, turning downcourt, yelled "Shitttt!"

Detroit was still down 3. 36 seconds left. Chicago zipped the ball through the backcourt. Mahorn stood next to Pippen, and nudged him with his forearm. Whistle. Mahorn got called for the forearm. He was stunned. So was Pippen. Jordan sank both shots. The game was over.

McCloskey, Daly, and Suhr followed the players back into the locker room. Daly was quiet, but McCloskey acted upbeat and confident. That was his role. Then they left the players and went into the coaches' room. As they sat there, Suhr said, "When was the last time we lost a game?" McCloskey and Daly looked at him blankly. They couldn't remember. "April fourteenth," said Suhr, "in New York. Almost six weeks ago. The last time we lost at home was January twenty-seventh."

"Cleveland," said Daly.

McCloskey and Daly brightened a little. Suhr's remark had reminded Daly that teams can win *too* much—and go soft from it. Daly went out to face the press. He singled out missed free throws in the stretch as the cause for the loss. Everybody knew he meant Mahorn, but nobody asked him to get specific—that would violate the protocol of mantalk.

In the locker room, reporters milled around Mahorn's cubicle, waiting for him to come out of the shower. They needed their goat. Mahorn peeked around the corner and a sportswriter called, "You coming out pretty soon?"

"Next week," he said, and ducked back in.

But they waited him out, and he sat down and served up his jock-isms: "Just one of those days," and, "Just part of the ups and downs of the NBA," and "Give Chicago credit." Finally, Aguirre leaned over from his adjacent locker and shouted, "Hey, leave the man alone, okay?"

Mahorn smiled weakly, got up, and said, "I'm gonna go home and kick my dog."

The players scattered quickly, as they usually did after a loss. Isiah Thomas hopped into his massive black four-wheeler and went straight back to his castle in Bloomfield Hills. He couldn't sleep. He never could when they lost. He sat in front of his TV and plugged in the game. He'd missed 15 out of 18 shots. *Fifteen* out of *eighteen*. Almost all the shots he'd taken had been good shots—there were only two stinkers. He kept replaying each shot, looking for a flaw. He couldn't find any. Everything was perfect. So . . . *what went wrong?*

A few miles away, across a strip of lakes and hills, Leslie McCloskey sat outside their condo, watching the lake as night fell. Inside, Jack McCloskey sat in front of the TV. He was only vaguely aware of what was on. He was thinking about Mahorn. And about Edwards, who'd only played 11 minutes. And about Vinnie Johnson, who'd shot 3 for 11. He replayed the game in his head. He felt the dream of his life dematerializing, becoming once again fantasy. If it did disappear, it would be time to rebuild—"to start over." The game had been in the afternoon, so there was plenty of time to think.

Leslie McCloskey sat outside until it was dark.

Rodman's team was losing, and Rodman *hated* to lose. It didn't mat-ter that this was just practice, a tune-up before the next Chicago game. The Killer B-Team often beat the starters in practice, and they'd had a chance to win this scrimmage. But they'd been too tight—a carryover from the Chicago loss. Detroit was suffering from its first case of nerves in a long time. Passes were going into the seats, a sign of trying too hard. So when it became apparent to Rodman that the B-Team was going to lose, he delicately let go of the ball about waist-high, and—*bam!*—drop-kicked it as hard as he could. With his phone-pole thighs, he launched it on a tremendous rising curve, over the first section of seats, over the lower deck of suites, into the upper level.

"Damn, Dennis!" yelled McCloskey from the sidelines, "we don't need *that* crap! Cut it out!" McCloskey took Rodman aside and said a few words to him. The subject was maturity. McCloskey loved Rodman's furious enthusiasm—it was the quality Trader Jack was constantly searching for—but there had to be a needle-sharp focus to it. They were suddenly facing the biggest threat of the season, and if they didn't overcome it, this group of players would never get another chance. No time to lose control.

After practice, Daly met reporters in the concrete-block hallway between the coaches' room and the locker room. There was a crowd of out-of-town and national reporters at the games now, and the sixty-foot-long CBS truck was semipermanently parked in the loading dock. The quiet, intimate feeling of earlier in the year was gone. Daly loved it.

Daly told the reporters that he was already dreading the games in Chicago. "It's a great home court for them," he said, "as good as there is in the league. We've put ourselves in a very difficult position by surrendering the home-court advantage. Right now we've got to hope for seven games to get it back. There's tremendous pressure on us tomorrow night. We *gotta* win." Daly was speed-rapping in his breathless, sound-bite style. "If we don't," he huffed, "it's Katie bar the door." Some of the young reporters looked at each other questioningly. Katie?

While Daly held forth, McCloskey bounded up the back stairs to the front office and ran into Tom Wilson.

"How'd they look?" asked Wilson.

"A little frustrated," McCloskey said. "Like something happened to us yesterday that hasn't happened in a long, long time. Like—maybe they don't have all the answers."

"Is that good?" asked Wilson. He was at least *trying* to be an optimist.

"No," said McCloskey, "it's not good." Wilson raised his eyebrows. He felt tormented. As badly as the team—the players and coaches—needed the Championship, the franchise needed it more. If they could win it, the franchise could ride the win for ten years, like Portland had done. But if they lost it again, particularly this year—after compiling the seventh-best record in NBA history—the fans, Wilson felt, would feel betrayed. And that feeling would last for years, too. Wilson had spent the day closeted with Ciszewski and Auker—the brain trust—working on next year's Bad Boys promos. The idea was to make the image more positive, and less associated with concussions and ripped knees. With impressions like "Bad Boys don't drive drunk," and "Bad Boys don't do drugs." It had been almost impossible for them to concentrate, but they'd had no choice. Win or lose, the franchise went on.

McCloskey was exhausted—all night long he'd dreamed he was defending Jordan, and he'd woken up with stiff, aching muscles. He flipped through his stack of messages on Nancy Maas's desk and race-walked to his car for a short lunch. It was Monday, so the Palace's excellent restaurant was closed. On the way to Pettijons, a nearby restaurant McCloskey liked—mostly because it was fast—he popped the sunroof and flipped a tape into his black Cadillac's high-end sound system. A John Philip Sousa march began blaring into the quiet Michigan countryside. For the first time in an hour, he smiled. "I love John Philip Sousa when I'm depressed," he shouted, leading an imaginary band with his free hand while the wind blasted his hair and tie. "Gets your adrenaline going. Once we were doing really badly, so I was desperately looking for a John Philip Sousa tape. I stopped by a music store and I said, 'Miss, do you have any cassettes of John Philip Sousa?' And she says, 'Is that a group or a single?' I felt *old*."

Over a turkey sandwich and cup of soup—a light enough lunch to stay in game shape—McCloskey worried out loud. He was afraid that this might be his last, best chance to reach his life's goal. At sixty-two, there wouldn't be many more NBA seasons for him. They were so close now, but still the odds were against them. Even if they got by Chicago, there was L.A. to beat, and McCloskey thought L.A. was "playing the best basketball on the planet."

"If we don't make it this year," McCloskey said, "then I've got to make a decision: Hey, if we can't make it with these guys, maybe I should break this team up and start over again. Maybe I ought to change things around. Drastically.

"We either have to play better, or dismantle. Start over. Change faces. Somewhere along the line, we're just not doing it—because this is three years, the third time around."

How would he rebuild the team?

"You'd trade stars for stars."

Will Robinson and Stan Novak were having their pregame dinner with Jack and Leslie McCloskey and George Blaha, as they always did when they were in town on game day. They'd feasted on prime rib, and were now breaking their diets with lemon meringue pie and trying to talk about anything but the Bulls. Robinson brought up a player they'd almost drafted who'd just been shot over a drug deal. "He was good, too," said Robinson, "but they kicked him out of the CBA for drugs."

"You never know how they'll handle money," said Novak. "Maybe they'll take drugs. Or if they've never had any money and were into stealing, maybe they'll stop stealing."

"Yeah," said Robinson. "A kid like Sean Kemp. I bet he turns out to be a real citizen." Robinson was in love. After dragging his ass all over the country to look at stiffs, he'd suddenly found a real prospect. Robinson had been doing character research on Indiana's Jay Edwards and in the process had uncovered information about a nineteen-year-old center at a tiny junior college who wanted to quit school and play ball. He'd tracked down some tape on the kid, and it was *love*. The real thing, this time. The kid was six-ten, and he could run, could shoot, could rebound, and was strong as hell. Best of all, he might still be around at the bottom of the draft, because he hadn't had good enough grades to play in junior college and was a question mark. Even more damaging to his reputation, he'd unexpectedly left the University of Kentucky team the prior year after an apparent theft. But Robinson could overlook that. "He wouldn't be the first kid who'd stolen something," Robinson said. "Or the last."

"But, Will," said Novak, "it looks like he stole from the *coach's son*. That's not very bright."

Robinson picked at his pie. "Six-ten. And he can *shoot*." Robinson was getting desperate. All those frequent-flyer miles, all those Holiday Inns, all those invisible rent-a-cars—and no real prospects. Just suspects. It looked as if McCloskey would have to trade someone to move up high enough in the draft to get a good prospect. But who would that be? A Michael Williams, to move up a couple of notches? Or a John Salley, to get a lottery pick?

McCloskey looked grim, preoccupied. He got up from the table and headed toward the locker room. Before he got to the door, he headed back. "I forgot my kiss," he said to Leslie. He bent down and she kissed him lightly on the mouth. "Good luck," she said. He smiled. He didn't need the kiss, he needed the luck.

At tip-off, there was a new sound in the Palace, one that hadn't been there all season. It was the high-pitched wail—like a disaster alarm—as if every fan's voice had suddenly risen two octaves. The opening action was intense, like fourth-quarter action, with Thomas and Jordan trading baskets. Jordan hadn't told anyone, but he had the flu; he was clammy and his whole body felt like it had been beaten with sticks. It would be a long night.

With the score tied at 8, Scottie Pippen drove toward the hoop, knocked down Aguirre, popped up a four-footer, and stepped back behind Laimbeer as the shot went down. But as he stood behind Laimbeer, he drove the bone of his knuckle into Laimbeer's elbow. Pain shot straight up to Laimbeer's head as he grabbed his arm. It felt dead. He tried to run downcourt, but Daly saw him holding his arm and pulled him. Laimbeer came to the bench and held a towel over his face as Mike Abdenour probed the arm.

Isiah kept throwing in jumpers, but Jordan was fighting through his illness to score and to pass off when he was triple-teamed. Pippen was hitting almost everything, and that terrified Daly. Daly had to leave Pippen open to double- and triple-team Jordan, and if Pippen and the others started hitting, Detroit was screwed. But what else could he do? Jordan was the franchise. At the end of the quarter, Jordan went up on a fast break, and stayed seemingly frozen in air for .84 of a second—his longest hang-time of the night. About halfway through Jordan's leap, Laimbeer—back in the game with a numb arm—jumped up with both hands poised over his head like clubs, and smacked hell out of Jordan. But still Jordan stayed in the air, and at the last moment jammed down his shot, his right hand still above the rim. The Palace went silent. Applause from the Chicago bench echoed across the floor.

In the second quarter Chicago tied it with a corner shot by Charles Davis. Charles Davis? Charles Davis—who had been waived by two teams and had a career 6.1 scoring average—was already in the game for Chicago, and had just pulled his team even with the deepest team in the league, a team he almost certainly wouldn't be able to make. It was a bitter moment—McCloskey's phenomenally deep Pistons, representing the work of a decade—had just been tied by a one-man team. McCloskey was trying to change history—by winning without a superstar. But so was Jerry Krause—by winning with *only* a superstar.

As the lead continued to seesaw, John Ciszewski couldn't stand it. He ran into the dark blue late-spring night. His nerves were shot; earlier he'd been in the bathroom throwing up. "If we win tonight," he had said at dinner, "I'll go to Chicago. If we don't, I won't even watch on TV. It's like, do you want to watch your child being beaten?"

In the parking lot, though, the game was blasting over loudspeakers, so he walked all the way to Lapeer Road. Before he got out of earshot, he heard George Blaha cry out, "Isiah's still down!" He ran back to the arena.

Isiah Thomas was lying on the floor under the basket, his legs spread wide. He'd just gone for a lay-up, but while he'd been in the air six-ten Horace Grant, a block of muscle, had cut crosscourt, leaped toward little Isiah, and had kneed Thomas square in the chin. Then he'd ridden Thomas down to the floor, his legs straddled over Isiah's neck, and had hit the floor hard with his knee against Thomas's testicles.

As Thomas lay there, Grant grabbed Thomas's broken hand and tried to pull him up. But Thomas was limp, and Grant just dragged his body along the floor. Play resumed with no foul, but Thomas was so destroyed that he grabbed the first Bull to come near him, to get a foul and stop play. He tried to walk back to the bench, but only got halfway there. He stopped, bent over, and put his hands over his balls, with his face straight up to the ceiling. Abdenour ran out and helped him to the bench. Thomas sat there blankly, rubbing his injured hand. With Thomas out, Jordan started scoring again, and by halftime it was tied.

McCloskey left just before the horn, looking like he'd been slapped. In the hallway, he saw Tom Wilson, who looked sad and scared. They didn't speak.

Halfway through the third quarter, Detroit by 3. Jordan had been driving through masses of arms and legs to score, and Chicago's Horace Grant, their Muscle Beach forward, had been pushing everyone out of his way to grab an eventual 16 rebounds. *Oakland Press* sports editor Keith Langlois turned to reporter Steve Addy and said, "They're in trouble."

"I dunno why," said Addy, "but I think they're gonna win it." Addy's confidence was, in part, born of indifference. His attitude was, "They're not cutting me in for a playoff share. Why the fuck should I care?" Addy was sick of getting bitched at by Laimbeer.

So Addy felt no remorse when Laimbeer, at the end of the third, went up for a rebound against Pippen, straight-armed him onto his butt, and got thrown out. Laimbeer walked off the court with his face twisted up. Now it was up to James Edwards. After eleven years in the league, Edwards was desperate for a ring. And this was his best shot to get on McCloskey's protected list. The way it looked now, he was the most likely to get axed. Edwards didn't feel nervous, though; he'd plugged his mind into his specific duties: keep Cartwright from scoring, and help out on Jordan when he comes around the curl toward the center.

Before Edwards could do anything, the quarter ended, but he started the fourth quarter with a turnaround jumper from the corner. The shot came off the rim, Grant went up for it, and Salley karate-chopped Grant to the floor, where he sat, stunned, his pain palpable from courtside. After that, Chicago started to slow down. Jordan felt like hell with his flu, Pippen had left the game with a strained arch, and the Chicago starters, pressed to play heavy minutes, were all puffing and slick with sweat. Still, they kept coming, and with 6:57 in the game, Jordan—on pure instinct, with Dumars's hand covering his eyes—arched a seventeen-foot jumper that ripped the net, bringing Chicago to within 1. McCloskey was racked with anxiety. If the game was close in the last few minutes, Jordan would take over. The mind is everything, as Doug Collins said, and Jordan's mind had a level of focus most people couldn't comprehend.

But Isiah Thomas decided to take over. He was obsessed with winning the Championship, and no one else was getting the job done. For good or ill, he was going to take over.

Like Jordan and a few others, Thomas could tune out everything. Thomas started dancing to his own private rhythm and his presence on the court seemed to expand, even engulfing part of Jordan's. With 6:19 in the game, Thomas drove downcourt on Jordan, reversed field, reversed again, spun to his right, shoulder-faked, leaped, and laid it off the glass. He'd gone one-on-one with Michael Jordan and beaten him. His dance intensified. By 2:03, Thomas had built a 10-point wall. McCloskey felt the muscles in his neck begin to unknot. Half a minute later, the lead was 13, and Doug Collins pulled Jordan. A giant, mass sigh, almost a "whoosh," swept through the arena. Just before it ended, Daly took Isiah out, and the crowd boomed. Thomas had 33 points, with 4 assists and 2 steals.

Isiah Thomas's eyes were wide. "Okay, all the coaches—out!" he yelled. He wanted a players-only meeting. McCloskey left unhappily. He was worried that "in an open meeting, everybody gets to say what they feel—and I don't know if that's good in the middle of the playoffs."

In the coaches' room, despite their concern about the meeting, the mood was one of vast relief. Daly looked at peace. "You know," he said to McCloskey, "we're gonna *beat* those guys." McCloskey was shocked. It was totally out of character for Daly. "A pessimist is an optimist with experience." But for now, Daly felt he'd figured out how to beat Chicago. He put on his pessimist's face and went to meet the press.

The team meeting was over quickly. Thomas sat by his locker naked except for a towel over his midsection and talked about what he'd said. "I said it's not good for a basketball team when one guy has to score as many points as I did tonight. What makes our team good is that we've got six or eight guys that can get in double figures, or seven to nine points, and that's when we can look at the stat sheet and say, okay, this basketball team's playing pretty good. The problem with these last two games is, we're just passing by guys in the night. You can't set a screen if you just pass by a guy—you've got to *stop* and *set* it.

"In terms of us being tested, and the layoff and all that, that's just writing, that's just conjecture. It's just a matter of getting out on the basketball court and *setting* the damn *screen*." It was typical Team-First Thomas talk, and was delivered slowly and quietly, with only rare flashes of his ghetto-boy ferocity. Ever since the Bird Disaster, Thomas had learned to weigh every word.

When he'd finished, and the TV lights were off, one of the reporters said, "Great game, Isiah." Thomas glared at him.

The next day, after practice, the national and out-of-town reporters left early, pausing only to soak up a few minutes of mantalk by Daly. One good quote made for a day's work, and Daly, with his background in media, knew how to supply product. Now he was using, "We're off the critical list, but we're still in intensive care." He'd given it to several reporters, so it was no longer the highly prized "virgin quote," but the sportswriters he'd given it to didn't have crossover readership, so everyone was happy. The local beat reporters—Drew Sharp, Terry Foster, Jim Spadafore, Steve Addy, Scott Wahle—hung around the locker room longer, looking for the features their bosses needed to fill two or three pages. The Championship drive was the biggest Detroit sports story in years.

The last out-of-towner to stay in the locker room went up to Mahorn with a big Styrofoam hand with the index finger sticking up, and said, "Will you sign my Number One Hand?"

Mahorn locked on his Badass Rick face. He hadn't scored a single point last night and was touchy. "Will you sign my Number One Snake?" he said, reaching into his underpants. The guy backpedaled, keeping Mahorn in his field of vision. Foster and Spadafore, who'd learned to enjoy Mahorn, swallowed their smiles. They were next door to Mahorn, on either side of Laimbeer, trying to get something out of him other than mantalk: We won yesterday, and we wanna win tomorrow, because that would give us two wins. But he was mute.

"I already talked to you guys," Laimbeer said. "You guys" meant reporters in general.

"Talk to the press, you white bitch," Mahorn yelled at Laimbeer. "Get some image. That's why you got your ass kicked out of the game."

Laimbeer relented. When Mahorn made a suggestion, even Laimbeer listened. Laimbeer talked about the effect of Isiah's players-only meeting. "He was right to call it. We're not in the right frame of mind. You gotta understand, athletes and teams are very fragile as far as playing to their peaks. You all have to be in tune together, and we're not right now. It's scary."

At the other end of the row of lockers, Mark Aguirre studied the sportswriters and looked very serious. "I don't mean to get on any of you," he said to the few remaining reporters. "Personally, I mean. But . . ." He stared at the floor, scanning the reporters' loafers, sneakers, and Hush Puppies. "But why do you wear *those* kinds of shoes?" Aguirre, at the moment, was wearing red-leather Italian pumps.

Mahorn, in hot-pink dress shoes with Day-Glo purple socks, jumped in. "They'll say, 'Cuz they're *com*-fortable.' "

Any of the reporters could have replied, "No, it's because we don't make a million dollars a year." But no one did. Sportswriters hated to point up the earnings gap between themselves and the men they passed daily judgment on. Instead, Terry Foster, looking half angry, jumped up and said, "Just 'cause I don't go pimpin' around in some Gucci shit, right?" He launched a spirited defense of comfortable footwear while Aguirre watched, his jaw sagging by the second.

When Foster had calmed down, Aguirre turned to the white reporters and said, "Brothers go *crazy*, man. Thank *you* all for just havin' a normal conversation."

Mahorn pointed at Scott Wahle. "Scott Wahle in his pink shirt and maroon shoes," he said. "That shit doesn't *go*, man. But I'll bet it's real *com*-fortable." Wahle blanched. He'd thought his color combinations were dynamite—hell, they were both shades of red, weren't they?

Mahorn was trying to decide which of two outfits to wear. "Fuck Isiah," he said to Aguirre. "*We* should be on the cover of *GQ*."

Aguirre nodded. "They ought to let somebody on who knows how to *wear clothes*."

"Wear *clothes*, man," mimicked Spadafore, who started doing the pimp-walk around the locker room. But Spadafore was white, and it didn't quite go over.

"Shut up, bitch," Mahorn yelled at him. Mahorn settled on blue-and-cream shorts, with a matching baggy top, and headed out. Aguirre called, "Wait for me."

When just the reporters remained, Foster said, "Spad, what you've gotta do, go home and get a book of jokes and start memorizin' 'em. Then when Horn hits you—bing! bing! bing!—wear him out. Get him playin' your tempo. Take the game to him."

"Know what I think," said Drew Sharp. "I think now the pressure's on Chicago to win two at home." Nobody agreed. The rest of them—Detroit's corps of Piston experts—thought the Pistons were in deep, deep trouble:

"I think," said Foster, doing a speed-rapping Chuck Daly, "it's Katie bar the door, Katie bar the door."

An hour before tip-off, in Chicago Stadium, Horace Grant sat in front of the TV in the Bulls' crumbling old locker room, watching a replay of

Laimbeer stiff-arming Pippen. "*Watch* this shit," he said to Charles Davis. On the screen, Laimbeer knocked Pippen down. Grant rewound it, and Laimbeer did it again. "I woulda *hit* him if he hadn't got the foul." And again. "Id'a put the motherfucker *down*."

"Laimbeer doesn't want to fight," said an old Chicago reporter sitting next to Michael Jordan, who was ignoring the histrionics. "We *use*-ta have guys that would fight *anybody*," he said. "Van Leer. He didn't care."

From a cramped cubicle off the locker room—built back when six-six was good size—Pippen peered in at the TV. Lying on a table in front of trainer Mark Pfeil, Pippen's leg had what looked like a cast halfway up his calf; it was adhesive tape to support his injured arch. "Could you jump off it Wednesday?" asked Pfeil.

"I couldn't *walk* off it, man," said Pippen, wincing as Pfeil touched the leg. "I was on *crutches*."

Jerry Krause—who had the same oval body and big eyes as Alfred Hitchcock—walked into the locker room and hurried past Jordan without speaking. There was tension among Krause, Jordan, and coach Doug Collins. No one was certain who was running the show. Jordan called Krause "the boss," but now he was pushing Krause for a voice in the draft selection, opening the old hostilities between himself and the GM. Collins was caught in the middle, and was ambitious for power himself. Collins was already locked into a battle with Krause and the Bulls' owners over seven-foot stiff Will Perdue. Krause had spent the eleventh pick of the 1988 draft on Perdue, and Collins refused to play him. Something had to give. But for now, with the series tied 1–1, they were in it together.

The Pistons emerged from the dark basement of Chicago Stadium to an ugly greeting from the crowd. Courtside fans were wearing silk-screened "Fuck the Bad Boys" T-shirts, and when Laimbeer did his opening ritual—a rim-rattling dunk followed by a hard bounce of the ball toward the rafters—the old stadium quivered with sonic vibration.

Scottie Pippen, his leg mummified, was introduced into the starting lineup. He'd been called doubtful in the Chicago papers for the last two days, and his intro set off the stadium's unique high, hysterical squeal: the dog whistle. After tip-off Jordan got the ball and held it away from his body with one hand while three Pistons collapsed on him. He went up anyway and softly curled it in and the dog whistle started in again. Then Mahorn yelled "Bullshit!" at a call and got a technical and the dog whistle shrieked again and never entirely went off. The Chicago fans, the best in the league, kept pouring waves of adrenaline down onto the players until even the never-play guys on the Chicago bench were jiggling their knees and squirming. It was pure Basketball Belt. But for Horace Grant it was too much—late in the first quarter, his nerves raw, he ran back down to the Bulls' locker room and vomited into a toilet. Grant's absence put Charles Davis in the game early again, and with 1:55 left in the quarter, Davis took advantage of a triple-team on Jordan for an easy lay-up. Just after that, Jordan flashed downcourt, a blur, ducked his head for a drive to the hoop, collected his defenders, went up—and shot a fastball pass to Davis in the corner, who took his time and swished it. Daly looked sick. Charles Davis? The quarter ended with Detroit up 1 and the dog whistle screaming.

In the second quarter Detroit's depth finally started to pay off. Charles Davis, who'd scored 6 in the first quarter, was held scoreless, and Chicago subs like clumsy Dave Corzine and slow John Paxson were mauled by the Killer B-Team. Every time the Bulls cut into Detroit's 8- to 10-point lead, Johnson and Salley and Rodman would come in to rain jumpers and smash down blocks. When one of them tired, Daly shuttled Aguirre back in, and he was nailing everything in sight; he'd have 18 points before the half was over. It made the Trade look like a stroke of brilliance. The lead hit 14, but just before the half Jordan cut it to 11. The Chicago dance team—the Luv-a-Bulls—came out at halftime, but they were amateurish and so anorexic that their Lycra hung in folds on them, and there was a general sense of the Chicago Bulls returning to reality.

It was more of the same in the third quarter. The Piston bench would score 27 points by the end of the third—8 each for Salley and Johnson and 6 for Rodman. But Rodman was also making his Dumb Dennis mistakes; with 1:42 left, he committed his second goaltend within 45 seconds. Daly screamed, "That's two!" and tapped his head with his forefinger. But then Rodman jumped over Corzine and Davis and Laimbeer and Aguirre to grab his eighth rebound of the quarter, passed off, ran downcourt, took a rifle pass from Dumars for a lay-up, and stayed in the game.

By halfway through the fourth, the lead was 12, and Benny the Bull, some short person in a plastic bull's head, was having a hell of a time trying to get the dog whistle cranked back up.

Then Michael Jordan began to tune out the world. He didn't hear the crowd, or feel any fatigue. He felt happy, at home, confident. With 4:09 left and the lead still at 8, he took the ball at the top of the key, drove past Rodman, drove past Aguirre, and drove past Laimbeer for a lay-up that was suddenly uncontested. Then he stole the ball from Dumars, streaked downcourt, started the same drive, pulled up, and drew a foul from Vinnie Johnson. He sank both free throws. The dog whistle began to wail through the stadium. Daly sat down.

"We couldn't *blow* this game, could we?" Stan Novak shouted to Will Robinson, sitting next to him in the stands.

"Nah—that won't happen." They both sat stolidly, without emotion—an old coach's habit.

With 2:15 in the game, Rodman made a lay-up to put the lead back at 6, but then Jordan dribbled to his favorite spot on the right side of the free-throw lane, eyed the congestion underneath, leaped up, and canned a perfect sixteen-foot jumper. The lead was 4. It stayed at 4 until 52 seconds were left. Jordan got the ball from Cartwright at his favorite spot. He drove around Rodman and he ducked ahead of Dumars. Salley came leaping in at him with his hand almost twelve feet in the air. It didn't matter. Jordan went higher and scored. It was his forty-fourth point. The lead was 2.

The dog whistle was fierce. Laimbeer crooked his finger at the crowd, daring them to make more noise, yelling, "C'mon! C'mon!" Dumars brought the ball down and worked time off the game clock. The shot clock was at 14 seconds, then 12, 10, 8—nothing opened up. Dumars flipped it over to Laimbeer—5, 4, 3—Laimbeer threw up a desperate shot that caromed steeply off. Rodman went up for it. So did Horace Grant. Their bodies were pasted together as Rodman came down with the ball. Referee Bill Oakes blasted his whistle and shot his arm toward the Chicago end: foul on Rodman. Grant went to the line and sank both shots. Tie game. Piston ball. Daly sat miserably on the bench, holding his face up with one finger.

Thomas and Jordan faced each other at the top of the key. Thomas looked into Jordan's eyes, and drove in. A whistle. Daly's mouth fell open. Jordan pointed toward the Chicago end. Then referee Jack Madden did the same. Laimbeer, helping Thomas, had brushed Jordan with his hip. Daly's head dropped, and he covered his face with his hands. He couldn't believe it. A hip-brush foul! Away from the ball! In the last seconds of the game! The refs must have Laimbeer under a microscope, just like Mahorn. Red Auerbach had predicted it—probably prayed for it. It was the Curse of Auerbach.

A dozen yards behind Daly, in the stands, Jack McCloskey closed his eyes. The lifetime dream of both of them, which seemed so tangible fifteen minutes before, was suddenly again a fantasy. There were 9 seconds left. Daly walked over to the scorer's bench and looked at the press table. He made eye contact with a journalist—a very unusual thing for him to do. The dream of a man's life—coming down to 9 seconds.

In the Chicago huddle, Doug Collins yelled, "Get the ball to Michael, and everybody else get the fuck out of the way!"

Michael Jordan went off into his own mind. He saw himself getting the ball. He saw the defense collapsing on him. He saw himself jump. He saw the shot. It hit the glass. It swished.

Jerry Krause sat stoically behind the bench. He knew Jordan would be the shooter. A wave of optimism swept him. He thought to himself, "The son of a gun's gonna make it."

Jordan got the ball at his favorite spot. He felt good. He didn't feel nervous—he felt happy. He'd already seen the end of the game, and now his basket seemed inevitable. He danced to his left. Rodman and Dumars were in front of him, flashing their arms and leaping. Salley was behind them, his immense arm snaking almost as high as the rim. Jordan rushed toward the baseline. He leapt up and defied momentum by slicing backward, to gain his only possible angle. He shot. The ball darted toward the hoop in a dangerously flat trajectory. It hit the glass. It swished. The dog whistle screamed. It seemed to get louder and louder. There were 3 seconds left. Chicago by 2.

"There's a *lotta* time left," Will Robinson shouted to Stan Novak.

"*Oh* yeah," said Novak. "Lots."

Daly put in his shooters: Dumars, Thomas, Johnson. Laimbeer got it to Dumars. Dumars shot a high, curving 3-pointer. It hit the glass in perfect alignment with the rim. It came down toward the hoop—the dream of a man's life—and popped off the rim. The buzzer blasted.

Daly walked rock-faced toward the Piston locker room while the stadium shivered with screams. Jack McCloskey sat behind the bench, his stomach hollow. Jerry Krause clenched his fist, and, for an instant, thought about McCloskey.

Doug Collins raced across the floor with his fist high in the air, his face lit with youth and joy. It would be his last happy moment with the Chicago Bulls.

Trader Jack McCloskey stood and watched his team—*this* year's team—descend into the moldy basement.

FIFTEEN

"Democracy"
The Chicago Series, Part Two

MICHAEL JORDAN—famous, in part, for doing his own housecleaning—was buried in petty paperwork as almost forty million people around the globe began gathering in front of TV sets to watch him play the most important game of his life. Jordan was sitting at his corner locker—the athlete's equivalent of a corner office—hunched over a floor carpeted with tickets. The other Chicago players had long since shuffled their allotted tickets into envelopes and checked them off against their lists of requests, but Jordan had more tickets to give, more people to please, and more people to piss off.

CBS commentator Pat O'Brien, already in his navy blue on-air blazer, wandered by and said, "Hey, Michael, I went to my favorite store yesterday and dropped a bundle on clothes. I spent *your* kinda money." Jordan, resplendent in a pink silk sport shirt, a white watch with a white band, raw silk pants, and satin loafers with no socks, gave O'Brien the little corner-curl smile that's so often on his face when he's not playing. But he didn't look impressed.

"Michael," said Bill Cartwright, suddenly towering overhead, "gimme two tickets." Cartwright reached down tentatively toward a pair of tickets set off to one side.

Jordan flashed the corner-curl smile and put the toe of his loafer over the tickets. "Not *those*, man. You'd be fuckin' with Oprah."

"*I* wouldn't fuck with Oprah," said Charles Davis.

Cartwright jerked his hand back.

"Sor-reee. What about those?"

"For my family."

"Fine," said Cartwright, reaching for them. This time the toe of the loafer came down on Cartwright's fingers, just as Jerry Krause entered the room. Krause glanced over at his star standing on his center's hand, and rolled his eyes.

Krause and Collins didn't want Jordan to be one of the guys. They wanted him to be the team leader, the enforcer. Jordan had been resisting the role. His attitude was, "I can tell guys, 'Look, you need your rest,' but that's all I can do. If they don't listen, they don't listen." That wasn't good enough for Krause and Collins. Jordan had often trained his power on them, and they wanted him to aim it where they thought it would do more good.

Instead, Jordan was meddling in their terrain, trying to "help" with the fast-approaching college draft—which would be team-shaking, since Chicago had a lottery pick and two other first-round choices. Earlier, Krause had been talking about Jordan's role in the draft. "He's more than a player," Krause had said. "Michael's a really bright young man who really has a comprehension of what's going on. I'd be a damn fool not to listen to him. We run a democracy—until the last minute before the draft."

Krause ducked around the corner to talk to Doug Collins, and Jordan peeled off his street clothes and ruminated about power and privilege. "Jerry's the boss," said Jordan. "He's in charge of the team. He makes the moves—brings players in, moves players out. I'm *not* the boss, and I know that. This is not a team that I want to run. But if you want my opinion, I'm going to give you my opinion. Being the leader of the ball team, they ask my opinion."

Jordan was still testing the limits of his power. When Krause had traded Oakley for Cartwright, Jordan had exploded, and had demanded a meeting with Krause. The trade, which had reignited Jordan's rookie-year war with Krause, was to be the *last*—Jordan had made clear—without his prior consultation.

Jordan was also having problems with Doug Collins. Jordan had accepted the move to point guard, because it had made the Bulls tough as hell to beat. But it cut into Jordan's scoring, and he didn't take that the same way someone like Team-First Thomas did. Jordan felt Collins was too intent on him doling out points to everyone else early in the game—when baskets came easy—while saving Jordan for the crunch, when everyone knew he'd get the ball. This conflict had set off a battle of egos. Collins was genuinely likable—it was part of his Will Robinson heritage—but he'd been a superstar player and still carried the superstar arrogance. He knew how to bust balls. He wasn't at all afraid to fight Krause over the Will Perdue issue.

Jordan and Collins were also at odds over Collins wanting Jordan to crack the whip. Jordan wouldn't have anything to do with it. He just wanted to be left alone to play—to be the king of the playground—and as he finished his paperwork, the hot, exciting pleasure of the game started to bubble in him. Even though it was the biggest game of his life—the chance to gain a virtual lock on the title—it was a fun day, full of "wild expectations." He felt nervous—"but it's a good kind of nervousness. Excitement."

Jordan had the reporters excited, too. He was good for business—especially the TV business. Hubie Brown, working the game for CBS, stood on the court during warm-ups, his sun-bright blue eyes flashing, talking about Jordan. "He has the ability to almost make his body disappear," gushed Brown. "He comes at you one way, then in midair he shifts his body to make himself smaller. It's breathtaking. And that last game! That last game, on one shot he actually shot *down* on the basket. He was so pumped that when he elevated—it was in the first quarter—he got so high that he actually shot *down*. I thought, this is incredible. Hell, this just isn't *normal*."

Jerry Krause was also attracting a lot of media attention. As he stood by the Bulls' bench, a crowd of reporters began to gather. The team he'd almost totally rebuilt over the last two years had become the year's best Cinderella story—front-page news across the country. Krause's boys were now poised to crash their way into the Finals. With Chicago up 2–1, Detroit would have to win three out of the next four, including two here in the dreaded Chicago Stadium.

"The margin of victory in this game is *so* slim," said Krause, raising his voice over the nervous rumble of the assembling crowd. "You're hanging on a precipice, and you're a genius if you win by one point and you're a bum if you lose by one point. It's amazing how over the last two weeks I've gotten handsomer and skinnier. All of a sudden, it's, 'Jeez, you've lost weight, you're looking better.' A guy just told me, 'Boy, you really look *good* on television.' I said, 'Well, they couldn't take out the two chins,' but he's like, 'No! You looked *good*, you looked *skinnier*!'

"Don Zimmer described it real well, the difference between winning and losing. Zimmer said when you win, your wife looks like Gina Lollobrigida, your hamburger tastes like steak, and your beer tastes like champagne. When you lose, your wife looks like Phyllis Diller, your steak tastes like dog food, and your beer tastes like piss.

"I really felt for McCloskey the other day, when we took it at the buzzer. He was sitting over there"—Krause nodded at a seat behind the bench, where a few fans now stood, staring at Krause and watching the warm-ups. "What goes through your mind in those situations is unbelievable. You're trying not to yell because you know people are watching you, and there's times when players make mistakes and you want to yell, 'God-*damn*-it!' But you can't let your emotions go, because you're right out in the stands. You're naked.

"I've been there, on the other end of it. Nineteen eighty-three. I was GM of the White Sox. The Sox were one win away from being in the Series against the Dodgers. So I was in Philadelphia, scouting the Dodgers. I'd seen the Dodgers like twenty-six straight times. I had their signs, I had everything. I was ready to write as good a book on them as exists. Then. Tenth inning of the Sox game. That little pisser Tito Landrum hits a home run and the Sox lose. Season's over. It was off a slider by Britt Burns. I've never felt so low in my life. When Tito Landrum hit that goddamn ball I've never felt so empty. I'll never forget how I felt going to the airport that night with my report on the Dodgers. That report is still laying in my basement someplace. I'll never forget that empty feeling." Krause's eyes went distant and for a second he was gone. Doug Collins walked by. Krause snapped out of it and they huddled. But they left the floor separately.

As Krause strode off, as many fans were gawking at him as at Collins or the players. The Chicago *Sun-Times,* which had previously crucified Krause for the Oakley-Cartwright trade, had just run a story on what a savvy move the trade had been. This was Krause's moment in the sun. Meanwhile, in the Detroit papers, it was being argued that if Detroit lost, it would be McCloskey's fault, because of the Dantley trade.

From out of the mildewed basement of the stadium came Jack McCloskey. McCloskey looked haggard, his face cut with lines. He'd just met with Daly. Their meeting hadn't accomplished anything. They'd tried to talk in depth about how to neutralize Jordan, but they'd kept returning to the subject of referees. They were both enraged over the devastating calls on Mahorn and Laimbeer at the end of the first and third games—the Curse of Auerbach. But they had already done everything they could do to pressure the refs. After Laimbeer's hip-brush foul at the end of the third game, Daly had gone to work on the press, giving them a feast of juicy quotes to fill the feature stories he knew they had to write. Daly's barrage resulted in a number of stories like "Are the Referees Cutting the Pistons?" and "Pistons Suddenly Find Bad Boy Image a Burden." In the articles, Daly bitched about the soft fouls on his guys and about preferential treatment for Jordan. He accused the refs of letting the Bad Boy image influence their calls. Daly and McCloskey were hoping that the glare of attention would force the refs to give Detroit a few breaks. The league hated to see refereeing become an issue, and the refs knew it.

Jesse Jackson ambled past in a sweater and slacks, looking as if he wanted to be recognized. "Maybe Jesse's gonna referee," said McCloskey. "He might not be so impressed by our local celebrity." McCloskey nodded toward Jordan, who was sinking corner jumpers quickly and rhythmically. "Worst case of stargazing I ever saw," said McCloskey, "was a couple of years ago in the playoffs in Boston. There was a scuffle for a loose ball, Bird went down, and Isiah comes up with it and goes downcourt. Out of the corner of my eye I thought I saw the ref, Jess Kersey, helping Bird up. I thought, that's impossible, that couldn't happen. I couldn't wait to see the tape. And sure enough, there's Jess Kersey helping Bird to his feet. I sent the tape to the league office. I'm pretty sure Jess heard about it from the league." McCloskey stopped abruptly, his brief reminiscence no longer enough to ward off anxiety.

"They look so *loose*," he said, watching his players clown around and laugh as they shot baskets. Just off the floor, Salley was schmoozing with a Hollywood pal, actor John Cusack. "Man, I'd be so intense. But they're still confident. They still think they're the better team." McCloskey did, too. That was part of his pain. He had built the best team in the league. So why were they on the verge of yet another failure? Why did he have to be thinking about tearing the whole team apart, and starting over? And how would he rationalize their failure if it was ultimately caused by the Bad Boys image, which was supposed to be just a marketing gimmick?

Tom Wilson, father of the Bad Boys campaign, walked up to McCloskey. Wilson, his boyish face rigid and puffy, finally looked his age. A number of times the night before, he'd come suddenly awake, had realized his situation, had cursed, and then fought his way back into a troubled sleep. McCloskey had done exactly the same thing. Daly hadn't slept at all, not a wink.

"How you feeling?" Wilson asked.

McCloskey grinned. "Never better!" he boomed. McCloskey said it with such gusto that Wilson believed him. But Wilson always took McCloskey at his word. He trusted him implicitly, just as he trusted Daly. That was one thing about the Pistons' management—they didn't second-guess each other, and they didn't jockey for power. That could kill a team. And then kill the franchise.

*   *   *

"And at center," boomed the PA announcer, "Bill . . ." A sudden rush of boos obliterated the rest of Laimbeer's introduction. The swell of sound grew so deafening that it seemed somehow to take material form, like a rolling black cloud. At courtside the booing segued into a sharp chant: "Fuck-Laim-*beer*! Fuck-Laim-*beer*!" It was a variation of the familiar "Laim-beer *sucks,*" performed by the group wearing "Fuck the Bad Boys" T-shirts.

The Chicago players were brought out and the shrieking dog whistle greeted each intro. Except Jordan's. His introduction was totally drowned out. Jordan was used to it; he just waited until Craig Hodges was introduced, let the dog whistle shoot swiftly up the sonic scale, then raced out and slapped his teammates' hands.

The game started at a frantic pace. That worried Krause. He'd wanted to keep the team from coming out "too high"; but there was nothing he could do now. Just after tip-off, Mahorn and Cartwright collided, and Mahorn slapped Cartwright's ribs so hard it echoed. Cartwright stared at referee Jess Kersey but Kersey just stared back. Shortly after that Jordan came downcourt and Dumars hand-checked him, then Jordan darted sideways and crashed into Isiah Thomas. Kersey hit his whistle—and pointed at Dumars. Dumars turned on Kersey, said "Real fine game so far," and applauded derisively. Daly came off the bench and met Kersey near the scorer's table. "Come *on!*" Daly yelled. Kersey walked away.

A few minutes later, with Chicago up 4, Thomas drove on Jordan. Thomas thought he could beat Jordan off the dribble, and that he had to for his team to win. This time, he did. He jerked past Jordan, causing Jordan to lean in and bump him with his chest. Kersey called Jordan for the bump. Both of Jordan's hands shot up, acknowledging guilt, then he brought them halfway down and balled his hands into fists. Daly clapped and yelled, "Let's go!" A bump foul on Jordan was a good sign.

As the quarter raged on, Jordan kept fastballing passes to the other players, marshaling them as a unit. Though Detroit had beaten Chicago all six games in regular season, that had been without Jordan at the point. With all the Bulls hitting their jumpers, Chicago pulled to a 5-point lead, then 7. Daly looked stunned. If Chicago's supporting cast stayed hot, Daly's dream was dead. But Detroit kept slashing away, wearing Chicago down with body blows and lung-burning wind sprints. Mahorn hammered at Cartwright and even Jordan, beating them with his arms and legs and chest and ass until they both started moving away from him. Toward the end of the quarter, with Horace Grant's chest heaving, Collins had to send in Jack Haley. Jack Haley? (Jack Haley: fourth-round pick; 2.2 scoring average; six-ten, 240. A "badminton champion and surfer." White.)

"You never know where Doug Collins is gonna go to get people," CBS's Hubie Brown shouted into his microphone when Haley came in. "We may even see *Will Perdue* before it's over." Haley lumbered downcourt, dropped anchor under the basket, grabbed John Salley with both hands and shoved him out of the way. Foul on Haley. Twelve seconds later, Haley went up for a rebound and piggybacked on Dennis Rodman. Foul on Haley. Haley out, Grant back in. But there was no one to substitute for Jordan. As they walked to the Detroit end for Rodman's free throws, Jordan was sweating so hard his skin was laminated. The quarter ended with Chicago up 4.

At the break just before the second quarter, the Brow appeared magically at courtside during the Lycra show, with "PISTONS" stapled in a strip to his tie. He didn't have a ticket, but he'd talked his way past security, telling them he was a "Pistons mascot." He started dancing in the aisle next to the floor, his porkpie hat bouncing, while the fans screamed, "Pistons suck!" and "Sit down!" He peered into the stands and yelled, "What a madhouse!" at a kid in a "Michael Jordan" T-shirt and Spuds McKenzie cap. The kid yelled, "Eat shit and die!"

"Great crowd!" the Brow cried.

Detroit kept up its body-jarring defense as the half approached, denying Jordan the ball and full-court-pressing him. At one point, Rodman outquicked the much smaller John Paxson so badly that Paxson fell on his butt in the middle of a dribble. Salley scooped up the ball and set up a play, but Chicago broke the play and grabbed the rebound. Then Chicago tried a play and Detroit broke it up; Salley passed it out to the wings, but suddenly there was Jordan, wailing through the air like a line drive, with no apparent arc to his leap, grabbing the ball in midair. The whole quarter was one long highlight-film on defense.

The baskets came hard. With Chicago up 4, Thomas got the ball at a half step inside the 3-point line, with two defenders in his face. He faked, leaped—it was the kind of shot only a supreme egotist would try; Daly was screaming, "Zeke! Zeke!"—and set the ball on a low, perfect arc. It swished, and Thomas cranked his elbow to his hip in triumph. Next time down, Thomas tried it again; it was off, but Laimbeer and Rodman went up for it and Laimbeer grabbed it. As they came down, though, Rodman kept clutching for it, as if his brain couldn't convince his hands to stop. The ball careened to Chicago. They raced downcourt, Laimbeer yelling at Rodman, "Get out of my way!"

As the dog whistle went into a solid, ceaseless blast, the two teams clawed back and forth. With a couple of minutes left in the half, Chicago had a 5-point lead, but then Thomas—who Daly thought had been taking the Team-First concept *too far*—reverted to his old, ball-hog ways.

He took the ball all the way downcourt, jumped into a nest of Chicago defenders, and banked it off the glass. "Now *that*," Hubie Brown crowed, "is Isiah Thomas!" Moments later, at the Chicago end, Thomas ran up behind John Paxson, batted away the ball, and was four steps toward the Detroit end before Paxson knew he was naked. Thomas rushed down, kept the ball, shot a pull-up jumper, grabbed his own rebound, then worked time off the clock as the buzzer approached. For almost 20 seconds he stood at the 3-point line, dribbling slowly, scanning. His teammates kept breaking open and looking for the ball—12 seconds, 10, 8—Isiah dribbled slowly. Four, 3, 2—1 second left; Thomas jumped, lofted a 3-pointer, and buried it. His face a total blank, he walked offcourt as the horn blared. Detroit had its first lead.

The PA announcer gave the halftime stats as the Chicago fans went after their bratwurst and beer. Thomas had 15 points. Rodman had 12 rebounds. Jordan had only 12 points, but was getting good help from the other Chicago starters. The Chicago bench hadn't scored.

At the start of the third quarter, Pippen, Cartwright, and Hodges kept hitting, as Daly sat solemnly on the bench, making funny shapes with his mouth and watching his defensive strategy get picked to pieces. His strategy revolved around what Daly was calling the Jordan Rules, a complex set of defensive options centered on one basic theme: "When Jordan goes to the bathroom, we go with him." Jordan was constantly double-teamed now, often by the towering Salley and Rodman, and he'd gone almost twenty minutes without a basket. But he was firing passes to Pippen and Hodges, and Pippen was on fire, pushing Chicago on a 10–2 run.

With 4:52 in the third, James Edwards came in and started making his low-post moves to the hoop, the kind most elite teams revolve around, and which Detroit would lack totally if McCloskey let Edwards go in the expansion draft. Edwards got to the hoop so fast that Corzine, smaller but clumsier, had to hack Edwards to prevent a sure basket. While Edwards shot his free throws, Doug Collins and his two assistants huddled nervously. But they couldn't find a way to control Edwards. On defense, Edwards was practically wearing Corzine—he stuck a hand so close to Corzine's eyes that Corzine threw a pass into the stands. Then Edwards waved for the ball down low, dribbled it with his back to the basket, and flipped up his soft turnaround jumper—the shot that made him $700,000 a year—to finally put Detroit 3 points ahead. At the end of the quarter, still ahead by 2, Vinnie Johnson dribbled slowly at the 3-point line, killing time. He waited until 3 seconds were left and went up with three Chicago defenders. But he suddenly whipped the ball sideways to Thomas—all alone just inside the 3-point line—and Thomas sank it at the buzzer. Four-point lead—one quarter left to stay ahead. Or the season would be all but over.

Tom Wilson sat in the stands, his stomach churning, waiting for the last quarter to start. "It's been a good whistle so far," he said, "but I'll bet Chicago's in the bonus situation in four minutes. Because of that damn Bad Boy thing."

All of Collins's players were staring at him as the Chicago huddle came to a close. "Rodman and Salley are *killing* us," said Collins—they had 11 offensive rebounds, 4 more than the whole Chicago team. "Keep 'em off the *glass*," said Collins. The whole Killer B-Team was torturing Chicago—they had 23 points, compared to 2 by the Chicago bench.

Isiah was the only starter to take the floor; he was flanked by Rodman, Edwards, Johnson, and Salley. Right away, the B-team started firing in shots, expanding the lead to 9. But they needed a cushion, McCloskey was thinking, because if Chicago was within 3 or 4 with a minute left, Jordan would murder them. The mind is everything, and Jordan had a mind like no one else.

With about eight minutes left, Hodges drilled a long 3-pointer to pull Chicago to within 5. And Chicago was already in the bonus situation—Wilson had called it right. But the Chicago starters were beginning to droop and shake with exhaustion, and Collins was no longer putting in his Jack Haleys and Charles Davises.

Detroit seemed to get stronger and stronger. Most of the starters were still on the bench, and none of them was sulking. When Daly called time, Laimbeer jumped up, bouncing lead-footed to the PA music and yelling to Edwards, "Kick his ass, boy, KICK HIS ASS!" The fans were getting tense. Someone threw a whiskey bottle onto the floor where it exploded into glistening needles, and fans tossed popcorn and Coke cups at Wilson and Ciszewski.

With less than a minute to go and Detroit up by 6, Daly still couldn't relax. Hodges could shoot for 3, and there was Jordan to worry about, always Jordan. With 32 seconds left, Dumars drove in hard then hooked it backward to Edwards, who had a chance to put the game away. Edwards bounced upwards and let go—it bucked out. Craig Hodges grabbed it. "Fuck!" snarled Daly.

The inbounds play was to Jordan. Dumars flew up after it, batted it away, then he backflopped to the floor with a hollow, ugly thump. Jess Kersey blew his whistle. Foul on Dumars. "I can't fuckin' *believe* it," Daly screamed. Jordan went to the line breathing hard. He hit his shot. Five-point lead. The second shot went up and banged off the front of the rim. Edwards grabbed it. The game was over.

McCloskey sagged in his seat. They'd survived. Thank God for Edwards. How could he get rid of a guy like that?

It was great to be home. They still had to win two out of three, but two of them would be in the Palace, where the adrenaline would be on Detroit's side. McCloskey, sitting in his office, jolted out of his chair and hurried over to the business side of the hall, where he corralled the brain trust. "I've got a great idea," he said.

"What kind of great idea?" asked Dave Auker.

"If we make it into the Finals," McCloskey said, "after they introduce the L.A. players, before they introduce our players, let's send out a guy from the locker room with a big Bad Boy flag and run him around the arena and stop at center court. I think the crowd will go crazy."

"The crowd *will* go crazy," said Auker. "But are you sure you're okay? This doesn't sound like you." For months, McCloskey had ragged at the brain trust to cool it with the Bad Boys campaign. Maybe it was making money, but it was a red flag to the refs. But something in him had snapped.

"There might be some press criticism," said John Ciszewski. "I can just hear Joe Falls."

"I don't give a damn," said McCloskey.

Doug Collins was laughing with burly Charles Davis as the postcocktail crowd drifted down from the plush Palace bar. Collins was sitting in his coach's seat along the sidelines, his big hands wrapped around a basketball, waiting for game time. "You think I can't make it from here?" he asked Davis.

"I *know* you can't."

"Bet me."

"I bet you dinner." Collins eyed the basket and started to stand up. "No! No!" said Davis. "Sitting *down*."

Collins thought about it, sat down, stared at the hoop, and vaulted a high perfect shot that ripped the net. Collins grinned.

Vinnie Johnson, who'd been standing to one side, said, "That's not shit. Check this out." He walked most of the way to halfcourt, leaped onto the scorer's table, faced the basket, and launched a missile that went as high as the first level of suites before plummeting through the hoop.

Collins and Davis applauded slowly. They all looked very relaxed. None of them was acting as if their careers were on the line. But they were.

When the game started, the air of relaxation continued. The crowd was quiet and cheerful and politely applauded Jordan—the greatest possible threat to their team. Chicago promptly ran up a 10-point lead. The Pistons were popping up jumpers, not bothering to drive to the hoop. Daly was frantically crying out plays, but the team was as sluggish as the crowd. It seemed suddenly as if the season had already ended— not just now, but in April, when no one was looking and the future seemed remote and golden.

Toward the end of the quarter, the Detroit ball movement tightened and they got nastier on defense. With less than a minute left, Salley even challenged Jordan on the dribble, and managed to poke the ball away. Salley looked for someone to take it to the Detroit end, but no one was back there, so he started a tortured, ungainly drive to the hoop, darting looks for someone who could actually dribble. Salley finally got close to the hoop, leaped, tried the kind of scoop lay-up that Thomas made look easy, and watched with big, scared eyes as the ball bammed off the glass. He tried to shove it back in, but it caromed back to the 3-point line. Salley jumped backward and dived for it, knocking it out of bounds. Daly watched pensively, with his thumb under this chin and his forefinger laid alongside his nose. Then he laughed. "E" for effort. The quarter ended. Eight-point Chicago lead. Daly didn't get it; they lost this one, they'd have to win two in a row, including one in the Chicago Pit. And his guys were acting like they didn't give a damn.

The Bulls got 10 up and the crowd was becoming paralyzed. Ken Calvert bleated over the ultratech sound system, "Let's let the people around the country know we can make some *noise,* for *your . . . Detroit . . . Pistons!* The crowd cranked it up, then it fizzled. Dave Auker was tense. He was supposed to choreograph the home-court adrenaline, and he was falling on his face. He kept frantically plugging in all his blue-chip hype songs—"Footloose," "Eye of the Tiger"—but the building was dead. The franchise's history—"They'll break your heart"—seemed to be weighing on the crowd, and even the team.

But Mark Aguirre was new here. Aguirre was unacquainted with the legacy of failure, and he was *damned* if they were going to lose—not after all the crap he'd endured to get here. He started pouring in jump shots with his flawless, gifted stroke, and for long moments he seemed to be in his own world, unaware of the stadium or the score. He was lost in a childhood dream: the king of the playground.

Aguirre brought Detroit to within 7, then he had the ball at the top of the key with Pippen in front of him. Aguirre shuttled the ball from one hand to the other, head-faking and shoulder-faking for a good seven seconds, maybe ten. Pippen stayed with him, then Aguirre zigged while Pippen zagged, found a moment of freedom, and popped it in. Five-point lead. Next time down, Brad Sellers was hanging all over Aguirre, grabbing at him and pinching his jersey, but Aguirre ducked away from Sellers and sailed it over to Laimbeer, who drilled it. Auker went with the "Hey" song, the crowd started to wake up, and Rodman soaked up the adrenaline and started making Jordan miserable. Jordan was getting virtually no shots, and those he took were with Rodman's hands over his eyes. Jordan was passing off more than he was shooting—against Doug Collins's wishes. Collins and Jordan had talked, and Collins had told Jordan he could shoot more. Collins thought that was what Jordan wanted. But Jordan wasn't doing it, and Collins could only watch in frustration, digging the heels of his black sneakers against the front of his chair. Everybody from Chicago was wearing black sneakers, like Jordan always did. It was Jordan's idea—to promote "team unity."

At the end of the third quarter, Vinnie Johnson threw up a ridiculous shot—a leaning, off-balance catapult—the kind that usually made Daly yell "Go get Vinnie!" But it went in. Daly's intuition told him to stay with Johnson. Daly believed that about 90 percent of the time he could tell when Johnson was hot. He thought he was now. He better be.

When the fourth quarter started—Detroit down 1—Johnson was still in the lineup. Johnson got the ball on the left side and curled into the lane against a wall of three Bulls, with Corzine behind. Johnson jerked, faked, shot through a crack in the wall and went straight against Corzine, who was at least nine inches taller—depending on how much Johnson lied about his height. To get off a lay-up over Corzine's huge, high hand, Johnson leaned backward in his jump until he was practically parallel with the floor. He rolled the ball off his fingertips as he started his hard crash down. The ball banked off the glass and in. Corzine pushed Johnson as he fell. Foul. V.J. picked himself off the floor, glared at Corzine, shook his arms, and sank his free throw.

Down at the other end, Corzine got the ball under the hoop and went up, but Salley went with him and rode Corzine to the floor. He bulldogged him, broke him like a steer. Payback for Vinnie. Salley got an instant replay on the scoreboard, and the crowd started to scream.

Then a remarkable thing happened. Michael Jordan got the ball at the free-throw line. Dumars was between him and the basket. Jordan didn't try a sweep or drive or even a leap. He just jumped and shot. The shot was a foot long and to the left. Airball. *Airball!* By Michael Jordan. Something was wrong with Jordan. The endless, bone-cracking season was finally settling in.

But Vinnie Johnson felt perfect. He had entered the zone of altered consciousness. His every move was in rhythm and his shots were Zen perfect. He'd get the ball halfway in, drive out to the perimeter, spin suddenly, and shoot—the kind of shots defense dares you to take—and they were ripping net. Detroit ran up a little lead. Auker played "Shout" and the fans stomped on the beat and screamed the "Hey-ay-ay-*ay*" refrains. Rodman was getting every Detroit rebound—he'd have 10 for the quarter. With 4:30 left, Johnson sank a short jumper to put Detroit up by 8 and Auker played "Mony, Mony." McCloskey stood with his arms folded while everyone in the stadium clapped with the song. Just before McCloskey sat down, he jabbed his fist in the air.

At 2:22 Detroit was up 7. Jordan time. Daly went with his best defenders. Chicago ball. Hodges—their 3-point man—got it at the 3-point line. He found Jordan to his left and whipped it over. But Dumars bolted in and grabbed it. Doug Collins threw a white towel to the floor. Detroit went downcourt. V.J. had it, in to Edwards, back to Johnson—the 24-second clock was running out—Salley got it in the corner. Two seconds to shoot. Salley dribbled behind the backboard—the buzzer began to sound—Salley was shooting. *Swish.* 89–80 Detroit, with just over a minute. Auker put "Mony, Mony" back on. Everyone in the Palace was up and clapping. Jack McCloskey unfolded his arms. He began—for the first time all year—to clap along with the song.

In the locker room, reporters were clotted around Vinnie Johnson. Off to one side, Rick Mahorn tugged glumly at his socks. He'd played ten minutes, hadn't scored, had 2 rebounds and 4 fouls. He thought the refs were killing him. He made $800,000 a year, and they were trying to take it away.

Laimbeer leaned over to him. "Hey, don't worry about it," he said softly. "Next time it'll be me."

Mahorn stared at his feet. "Ain't it a bitch."

In the interview room, Doug Collins, his wide round eyes full of hurt, tried to explain why his team had lost. The answer was pretty obvious; Michael Jordan had taken 8 shots. One of the Chicago reporters, a TV guy, boomed in his TV voice, "Doug, why is Michael Jordan the highest-paid decoy in the NBA?"

Collins flinched. "I think that's a pretty crass thing to say." His voice was high and tough. "The highest-paid decoy in the NBA! That's really a cheap shot. What do you want him to do? Shoot against three guys? You guys are amazing! When he scores forty-six points he's a one-man team, when he only takes eight shots he's the highest-paid decoy in the league."

Most of the reporters in the room stiffened. They were used to being condescended to, lied to, made fun of, and made to feel like wimps. But a direct attack violated protocol.

A few moments later, Collins began to look worried. "Look, if I've offended you, I didn't mean anything by it at all. You know what I'm saying. I'm not trying to offend you in any way." Even in his misery, Collins smiled at the reporter who'd pissed him off.

Doug Collins needed all the friends he could get.

The next morning, McCloskey, Will Robinson, and Stan Novak sat in front of McCloskey's desk, watching videotape on the TV set in the wall. They were all still worried about the Chicago series, but they had to push that aside to arrange next fall's rookie camp. They had to think of the franchise, not the team. On the screen was Jay Edwards, the hotshot Indiana guard who was Player of the Year in the Big Ten. It was conceivable that Edwards would still be available when McCloskey's draft pick came up, because he'd been accused of stealing, was rumored to be using drugs, and had beaten up a girlfriend. Those kinds of stories scared hell out of GMs, particularly since Len Bias's death. If Red Auerbach could get burned, anybody could.

"Your buddy out there at Cal Irvine is coming to camp," McCloskey said to Robinson. "Pronounce his name. Doctor-sick?"

"Dock-*tor*-chick," said Robinson. "Doktorczyk can shoot the ball, for six-nine."

"Good Irish name," said McCloskey. "What about Ralph Lewis?"

"He'd be worth bringing to camp. Very much worth it."

"I'll ask Nancy to call. And I'm calling Ken Johnson."

"You know Darryl Dawkins was down at the Orlando Magic camp?"

"Is that right?" said McCloskey, showing no special interest.

"Yeah. He gets off the plane and they got all the television people there, and he goes to see Pat Williams, and tells Pat that he doesn't want to participate, because some of these guys are gonna *hurt* him. *Hurt* him! He'd have to get hit by a *train* to get hurt. So he didn't participate, he walked out of camp. His agent calls and tells them, well, he'll go if they get an insurance policy. So Pat says, how we gonna get an insurance policy in one or two days—on a guy that's had *back* surgery? Never did participate."

"How'd Darryl do overseas?"

"He didn't do well overseas, for this reason," said Robinson. "He's bigger and more experienced than the opposition. Not to mention more talented. Plus the fact that they only play twice a week and practice not that much. So how *could* he do well? Dawkins doesn't really have any wish to play. He wishes to steal some money."

"Jack," said Stan Novak, scanning a list, "you said you had five guys for camp, and there's only four names here."

"Plus Bedford," said McCloskey.

"Bedford. I forgot about him."

"I didn't." McCloskey looked bitter.

As McCloskey and his scouts concluded their meeting in the front office, players downstairs were streaming from the court into the locker room. Their shirts—an odd assortment of college jerseys, promo shirts, and designer T-shirts—were stuck to their muscles with sweat. Fifty yards to the rear was Daly, who stopped in the hall outside the coaches' room to meet the reporters.

"Chuck," said anchorman Scott Wahle, "what do you make of Vinnie? He takes those shots and on the way up you kind of say, 'No—not that one,' and then they fall and they look pretty."

"I said it to the team the other day—it's great to coach a guy like Vinnie because he's uncomplicated. If he's supposed to pass, he passes and if he's supposed to shoot, he shoots. And when he gets into that zone, there's nobody like him. I've seen him make the most incredible shots, you know, falling down, up and under. Hey, a lot of people forget the shot he made down the stretch in Chicago when we were struggling to score—he went from the right side and came back up on the left. *Nobody* can make that shot, but he made it." Daly was talking like a coach who wanted to send his GM a message: Don't let Vinnie go.

"Chuck, do you want to tell us how you stopped Jordan?"

"Doug had said the day before that they were going to go more inside, pound the ball to Cartwright, look for him to create, go inside-outside. That means Jordan becomes more of a passer. But I can assure you, you will see them play their most intense game next time, and Jordan will absolutely give everything he's got to win that game. It's bottom line, back against the wall. Every series, they've managed to win somehow. Jordan has appeared, and he's won. I mean, there's never been a player like him." Most of the TV guys snapped off their lights. All they needed was one good sound-bite on Jordan to justify their morning's work. The print guys stayed; the Detroit writers had three pages to fill.

"Is Detroit playing better now than earlier in the playoffs?" asked Terry Foster.

"Basically, we've played the same all year. Outstanding defense, erratic offense. We live and die with the jump shot, and the jumper can be erratic." Daly wasn't saying it, but he thought part of the reason the jumpers weren't falling now was nerves; the jump shot was a finesse shot, and Detroit's 40 percent shooting was indicative of the Fear of God. "When I substitute," said Daly, "I bring in two guys, Salley and Rodman, who are basically nonoffense players. That's what makes coaching hard. The All-Star teams came out today, and I didn't see any of our guys on the team, not even the third team."

"That ought to make you feel good, though."

"It does. It talks about teamwork. And defense. But you've gotta *sell* defense. Coaches today, all of us are salesmen. It's a sales job, and our people here have been willing to accept the sales pitch."

"What's the pitch?"

"Defense is macho. It's masculine. It's tough. It goes with our so-called image, which I won't mention, 'cause I'd like to get rid of it. Plus, they've seen results. Right now, there are only three teams in the world still playing. Europe's all done, everybody's done. If you want to watch basketball, you have to watch us."

Most of the print reporters were drifting into the locker room to collect their requisite jockisms. Daly didn't like playing to a small crowd. "Anything else?" Daly asked. No one responded. "Great." Daly ducked into the coaches' room. He hadn't mentioned that the Coach of the Year voting had also come out. He'd finished a distant second behind Phoenix's Cotton Fitzsimmons—despite his team's historic record, all its injuries, its shake-up from the Trade, and its lack of All-Stars. None of the reporters had brought the subject up. Why bother? Daly would just say: Cotton deserved it, winning is what's important, I'm just playing one game at a time. After all, it had been his own personal defeat, so now it would be his responsibility to bury it in jocktalk.

Game day. Back in Chicago. McCloskey needed to pull his mind away from it, at least for a couple of hours. So after the morning shoot-around, he and Stan Novak left the Westin Hotel, where the team was staying, and walked over to a tennis court next to Northwestern Hospital. While they were hitting the ball around, two guys in wheelchairs took the adjacent court, and a nurse hit balls to them. After a few minutes, McCloskey approached her and said, "Want me to try that?" He started lobbing in shots, and one of the guys, who'd been paralyzed since he was fourteen, was pretty good. The other guy, who was only eighteen and had a fresh scar thick as a Band-Aid from his neck to his tailbone, had fallen asleep at the wheel just four months before and was having difficulty.

After they'd finished, McCloskey said to Novak, "Puts the game in perspective, doesn't it?" Novak agreed. But within minutes, McCloskey was climbing the walls again.

In the basement of Chicago Stadium, McCloskey, Novak, and Will Robinson stood against a forklift, eating their pregame meal off the machine's grimy flat surfaces. The folding tables next to the buffet were full, so the three of them had wandered over to the forklift. Novak picked at his food, eating his cookies first, and tried to edge away from a pool of water, dark and thick as maple syrup, which smelled like stale urine. They all looked scared and disoriented—as if the phone had just rung in the middle of the night. But McCloskey felt good. "If you don't get a thrill out of being here, as a player or a coach or a general manager, you're in the wrong business. I think this whole thing"—he waved his arm expansively, taking in the locker room and the reporters and his buddies and the piss on the floor—"is the greatest experience in the world. I mean—damn!—this is *fun.*"

Will Robinson was studying a *Sun-Times* sports page. "You know," he said, "I think Pitino did exactly the right thing. Leaving the Knicks. Here's why. He's in for a million a year at Kentucky. Right? Okay. He's *got* no pressure. Right? And he can come back to the NBA anytime he wants." Robinson, perhaps in deference to McCloskey, didn't mention another factor: Pitino would never have to speak to Knicks GM Al Bianchi again.

"Sounds like you've got that figured, Coach," said McCloskey.

Around the corner, the Pistons were climbing the steep, narrow stairs to the floor. Mahorn stood by the steps, slapping the ass of every player that went by—hitting them hard: Pop! Pop! Pop!—growling, "Let's go, pal!" in a voice that sounded like a threat. Inside the locker room were a few crumpled cups, and a blackboard on which Daly had written: "7th Game Intensity—Control the boards—Energy—Intimidate—Dominate —FOLLOW THE JORDAN RULES."

A four-part harmony group tried to sing the national anthem, but their music was obliterated by the dog whistle, now at a new level of frenzy. When they finished, Laimbeer bounced the ball twenty feet into the air, just to piss off the crowd, and came to the bench with his need-to-win scowl.

The game started with a furious burst of shoving and smashing. A shot came hard off the backboard and Laimbeer, Scottie Pippen, and

Horace Grant went up for it. Laimbeer tipped the ball with his left hand, then dropped his elbows and shot back up to seize it with both hands. But as he'd dropped his left elbow, it had cracked squarely into Pippen's face, right between his eyes. Laimbeer clutched the ball as Pippen grabbed his face and collapsed backward. As sneakers thudded around Pippen's head, referee Joe Crawford grabbed Pippen's arm and dragged his limp body off the floor. The fans started to scream. Pippen lay in a silent pile. Doug Collins would later call it "another cheap shot from Laimbeer." Laimbeer would say that Pippen "just happened to be in the wrong place." Collins sprinted onto the floor and hovered over Pippen, who was still as a corpse. The trainer and the team doctor bent over Pippen. After a couple of minutes, Pippen began to mumble and stir. The doctor had to put his ear close to Pippen's mouth to hear him because the stadium was vibrating with "Laim-beer *sucks*—Laim-beer *sucks*." Finally, Pippen staggered up and was carried off to a hospital, for treatment of a concussion.

Brad Sellers replaced Pippen. Sellers, with a 3.2 scoring average, sloping little-girl shoulders, a concave chest, and scrawny legs, looked like his bones had stretched during a growth spurt and his body had never caught up. Chicago went on an emotion-fired scoring binge—win one for the Gipper—that crescendoed with Michael Jordan getting the ball on a fast break, sailing downcourt so fast his sweat flew straight back—like raindrops on a jet window—then soaring through the air backward and jamming the ball down blind, by feel. Chicago raced to a 12-point lead, while Daly stood at the sidelines yelling, "Work for good shots! Work for good shots!" With a couple of minutes left in the quarter, Collins gave Jordan a breather. Disaster. Detroit scored 10 straight, and was only down 2 at the end of the quarter.

The Pistons started coming at Chicago in waves. Mahorn and Laimbeer would pound at Sellers's shoulders and hips, then Rodman and Salley would come in and leap over him, then Edwards and Aguirre would shuttle in and show Sellers skills he could only dream of. Dumars and Rodman would clamp down on Jordan, then Thomas and Salley would work him over, then Vinnie Johnson would come in and sap Jordan's energy with wild drives to the hoop. At the same time, Daly kept working on the refs. Early in the second quarter he intercepted referee Earl Strom at the sidelines and yelled, "What about walking, on Jordan? He's been walking!"

"If I see it I promise I'll call it," said Strom.

The Chicago starters withered. The Killer-B players kept coming. Just before the half, Daly pulled Laimbeer and put in John Long, even though there were already two guards on the floor. Laimbeer ran off the floor yelling at Daly, "You don't have any matchups!" Daly nodded and turned away. He liked seeing Laimbeer rabid, even if he had to absorb some of it himself. He didn't feel any real threat to his authority. The lines of power in the Pistons organization were clear and inviolable.

John Long looked perfectly at home on the floor. Why not? He had a 15.5 career scoring average. He was the Pistons' eleventh man, but Doug Collins would have loved to have had him. At the half, Detroit by 2.

In the third, Jordan tried driving to the hoop, but when he did Salley would jump in front of him. Twice Jordan cracked his elbow into Salley's nose and twice Salley was called for the foul, but it was taking Jordan out of his rhythm. Meanwhile, Edwards came in and racked up points with his soft low-post shots, and Rodman crashed the glass. With the quarter almost half over and Detroit up 5, Chicago called time and huddled. "Look," Collins cried, "this is the time when we can't let it get away from us. Please! This is the most important time of the game. We *can't* let it get away now!" Collins looked desperate.

In the Detroit huddle, the mood was different. Cocky, but totally focused. Laimbeer shouted, "C'mon! We don't wanna take these guys home!" A fan went to the halfcourt line to shoot for a new car. As Daly scribbled, Salley was scowling, Rodman was clapping, and Mahorn had his elbows on Brendan Malone's shoulders. "Bill," said Daly, "if Jordan . . ." The fan heaved his shot; it clanged down through the hoop and the stadium went crazy. Nobody in the Detroit huddle noticed. Daly kept talking and Rodman kept clapping.

Chicago couldn't keep up. They needed Pippen—in a twenty-three-minute span, their frontcourt only scored one field goal. They also needed a bench. The quarter ended with Chicago down 8 and Jordan on the bench, a towel over his shoulders, his mouth twisted into a strange grimace.

At the start of the fourth, Rodman got the ball down low, leaped up, and threw up a horrendous shot that almost missed the top of the backboard. "Shit!" screamed Daly. "Oh my God! Goddamnit!" He slapped the computer terminal on the scorer's table and grabbed his head. To lose this now and force a seventh game—all because of Dumb Dennis mistakes—would be an unspeakable déjà vu. Daly pulled Rodman, and Rodman moped back to the bench and kicked the scorer's table, his eyes caught on the ceiling.

Jordan went on a rampage. He hit perfect slow-motion jumpers and knifed through triple-teams for gravity-free drives. By 8:39, Detroit's lead was 2. Collins called time. He gathered his players in closely and screamed, "*Do* not let our fans down! Keep the fans in the *game*!" He went over a few technical points, but he was mostly worried about emotion: The mind is everything. On the sidelines, fans stripped off their "Fuck the Bad Boys" shirts and whipped them in circles.

Isiah Thomas came out of the time-out with his face rigid, looking a little amused, if anything. Then he took over the game. He hit a jumper, then drove on Jordan, drew a foul, and made both shots. Then he hit another jumper and grabbed a rebound. As he came down with the ball, Daly put his palms out flat: slow it down. Isiah worked John Paxson into a frenzy, collected another foul and swished both. Suddenly, the lead was 10. Jordan missed a free throw, Isiah pumped in another jumper and now the bench was standing, grinning. Salley, Vinnie Johnson, and Fennis Dembo were wiggling their fingers at each other.

The dog whistle died. Mahorn was up, waving his towel. With a minute left and the lead frozen at 10, Jordan came out. He sat down and Collins came up to him and put his hands around Jordan's face.

When it ended, Isiah Thomas threw his arms around Mark Aguirre. "I got us in it," said Thomas. "Now you've got to win it for us."

They ran down to the locker room. The first person in after Aguirre and Thomas was McCloskey. McCloskey stopped briefly to grab Dumars's hands, then put both his hands around Aguirre's face, just as Collins had done with Jordan. Aguirre bellowed, "Yeahhh!"

CBS's Hubie Brown watched Aguirre and McCloskey and shouted over the growing bedlam, "Jack McCloskey! The architect! They used to be, in '83 and '84, one of the highest-scoring teams—he changed the chemistry. They drafted Dumars, Salley, Rodman, went out and got Dantley, and then traded him for Aguirre. And McCloskey made a big trade for the Microwave, Vinnie Johnson, and another trade for James Edwards. He controls the purse strings, and changed the face of this team—and now he deserves the credit." McCloskey skip-stepped across the room to high-five Daly. Daly was glowing, his face totally different from the mask he'd kept on as he walked off the court. Then McCloskey shook hands with all of his players, spending extra time with his veterans—Mahorn, Edwards, Vinnie Johnson.

At that instant, he loved all of them, not the same way he loved his own sons, but just as certainly.

Which of them would he get rid of? And how would he do it?

For a moment, as McCloskey finished thanking his players—all so young and so certain of the inevitability of success—he was flooded with memories of his early Piston players. They were no longer young, and they'd lived mostly without success. He saw the faces of Ronnie Lee— the Kamikaze Kid—and Kent Benson, Terry Tyler, Phil Hubbard, and Tripucka, the White Hope. They were still part of the franchise. They always would be. Where were they? Were they watching the game?

Tom Wilson stood off to one side. He always tried to maintain distance from the players, and it had never been harder than right now. It was a transcendent moment for the team. And—more important—for the franchise.

After things had quieted a little, Jerry Krause and Doug Collins came in. Both were drained and white. They congratulated Daly and McCloskey and some of the players. They left separately.

Doug Collins had coached his last game for the Chicago Bulls.

SIXTEEN

"How to Win"
The L.A. Series

"Nancy," JACK McCloskey called to assistant Nancy Maas, "would you ask Frank if he's got the flag yet?"

"Sure." She punched a number into her phone and put her hand over the mouthpiece. "What flag?"

"He'll know what I'm talking about."

A few moments later she said, "It's behind your door."

McCloskey closed his door and locked it. Standing in back of the door was a tall steel pole wrapped in black. He unfurled it. The flag was a white skull-and-crossbones, big as a picture window, on a bed of deep black. He grabbed the end of the pole and began waving a figure eight. The flag rippled and popped in the quiet of his office. His face brightened, then cracked into a grin.

"Tonight!" said McCloskey, his eyes on fire, "Pistons versus Lakers! World Championship! *Be there.*" He laid the flag on his conference table and began rolling it up. "This is as it should be," he said. "The two best teams fighting it out." As he stowed the flag, he became reflective. "The beauty of athletics," he said, "is that it's the *one* business where you can find out if you're the best. An attorney *never* has the chance to find out if he's the best attorney in the world. A doctor doesn't have it. A bricklayer doesn't.

"But a chance to win, you know, is also a chance to lose. And if we lose, I'm gonna be . . . I don't know—devastated." He seemed to shudder a little. "There are some people who feel like just getting in the Finals is the main thing. I can't understand that. I've always said, don't come to play, come to win."

McCloskey looked at his watch. It was eleven-fifteen—time for the last shootaround before the Finals began. It had only been three days since the Chicago series, and Daly hadn't been working the team too hard. They were still pretty banged up. Rodman's back was a knot of twisted muscles and pain. Laimbeer's shooting hand felt dead, and Isiah had an aggravated hamstring.

Down on the court, the players were talking to reporters. Now the full glut of international media was in Detroit—about two hundred American sports reporters and crews from Italy, Spain, France, and other countries where NBA games were broadcast. They were falling all over each other to pick up identical snatches of mantalk. The largest clot of sportswriters was surrounding Isiah Thomas. But Thomas, stimulated by the limelight, had backed off the mantalk and was actually trying to communicate. Little of what he said, though, would see print. It didn't boil down to a good twenty-word quote with a feisty punch line. Thomas was talking about what was foremost in his mind—the psychology of winning. "Kevin McHale gave me some good advice," said Thomas, "as I was leaving the court last year after we beat Boston and got into the Finals. He said, 'Don't be happy to be there. Go there to win it.' I heard him, but it didn't compute. It just didn't register. Now I understand his advice fully. I guess that's something you learn from losing.

"You know, Magic has learned a lot from going through hard times, too. I remember you writers calling him Tragic Johnson and saying how he choked and how he could never be a really great player. You didn't always treat him as nice as you do now. But now I understand that that's part of the process. You need that.

"I used to go into the Laker locker rooms after they'd won the Championship, and I'd be trying to figure out what made those guys winners. But I'd end up standing around talking to Jack Nicholson or somebody when I really wanted to be talking to Magic. But Magic wanted to be with his teammates, which I can understand. Maybe *not* being part of it, though, was what helped me to figure out their secret."

"What is it?" asked one of the writers, looking up from his notepad.

"It's a secret." Thomas flicked on his high-beamed smile. "I'll say a few things, though. It's not about physical skills. Goes far beyond that. When I first came here, Jack McCloskey took a lot of flak for drafting a small guy. But he knew that the only way our team would rise to the top would be by mental skills, not size or talent. I knew the only way we could acquire those skills was by watching the Celtics and Lakers, because they were the only teams winning year in and year out.

"I also looked at Seattle, who won one year, and Houston, who got to the Finals one year. They both self-destructed the next year. So, how come? I read Pat Riley's book *Showtime,* and he talks about 'the disease of more.' A team wins it one year and the next year every player wants more minutes, more money, more shots. And it kills them.

"Our team has been up at the Championship level four years now. We could easily have self-destructed. So I read what Riley was saying, and I learned. I didn't want what happened to Seattle and Houston to happen to us.

"But it's hard not to be selfish. The art of winning is complicated by statistics, which for us becomes money. Well, you gotta fight that, find a way around it. And I think we have. If we win this, we'll be the first team in history to win it without having a single player averaging twenty points. First team. *Ever.* We got twelve guys who are just totally committed to winning. Every night we found a different person to win it for us.

"Talked to Larry Bird about this once. Couple years back, at an All-Star Game. We were sitting signing basketballs, and I'm talking to him about Red Auerbach and the Boston franchise and just picking his brain. I don't know if he knew I was picking his brain, but I think he knew. Because I asked one question and he just looked at me. Smiled. Didn't answer me."

"What was the question?" asked one of the writers.

"Not gonna say." High-beamed smile. "I already said too much. I'll tell you one thing about how to win, though, and that's that you don't push the other team's button. Like, you don't say, we're gonna win in six games. That's why I was surprised when I read that Byron Scott said they're gonna win in six. I've been following the Celtics and Lakers a long time, and that's the first time one of their players said we're gonna win in X number of games. I was surprised. You have to ask yourself, why would that statement be made? Either he feels confident, or it's a shield. Either way, it's a mind game."

"Did you hear?" asked a reporter. "He's not playing tonight. Hamstring."

Thomas ignored the remark. If the injury—announced only a few minutes before—was a shock to him, he hid it. In the silence, a reporter asked, "Is there any part of you that wished he was playing?"

"No." Isiah's face was deadpan. His eyes were smiling.

*   *   *

Dave Auker almost never used the theme song from *Rocky*. Too dated. But for this it was perfect. The warm-ups were over and the crowd was crackling and antsy. Auker slowly dimmed the lights—the arena went black. "Cue 'Rocky,' " Auker said into his headset. The music started to boom through the stadium. Suddenly a spotlight exploded onto the floor and everyone in the Palace found themselves looking at a Piston ball boy holding a huge black flag. The music peaked and the ball boy began a hard run around the perimeter of the floor. The flag unfurled. The skull and crossbones appeared. A tremendous cheer jolted the building. McCloskey watched with the corners of his mouth curling up.

Auker blended "Rocky" into "Eye of the Tiger" and had the crowd chanting "Beat L.A." as the game started. The players looked galvanized. Rodman was bouncing around the bench, Laimbeer was grimacing, Mahorn's fists were tight, and Aguirre was clapping and yelling, "Let's go, let's go, let's go!" Detroit came out hot and hit 7 of their first 9 shots. L.A. looked clumsy and uncertain. Kareem was missing his skyhooks and coach Pat Riley quickly yanked him. Orlando Woolridge came in. "Here's a young man, Orlando Woolridge," CBS announcer Dick Stockton shouted into his mike, "who was in drug rehabilitation last year out in Los Angeles, and felt that L.A. would be the place to play. Now he finds himself in his first NBA Finals. Laker GM Jerry West over the years has done a terrific job, picking up Bob McAdoo, Mychal Thompson, and now Woolridge."

Stockton's color man, Hubie Brown, jumped in. "Jerry has been a real architect because he's *brazen* about the moves he makes. Then Pat Riley takes them and puts them into this chemistry—which stresses that winning is *paramount* here. You submerge your talents into *winning*."

Woolridge got the ball on the left perimeter and started backing toward the basket with Rodman behind him. He could bull his way because he had a perfect basketball body: big molded-steel biceps, bodybuilder muscle definition, arms that hung halfway to a pair of glittery blue knee braces, and a heavy scowl to top it off. As he got close to the hoop he spun and shot. Whistle. Rodman had bumped Woolridge's hip—a classic soft foul, courtesy of an image-conscious league. "God!" Daly cried, balling his fists. "Jesus Christ!" He stomped back and forth in front of the bench. Daly had been spooked by the refs in the Chicago series, and he wanted his guys to cool the rough stuff. But if the refs kept calling it that close, Detroit was screwed. Woolridge made both his shots, but the Pistons were still up 6.

There was a TV time-out and the Pistons gathered around Daly. Daly motioned for Dumars to sit down and beckoned Isiah. "Who, me?" said Thomas, and Daly nodded. Isiah had the special detached look he got when he was fixated on a win, and after eight years Daly could read all of Thomas's looks. "You want Vinnie on Cooper," Isiah told Daly. Isiah wanted to guard Magic.

"You're on top," Vinnie said to Rodman. Rodman's head bobbed in quick staccato nods.

"Let's do it!" Laimbeer yelled, and they took the floor as Auker lowered the volume on "Twist and Shout." Isiah got the ball at the top of the key and fired it in to Vinnie Johnson, who curled around the free-throw line. Johnson leaned back and heaved it up. He sank it, but Daly scowled. "Take the shot all the way in!" he yelled. "It's your shot!" Vinnie gave Daly a quick, hurt look. He was a prime candidate to get axed in the expansion draft, and he knew it.

Next time down, Johnson got the ball in the same spot, but this time he drove in and leaped up with Michael Cooper and Mychal Thompson in his face. Nine inches shorter than Thompson, Vinnie kept rising until he was over Thompson's outstretched arm, then he popped it off his fingertips and the ball arched high and swished. But referee Jess Kersey blew his whistle and pointed at Cooper. The foul nullified the basket, but Cooper was pissed. "I didn't touch him!" he yelled. Cooper already had three fouls. So did Woolridge and Jabbar. Pat Riley chewed his gum frantically. Three of his top seven men were in foul trouble, and those seven were the only real players he had. After them, he was looking at guys like Tony Campbell, who'd spent last year in the CBA, and Jeff Lamp, who had a 5.6 career average. Laimbeer passed it in to Isiah, who stayed deep and immediately swished it. "The Detroit guards are makin' all their jump shots," shouted Hubie Brown. "When that happens, *watch out*."

Magic Johnson, who had just won the league's MVP award, pulled Isiah's basket out of the net and danced downcourt. He drove on Isiah in the lane, spun 360 degrees and flipped it up. No good, but a foul was called on Thomas. Daly hated to see that kind of penetration. He cupped his hands to his mouth and screamed, "They're gonna kick our *ass* with that." No one on the floor heard him. But the bench did.

As the first half wound down, Tony Campbell came in. Campbell had played his first three years in Detroit, and still blamed his stunted career on Daly's lack of faith in him. The crowd chanted, "To-ny, To-ny, To-ny." Over the season, they'd learned—mostly from Leon the Barber—the value of a little sarcasm. Campbell got the ball at the top of the key and drove. The defense collapsed, he leaped, and there was a sick slapping sound as the Pistons clubbed him down. He tossed the ball into the air to get two free throws. He stood at the line, shaken, blowing air through pursed lips. His first shot banged off the front of the rim. He took four steps backward, shot again, and it bounced to the left. Riley looked at the ceiling. Rodman grabbed the rebound. Thomas dribbled to the free-throw line, touched bodies with Campbell, then threw it in over Campbell's head. Daly wanted more. Campbell, a great shooter, was weak defensively and they had to exploit that. "Shit," Daly shouted, pointing at Campbell. "*I* can beat him on the dribble!" Campbell looked worried. He was in over his head.

Just before the end of the half, Thomas got the ball and Campbell rushed at him, grabbing wildly. Thomas clamped his free hand around Campbell's arm and started to dribble past a Laimbeer pick. But Thomas bumped Laimbeer and fell to the floor, losing the ball. Magic Johnson swooped after it. Isiah, flat on his back, grabbed hold of it. Magic groped for the ball, his huge arms as lightning fast as a lightweight boxer's. Isiah, without using his hands, made an incredible gymnastic flip onto his stomach, with the ball under his belly. Magic encircled Isiah with his arms and the ball slid out of bounds.

Magic got up grinning his million-dollar smile. "Man, oh man," he said to Isiah. For a moment, it was as if they were on the playground and it was Just a Game. Isiah grinned back. Their two brilliant smiles lit the stadium. It was a moment of peace.

Then Jess Kersey blew his whistle and pointed at Magic. "What!" Johnson blurted. *"What!"* It was a business again. Thomas made both shots. Detroit was up 9. The Lakers were struggling to keep it even that close, and they were losing their grip. Just two weeks ago, the nation's sports intelligentsia had said L.A. was playing "the best basketball on the planet." But that hadn't been against Detroit.

In the third quarter, the game ended. Detroit zoomed out 15 ahead, then 18, then 20. Magic Johnson didn't score in the third quarter and ended up with 17 in the game. Detroit was superior in every category. They outrebounded L.A. 45–32, they shot .554 to L.A.'s .467, and they had 26 assists to L.A.'s 21.

The Lakers, of course, were playing without Byron Scott. But Thomas, Laimbeer, and Rodman also had serious injuries; Laimbeer and Rodman only scored 4 points each. The difference between L.A. and Detroit was that L.A. had no one to take Scott's place—except for Michael Cooper, who couldn't shoot. But Detroit had Salley, Rodman, Edwards, and Vinnie Johnson. Once again, the depth McCloskey had built was the difference.

After the game—so much of a blowout even Fennis Dembo got in— Isiah drove his buddy Buck Johnson back to Magic's hotel. It was a ritual. One of them always drove the other home. They talked about the game, as they always did. Johnson vowed to do more in the next game. If he had to, he'd take it over. He wasn't too worried. This was, after all, only one game.

Magic Johnson had no idea that the Lakers' wave had crested. Already, it was rolling back. The Pistons hadn't come to play—they'd come to win. And now they knew how.

The next day, McCloskey met with the coaches. They had to start deciding which four players to leave unprotected in the expansion draft. Dembo, Williams, and Long were the easy choices. But who else? Maybe James Edwards. Maybe Vinnie Johnson. Those were the obvious candidates. They weren't starters. They were both getting older. They had expensive contracts. The beat reporters believed that McCloskey had left Vinnie unprotected last year. Charlotte, though, had taken Ralph Lewis, a springy young six-six guy. Not only was V.J. old and expensive, but he was a little temperamental. Bill Musselman, coach of the new Minnesota team, was dubious about Vinnie. Musselman thought V.J. might not be very inspired by a losing team.

So maybe the best strategy was to put Vinnie on the list, hoping that the expansion teams would pass him up and go for someone cheaper and younger, like Michael Williams. The new teams had to look to the future, but McCloskey was more concerned about next year. Next year, Detroit would be in the thick of the race again, and V.J. would be valuable.

Or maybe it should be Aguirre. The media would kill them for that, but possibly Aguirre would be the easiest to replace. Another possibility was Mahorn. He was a starter, but what if his back suddenly exploded?

McCloskey had each of the coaches, along with Stan Novak and Will Robinson, choose the fourth player to leave unprotected.

They all did it, and one by one they told McCloskey their choice. It was unanimous.

McCloskey nodded. "That's who I chose, too," he said.

Pacing, gnawing the insides of his own cheeks, folding and unfolding his arms, Pat Riley glowered at center court. There the Piston ball boy stood in the spotlight, waving the Bad Boys flag. The crowd howled. Riley, according to his players, had been a "madman" over the last two days, digging frantically for a way to derail the Pistons' momentum.

Even before the end of the first game, a sense of inevitability had set in. Detroit was just too good, too deep, too hungry. Riley was a master motivator—a classic overachiever who'd played nine years in the NBA with just a 7.4 scoring average. But he'd exhausted his bag of motivational tricks: win one for Kareem, be "the Team of the Eighties," and "three-peat" (a phrase he'd copyrighted). By now, it all sounded pretty hollow. The only thing with any punch at all was the sentiment for Kareem, and that didn't go far. Jabbar had spent most of his career as a remote, forbidding cynic—an angry young man with little to be angry about—and it was pretty hard to get all misty about him now. The only reason he was on the team was to collect his $3 million—because he'd screwed up his finances—and he'd put the team through hell by coming to fall camp puffed with blubber.

So Riley had done what he often did—tossed it in Buck Johnson's lap. If there was one person who knew how to win, it was Buck. Johnson had unparalleled physical skills—he had almost as much liquid grace as Michael Jordan but packed twice Jordan's muscle. It was his mind, though, that set Johnson apart. Like Thomas, he was obsessed with winning; that had been their initial bond when they'd first met in 1979, introduced by mutual friend Mark Aguirre. That wasn't all they had in common, though. They both had an extraordinary capacity for focus, which made them brilliant in crucial situations. They were both handsome and articulate, traits that had little to do with basketball but a great deal to do with being a sports god. They were also both natural leaders. Johnson had the unique ability to charm and kick ass at the same time. He was one of the few people who could have taken over a team long dominated by Jabbar.

And now, Magic Johnson believed, it was time for him to take over this series.

Johnson led the Lakers onto the floor as Dave Auker blasted out Generic Hero Music. Even as his lips brushed Isiah's cheek, in their now-famous pregame kiss, Johnson's eyes were locked in a thousand-yard stare. His eyes were hot. His stride was long, exaggerated, as if he had someplace to go. Even Kareem was kinetic, bouncing off the balls of his feet and jerking his shoulders.

Just after tip-off, Aguirre took position under the hoop with his back to A. C. Green, working Green over with his big beefy ass and his elbows. Green's hands searched for a point of leverage on Aguirre then suddenly Aguirre jerked his elbow and Green's head rocketed backward. Green's hand flew to his mouth, touching a front tooth that Aguirre had knocked loose in the last game. Referee Joe Crawford whistled Aguirre but Aguirre looked happy. He didn't get too many chances to set the "tempo" of the game—that was usually Mahorn's job. It was one of the many dirty jobs Mahorn did without recognition.

Riley put in six-foot-nine Orlando Woolridge and six-ten Mychal Thompson and left in Jabbar. Daly looked stricken. He yelled, "Size! They got too much size." He got Dumars's attention. "Joe! Joe! Time-out!" The team huddled and Daly countered with Edwards and Rod-man. "Now you guys are in the *Finals*!" Daly shouted as they crowded around. "You gotta stop 'em!"

Back on the floor, Edwards started torturing Kareem, butting and grabbing at him. Daly clapped his hands. Kareem's forearm sailed up by Edwards's head and his elbow hooked into Edwards's eye. Edwards brushed his hand over the eye and kept battling. For the next few minutes, someone hit the floor on almost every possession. "Intensity!" yelled Daly. But then Michael Cooper hit a 3-pointer and then a fifteen-foot jumper and Daly deflated. He turned toward Brendan Suhr. "We don't want to compete tonight. I can see that." Suhr gave Daly a blank look. It was no time to contradict him. Cooper's jump shot put L.A. ahead by 10.

But pretty soon Jabbar was stiff-legged with fatigue and Cooper and Green each had two fouls. It was Tony Campbell time. Riley called time-out. In the Detroit huddle Mahorn, fresh from a rest, boomed, "Let's keep up the intensity."

"Keep playing hard for forty-eight minutes!" yelled Laimbeer, a deep frown wrinkling his face.

"Bill," said Daly, his eyes on his clipboard, "meet Kareem early on defense."

They came out looking fresh and mean and began chipping away Coalminer Style at the Laker lead. Dumars grabbed a rebound right under the hoop and looked up to see Jabbar towering over him. Jabbar's massive torso—much more muscular than it looked on television—cast a shadow that covered Dumars's entire body. Dumars darted toward the corner, then curved back to the top of the key. No one was following him—an apparent violation of the zone defense rule. "Illegal defense!" Daly screamed. "Illegal!"

Without looking at Daly, referee Joe Crawford said, "I don't need your help!"

"Damn it! It's illegal!"

Mahorn tried to break open to help Dumars, but A. C. Green had knitted arms with Mahorn and Mahorn struggled like a bulldog on a chain. "Fuck," Mahorn snarled. But Dumars, still on the fly, lofted the ball over Tony Campbell's head; it plunked against the glass and ripped the net. Next time down Dumars scored over Magic's head, then he faded on Campbell and hit again. Dumars could tell he was sliding into the zone of altered consciousness, but he tried not to think about it. He didn't know how many points he had and didn't want to know. He had no idea who was guarding him. He drifted off, and for long minutes he felt as if he were in the stadium's top row, in a silent booth, watching the game without passion or any physical sensation. The Laker lead dwindled to almost nothing. Dumars finished the half with 26 points—8 for 11 from the floor and 10 for 11 from the line.

Third quarter. Lakers by 1. Magic Johnson hurried the ball downcourt. He passed off to A. C. Green, who barreled down the middle of the lane. As Green soared for the hoop, Isiah brushed him. Green kept going and jammed. Whistle. Foul on Isiah. Leon the Barber leaped up. "Oh, bullshit!" he cried. "*Bull*shit!" The crowd picked it up. "Bull-shit! Bull-shit!" It got louder. "Bull-*shit*! BULL-*SHIT*!" It was hard to believe the Palace had ever been quiet. All those quiet early-season games were just a vague memory now. "BULL! *SHIT*! BULL! *SHIT*!" Dave Auker looked up with satisfaction. A. C. Green took his free throw. The fans behind the basket writhed in frenzy. Green missed.

Detroit brought the ball down, Isiah dribbling past Laimbeer, who sat on the bench holding his arm out for team doctor Ben Paolucci—the arm was numb, just pins and needles. Isiah knifed down the middle, flipped it in underhanded, and took a foul. Pat Riley chewed his gum like a condemned prisoner. "The Lakers can't run away," Hubie Brown crowed into his mike.

Magic brought the ball across the halfcourt line and fed Mychal Thompson on a pick and roll. Thompson's shot missed and Salley batted it to Isiah. Thomas streaked downcourt, threatening to break free.

Magic pivoted and ran alongside him. They were almost alone, each floating on graceful, gravity-free strides—beautiful strides that burst off the floor and then sailed. Step for step, they flew down the floor. Now it was just a simple footrace between two close friends. Just a Game. Just for fun. They ran with abandon and joy. Side by side, in midair, they floated.

Suddenly Magic Johnson grabbed his leg. A look of shock hit his eyes. Isiah kept going. Johnson staggered to a halt. Magic clutched the back of his thigh. Riley screamed for a time-out. The Laker trainer rushed out and put his hand on Johnson's back. Johnson jerked away. He shot his arm upward in disgust. Tears glassed his eyes. He walked in a small circle, his face twisted in rage. He knew it was his hamstring. And he knew what that meant.

*　　*　　*

The streets of Marina del Rey, the classy coastal encampment just south of Beverly Hills, were paved with flowers. This was the Lakers' neighborhood. Such beauty! Such an air of wealth! The Detroit Pistons scuffed through the flowers.

The flowers had fallen from the overhanging jacaranda trees, and they colored the streets lavender. Their scent mixed with the salty coastal air as the Pistons and the press boarded separate buses for the short ride to practice at Loyola Marymount. The Pistons were loud and happy, high on the hot, perfumed air and their increasing sense of confidence.

The mood on the press bus was subdued. The story had ended. Just like that. The Lakers were down 0–2 with Magic Johnson and Byron Scott crippled. The outcome of the series was almost certain. No more tension, no drama: no story. At this point, the best they could do was a decent feature story. The best one available was Kareem's farewell, so when they got to the gym, where the Lakers were just finishing, they surrounded him. They wanted something bittersweet and heart-rending—sort of a sports version of *The Old Man and the Sea*, with the Championship Trophy substituted for the fish. But Jabbar wasn't going to give it to them. For the most part, he stuck to mantalk: "Winning's the bottom line," "I'm just going to play as hard as I can," and "All we have to do is go out and play our game." The writers who'd dealt with him during his long Silent Era scribbled happily; for them, it was a real Jabbar word feast. But most of the writers were too young to have dealt with him then, and they got bored quickly. A few drifted over to Pat Riley—he knew movie stars. Maybe he'd be good for a Hollywood anecdote.

The reporters who stayed kept digging at the nostalgia angle. One asked Jabbar if most of his friends in the game had retired. "Yeah," Kareem said, "most of my best friends are like *long* gone. People you probably never even heard of. I saw that Oscar Robertson's daughter was in college, and I remember her in pigtails—it's like a time warp. Back to the Future, definitely. Sometimes, these days, I feel like I've just sort of been dropped into this game. In the back of my mind I'm looking for faces that I'll never see: Nate Thurmond, Dave Cowens, Bob Lanier, Willis Reed, Wes Unseld, Bill Walton. Though I never really got to know Walton like I did those other guys. I met him at UCLA, but he had a different attitude about things. We weren't what you'd call simpatico."

The reporters fidgeted restlessly. Jabbar was right. To them, those names were ancient history. They needed more *contemporary* nostalgia— hot, "now" kind of nostalgia. One of them took a last stab. "What's going through your mind in this last week of your career?"

"My defensive assignments." Jabbar looked apologetic. He shrugged.

He knew the reporter wanted a ten-word tearjerker, but focusing on mechanics instead of sentiment was what it took to win. Jabbar wasn't going to drop that now.

"Do you feel *any* nostalgia?"

"No."

Jabbar's last answer hung in silence, and the few remaining reporters took off. Jabbar bent down to cram some stuff into an old gym bag: an extra pair of shoes. A baseball cap that said, "1989 NBA Finals." Sunglasses. On his way out, one of the reporters said, "Hope you win tomorrow."

Jabbar paused. "Me *too*," he said with genuine enthusiasm. The world's media was focused on Jabbar, but Jabbar was focused on winning one more game.

A few minutes later, the Pistons came out of their locker room. The largest crowd of reporters clotted around Isiah. "Do you hope Magic can play tomorrow?" asked a dark, long-haired reporter from Spain.

"If he does, fine. If not, fine. At this point, I'll settle for beating the Little Rascals—I don't care." The Spanish reporter looked confused. Little Rascals?

"Does the Pistons' success," boomed a radio reporter in his on-air voice, "mean the teams of the future will have to be bad boys? Play dirty?"

Thomas's eyes narrowed. He paused, as he often did with a question that pissed him off. "Playing aggressive is just *part* of what we do," he said softly. "If you're really interested in how we changed the future of basketball, look at the fact that no Championship team ever before has been built around a guard. Never been done. We've proved you don't have to have a dominant center to win. The traditional way of thinking is, you've got to have an *inside* game to get the *outside* game. Jack McCloskey came along and changed that. McCloskey took an untraditional approach, and built a team that has a whole different way of thinking.

"Look at our team statistically. We're one of the worst teams in the *league*. So now you have to find a new formula to judge basketball." Many of the reporters looked impatient. They needed quotes, not answers. But Thomas had gotten wound up. He'd waited eight years for this audience and he knew exactly what he wanted to say. "There were lots of times I had my doubts about this approach," he said, "because all of you kept telling me it could never be *done* this way. Statistically, it made me look *horrible*. But I kept looking at the won-lost record and how we kept improving and I kept saying to myself, Isiah, you're doin' the right thing, so be stubborn, and one day people will find a *different* way to judge a player. They won't just pick up the newspaper and say, oh this guy was nine for twelve with eight rebounds so he was the best player in the game. Lots of times, on our team, you can't *tell* who the best player in the game was. 'Cause *everybody* did something. That's what makes us so good. The other team has to worry about stopping eight or nine people instead of just two or three. It's the only way to win. The *only* way to win. That's the way the game was *invented.*''

The circle of reporters around Thomas was thinning. "But there's more to it than that. You also got to create the *environment* that won't accept losing. Three years ago Chuck came to me and said, 'Isiah, our basketball team is in the process of making a transformation, and I'm gonna have to be a different coach.' He said, 'I gotta drive more, push more.' So there were more verbal confrontations with players, and he started sort of slapping people and shoving people and *that* drove us to where we are today. Plus, when I first got here, Jack McCloskey said two things to me. He said, 'Isiah, you got a chance to be a great bas-ketball player in our league, and a great player in our community—and I drafted you for *both* reasons.' I didn't understand that then, but I do now. I know now that what really makes a basketball team great is the amount of pressure the *community* applies. That's happened with the Celtics and Lakers. They got that *environment.* Jack kind of suckered me into that community aspect, but I see now we couldn't have gotten here without it. It's part of what forces you to play unselfishly.''

Most of the reporters were gone. A number of them had collected around John Salley. His one-liners filled their needs better. One asked, "What do you like best about L.A.?"

"The women don't wear pantyhose." Salley grinned at the reporter. "I guess your ass can't write *that* shit, huh?"

The reporter shook his head. "What do you like about Hollywood?"

"All the Caucasians have tans."

Another reporter asked him what he'd been doing during a mild earthquake yesterday. "Let me just say, I was being as black as possible when it happened. If that answers your question." The reporter, a young sandy-haired kid from a small, rural newspaper, looked puzzled. "I think," Salley said, "that this will answer you: I got engaged right afterward. Okay?" It still didn't register; the Detroit beat writers were laughing. Salley tried again. "The *earth* moved, man. Then afterward, she gave me all kind of money—here, I'm payin' *you,* instead."

The reporter smiled tightly. He got the joke. But he still didn't have a good quote.

Vinnie Johnson walked up. "I thought that quake was just Mahorn in the floor up above—shakin' his big fat ass."

The sandy-haired reporter smiled. Good short quote. He'd just change "ass" to "butt," or maybe to "bleep." That would give his paper some *vintage* Bad Boys stuff. The real thing.

On game day, McCloskey got the expansion draft list. All the players that would be available in the draft were on it, except for Detroit's and L.A.'s. As soon as the Finals were over, McCloskey would have to hand in the names of his four players.

The list of the other teams' players was slightly encouraging, because it had several power forwards on it. McCloskey now believed he was going to have to ax one of his own power forwards. Rick Mahorn. When McCloskey had asked his coaches and scouts for their recommendations, the player they'd unanimously put forward was Mahorn.

McCloskey called a meeting. Chuck Daly, Brendan Suhr, Brendan Malone, Stan Novak, and Will Robinson came. McCloskey wanted to go over their choice once more. The decision was tearing him up.

For more than an hour they went over their rationale. It boiled down to one main thing: Mahorn would be the least difficult player to replace. "We just don't *have* anybody from within to replace Vinnie or James," McCloskey said. "Nobody can give us the scoring down low that Edwards does. You give him the ball, he's gonna score. On the perimeter, same goes for Vinnie. But in Rick's case, we've got Salley and Rodman and also Edwards who can play that position." The others nodded. That's why they'd each put Mahorn's name on the list.

There were other factors, too. The most important was Mahorn's back injury. It could flare up again at any time, and if it did he'd be finished. Also, the refs had put him on a hell of a short leash ever since Mark Price's concussion. One of his biggest contributions—intimidation—had been severely compromised. They also had to consider that the Pistons had almost won the Championship Series without him last year; if he was truly indispensable, they couldn't have.

On the other hand, nobody they had could replace his fierceness under the hoop. Salley didn't scare people. Rodman didn't. And how would Laimbeer do when he had to face the league's intimidators alone? Without Horn, it might be open season on Laimbeer next year.

No matter what happened, they were screwed. Lose Vinnie, and lose the three-guard rotation that was the core of the team. Lose Edwards, and lose the hardest-to-replace element in the Killer B-Team—a backup center who could score. Lose Mahorn, and lose the soul of the Bad Boys. It was a miserable choice.

McCloskey liked to end meetings on a positive note. He told the coaches that he might be able to work something out. It would mean losing Michael Williams, but if he could pull it off, they could keep Mahorn.

That was good news. Nothing could please the coaches more. Except winning the next two games.

Strapless tops and tight skirts, sunglasses and polo shirts, swirls of hair, lots of endangered-species cowboy boots, money everywhere. The Great Western Forum. It had been the Fabulous Forum until a couple of months ago, when the Great Western Bank paid $1 million to change the name. When Mychal Thompson had heard about the proposed name change, he'd advised the bank to save its million, and change its own name to the Fabulous Bank. In L.A., that might have worked.

Jack Nicholson and Anjelica Huston arrived just before tip-off and sat at their $3,000-a-game courtside seats just down from NBC chief Brandon Tartikoff. None had as good a seat as talent agent Michael Ovitz, the most powerful man in Hollywood, who was adjacent to Red Auerbach and Dyan Cannon. Upstairs, Dancing Barry was adjusting the Carmen Miranda outfit he'd spring on the crowd in an hour. In the small, dark Piston locker room, Daly was saying, "We can put it away today, or we can take a chance on Isiah going down and Bill going down and letting it slip away again. It's your choice." In the Laker locker room Magic Johnson lay on his back as a trainer mummified his thigh. Kareem sat in front of his locker and stared at the floor.

Minutes later it began. The Lakers charged off to a small lead. Magic was hobbling. From the sideline, Riley yelled, "Buck, how you feelin'?"

"I'm hurtin', coach," Johnson said, "but I'm gonna play for ya."

But he couldn't. Minutes later, he limped to the bench. It was up to Kareem to keep them alive. Jabbar began playing like a twenty-year-old. He catapulted after rebounds with his huge thighs spread wide and his elbows churning, carving out room. The skyhook was ripping the heart of the net, and there was an ice-hard look in his eyes. He would finish the game with 24 points and 13 rebounds. He inspired his teammates, aroused the crowd, and every move he made was strategically correct. Jabbar knew how to win. But it wasn't enough. L.A. lost. There just weren't enough weapons in the Laker arsenal. By now, the Pistons knew how to win, too. And they had the weapons to do it.

McCloskey sat down with the coaches and explained the deal he was trying to work out. He'd been calling all over the league, trying to find a way to keep Mahorn. It was a complicated deal, and had required all his knowledge of the other teams in the league.

But the deal hung on a thread. It was full of variables. First, one of the two expansion teams would have to agree to choose Michael Williams from McCloskey's list, passing up Mahorn. That team would then trade Williams to Indiana, along with their first-round pick, which would be the tenth or eleventh pick. Indiana would give the expansion team its own first-round pick, which was the seventh pick.

For the expansion team, moving up three or four positions could mean moving from a good small man—somebody like Mookie Blaylock or Pooh Richardson—to a good big man, like Randy White, who'd been compared to Karl Malone. They might even get someone like Stacey King.

McCloskey thought it was a pretty tempting package. It would solve Indiana's point-guard problem, it would give an expansion team a shot at a quality big man, and it would keep the Piston core together.

"It's most likely to happen," McCloskey said, "if Orlando takes Sidney Green with their first pick. Then, if Minnesota goes for somebody other than Rick, I think Orlando will take the deal with their second pick. Because they'll already have their power forward, and they'll say, let's get a good young guard."

Green was a likely first choice for Orlando because he was three years younger than Mahorn, and he could be a monster on the glass. Once he'd pulled down 31 rebounds in a game. Though Green and Mahorn would be the two best picks in the draft, there were other solid players. Like Reggie Theus—Atlanta's experiment with multistars had failed.

The hard part was going to be getting Mahorn past Minnesota. The new Minnesota coach was Bill Musselman, the former Cleveland coach who'd reportedly had his players chanting "Kill! Kill! Kill!" before the infamous stomping of Luke Witte. Mahorn was the kind of player Musselman *loved*. For years, Musselman had been in exile from the NBA. But he'd put together a historic series of championship titles in the CBA and had fought his way back to the League. He didn't intend to blow his chance, and thought Mahorn represented his best shot. He liked Mahorn's physical skills, but he loved his outlook and leadership. Mahorn had learned how to win. You needed that quality on an expansion team.

McCloskey was desperate to work something out. He had tremendous regard for Mahorn. Mahorn had sacrificed not just his glory to the Pistons' system of defense and teamwork, but also his body. Mahorn had a back that might torture him for the rest of his life, and he'd gotten it bouncing the league's terrorist-forwards out of the way for Isiah,

Dumars, and Laimbeer. He'd kept the team optimistic when they'd started to get down, he'd befriended the rookies, he'd scared hell out of slackers and troublemakers, and he'd been great in the community. McCloskey was interested in him as a future assistant coach. Letting him go would be the hardest thing McCloskey had done since the time he'd waived Charlie Davis at Portland. Back then, McCloskey had ended up crying with Davis. That was almost how he felt now.

McCloskey tried never to let emotions influence his decisions. But that didn't mean he didn't feel them.

Nonetheless, if he had to let Mahorn go, he would. The franchise came first.

By the fourth game, the outcome of the series was a foregone conclusion. No team had ever come back from 0–3, and with Magic and Scott out, the Lakers weren't going to break tradition. So the event wasn't as much a game as it was a set of images, impressions, and actions. A collage. Or, as Ron Campbell had put it exactly one year earlier: "Just drama for television."

Scene before the game: John Ciszewski and Tom Wilson stand at the ticket window. Ciszewski: "I'm not getting my hopes up yet." Wilson: "There's a light at the end of the tunnel. But it could be a freight train." Ciszewski nods grimly.

At courtside, McCloskey, in a suitcase-creased pinstripe shirt, talks with Raider boss Al Davis, godfather of the Bad Boys image. Davis: "Think it's inevitable now?" McCloskey: "My god, it ought to be. It ought to be."

The national anthem plays. The Pistons are stuck in the tunnel leading to the locker room. All of them hover back toward the hallway, out of range of hostile fans, except for Vinnie Johnson. Johnson stands at attention in the middle of the tunnel, hands clasped behind his back, staring at the American flag. A fan leans over the tunnel and hisses, "'Vinnie! Miss! Miss! Miss!" Johnson thinks this is his last game as a Piston. He thinks his name is on McCloskey's list.

The opening minutes: Rick Mahorn pushes A. C. Green and Green lunges for Mahorn. A referee grabs Green and holds him back. Mahorn, over his shoulder: "Wanna fight? Huh?" He walks away laughing: the tempo is set. The Laker girls do a too-hip, modified striptease break dance with satin Laker jackets. The Lakers lead by 13. Jack Nicholson grins his devil's grin.

Dennis Rodman crouches on his hands and knees in front of the Piston bench, his back burning with pain. Trainer Mike Abdenour holds a bag of ice on Rodman's back with one hand and keeps stats with the other.

The Lakers hold their lead. The fans begin to chant, "Three-peat."

James Edwards comes in the game and starts nailing shots over Kareem's head. Edwards melts the lead, feeling a strange mix of exhilaration and melancholy. He believes he is on McCloskey's list.

Watching Edwards take over the game, McCloskey is reassured that he's made the right decision. But Mahorn is having a great game, too— 5 for 7 from the field, 3 offensive rebounds.

Dancing Barry bursts out of the stands and cavorts with some belly dancers. The crowd goes dead. Jack Nicholson saws his finger across his neck. He yells, "Cut." The Lakers, pioneers in the Basketball Disneyland approach, have been left behind in showmanship.

Kareem rips down a rebound and pivots his elbows back and forth. Mahorn grabs for the ball but Kareem fires the last outlet pass of his career.

The Pistons begin to pull away. Mahorn drives past Jabbar, is fouled, and hits the basket. Mahorn pumps his fist. He looks at Jabbar and mumbles, "Old motherfucker."

John Ciszewski to Tom Wilson: "I think we've got a *chance.*" Wilson says nothing. He doesn't want to jinx it.

At the Palace, twenty-one thousand fans—more than in the Forum— watch the broadcast on the huge scoreboard. They chant, "Sweep! Sweep! Sweep!"

Minutes before the end, Pat Riley removes Kareem. A shudder of emotion ripples through the stadium. Fans stand and cheer. All of the Pistons stand and applaud. Mahorn, with a welt over his eye from Kareem's elbow, claps the longest.

When Kareem leaves, Isiah realizes the Lakers have conceded. His eyes fill with tears. He holds back. Fennis Dembo quietly says, "Let it out." Thomas begins to cry.

The Piston bench links arms. They sing, "Bad-Boys-Bad-Boys-Bad-Boys."

It ends. As Joe Dumars runs the court, he shouts to a camera crew, "I'm goin' to Disney World!" He's won the Series MVP. How different from last year, when Dantley had haggled over the Disneyland money. The Pistons had been planning to give Dantley a Series share and a Championship ring. But that week he'd told CBS, "I got screwed in the trade." It cost him a ring.

The emotion of the game merges into the emotion of the locker room. Mahorn leads a chant of "Bad-Boys-Bad-Boys" and sprays owner Bill Davidson with champagne.

Isiah and Laimbeer spout some happy mantalk to CBS's Brent Musberger and then get him out of the way. Salley grabs the Championship Trophy and whispers, "Yo, baby, how you doin'? Lookin' good, baby. You want to come home with me tonight? Yes you do. Yes you do. Gimme little kiss—c'mon now. Kiss my gal," he says to Laimbeer. Laimbeer kisses the big gold basketball. Isiah licks champagne off it.

Aguirre sits in the front of his locker, tears running down his face. "I don't know why I'm doing this," he says. "This is the happiest day of my life. Why am I crying? I guess because I thought this was never going to happen for me." Thomas comes over and puts his arm around Aguirre.

PR head Matt Dobek stands at the door of the locker room, keeping out a roiling knot of people in the hallway. Boxer Thomas Hearns stands out there. So does *Do the Right Thing* director Spike Lee, who is a friend of Salley's and is better known to basketball fans as the Nike commercial's Mars Blackmon. But the room begins to pack with hot bodies and steam.

John Ciszewski and Tom Wilson stand by the showers in champagne-soaked suits. Ciszewski: "It hasn't sunk in yet." Wilson: "I know." Ciszewski: "I always get choked up when I watch this on TV."

Chuck Daly: "All those years . . . I watched everybody else . . . everybody else . . . everybody else. . . ."

Joe Dumars, who'd averaged 27 points in the Series, sits quietly.

Jack McCloskey, his gunmetal-gray hair matted from champagne and steam, locks his arms around his son Tim. Over his son's shoulders, he sees Mahorn, grinning.

The deal to save Mahorn isn't working. He reaches toward Mahorn, embraces him. He thanks Mahorn. His eyes are full of tears.

Epilogue

"**Y**O!" YELLED John Salley over the racket of the band, "Mr. Davidson! You drunk yet?" Owner Bill Davidson, probably the only person at the postgame party with a sport coat on, looked up. "You *drunk* yet?" Salley again yelled. Without waiting for a reply, he shouted, "Good! Let's negotiate my new contract. I got a pen, you got a room." Salley grabbed Davidson and hugged him.

The band was off on a special song, written just for this occasion, that consisted of nothing but "Salley's got a big butt, doot-doot-doot—Rickey's got a big butt, doot-doot-doot—Vinney's got a big butt, dot-dot-dot—Fennis's got a big butt, dit-dit-dit. . . ." And so on, down the roster. The players, most of them dancing up close to the band, hardly seemed to hear. They'd just drunk their first alcohol since the playoffs had begun, and the booze had mixed with euphoria and exhaustion to put a special glaze on the evening.

At the door to the big ballroom in Marina del Rey, beat writer Terry Foster caught Mahorn's eye. Foster was chest to chest with a security guard, who was restraining a pack of Piston fans. Mahorn, in a loose white shirt, sauntered over. "You got to let our media in," he told the guard. Then, to Foster, "Now you punks better write nice stuff about me for the rest of your life." Mahorn felt fantastic. He'd had his best game of the playoffs—13 points and a team-high 7 rebounds. And now the ring. He felt invincible.

Foster grabbed a drink and strolled the fifty yards of food: chilled shrimp, prime beef, intricate little hors d'oeuvres, Alaskan king crab, two dozen exotic desserts, lots of champagne.

Bill Laimbeer, in a black skull-and-crossbones T-shirt and a white Finals cap, collared columnist Mitch Albom. "They said I made a fool of myself at the postgame press conference," said Laimbeer, grinning. "I told 'em this proved people wrong for all the stupid stuff they've written about us all year."

"You said that to the national media?" Albom asked.

"You think I made a jerk out of myself?" Albom wouldn't commit. "You know what?" said Laimbeer. "Screw 'em!" He grabbed a long-necked beer bottle and sucked it half-dry in a gulp.

Salley, in a white "World Champion" T-shirt and his glasses, vaulted onto the stage and grabbed a mike. "*January, February, March-April-June,*" he rapped, "and soon you *will* be finding *out* why we *are, dy*-na-mite. We *are*, will *be*, gotta *be* number-*one*—gotta have our *fun*, gotta get *mo*! mo! mo-mo-*money*, mo money, mo *money money money!*" At Salley's feet, Rodman, still in his game uniform, bumped butts with James Edwards. Fennis Dembo danced by in a pair of cowboy boots, a reminder of his University of Wyoming, *Sports Illustrated* cover-boy days, when he'd been more than just a well-paid mascot. Dembo was floating; he knew he'd be on the unprotected list, but probably wasn't good enough to be chosen. Failure had its privileges.

The band jumped into fast rock, and Jack McCloskey and his wife Leslie leaped up to dance. Isiah danced over. He started dancing with the two of them, and then with just McCloskey. Thomas grinned. He felt silly, and perfect. McCloskey grinned, too. But he didn't feel perfect. He felt preoccupied.

Outside the door, the Brow sat slumped in an easy chair. He couldn't get in. The other Detroit fans in the hallway also looked a little bleak. They'd assumed their $10,000 to $20,000 season tickets—and their trip to L.A. to support the team—had made them part of things. Mahorn came over to the security guard and whispered something. He seemed to be the only person inside who was aware there were people outside. Mahorn pointed at a couple of people, including the Brow. They all watched the guard intently. He shook his head and mumbled something about fire code.

Mahorn shrugged, shook a few hands, and went back to the party. Soon he was dancing and yelling. It was *good* to be on the inside.

*   *   *

John Ciszewski, with his walkie-talkie to his ear, piled players, coaches, and franchise employees into buses as he looked warily at the drippy gray skies. The Pistons' celebration parade was an hour away. "God," said Ciszewski, "I hope somebody's going to *be* there for it. You don't want to be embarrassed."

As the caravan of buses headed from the Palace for downtown, though, Ciszewski's fears were laid to rest. Just the line of buses with its police escort was treated like a parade. Construction workers stood on top of buildings and waved, and all along the freeway drivers pulled over and honked and blew kisses as the Pistons drove by.

When they got downtown and loaded onto floats, the real hysteria started. Hundreds of thousands of people were lining the streets. They looked ecstatic. People threw confetti from the offices overhead, clapped and danced with the school bands, hugged each other, reached out to touch the players. They screamed. A few brushed away tears. A great many of them were black and many were poor—this was, after all, downtown Detroit, not Auburn Hills. This was the old Cobo Hall crowd, the Silverdome crowd, the "thirty thousand crazy carmakers" who couldn't afford the Palace. But they had followed the team on TV and radio and were an indispensable part of its revenue stream. They were the masses: They made possible the huge salaries, the luxurious Palace and the private plane. They were, in a real way, the heart of the franchise, no matter how far physically removed from it they were: until now. This parade wasn't just the Pistons' payoff—it was theirs, too, and they knew it. Tough men stood in front of red-brick taverns with mid-day drinks in their fists and looked all choked up as Mahorn and Isiah and Rodman and the rest cruised slowly by, waving and laughing. The people on the streets were proud as hell. Now they had bragging rights over every damn city in the whole damn country, and for many of them, that was the best thing this year would offer.

The closer to the city's center the parade got, the louder and more frenzied it became. Police on horseback tried to keep the crowd from surging past barricades, but people danced out into the streets, cursing the cops and laughing, jumping for joy. Screaming—always screaming. Mahorn and Laimbeer, waving their "sweep" brooms, got huge sections of the mob chanting in unison: "Bad-Boys-Bad-Boys." To Tom Wilson, riding behind the wheel of a giant car mock-up, it looked like Beatle-mania. He'd never seen anything like it. "We made it," he thought to himself. "We'll never be nothing again."

Joe Dumars, on a float with McCloskey, Stan Novak, and Will Robinson, looked stunned. Dozens of beautiful women kept running up to his float and throwing him scraps of paper with their phone numbers.

One of them wailed, "Don't get married, Joe!" He beamed at the crowd. At last, no one was asking why he was so underrated. Maybe they never would again.

Assistant coach Brendan Malone looked at the float behind him. There was Jack McCloskey, with one finger plugged into his ear, a cellular telephone jammed against the other. Malone knew what the phone was for. The expansion draft was just three hours away. McCloskey was negotiating with Minnesota's Bill Musselman, sweetening the deal to keep Mahorn. McCloskey was ready to throw in his own first-round draft pick. That would give the expansion team Michael Williams plus two first-round picks. It was a hell of a deal. McCloskey thought Musselman was ready to grab it.

McCloskey was smiling. He was nodding his head up and down. His smoke broke into a grin.

"My God," Brendan Malone thought. "He *did* it."

Malone looked ahead, at the huge joyous mob, the snow of confetti, the gleaming brass bands and Mahorn and Laimbeer waving their brooms. He'd never been happier.

Two hours later, the Palace went dark. A hush fell on the fifteen thousand people who'd come for the finale of the Championship celebration. Dave Auker, at his courtside seat, wearing his headset, said, "Okay. Start it!" A video flashed onto the scoreboard to the strains of Generic Hero Music. Auker segued into "Shout" and the crowd clapped in unison as images of the Pistons lit the stadium: Rodman diving for a loose ball. V.J. hitting a long jumper, then another, another, another. Laimbeer pumping his fist. Isiah spinning, floating, jamming. Mahorn bellowing at some huge terrorist-forward. Clips from the Finals started. The crowd chanted, "Beat L.A." On the scoreboard, Edwards hit over Jabbar. Aguirre made a magical spin that ended in a jam. Salley blocked Woolridge. Then the locker room scene: champagne, embraces, tears.

It went black. A drum roll. The Bad Boys flag appeared in a solo spotlight and a ball boy ran the floor with it as the crowd went wild.

"Okay," John Ciszewski said into his walkie-talkie, "let 'em go." Announcer Ken Calvert: "Ladies and gentlemen, your World *Champion* Detroit *Pistons!*" The players, coaches, and general manager emerged, one by one, from the tunnel outside the locker room, and ran onto a raised stage. Ciszewski was standing among the players, but none of them were paying him any special attention, except for Mahorn. Mahorn was a good friend and kept a picture of Ciszewski's daughter above his locker. Mahorn and Ciszewski grinned at each other. "Hey, Rick," said Ciszewski, "you don't know how much I . . . appreciate this. I've been waitin' eleven years. . . ." Mahorn shook his hand. Neither said anything else.

Jack McCloskey took his place on the stage, and looked at the roving spotlights that were swirling over the crowd. It was the moment he'd waited his entire life for. In a couple of days, they would go to the White House and would meet the President. It would prove to be a memorable experience, a rare moment in McCloskey's life. But it was still just a public formality. A few days after that, he would make his selection in the college draft. In that situation, he would end up trading Michael Williams to Phoenix to move up in the draft, and he would snare Anthony Cook, the kid who had jumped so high down in Orlando. Landing Cook would be a real coup, and would earn Trader Jack accolades. But McCloskey had gotten good press before, and made a point of not being seduced by it.

But this moment was different. The people cheering now were the ones who'd supported them all season; many were people who'd been loyal during the grim early years. This was a moment to let down your guard and share your happiness.

George Blaha, emcee of the show, stepped to the microphone and said, "Ladies and gentlemen, the man who built the Pistons, General Manager Jack McCloskey."

The Palace shook with cheers as McCloskey stepped forward. There was only one thing he wanted to say. "When I first came here," he boomed over the stadium's great sound system, "everybody said the Pistons were losers. The players were losers. The coaches were losers. The front office people were losers. I say this to you! Sometimes winners are losers who *just . . . won't . . . quit!*" He sat back down while they were still cheering.

Each of the players came forward and said something. Laimbeer said, "Everybody calls us thugs, bad boys. I call us World Champions." Isiah, in a black Pistons warm-up suit, stood at the microphone and applauded the fans. Aguirre said, "I want to thank everybody on the team for making me love basketball again. The first night I was here was the beginning of my career." John Salley said, "I'd like to thank Jack McCloskey for not trading me." Fennis shouted, "Party time!" Then Blaha said, "Here's a man who loves you as much as you love him," and Dennis Rodman stepped to the microphone. He started to say something about the family in Oklahoma who had taken him into their home. But he couldn't go on. Tears began rolling down his cheeks. For long moments, he stood there. He opened his mouth to start again, but nothing came out. The tears were spilling onto his shirt. The crowd was standing and cheering. Isiah came up and embraced Rodman, and together they sat back down. Chuck Daly, watching, swallowed hard and blinked his eyes. It was Mahorn's turn. Mahorn led the crowd in a "Bad Boys" chant, then walked over to Daly and shook his hand. "Thank you for having faith in me," he said. Mahorn looked deep into the crowd, picking out familiar faces. "I'd like to thank God and my family," he said softly. Then, grinning, he said, "I'm glad to be the baddest Bad Boy you've ever seen." The crowd went wild. Then he walked over to Mc-Closkey. "I'd like to thank Jack McCloskey," he said. To McCloskey: "Thank you for sticking with me through my weight problem." He held out his hand, and McCloskey grasped it.

McCloskey felt as if his heart was breaking. He felt sick. Musselman had turned him down. Musselman was taking Mahorn.

The team stood up together. For the last time, the crowd cheered them.

Mahorn and Salley burst into the locker room, leading the other players as they all climbed off the stage. From outside came the muffled sounds of clapping and rock music. "God damn!" said Mahorn to John Ciszewski, "that was *great*! Can you get me a tape of that?"

"Me, too," said Salley.

"No problem," said Ciszewski. He took off for the media room to see about getting tapes.

McCloskey walked into the locker room, which was filling with grinning, shouting players. This was just the beginning of their celebration. In an hour, there would be a buffet in the Palace, then a round of private parties would start. Mahorn was hosting one at a nightclub downtown, and Salley had one set for tomorrow night. "Rick?"

McCloskey asked Mahorn to step into the coaches' room. Mahorn looked confused. He followed McCloskey through the door. Then he saw Daly, Brendan Suhr and Brendan Malone. They were stone-faced. His face tightened. He knew the expansion draft had just taken place. But he hadn't been worried about it. He was a starter. A star. Every so often he'd gotten paranoid, but . . .

"Rick, the news I've got for you isn't very good," said McCloskey.

Instantly, Mahorn realized everything. He exhaled. "Where am I going?" he asked softly.

"Minnesota," said McCloskey. "I'm sorry, Rick. We did everything we could."

"We tried our best, Ricky," said Daly.

Mahorn looked terribly sad. McCloskey said a couple of things about what Mahorn had meant to the team, and how grateful they were. Those things never took the hurt away, but if you didn't say them, it could make the hurt worse.

A few minutes later, Mahorn walked back into the locker room.

"Oh, Rickeeee?" sang Aguirre. Ciszewski came back from the media room. Mahorn cleared his throat. "I'm goin' to Minnesota," said Mahorn. "Look, I . . . uh . . . enjoyed playing with you guys. Okay? Good luck next year."

Vinnie Johnson, who still thought he would be leaving the team, didn't appreciate Mahorn's remark. "Stop screwin' around," Johnson said. Michael Williams didn't even look up at Mahorn—Mahorn was always joking around.

Ciszewski paid little attention and headed back into the coaches' room. Trainer Mike Abdenour was in there. He looked stricken. Tom Wilson was in there, too. Wilson was in tears. It hit Ciszewski. Mahorn wasn't kidding. Ciszewski felt like throwing up. Dave Auker walked in, looked at the faces, stopped dead. "Jesus," said Auker, "what the hell happened?"

The players began to gather around Mahorn. Michael Williams, who had thought he'd be gone after today, had prepared himself for the blow. Now that it wasn't going to come, he felt numb, confused. James Edwards was pissed off. He'd been almost sure he would be gone, and that hadn't made him angry. In a way, it would be his last contribution to the team. But losing Mahorn pissed him off. They *needed* Mahorn. Mahorn was too important to the team. The irony of Edwards's anger never occurred to him. The team feeling ran that deep.

In the hallway outside, McCloskey was surrounded by reporters. Once again, it was just the local guys—Terry Foster, Drew Sharp, Charlie Vincent, Mitch Albom, Steve Addy. "It's a sad, sad day," said McCloskey. "We feel like we're being penalized for having depth. It's heartbreaking." McCloskey pulled away as quickly as he could. He knew that the fans and media would be incensed. Over the next few days, he would be bombarded with hate mail, vilified in the papers, and even picketed outside his office by protesting fans. He had gone from being the brilliant architect of the team to being a heartless fool in less than an hour.

The reporters gathered in a few quotes. It was a good story. They should have been happy. They didn't look it. Mahorn was still in the weight room, and they had to stick around to try to get a comment.

From the weight room came a sudden jarring crash. Then silence. A couple of minutes later, Mahorn burst through the door and double-timed for the exits. The writers trailed him halfheartedly, calling out a few questions. No reply.

When Mahorn got outside, the fans from the celebration spotted him and started to cheer and chant, "Bad-Boys-Bad-Boys." The draft hadn't been announced; they had no idea anything was wrong. "Ricky," cried a young woman, pointing to her girlfriend, "she *loves* you." The friend put her hands over her face and spun around. A crowd of kids formed around Mahorn as he hurried to his car. "Ricky," said a little black boy, "will you sign this?" He thrust out a piece of newspaper. Mahorn stopped and smiled. But with the smile, tears came to his eyes. He signed the paper and kept going.

Beat writer Drew Sharp stayed with him. "You okay?" Sharp asked.

"It's a business deal," said Mahorn. "I'll be all right." Mahorn stepped into his car. He started it, and looked around to see if any of the kids were in the way. Then he was gone.

That night, John Ciszewski called Tom Wilson. "Isn't this just like the Pistons?" he said.

"What do you mean?" asked Wilson.

"They'll break your heart."

It could have been the worst day of Jack McCloskey's life. The celebration had turned into an ugly, gloomy wake. He'd gone to the buffet in the Palace, picked at a few pieces of food for a couple of minutes, then he had found Leslie and left. Leslie had been crying all evening.

Once again, he'd had to make a gut-wrenching decision. One he knew would hurt people. One that would make thousands of loyal fans—the heart of the franchise—feel betrayed. One that had wounded a player he cared deeply about. One that would probably make all the players a little more cynical.

The criticism of him had already started on the TV and radio. To-morrow morning, in the newspapers, it would get much worse. It was bitter and very personal. If his decision didn't work out, he might begin to lose his grip on the franchise. He might even eventually lose his job. The only security in the NBA was success.

. . . But they'd done it. They'd won the World Championship. They had learned how to win. They had proven they were the best in the world.

So many great teams had tried to beat them. For almost the entire season, the odds had been against them. They had been called dirty and vicious but had kept their dignity and focus. They'd fought among themselves, but learned to work together. They'd experienced terrible doubt and learned to believe in themselves. Men with powerful egos and a great deal to lose—men whose only business in life was basketball—had played as if it were just a game, with abandon and joy and generosity. In the purest sense, they had become a team.

The shared dream that had finally brought them together had begun long ago, in many distant places. It had begun in the dirty red-brick slums on Chicago's West Side, where Isiah Thomas and Mark Aguirre had played basketball to stay out of trouble and had found their gift. It had begun in Louisiana and Florida, where Joe Dumars and Darryl Dawkins had played on dirt courts. It had started when a white family had shown kindness to young and troubled Dennis Rodman. When Adrian Dantley had starved himself into fitness at Notre Dame, part of the dream had been born. When kids had made fun of little Rick Mahorn and Bill Laimbeer for being fat, it had begun. And the dream of the Championship had also begun long ago in Punxsutawney, when coalminers' kids with no real talent had been taught how to win. And it had begun in Mahanoy City, when Jack McCloskey had watched his mother try to protect his father's feet with waxed paper.

The dream of Jack McCloskey's life had finally become real. His franchise had won it all. No one could change that.

The win hadn't been luck. They were good. Good enough to maybe—just maybe—win it next year, too.

It was the best day of Jack McCloskey's life. He was at peace. Until next season.

Appendix:Statistics

1988 – 1989 PLAYOFF STATISTICS PISTONS (15–2)

PLAYER	G	MIN	FG-FGA	FG%	FT–FTA	FT%	REB	AST	AVG
Isiah Thomas	17	37.2	115–279	.412	71–96	.740	4.3	8.3	18.2
Joe Dumars	17	36.5	106–233	.455	87–101	.861	2.6	5.6	17.6
Vinnie Johnson	17	21.9	91–200	.455	47–62	.758	2.6	2.5	14.1
Mark Aguirre	17	27.2	89–182	.489	28–38	.737	4.4	1.6	12.6
Bill Laimbeer	17	29.2	66–142	.465	25–31	.806	8.2	1.8	10.1
John Salley	17	23.1	58–99	.586	36–54	.667	4.6	0.5	8.9
James Edwards	17	18.6	40–85	.471	40–51	.784	2.1	0.7	7.1
Dennis Rodman	17	24.1	37–70	.529	24–35	.686	10.0	0.9	5.8
Rick Mahorn	17	21.8	40–69	.580	17–26	.654	5.1	0.4	5.7
John Long	4	2.0	1–1	1.000	3–3	1.000	0.0	0.0	1.3
Fennis Dembo	2	2.0	1–1	1.000	0–0	.000	0.0	0.0	1.0
Michael Williams	4	1.5	0–0	.000	2–2	1.000	0.5	0.5	0.5
TOTALS	17	—	644–1361	.473	380–499	.762	44.2	22.6	100.6
OPPONENTS	17	—	583–1300	.448	368–491	.749	37.6	21.0	92.9

Three-point goals: Johnson 10–24 (.417), Laimbeer 15–42 (.357), Aguirre 8–29 (.276), Thomas 8–30 (.267), Dumars 1–12 (.083), Edwards 0–1 (.000), Rodman 0–4 (.000). Totals: 42–142 (.296). Opponents: 45–160 (.281).

1989 STATISTICAL LEADERS

Scoring	Michael Jordan, Chi.	32.5
Rebounding	Akeem Olajuwon, Hou.	13.5
Assists	John Stockton, Utah	13.6
Steals	John Stockton, Utah	3.21
Blocked Shots	Manute Bol, G.S.	4.31
Field Goal Pct.	Dennis Rodman, Det.	.595
Free Throw Pct.	Magic Johnson, LAL	.911
3-Pt. FG Pct.	Jon Sundvold, Mia.	.522

1989 PLAYOFFS

EAST   **WEST**

(1) Detroit   Lakers (1)
                Pistons   Lakers
                3–0   3–0
(8) Boston   Portland (8)
                         Pistons   Lakers
                         win 4–0   win 4–0
(4) Atlanta   Seattle (4)
                Bucks   Sonics
                3–2   3–1
                                           FINAL
(5) Milwaukee   Houston (5)
                                  Pistons   Lakers
                                  win 4–2   win 4–0
(3) Cleveland   Phoenix (3)
                                           Pistons
                                           win 4–0
                Bulls   Suns
                3–2   3–0
(6) Chicago   Denver (6)
                         Bulls   Suns
                         win 4–2   win 4–1
(2) New York   Utah (2)
                Knicks   Warriors
                3–0   3–0
(7) Phila.   Golden St. (7)

DETROIT PISTONS
1988–1989 REGULAR-SEASON STATISTICS

WON 63, LOST 19

PLAYER	G	GS	MIN	FIELD GOALS			3-PT. FG			FREE THROWS			REBOUNDS			AST	PF	DQ	STL	TO	BLK	PTS	AVG	HI
				FG	FGA	PCT	FG	FGA	PCT	FT	FTA	PCT	OFF	DEF	TOT									
AGUIRRE (TOT)	80	76	2597	586	1270	.461	51	174	.293	288	393	.733	146	240	386	278	229	2	45	208	36	1511	18.9	41
AGUIRRE (DET)	36	32	1068	213	441	.483	22	75	.293	110	149	.738	56	95	151	89	101	2	16	68	7	558	15.5	31
DANTLEY	42	42	1341	258	495	.521	0	0	.000	256	305	.839	53	111	164	93	99	1	23	81	6	772	18.4	35
THOMAS	80	76	2924	569	1227	.464	33	121	.273	287	351	.818	49	224	273	663	209	0	133	298	20	1458	18.2	37
DUMARS	69	67	2408	456	903	.505	14	29	.483	260	306	.850	57	115	172	390	103	1	63	178	5	1186	17.2	42
JOHNSON	82	21	2073	462	996	.464	13	44	.295	193	263	.734	109	146	255	242	155	0	74	105	17	1130	13.8	34
LAIMBEER	81	81	2640	449	900	.499	30	86	.349	178	212	.840	138	638	776	177	259	2	51	129	100	1106	13.7	32
RODMAN	82	8	2208	316	531	.595	6	26	.231	97	155	.626	327	445	772	99	292	4	55	126	76	735	9.0	32
EDWARDS	76	1	1254	211	422	.500	0	2	.000	133	194	.686	68	163	231	49	226	1	11	72	31	555	7.3	18
MAHORN	72	61	1795	203	393	.517	0	2	.000	116	155	.748	141	355	496	59	206	3	40	97	66	522	7.3	19
SALLEY	67	21	1458	166	333	.498	0	2	.000	135	195	.692	134	201	335	75	197	1	40	100	72	467	7.0	19
LONG (TOT)	68	1	919	147	359	.409	8	20	.400	70	76	.921	18	59	77	80	84	1	29	57	3	372	5.5	25
LONG (DET)	24	0	152	19	40	.475	0	0	.000	11	13	.846	2	9	11	15	16	0	9	9	2	49	2.0	17
WILLIAMS	49	0	358	47	129	.364	2	9	.222	31	47	.660	9	18	27	70	44	0	13	42	3	127	2.6	11
DAWKINS	14	0	48	9	19	.474	0	0	.000	9	18	.500	3	4	7	1	13	0	0	4	1	27	1.9	8
HARRIS	3	0	7	1	4	.250	0	4	.000	2	2	1.000	3	4	7	5	1	0	1	7	0	4	1.3	4
DEMBO	31	0	74	14	42	.333	0	0	.000	8	10	.800	8	15	23	5	15	0	1	0	0	36	1.2	8
MANNION	5	0	14	2	2	1.000	0	0	.000	0	0		0	3	3	0	3	0	0	0	0	4	0.8	4
ROWINSKI	6	0	8	0	2	.000	0	0	.000	4	4	1.000	0	2	2	0	0	0	0	0	0	4	0.7	4
PISTONS	82		19830	3395	6879	.494	120	400	.300	1830	2379	.769	1154	2546	3700	2027	1939	15	522	1336	406	8740	106.6	132
OPPONENTS	82		19830	3140	7022	.447	158	554	.285	1826	2325	.785	1131	2188	3319	1855	2088	28	646	1225	341	8264	100.8	133

1988–1989 NBA STANDINGS

	ATL	BOS	CHA	CHI	CLE	DAL	DEN	DET	GS	HOU	IND	LAC	LAL	MIA	MIL	NJ	NY	PHI	PHO	POR	SAC	SA	SEA	UTA	WAS	W	L	PCT.	GB
NY	2	3	2	2	2	0	1	0	2	2	5	2	1	0	1	3	x	4	1	2	1	2	1	1	5	52	30	.634	—
PHI	2	3	3	2	1	1	2	1	1	2	4	1	0	1	2	4	2	x	2	1	1	1	1	1	2	46	36	.561	6
BOS	3	x	6	3	4	1	2	3	1	1	3	1	1	2	2	5	3	3	2	1	2	1	0	1	4	42	40	.512	10
WAS	1	5	5	1	1	1	0	1	1	2	3	0	1	1	2	5	1	4	1	1	1	1	0	1	x	40	42	.488	12
NJ	1	1	4	0	1	0	1	0	0	0	2	1	0	1	0	x	3	2	0	0	0	0	1	1	1	26	56	.317	26
CHA	1	0	x	0	0	1	0	0	1	0	2	0	0	1	0	2	0	1	0	0	1	0	0	0	1	20	62	.244	32
DET	5	3	6	4	3	1	1	x	2	2	4	1	1	2	5	6	5	4	1	2	2	1	2	2	5	63	19	.768	—
CLE	2	4	6	3	x	2	1	3	2	1	4	1	0	2	4	5	2	3	2	1	2	1	1	2	5	57	25	.695	6
ATL	x	3	4	3	4	1	1	1	2	1	4	1	0	2	3	4	2	2	1	1	2	1	1	2	4	52	30	.634	11
MIL	0	2	4	4	2	2	2	3	1	1	4	1	1	1	x	4	2	4	2	2	2	1	1	2	5	49	33	.598	14
CHI	2	3	4	x	3	1	1	3	2	1	3	1	0	2	2	5	2	4	1	2	2	1	2	1	4	47	35	.573	16
IND	1	3	2	3	2	1	0	0	1	0	x	1	0	2	1	5	1	3	1	0	1	0	1	1	3	28	54	.341	35
UTA	1	1	1	1	1	3	3	0	2	3	1	3	1	5	1	1	1	1	3	5	5	4	1	x	1	51	31	.622	—
HOU	1	1	2	1	0	5	1	1	4	x	1	2	1	4	2	1	2	1	1	5	2	5	0	2	1	45	37	.549	6
DEN	2	2	2	1	1	3	x	0	4	1	1	2	1	5	3	1	1	1	2	5	4	4	1	2	1	44	38	.537	7
DAL	1	1	2	1	0	x	3	1	4	1	0	2	1	6	2	1	1	1	2	5	5	4	1	3	1	38	44	.463	13
SA	1	0	0	1	0	0	1	0	0	1	0	3	1	4	1	0	0	0	0	3	3	x	0	1	0	21	61	.256	30
MIA	1	0	1	1	1	0	0	0	1	2	0	3	0	x	1	1	0	0	1	2	2	2	0	1	0	15	67	.183	36
LAL	1	1	2	1	2	3	4	2	3	2	1	5	x	4	1	1	1	2	3	5	5	4	2	4	1	57	25	.695	—
PHO	1	2	2	1	1	4	3	1	3	1	1	5	2	4	1	1	1	1	x	4	5	5	3	4	1	55	27	.671	2
SEA	1	2	1	2	1	3	2	1	4	2	1	4	2	4	1	1	1	1	2	5	5	5	x	2	0	47	35	.573	10
GS	1	1	2	1	1	4	2	1	x	3	0	5	1	4	1	0	1	0	3	3	4	3	3	3	1	43	39	.524	14
POR	1	1	2	2	1	2	2	0	3	1	1	3	1	3	2	1	2	1	3	x	4	3	3	3	1	39	43	.476	18
SAC	0	0	1	1	1	3	1	1	1	2	0	4	1	2	2	0	1	0	1	2	x	3	1	4	1	27	55	.329	30
LAC	0	0	0	1	1	1	2	0	3	1	1	x	2	2	1	1	0	0	2	3	2	2	3	1	0	21	61	.256	36

1988–1989 TEAMS' STATISTICS

TEAM	G	FIELD GOALS MADE	ATT.	PCT.	3-PT. F. G.'S MADE	ATT.	PCT.	FREE THROWS MADE	ATT.	PCT.	REBOUNDS OFF.	DEF.	TOT.	AST	MISCELLANEOUS PF	DQ	STL	TO	BLK	SCORING PTS	AVG.
PHOE.	82	3754	7545	.498	168	481	.349	2051	2594	.791	1095	2619	3714	2280	1933	13	693	1279	416	9727	118.6
DEN.	82	3813	8140	.468	228	676	.337	1821	2314	.787	1206	2513	3719	2282	2088	26	811	1225	436	9675	118.0
N.Y.	82	3701	7611	.486	386	1147	.337	1779	2366	.752	1322	2265	3587	2083	2053	16	900	1572	446	9567	116.7
G.S.	82	3730	7977	.468	194	629	.308	1904	2384	.799	1323	2561	3884	2009	1946	21	831	1488	643	9558	116.6
LAL	82	3584	7143	.502	227	667	.340	2011	2508	.802	1094	2612	3706	2282	1672	2	724	1344	421	9406	114.7
PORT.	82	3695	7795	.474	216	645	.335	1789	2416	.740	1384	2381	3765	2212	2026	22	828	1435	388	9395	114.6
SEA.	82	3564	7478	.477	293	774	.379	1775	2379	.746	1397	2238	3635	2083	2027	12	864	1403	494	9196	112.1
PHIL.	82	3500	7201	.486	204	646	.316	1970	2504	.787	1143	2356	3499	2110	1721	8	689	1214	354	9174	111.9
ATL.	82	3412	7230	.472	110	397	.277	2168	2709	.800	1372	2316	3688	1990	1880	14	817	1310	474	9102	111.0
BOS.	82	3520	7143	.493	78	309	.252	1840	2349	.783	1179	2442	3621	2189	1876	16	639	1336	418	8958	109.2
MIL.	82	3399	7167	.474	179	567	.316	1955	2382	.821	1133	2472	3405	2071	1953	16	821	1305	323	8932	108.9
CLEV.	82	3466	6904	.502	170	474	.359	1821	2438	.747	1033	2475	3508	2260	1592	5	791	1323	586	8923	108.8
HOU.	82	3412	7196	.474	164	523	.314	1909	2527	.755	1211	2554	3765	2016	2026	26	789	1569	501	8897	108.5
WASH.	82	3519	7591	.464	52	243	.214	1789	2318	.772	1254	2354	3608	2048	2054	17	694	1291	325	8879	108.3
IND.	82	3385	6945	.487	202	615	.328	1795	2275	.789	1065	2497	3562	2012	2105	48	563	1547	418	8767	106.9
DET.	**82**	**3395**	**6879**	**.494**	**120**	**400**	**.300**	**1830**	**2379**	**.769**	**1154**	**2546**	**3700**	**2027**	**1939**	**15**	**522**	**1336**	**406**	**8740**	**106.6**
CHI.	82	3448	6968	.495	174	530	.328	1656	2106	.786	1018	2453	3471	2213	1855	17	722	1327	376	8726	106.4
LAC	82	3526	7428	.475	54	234	.231	1606	2220	.723	1156	2384	3540	2208	1937	17	815	1666	530	8712	106.2
S.A.	82	3469	7409	.468	63	293	.215	1651	2367	.698	1295	2181	3476	2037	2153	36	961	1712	423	8652	105.5
SAC.	82	3362	7351	.457	307	824	.373	1620	2104	.770	1141	2454	3595	1970	1877	28	624	1370	409	8651	105.5
UTAH	82	3182	6595	.482	114	380	.300	2110	2742	.770	1050	2607	3657	2108	1894	13	720	1532	583	8588	104.7
CHAR.	82	3426	7430	.461	134	430	.312	1580	2060	.767	1138	2200	3338	2323	2068	20	705	1318	264	8566	104.5
N.J.	82	3333	7226	.461	187	568	.329	1653	2260	.731	1204	2419	3623	1793	1966	12	773	1449	431	8506	103.7
DALL.	82	3244	6917	.469	211	681	.310	1785	2263	.789	1048	2397	3445	1867	1739	14	579	1233	476	8484	103.5
MIA.	82	3221	7116	.453	97	298	.326	1477	2103	.702	1309	2211	3520	1958	2124	38	744	1728	408	8016	97.8

OPPONENTS' STATISTICS

TEAM	FIELD GOALS MADE	ATT.	PCT.	3-PT. F.G.'S MADE	ATT.	PCT.	FREE THROWS MADE	ATT.	PCT.	REBOUNDS OFF.	DEF.	TOT.	MISCELLANEOUS AST	PF	DQ	STL	TO	BLK	SCORING PTS	AVG.	DIFF.
UTAH	3113	7170	.434	185	606	.305	1765	2342	.754	1220	2233	3453	1812	2086	26	779	1329	505	8176	99.7	+5.0
DET.	3140	7022	.447	158	554	.285	1826	2325	.785	1131	2188	3319	1855	2088	28	646	1225	341	8264	100.8	+5.8
CLEV.	3385	7346	.461	172	508	.339	1358	1748	.777	1214	2283	3497	2043	1970	19	685	1429	363	8300	101.2	+7.6
DALL.	3422	7304	.469	166	515	.322	1573	2090	.753	1231	2500	3731	2133	1869	11	660	1175	386	8583	104.7	-1.2
CHI.	3361	7098	.474	193	590	.327	1693	2300	.773	1078	2300	3378	2099	1781	13	686	1255	348	8608	105.0	+1.4
MIL.	3301	6901	.478	196	533	.368	1838	2369	.776	1094	2335	3429	2109	1935	14	707	1522	425	8636	105.3	+3.6
ATL.	3363	7124	.472	147	511	.288	1826	2329	.784	1261	2325	3586	2037	2109	23	687	1487	348	8699	106.1	+4.9
LAL	3541	7540	.470	194	587	.330	1542	2051	.752	1178	2222	3400	2157	1941	24	752	1263	432	8818	107.5	+7.2
HOU.	3413	7290	.468	187	534	.350	1806	2372	.761	1145	2428	3573	2015	2013	28	800	1455	439	8819	107.5	+1.0
BOS.	3475	7183	.484	133	459	.290	1780	2294	.776	1048	2222	3270	2124	1950	19	762	1191	387	8863	108.1	+1.2
MIA.	3384	6928	.488	148	432	.343	2021	2613	.773	1188	2366	3554	2062	1830	15	926	1543	553	8937	109.0	-11.2
SEA.	3437	7067	.486	169	543	.311	1915	2489	.769	1188	2252	3440	1958	1881	15	670	1553	413	8958	109.2	+2.9
N.J.	3560	7162	.497	158	512	.309	1749	2286	.765	1030	2412	3506	2134	1984	14	744	1376	485	9027	110.1	-6.4
PHIL.	3658	7296	.501	170	495	.343	1565	2023	.774	1149	2412	3561	2281	1984	26	640	1269	445	9051	110.4	+1.5
WASH.	3486	7235	.482	155	510	.304	1929	2510	.769	1132	2538	3670	2082	1921	19	655	1381	523	9056	110.4	-2.2
PHOE.	3589	7736	.464	181	568	.319	1737	2308	.753	1252	2458	3710	2166	2057	16	625	1368	427	9096	110.9	+7.7
SAC.	3589	7420	.484	181	573	.316	1747	2301	.759	1171	2604	3775	2107	1821	22	759	1284	442	9106	111.0	-5.5
IND.	3453	7400	.467	167	547	.305	2036	2606	.781	1288	2312	3600	2034	2029	15	836	1206	389	9109	111.1	-4.2
S.A.	3486	7148	.488	172	532	.323	2105	2714	.776	1256	2462	3718	2062	1938	21	915	1728	545	9249	112.8	-7.3
N.Y.	3636	7358	.494	152	534	.285	1834	2390	.767	1213	2326	3539	2292	1898	19	778	1688	433	9258	112.9	+3.8
CHAR.	3555	7113	.500	115	399	.288	2040	2629	.776	1191	2621	3812	2061	1791	10	710	1425	441	9265	113.0	-8.5
PORT.	3572	7322	.488	198	546	.363	1933	2504	.772	1151	2391	3542	2073	1960	17	738	1569	358	9275	113.1	+1.5
LAC	3747	7738	.484	197	576	.342	1834	2400	.764	1342	2550	3892	2384	1882	17	933	1440	551	9525	116.2	-9.9
DEN.	3701	7484	.495	157	446	.352	1977	2683	.737	1136	2864	4000	2136	2001	21	665	1597	485	9536	116.3	+1.7
G.S.	3693	8000	.462	281	821	.342	1916	2501	.766	1437	2639	4076	2215	1935	20	861	1554	485	9583	116.9	-0.3
AVG.'S	3482	7295	.477	173	537	.323	1814	2363	.768	1189	2412	3601	2097	1940	19	745	1412	438	8952	109.2	—

1988–1989 INDIVIDUAL LEADERS

SCORING AVERAGE

Player, Team	G	FG	FT	PTS	AVG
JORDAN, CHI.	81	966	674	2633	32.5
MALONE, UTAH	80	809	703	2326	29.1
ELLIS, SEA.	82	857	377	2253	27.5
DREXLER, PORT.	78	829	438	2123	27.2
MULLIN, G.S.	82	830	493	2176	26.5
ENGLISH, DEN.	82	924	325	2175	26.5
WILKINS, ATL.	80	814	442	2099	26.2
BARKLEY, PHIL.	79	700	602	2037	25.8
CHAMBERS, PHOE.	81	774	509	2085	25.7
OLAJUWON, HOU.	82	790	454	2034	24.8
CUMMINGS, MIL.	80	730	362	1829	22.9
EWING, N.Y.	80	727	361	1815	22.7
TRIPUCKA, CHAR.	71	568	440	1606	22.6
MCHALE, BOS.	78	661	436	1758	22.5
JOHNSON, LAL	77	579	513	1730	22.5
RICHMOND, G.S.	79	649	410	1741	21.7
MALONE, WASH.	76	677	296	1651	22.0
PERSON, IND.	80	711	243	1728	21.6
E. JOHNSON, PHOE.	70	608	217	1504	21.5
KING, WASH.	81	654	361	1674	20.7

REBOUNDS PER GAME

Player, Team	G	OFF	DEF	TOT	AVG
OLAJUWON, HOU.	82	338	767	1105	13.5
BARKLEY, PHIL.	79	403	583	986	12.5
PARISH, BOS.	80	342	654	996	12.5
MALONE, ATL.	81	386	570	956	11.8
MALONE, UTAH	80	259	594	853	10.7
OAKLEY, N.Y.	82	343	518	861	10.5
EATON, UTAH	82	227	616	843	10.3
THORPE, HOU.	82	272	515	787	9.6
LAIMBEER, DET.	81	138	638	776	9.6
CAGE, SEA.	80	276	489	765	9.6
THOMPSON, IND.	76	224	494	718	9.4
RODMAN, DET.	**82**	**327**	**445**	**772**	**9.4**
B. WILLIAMS, N.J.	74	249	447	696	9.4
GMINSKI, PHIL.	82	213	556	769	9.4
RAMBIS, CHAR.	75	269	434	703	9.4
LEVER, DEN.	71	187	475	662	9.3
EWING, N.Y.	80	213	527	740	9.3
DAUGHERTY, CLEV.	78	167	551	718	9.2
GREEN, LAL	82	258	481	739	9.0
PERKINS, DALL.	78	235	453	688	8.8

ASSISTS PER GAME

Player, Team	G	AST	AVG
STOCKTON, UTAH	82	1118	13.6
JOHNSON, LAL	77	988	12.8
K. JOHNSON, PHOE.	81	991	12.2
PORTER, PORT.	81	770	9.5
MCMILLAN, SEA.	75	696	9.3
FLOYD, HOU.	82	709	8.6
JACKSON, N.Y.	72	619	8.6
PRICE, CLEV.	75	631	8.4
THOMAS, DET.	**80**	**663**	**8.3**
JORDAN, CHI.	81	650	8.0
LEVER, DEN.	71	559	7.9
BOGUES, CHAR.	79	620	7.8
CHEEKS, PHIL.	71	554	7.8
K. SMITH, SAC.	81	621	7.7
CONNER, N.J.	82	604	7.4
GRANT, LAC	71	506	7.1
HARPER, DALL.	81	570	7.0
RIVERS, ATL.	76	525	6.9
JOHNSON, BOS.	72	472	6.6
PRESSEY, MIL.	67	439	6.6

STEALS PER GAME

Player, Team	G	STL	AVG
STOCKTON, UTAH	82	263	3.21
ROBERTSON, S.A.	65	197	3.03
JORDAN, CHI.	81	234	2.89
LEVER, DEN.	71	195	2.75
DREXLER, PORT.	78	213	2.73
OLAJUWON, HOU.	82	213	2.60
RIVERS, ATL.	76	181	2.38
HARPER, CLEV.	82	185	2.26
GARLAND, G.S.	79	175	2.22
CONNER, N.J.	82	181	2.21
ADAMS, DEN.	77	166	2.16
MULLIN, G.S.	82	176	2.15
HARPER, DALL.	81	172	2.12
MCMILLAN, SEA.	75	156	2.08
GRANT, LAC	71	144	2.03
WALKER, WASH.	79	155	1.96
HUMPHRIES, MIL.	73	142	1.95
JACKSON, N.Y.	72	139	1.93
PIPPEN, CHI.	73	139	1.90
W. ANDERSON, S.A.	81	150	1.85

BLOCKED SHOTS PER GAME

Player, Team	G	BLK	AVG
BOL, G.S.	80	345	4.31
EATON, UTAH	82	315	3.84
EWING, N.Y.	80	281	3.51
OLAJUWON, HOU.	82	282	3.44
NANCE, CLEV.	73	206	2.82
BENJAMIN, LAC	79	221	2.80
COOPER, DEN.	79	211	2.67
WEST, PHOE.	82	187	2.28
LISTER, SEA.	82	180	2.20
SMITS, IND.	82	151	1.84
WILLIAMS, DALL.	76	134	1.76
WILLIAMS, CLEV.	82	134	1.63
HINSON, N.J.	82	121	1.48
PARISH, BOS.	80	116	1.45
THOMPSON, MIA.	79	105	1.33
KONCAK, ATL.	74	98	1.32
GMINSKI, PHIL.	82	106	1.29
G. ANDERSON, S.A.	82	103	1.26
SMITH, LAC	71	89	1.25
MCHALE, BOS.	78	97	1.24

3-POINT FIELD GOAL PERCENTAGE

Player, Team	3FG	3FGA	PCT
SUNDVOLD, MIA.	48	92	.522
ELLIS, SEA.	162	339	.478
PRICE, CLEV.	93	211	.441
HAWKINS, PHIL.	71	166	.428
HODGES, CHI.	75	180	.417
E. JOHNSON, PHOE.	71	172	.413
BERRY, SAC.	65	160	.406
PRESSLEY, SAC.	119	295	.403
MILLER, IND.	98	244	.402
SCOTT, LAL	77	193	.399
TUCKER, N.Y.	118	296	.399
HIGGINS, G.S.	66	168	.393
EHLO, CLEV.	39	100	.390
SCHOENE, SEA.	42	110	.382
COOPER, LAL	80	210	.381
AINGE, SAC.	116	305	.380
SIKMA, MIL.	82	216	.380
FLOYD, HOU.	109	292	.373
RICHMOND, G.S.	33	90	.367
MORRIS, N.J.	64	175	.366

1989 DRAFT

TEAM	NAME	COLLEGE	HGT.
1. Sacramento	Pervis Ellison	Louisville	6–9
2. Clippers	Danny Ferry	Duke	6–11
3. San Antonio	Sean Elliott	Arizona	6–8
4. Miami	Glen Rice	Michigan	6–7
5. Charlotte	J.R. Reid	North Carolina	6–9
6. Chicago (from New Jersey)	Stacey King	Oklahoma	6–11
7. Indiana	George McCloud	Florida St.	6–6
8. Dallas	Randy White	Louisiana Tech	6–7
9. Washington	Tom Hammonds	Georgia Tech	6–8
10. Minnesota	Pooh Richardson	UCLA	6–1
11. Orlando	Nick Anderson	Illinois	6–6
12. New Jersey (from Portland)	Mookie Blaylock	Oklahoma	6–1
13. Boston	Michael Smith	Brigham Young	6–10
14. Golden State	Tim Hardaway	Texas-El Paso	5–11
15. Denver	Todd Lichti	Stanford	6–4
16. Seattle (from Houston)	Dana Barros	Boston College	5–11
17. Seattle (from Philadelphia)	Shawn Kemp	Trinity Valley CC	6–10
18. Chicago (from Seattle)	B.J. Armstrong	Iowa	6–2
19. Philadelphia (from Seattle)	Kenny Payne	Louisville	6–8
20. Chicago (from Milwaukee)	Jeff Sanders	Georgia Southern	6–9
21. Utah	Blue Edwards	East Carolina	6–5
22. Portland (from New York)	Byron Irvin	Missouri	6–5
23. Atlanta	Roy Marble	Iowa	6–6
24. Phoenix*	Anthony Cook	Arizona	6–9
25. Cleveland	John Morton	Seton Hall	6–3
26. Lakers	Vlade Divac	Yugoslavia	6–11
27. Detroit*	Kenny Battle	Illinois	6–6

* The Suns selected Cook for the Pistons, for guard Michael Williams and Detroit's pick at No. 27. The Pistons chose Illinois forward Kenny Battle for Phoenix.

1988–1989 ALL-NBA PLAYERS

ALL-NBA TEAMS
First Team
F   Karl Malone, Utah
F   Charles Barkley, Phil.
C   Akeem Olajuwon, Hou.
G   * Magic Johnson, LAL
G   Michael Jordan, Chi.
* 1989 Most Valuable Player

Second Team
Tom Chambers, Phoe.
Chris Mullin, G.S.
Patrick Ewing, N.Y.
John Stockton, Utah
Kevin Johnson, Phoe.

MASTER LOCK NBA
ALL-DEFENSIVE TEAMS
First Team
F   Dennis Rodman, Det.
F   Larry Nance, Clev.
C   Mark Eaton, Utah
G   Michael Jordan, Chi.
G   Joe Dumars, Det.

Second Team
Kevin McHale, Bos.
A.C. Green, LAL
Patrick Ewing, N.Y.
John Stockton, Utah
Alvin Robertson, S.A.

ALL-ROOKIE TEAMS
(chosen without regard to position)
First Team
Mitch Richmond, G.S.
Willie Anderson, S.A.
Hersey Hawkins, Phil.
Rik Smits, Ind.
Charles Smith, LAC

Second Team
Brian Shaw, Bos.
Rex Chapman, Char.
Chris Morris, N.J.
Rod Strickland, N.Y.
Kevin Edwards, Mia.

A Review of the 1980s
1980 DETROIT DRAFT CHOICES

1980—1, Larry Drew, Missouri; 2, Brad Branson, Southern Methodist; 3, Jonathan Moore, Furman; 4, Darwin Cook, Portland; 5, Tony Fuller, Pepperdine; 6, Tony Turner, Alaska-Anchorage; 7, Carl Pierce, Gonzaga; 8, Leroy Loggins, Fairmont State; 9, Terry Dupris, Huron.

1981 — 1, Isiah Thomas, Indiana; 2, Kelly Tripucka, Notre Dame; 3, John May, South Alabama; 4, Donnie Koonce, UNC-Charlotte; 5, George DeVone, UNC-Charlotte; 6, Vince Brookins, Iowa; 7, Greg Nance, West Virginia; 8, Joe Schoen, St. Francis (PA); 9, Ed Baker, Alcorn State; 10, Melvin Maxwell, Western Michigan.

1982 — 1, Cliff Levingston, Wichita St.; 2, Ricky Pierce, Rice; 3, Walker Russell, W. Michigan; 4, John Ebeling, Florida Southern; 5, Gary Holmes, Minnesota; 6, Dean Marquardt, Marquette; 7, Brian Nyenhuis, Marquette; 8, Kevin Smith, Michigan St.; 9, Dave Coulthard, York (Ont.).

1983 — 1, Antoine Carr, Wichita St.; 2, Erich Santifer, Syracuse; 3, Steve Bouchie, Indiana; 4, Ken Austin, Rice; 5, Derek Perry, Michigan St.; 6, Rob Gonzalez, Colorado; 7, George Wenzal, Augustana; 8, Marlow McClain, Eastern Michigan; 9, Isaac Person, Michigan.

1984 — 1, Tony Campbell, Ohio State; 2, Eric Turner, Michigan; 3, Kevin Springman, St. Joseph's; 4, Philip Smith, New Mexico; 5, Rick Doyle, Texas-San Antonio; 6, Rennie Bailey, Louisiana Tech; 7, Barry Francisco, Bloomsburg State (PA); 8, Dale Roberts, Appalachian State; 9, Ben Tower, Michigan State; 10, Dan Pelekoudas, Michigan.

1985 — 1, Joe Dumars, McNeese State; 2, Andre Goode, Northwestern; 3, Rich Johnson, Evansville; 4, Anthony Webb, North Carolina State; 5, Mike Lahm, Murray State; 6, Vincent Giles, Eastern Michigan; 7, Frank James, Nevada-Las Vegas.

1986 — 1, John Salley, Georgia Tech; 2, Dennis Rodman, Southeast Oklahoma State; 3, Chauncey Robinson, Mississippi State; 4, Clarence Hanley, Old Dominion; 5, Greg Grant, Utah State; 6, Larry Polec, Michigan State.

1987 — 1, Freddie Banks, UNLV; 2, Eric White, Pepperdine; 3, Dave Popson, North Carolina; 4, Gerry Wright, Iowa; 5, Antoine Joubert, Michigan; 6, Mark Gottfried, Alabama.

1988 — 1, Fennis Dembo, Wyoming; 2, Michael Williams, Baylor; 3, Lee Johnson, Norfolk State.

1989 — 1, Anthony Cook; 2 (no second round pick).

DETROIT'S DECADE-LONG CLIMB TO THE CHAMPIONSHIP

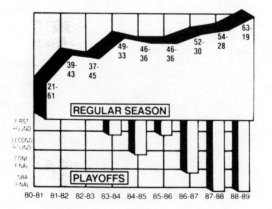

CHAMPIONS OF THE 1980s

1979–80	Los Angeles	Paul Westhead	Philadelphia	Billy Cunningham	4–2
1980–81	Boston	Bill Fitch	Houston	Del Harris	4–2
1981–82	Los Angeles	Pat Riley	Philadelphia	Billy Cunningham	4–2
1982–83	Philadelphia	Billy Cunningham	Los Angeles	Pat Riley	4–0
1983–84	Boston	K.C. Jones	Los Angeles	Pat Riley	4–3
1984–85	Los Angeles	Pat Riley	Boston	K.C. Jones	4–2
1985–86	Boston	K.C. Jones	Houston	Bill Fitch	4–2
1986–87	Los Angeles	Pat Riley	Boston	K.C. Jones	4–2
1987–88	Los Angeles	Pat Riley	Detroit	Chuck Daly	4–3
1988–89	Detroit	Chuck Daly	Los Angeles	Pat Riley	4–0

1980s TEAM SUCCESS RATE

TEAM	W-L	PCT.	AVG. WINS	AVG. DIV. FINISH
1. Boston	531–207	.720	59.0	1.3
1. L.A. Lakers	531–207	.720	59.0	1.1
3. Philadelphia	476–262	.645	52.9	2.0
4. Milwaukee	473–265	.641	52.6	1.9
5. Detroit	407–331	.551	45.2	2.6
6. Portland	404–334	.547	44.9	3.0
7. Denver	400–338	.542	44.4	2.5
8. Atlanta	399–339	.541	44.3	2.9
9. Phoenix	384–354	.520	42.7	3.0
10. Seattle	368–370	.499	40.9	3.7
11. Houston	361–377	.489	40.1	3.1
12. Dallas	358–380	.485	39.8	3.3
12. Washington	358–380	.485	39.8	3.8
14. Utah	353–385	.478	39.2	3.5
15. San Antonio	346–392	.469	38.4	3.8
16. Chicago	339–399	.459	37.6	3.9
17. New York	335–403	.453	37.2	3.6
18. New Jersey	312–426	.423	34.7	3.9
19. Golden State	308–430	.417	34.2	4.7
20. Sacramento	301–437	.407	33.4	4.4
21. Cleveland	289–449	.391	32.1	4.6
22. Indiana	280–458	.379	31.1	5.1
23. L.A. Clippers	221–517	.299	24.6	5.4
24. Charlotte	20–62	.244	20.0	6.0
25. Miami	15–67	.183	15.0	6.0

Bibliography and Sources

The primary research source for this book was several hundred interviews conducted by the author. The interviews were with all of the Piston players, coaches, scouts and primary front-office personnel. In many cases, key figures were interviewed twenty-five to thirty-five times. Also interviewed were a great many other NBA players, coaches, general managers, front-office executives, former players, media representatives, and agents.

In addition, a large number of printed reference materials were of great help. Of particular benefit was the daily coverage of the Detroit Pistons that appeared in the *Detroit Free Press,* the *Detroit News,* and the *Oakland Press.* The work of the three primary beat writers—Drew Sharp of the *Free Press,* Terry Foster of the *Detroit News,* and Steve Addy of the *Oakland Press*—was of special value because of its high standards of depth and accuracy. Also important, though, were the works of Detroit sports columnists and feature writers, including the *Free Press's* Charlie Vincent, Mitch Albom, Corky Meinecke, and Johnette Howard; the *Detroit News's* Jim Spadafore, Shelby Strother, and Joe Falls; and the *Oakland Press's* Keith Langlois.

Two magazine articles—Fred Waitzkin's "What Drives the Pistons" (*The New York Times Magazine,* January 8, 1989), and Jeff Coplon's "Bad Boys" (*Rolling Stone,* May 4, 1988), were of exceptional quality and provided significant insight.

In a few instances, quotations from Piston players and coaches that appeared in the aforementioned newspapers and magazines were used in this book. In virtually all instances, the reporter who recorded the quotation is acknowledged in the passage of this book where the quotation appears.

Other writers whose work was used in the compilation of this book include Terry Pluto (*Akron Beacon Journal*), David Kahn and Dwight Jaynes (*Portland Oregonian*), Jack McCallum (*Sports Illustrated*), Leo Martinosi (*The Holland Sentinel*), Dean Howe (*Flint Journal*), Lowell Cauffiel (*Detroit Monthly*), Loren Feldman (*GQ*), Bob Ryan (*The Boston Globe*), David Bradley (*Sport*), Gene Wojciechowski (*Los Angeles Times*), Roland Lazenby (*The Sporting News*), William Nack (*Sports Illustrated*), Sam Smith (*Chicago Tribune*), Scott Ostler (*Los Angeles Times*), Sam Goldaper (*The New York Times*), and Steve Kelley (*Seattle Times*).

Broadcasters whose views and information were of help include George Blaha and Greg Kelser, Fred McCleod and Tom Wilson, Hubie Brown, Dick

Stockton, Pat O'Brien, Brent Musberger, Steve Jones, Bill Schonely, Pat Lafferty, and producer-director Clark Attebury of Chuck Daly's *One on One* show.

Books that were used include David Halberstam's *The Breaks of the Game* (Alfred A. Knopf, New York, 1981); Bob Ryan and Terry Pluto's *Forty-Eight Minutes* (Macmillan, New York, 1987); Zander Hollander's *The Complete Handbook of Pro Basketball* (New American Library) series; *The Sporting News's NBA Register* and *NBA Guide* (The Sporting News, St. Louis, 1988); Jack Ramsay's *The Coach's Art* (Timber Press, Forest Grove, Oregon, 1978); Kareem Abdul-Jabbar's *Giant Steps* (Bantam Books, New York, 1983); Bill Bradley's *Life on the Run* (Bantam Books, New York, 1976); Larry Colton's *Idol Time* (Timber Press, Forest Grove, Oregon, 1978); Bob Cousy and Bob Ryan's *Cousy on the Celtic Mystique* (McGraw-Hill, New York, 1988); Leonard Koppett's *24 Seconds to Shoot* (Macmillan, New York, 1968); Pat Riley and Byron Laursen's *Showtime* (Warner Books, New York, 1988); and Isiah Thomas and Matt Dobek's *Bad Boys* (Masters Press, Grand Rapids, 1989).

Magazines that were used include Street & Smith's *Pro Basketball, The NBA News,* Dick Vitale's *Basketball,* Mike Warren's *College and Pro Basketball, Sports Illustrated, Sport,* and *The Sporting News.*

It should also be noted that many descriptions of GM Jack McCloskey's trading activities did not come directly or solely from McCloskey, but from other general managers, players, and informed and reliable sources.

Most direct quotes and dialogue in the book were tape-recorded by the author. Some were recorded through handwritten notes. In several instances, dialogue or remarks result from the recollection of the persons involved; because these instances are based upon memory, they may reflect the spirit of the dialogue or remark but may not be absolutely verbatim quotations.

A final important source of information for this book was the extensive file and media-service system of the Detroit Pistons.

Index